W9-BGL-322
Queensbury, NY 12804

DISCARDED

Secret Gardens, Satanic Mills

EDITED BY MARY JO MAYNES,
BIRGITTE SØLAND, AND
CHRISTINA BENNINGHAUS

Secret Gardens, Satanic Mills

Placing Girls in European History, 1750–1960

INDIANA UNIVERSITY PRESS
Bloomington and Indianapolis

This book is a publication of

Indiana University Press
601 North Morton Street
Bloomington, IN 47404-3797 USA

http://iupress.indiana.edu

Telephone orders   800-842-6796
Fax orders   812-855-7931
Orders by e-mail   iuporder@indiana.edu

© 2005 by Indiana University Press

All rights reserved

No part of this book may be reproduced or utilized in any form or by any means, electronic or mechanical, in-cluding photocopying and recording, or by any information storage and retrieval system, without permission in writing from the publisher. The Association of American University Presses' Resolution on Permissions consti-tutes the only exception to this prohibition

The paper used in this publication meets the minimum requirements of American National Standard for Infor-mation Sciences—Permanence of Paper for Printed Library Materials, ANSI Z39.48-1984

Manufactured in the United States of America

Library of Congress Cataloging-in-Publication Data

Secret gardens, satanic mills : placing girls in European history, 1750–1960 / edited by Mary Jo Maynes, Birgitte Søland, and Christina Benninghaus.
p. cm.
Includes bibliographical references and index.
ISBN 0-253-34449-2 (cloth : alk. paper) — ISBN 0-253-21710-5 (pbk.)
1. Girls—Europe—Social conditions. 2. Girls—Europe—History. I. Maynes, Mary Jo. II. Søland, Birgitte, date III. Benninghaus, Christina.
HQ777.S4 2004
305.23′082′094—dc22

2004002658

1 2 3 4 5   10 09 08 07 06 05

To Our Daughters:

Lili Yasmin Banihashem
Ella-Sophia Benninghaus
Lucie-Charlotte Benninghaus
Alice Susan Debarre
Sally Davin Easey
Hannah Lucy Gestrich
Sophie Maria Hardach
Vivienne Hastie
Tess Cox Hayton
Katherine Hodgkin
Isabella Torjussen Langhamer
Elizabeth Maynes-Aminzade
Johanna Alaimo Pacyga
Beatrice Marysia Pacyga
Anna Marta Søland-Guzowski

Contents

Acknowledgments   ix
Introduction   1

PART ONE   WORKING GIRLS' LABOR AND LIVES IN THE
PREINDUSTRIAL AND EARLY INDUSTRIAL ERAS

1. Bringing Up Girls: Work in Preindustrial Europe   23
   Deborah Simonton

2. In Search of Arachne's Daughters: European Girls, Economic
   Development, and the Textile Trade, 1750–1880   38
   Mary Jo Maynes

3. After Dark: Girls' Leisure, Work, and Sexuality in Eighteenth-
   and Nineteenth-Century Rural Southwest Germany   54
   Andreas Gestrich

4. An Industrious Revolution in Late Seventeenth-Century Paris:
   New Vocational Training for Adolescent Girls and the Creation
   of Female Labor Markets   69
   Clare Crowston

5. Work for Girls? The Small Metal Industries in England,
   1840–1915   83
   Carol E. Morgan

PART TWO   SPACES OF SOCIALIZATION OF MIDDLE-
AND UPPER-CLASS GIRLS IN THE EIGHTEENTH AND
NINETEENTH CENTURIES

6. Managing Girls' Sexuality among the German Upper Classes   101
   Irene Hardach-Pinke

7. Porous Walls and Prying Eyes: Control, Discipline, and Morality
   in Boarding Schools for Girls in Mid-Nineteenth-Century
   France   115
   Rebecca Rogers

8. Good Girls versus Blooming Maidens: The Building of Female
   Middle- and Upper-Class Identities in the Garden, England and
   France, 1820–1870   131
   Céline Grasser

PART THREE   REDEFINING GIRLHOOD: COMPETING DISCOURSES
ON FEMALE ADOLESCENCE, 1880–1950

9. The Authority of Experts: The Crisis of Female Adolescence in
   France and England, 1880–1920   149
   Kathleen Alaimo

10. Sex Education and Sexual Initiation of Bourgeois French Girls,
    1880–1930   164
    Mary Lynn Stewart

11. In Their Own Words: Girls' Representations of Growing Up in
    Germany in the 1920s   178
    Christina Benninghaus

12. Girls in Trouble: Defining Female Delinquency, Britain,
    1900–1950   192
    Pamela Cox

PART FOUR   CHANGING PATTERNS OF WORK AND LEISURE,
1880–1960

13. City Girls: Young Women, New Employment, and the City,
    London, 1880–1910   209
    Anna Davin

14. Girls in Court: *Mägde* versus Their Employers in Saxony,
    1880–1914   224
    Elizabeth Bright Jones

15. "Something for the Girls": Organized Leisure in Europe,
    1890–1939   239
    Tammy M. Proctor

16. Employment and Enjoyment: Female Coming-of-Age
    Experiences in Denmark, 1880s–1930s   254
    Birgitte Søland

17. Leisure, Pleasure, and Courtship: Young Women in England,
    1920–1960   269
    Claire Langhamer

18. The Emergence of the Modern Teenage Girl in Postwar
    Austria   284
    Karin Schmidlechner

Contributors   299
Index   303

Acknowledgments

When, in 2000, the editors of this book issued a call for papers for a scholarly workshop on girlhood in modern European history, we were hoping for a discussion that would allow us to address similarities and differences within the wide region characterized by western European patterns of marriage and generational relations. We also sought to include a variety of approaches and historical sources pertinent to the history of female youth. To our delight, the group of scholars who assembled in Columbus, Ohio, in October 2000 evolved into a lively transatlantic research collaborative. Participants represented a wide span of intellectual generations and a range of theoretical, disciplinary and national historiographic traditions. Members of the group (which was nicknamed "Eurogirls" although we include one male colleague who has been extremely good natured about this!) hail from across the United States and also from Canada, England, Scotland, France, Denmark, Germany, and Austria. We presented and discussed papers, exchanged views and comments, revised our work, and met for a second time in Bielefeld, Germany, in fall 2001, where we planned this book together.

Writing and publishing this book would not have been possible without the financial support from many institutions. The conference in Ohio in October 2000 was funded by a variety of institutions at the Ohio State University: the Department of History, the College of Humanities, the *Journal of Women's History*, the Office of International Education, the West European Studies Center, the Department of Women's Studies, and the Women's History Workshop. The conference in Bielefeld in October 2001 was funded by the Center for Interdisciplinary Research (ZiF) at the University of Bielefeld and the Deutsche Forschungsgemeinschaft.

Preparatory and subsequent editorial meetings in London and Minneapolis were made possible by funding provided through the Ohio State University College of Humanities Grant-in-Aid, the Forschungsinnovationsfond of the University of Bielefeld, and several units at the University of Minnesota: the Department of History, the College of Liberal Arts, the Comparative Women's History Workshop, and the Graduate School.

We would like to express our thanks to those people who contributed to the success of the conferences: notably Susan Freeman and Nancy Guzowski in Ohio and Marina Hoffman at ZiF in Bielefeld. We all appreciate comments on each other's chapters provided by the book's contributors. In addition, Ning de Cornick-Smith and Kerstin Kohtz participated in our conferences and generously shared their knowledge on the history of girlhood with us, and participants in the Comparative Women's History Workshop at the University of Minnesota provided feedback on the introduction. We would also like to thank the anonymous readers from the Indiana University Press for helpful and inspiring comments. We thank Marilyn Grobschmidt, former editor at IU Press, for her enthusiastic response to our proposal, and Robert Sloan, who initially took over as sponsoring editor when she left. Jane Quinet has been a wonderfully supportive editor in the most recent stages of production. Special thanks to Jen Grana and Marynel Ryan, graduate students at the University of Minnesota, for their help in preparing the manuscript for publication.

Secret Gardens, Satanic Mills

Introduction

Secret Gardens, Satanic Mills: Placing Girls in European History, 1750–1960 explores the history of young women in Europe during two centuries of profound social, economic, and cultural change. Our focus of attention is female youth, or, more simply, "girls"—that is, unmarried young women who were seen as no longer children but not yet fully adult.[1] European girlhood was grounded in changing social, economic, and cultural practices. It was structured by historically specific discourses and defined by the body and its history. What it meant to be a girl varied enormously across time and place and between classes. Yet, while paying attention to these variations, this book also offers insights into general patterns and broader tendencies characteristic of European girlhood.

This book focuses especially on those regions of Europe where the so-called "western European marriage pattern" prevailed—that is, where the age at marriage for both men and women was relatively late compared to most other regions of the world. Until the late nineteenth century, men in central and western Europe typically married in their late twenties and women in their mid-twenties; a substantial minority never married.[2] In contrast, throughout much of the rest of the world, some form of marriage was nearly universal, and it generally occurred not long after puberty. To make Europe's peculiarity in this regard clear, around 1800 about 80 percent of Chinese women were married by the age of twenty, whereas between 60 and 80 percent of women in central and western Europe were still unmarried at that age.[3] Thus in contrast with most other regions of the world, in Europe the time between puberty and marriage was relatively long—often up to ten years. During these transitional years between childhood and adulthood, young women played a distinctive role in European economic, social, cultural, and political life. In a world-historical frame the history of female youth in Europe thus has distinctive features.

Until recently, almost all studies of the history of European youth have focused on boys and young men. For example, Erik Erikson's pioneering psychological framework for approaching youth historically, which he laid out in *Childhood and Society,* restricted itself to the male psyche. Similarly, Philippe Ariès's *Centuries of Childhood* and John Gillis's path-breaking study *Youth and History* concentrated on boys.[4] Possible differences between male and female youth remained unexamined.

This book offers a corrective to these earlier interpretations by focusing on female youth. It analyzes adult-supervised institutions for the education and socialization of girls and parental and expert advice directed to them over the centuries. But it also looks at girls as historical actors who took up or rejected prescribed social roles, and who often challenged the limits placed upon them to venture into new places and new roles. The authors discuss many different dimensions of girls' historical experiences—as workers, students, and consumers; as readers and writers; as daughters, friends, and lovers; and sometimes as unwed mothers. They analyze the changing options open to girls in the economy, in educational institutions, in leisure, in the realm of sexuality, and in the realm of consumption. The book explores enormous social differences as well as often significant religious, national, and regional differences in the lives of girls.

As the title, *Secret Gardens, Satanic Mills,* suggests, many chapters in the book place special emphasis on the changing *spatial* dimensions—both literal and metaphorical—of growing up female. Spatial restrictions were more severe in some regions and classes than in others. For example, while in the 1780s young Fanny Burney was writing her novel *Evelina* to satirize the complex rules that dictated where respectable upper-class young Englishwomen could and could not be seen, working-class English girls were trekking public roads, unchaperoned, on the route from home to factory.[5] In Catholic Europe, convent walls were intended to close off respectable girls from most traffic with men, although they were not completely impermeable.[6] Gardens were, it seems, a liminal space in terms of gender and sexual propriety, but young girls in gardens behaved differently in different cultural contexts.[7] Constantly changing norms about place and propriety, the increasing and visible presence of young women in public—in city streets and shops, in offices and classrooms, in carriages and on trains, in theaters and dancehalls—appeared toward the end of the nineteenth century as a frightening or liberating hallmark of modernity.

Ultimately this book lays out the major shifts in the institutions, meanings, and experiences of European girlhood in the period between 1750 and 1960. Still, it does more than simply bring another aspect of female historical experience to light. It also offers insights into the ways in which girls mattered in the broad sweep of European history and reconceptualizes our understanding of significant dimensions of modern European history. Key features of European economic and cultural modernity—from factory work to typewriting, from novels to department stores, and from universities to cinemas—are fundamentally linked with the history of girlhood. By necessity or by choice, girls and young women were bearers of emergent European modernity.

Female Youth as a Life Stage: Changing Meanings and Understandings

> [T]here's different chapters in your life. Always look on it as different chapters. Like when you're a child and then you're in your teens and that's a different chapter and then you get in your twenties and you've different ideas then, and you're married, that's another chapter.
>
> —Mary, born in 1911 to lower middle-class parents in England[8]

Though long ignored by historians of youth, available evidence suggests that youth has been a distinctive and significant phase of the female life cycle for centuries. Already in preindustrial Europe, female youth was recognized culturally, linguistically, and economically as a distinct phase of life, even if that recognition was not always precise. In European languages, young unmarried women have been referred to by terms specific to their age and gender. In English, for example, they appear as *daughters, big girls,* or *young women;* in French as *filles, grandes filles,* or *jeunes femmes;* in German as *Töchter* or *Mädchen* or *Backfische;* and in Danish as *store piger* or *unge piger.*

Marks of crossing the boundary between childhood and youth for a girl included leaving elementary school, starting work full time, participating in the formal ceremony of religious confirmation, being presented at a formal ball, or adopting adult dress or coiffure, although none of these markers was universal and no girl experienced them all. In the eighteenth century, only a minority of girls went to school; female schooling and literacy generally lagged behind male rates throughout Europe.[9] Confirmation was more marked in Protestant than in Catholic regions. And, of course, whether a girl was presented at a ball or starting work as a servant or spinner depended on her social class. To more modern understandings, biological markers might seem more universal—the onset of menarche is seemingly the most obvious sign that a "little girl" has become a "young woman." But imposing this boundary across the board does not reflect changing historical experiences for a number of reasons. First, rooting human development heavily in biological markers such as menarche is a particularly modern construction, itself part of the historical transformation of female youth that this book documents. Secondly, in Europe's past young women often took on adult economic responsibilities and familial roles several years before beginning to menstruate. Finally, the onset of menses itself has a history: the average age at first menstruation has been declining in the West for two centuries. In the nineteenth century, it was as high as age fifteen or sixteen.[10]

In comparison, the end of youth as a phase of the female life cycle was usually much clearer. For most young women, as for young men, youth ended at the point of marriage, which brought full adult status and responsibilities. Yet for the significant minority of women who did not marry, or who married especially late in life, the end of youth might be fuzzy as well, unless marked, for example, by taking the veil or by giving birth outside of marriage.

During the course of the nineteenth century, the parameters defining youth, marking its beginning and its end, were becoming much clearer and institutionally defined for both girls and boys. By the end of the nineteenth century, most girls as well as boys attended school at least intermittently until at least age twelve or thirteen. More than any other phenomenon or institution, elementary schooling contributed to a certain "normalization" of the life cycle for most young people in Europe.[11] If schooling played a key role in creating more uniform patterns in the life cycle of young people, new cultural and scientific discourses emerging in the late nineteenth century also contributed to a redefinition of youth as a stage in life. Plays and novels increasingly portrayed young people in ways that symbolized modernist views of human development and its problems. In 1891, Franz Wedekind's play *Spring's Awakening* caused a furor when it opened in Germany because of its frank treatment of adolescent sexuality and the costs of sexual ignorance. Simultaneously, psychologists and anthropologists—still a new intellectual presence themselves—debated the meaning of what they now routinely termed "adolescence" as a formative period in people's lives. While this word was not new, it took on a new, specifically psychological meaning in this era, and crises of youth were reinterpreted in psychological terms.[12]

Much of this late nineteenth-century concern about youth initially centered on young men. The poor health of young men inducted into the military alarmed state authorities. The violence of street gangs in working-class neighborhoods was increasingly seen as a social problem, as were stress and suicide rates amongst male students.[13] However, new employment opportunities for girls, the campaigns of the women's movements for better education and vocational training for girls, and the decreasing birthrate in an era of competitive nationalism led to a new interest in female youth.[14] The growing number of female students and teachers produced considerable anxiety about the consequences of women's education for reproduction and generated a host of sociological and psychological studies focused on girls. As a result, girlhood was increasingly understood, among experts at least, in biological, medical, and psychological terms, to an extent much greater than boyhood was. By the early twentieth century, these changing perceptions of female youth would transcend the boundaries of expert discourse and increasingly inform broader understandings of the transition from girlhood to womanhood.[15]

The early twentieth-century reshaping of female adolescence was not merely a product of the writings of physicians, psychologists, social workers, and sexologists. Simultaneous changes in the labor market also functioned to change girls' options and call public attention to female youth as a social category. While most girls would continue to spend their youth working on farms, in workshops and factories, or as domestic servants in private homes, by 1900 a growing proportion of girls and young, unmarried women made their way into commerce and the service sector. Typically employed as sales clerks and office workers, these girls and young women formed a new and highly visible segment of the female labor force, which provoked considerable controversy in the early decades of the century. While some contemporaries lamented girls' flight from rural labor and domestic service, others were more alarmed by their increased earnings and their gradual acquisition of leisure time, both of which they seemed to spend unwisely and inappropriately.[16]

In a cultural context where meanings and understandings of female adolescence were clearly in flux, girls' sense of self, their expectations of what it meant to be young, and their dreams and desires were also shifting. In the early decades of the twentieth century, many girls were clearly beginning to perceive their youth as a unique stage in life with its own rules, responsibilities, and rights, including the right to leisure long claimed by their brothers.[17] During those same years, girls generally came to prefer the unstructured company of their peers to the supervised environments offered by adults, thereby laying the foundations for the establishment of modern female youth cultures, and the new definition of female youth centered on the "teenager" that would flourish in the second half of the twentieth century.[18] Throughout the two centuries under investigation in this book, youth has thus been acknowledged as stage in a woman's life, a transitional period between childhood and adulthood. Yet, the specific meanings and understandings of those years have changed considerably, as have the status, rights, and responsibilities of girls.

Girls' Labor: Necessary yet Suspect

I finished elementary school two years ago. Then I had to learn a trade. My wish was to become a seamstress. But my parents thought differently. I was supposed to become a worker and to help to earn a living. . . . I thought, no, I won't become a worker. But soon I thought differently. I looked for a job and soon found one. . . . I am really happy with my work. Perhaps much happier than if I had become a seamstress because now I know that I support my parents.

—Anonymous essay written by a sixteen-year-old German girl in 1926[19]

Work—paid and unpaid, in the household and the wage labor market—constitutes another central theme in the history of European girlhood. Although work was a reality in the lives of almost all girls during the years between leaving school and entering marriage, their places of employment, the type of work they performed, and the perception of girls' labor varied considerably over time and between classes. Work remained a central experience of growing up female in Europe and a crucial element of Europe's modernizing economy, even while it was often seen to be disruptive of proper gender roles or inimical to a girl's respectability.

The evidence presented in this book underscores the enormous significance of European girls' labor. In fact, we argue that careful attention to this aspect of girls' history demands that we rethink central aspects of European economic history and usual accounts of European constructions of femininity and female work. Not only was girls' work ubiquitous throughout Europe between 1750 and 1960, but girls were often and in many regions engaged in the new types of labor necessary for the economic transformations that characterized these years. Rural maids, for example, did milk cows, as countless folktales and cultural stereotypes depicted them doing, but they also were increasingly put to work mucking out stalls, carrying fodder, and at other tasks necessitated by the move of animal husbandry from pasture to barn that accompanied agricultural intensification in many regions of Europe. Moreover, they were critical as workers in the fields, where their weeding and hoeing proved crucial to the success of such newer commercial crops as sugar beets. Similarly, while it may not be a surprise to learn that girls spun in many regions of Europe, the centrality of their spinning to the growing prosperity of these regions emphasizes the role of young women as absolutely central, though generally ignored, characters in the story of Europe's path to industrial development. Furthermore, the fact that girls' labor was taken for granted in many sectors of, for instance, Birmingham's metal industries suggests that girls' labor was persistent and crucial to the operation of family economies. Even when child labor and the labor of married women came under attack throughout Europe from the middle to the later nineteenth century, girls' labor—that is, the labor of unmarried young women between their early teen years and their mid-twenties—remained a central component of both working-class family and entrepreneurial strategies.[20]

In many respects, girls thus were the advance guard of the early industrial wage labor force. Europe's textile industries were typically the first in any region to adopt the technological innovations we associate with the Industrial Revolution. Girls in textile labor—especially spinning—were prominent among the earliest recruits in factories. Despite increasing domestic containment of girls in the "respectable" classes beginning in the late eighteenth century, a growing number of lower-class girls began to work in non-family settings during these same years. In spite of the changing and more restrictive understandings of propriety and femininity that circulated in moral and pedagogic literature and in fiction, the European economy relied heavily upon the labor of girls.

The prominence of girls' labor grew even more marked in the era of advanced industrial capitalism. Many of the new technologies and practices of communication and administration that we associate with advanced capitalism—telephones and typewriters, the massive record keeping and management functions of public and private bureaucracies, the teaching of universal literacy—quickly became defined as the work of young women. And in contrast with their predecessors who led the workforce into factories, these young women claimed a new kind of respectability, independence, and visibility as a result of their employment.[21]

As several of the chapters in this book demonstrate, there was no single set of rules or norms governing girls' work between the eighteenth and the early twentieth centuries. Notions of respectability and its implications for girls' work varied along the lines of class, region, and occupation milieu, as well as over time. Not only the form and nature of work but also its location held moral as well as practical implications for many social commentators. Working girls were morally ambiguous and threatening figures. The factory remained a place of dubious moral character even while it continued to employ many young women. But for all of the ambiguity and contention around girls' labor, Europe's economic growth depended on it, both in the era of protoindustry and early industrialization and in later phases of economic development.

Because girls' labor was often regarded as merely life cyclic (as opposed to boys' labor, which was presumed to be the beginning of a lifelong engagement), families and employers were often tempted to go for the short-term gains from it instead of investing for the long run. Both families and employers thus had reasons to treat girls' labor as more readily exploitable. Moreover, in the patriarchal nexus of European families, girls were still expected to contribute their share to housework, from which their brothers were usually exempted, even in some situations when they were wage earners contributing to the household's earnings (although families did send girls and their labor away from home when there was a demand for it elsewhere). The "double burden" of housework and paid labor in or outside the home thus could weigh upon girls as much as on their mothers.

Still, some girls managed to acquire at least a minimum of formal training. In eighteenth-century France, for example, parents became increasingly interested in apprenticeships for their daughters as economic change brought new opportunities for skilled labor.[22] In other regions and eras where there was the promise of employment, the evidence reveals similar interest in teaching work skills to girls. There is also evidence that the move from household to wage labor may have given girls at least a temporary negotiating advantage in the family power nexus, making it possible for them to gain control over at least limited resources of time and money for their own use.

Girls' Sexuality: All Important yet Unmentionable

> I think that if I had a second home in a beautiful countryside, and the opportunity for enjoying it, waiting [to marry] would become impossible for me. Love is more intense [and] more expansive [. . .] under the sky and the trees than in a room or a drawing-room.
>
> —Claire Pic, eighteen-year-old French middle-class girl, writing in her diary in 1866[23]

In a cultural context where marriage typically did not take place until a young woman reached her mid-twenties, the regulation of female sexuality proved an issue of central importance.[24] The liminality of girls—sexually maturing but far from marriage and often no longer fully under a father's authority but not yet under a husband's—emerges as another central theme in the history of European girlhood. Yet, however significant, the sexual dimensions of growing up female are relatively undocumented. And with the exception of the girls who transgressed sexual norms as prostitutes or unwed mothers, girls' sexual practices and understandings remain elusive.

Throughout the period covered by this book, some aspects of girls' sexuality remained unchanged. Explicitly sexual relationships were regarded as the prerogative of married couples. However, although it was considered normal and even appropriate for unmarried young men to be initiated into heterosexual intercourse, often at a brothel, in most regions of Europe, young women were expected to remain chaste until marriage. Premarital or extramarital heterosexual activity seems to have been relatively uncommon in much of Europe, with, however, notable regional exceptions.[25]

The leeway given to young people was not only gender specific, it also depended on class, religious affiliation, and other factors. Furthermore, the means through which sexual activity was controlled varied enormously. In rural settings of the eighteenth and nineteenth centuries, village youth culture operated as an important agent in defining the boundaries of appropriate behavior, facilitating and controlling heterosexual encounters. Noble and bourgeois girls were subjected to other forms of control, some of which also varied regionally. While, for example, French girls seem to have been subjected to especially strict forms of surveillance, English or German girls were often expected to internalize norms of appropriate behavior, and they were generally allowed to partake in a broader range of mixed-gender activities. With the spread of more romantic notions of marital relationships beginning around 1800, young people of marriageable age were given the opportunity to meet and fall in love with appropriate partners. Parental controls over marriage became more circumspect, centering more on making sure their daughters met prospective partners of the appropriate class rather than selecting the partner.[26]

Given the long period of youth and the economic importance of girls' labor, working-class families of the nineteenth and twentieth centuries certainly could not afford to keep their daughters at home or in convent schools. However, the sexual behavior of working girls, though extremely suspicious in the eyes of bourgeois observers, was supervised by parents, fellow workers, and employers, certainly more intensely than that of boys. Moreover, toward the end of the nineteenth century, state control of girls' sexuality increased. While prostitution had long been of concern to the authorities and while states like Württemberg had for centuries punished single mothers, new institutions for delinquent girls (and female delinquency was often equated with sexual misbehavior) were established throughout Europe, particularly in urban centers. Following new concepts of adolescence, they did not only aim at punishing girls but were meant to prepare wayward girls for work and future motherhood.[27]

Increasing preoccupation with the dangers of puberty, emerging in the late nineteenth century, led to expressions of concern about sex education and about the emotional life of girls as they went through puberty. Mothers were expected to guide their daughters through the perils of adolescence by providing them with adequate information about appropriate behavior during menstruation and by helping them to deal with emotional problems. Still, whatever the level of official exhortation, the available evidence about sex education through the mother-daughter relationship suggests that continuities were more marked than discontinuities, and that the diffusion of "modern" attitudes about sexuality and sex education was limited. Instead, continued ignorance and suppression frequently remained the rule even in post-Freudian Europe.[28]

Perhaps more than in any other realm of the history of girlhood, the subject of girls' sexuality eludes definitive assessment. The evidence is scant and ambiguous or downright contradictory. For example, while some French evidence points to the repression of discussion of the subjects of sex, reproduction, and the female body within the intimate circles of the family, we also know that French women were among the first in modern European history systematically to limit births. Did men, then, control knowledge about sexuality, reproduction, and birth control? Were they the educators of wives who until marriage had been kept in ignorance? How do we sort out prescription and written record from practice? The discussion of sexuality thus raises in a particularly emphatic form issues that any historian of female youth confronts: How do we find historical sources that may provide answers to such puzzling questions as these?

Money, Time, and Spaces of Their Own: Girls and Consumer Culture

> [W]e have been able to observe these young craftswomen, for some time now, wearing on Sunday this precious thread (silk) that they spin on the other six days.
>
> —François-Félix de La Farelle, French economist, 1852[29]

If the evidence remains ambiguous concerning the level of participation of young women in sexual modernization, in the realm of consumption and leisure, they were key historical actors. Consumer taste, as Pierre Bourdieu pointed out, is a privileged marker of class. We would add of gender as well. Desires and preferences and tastes for certain foods, types of music or art, and styles of dress are of course products of socialization. They are acquired in a manner that reflects social structures. Tastes, in turn, are important mechanisms for perpetuating social and gender differences.[30]

The elites of modern Europe regarded good taste and artistic talent as important forms of cultural capital. Noble and bourgeois families took the aesthetic education of girls very seriously. Notwithstanding social and national differences, the education of girls from bourgeois and noble families emphasized not so much the skills of the housewife but rather the skills necessary for representing and securing the social status of the family. Their personal appearance and their ability to create a tastefully decorated and well-organized home were central to this endeavor.[31] Correspondingly, advice manuals of the nineteenth century included detailed descriptions on how to compose the trousseau and how to furnish and equip the family home. In addition, girls from upperclass families had to learn how to adorn themselves. Their debut into society and their marriage served not only as rites of passage but also as opportunities to represent their family's social status and ability to equip its offspring with material goods and cultural capital.

In contrast to bourgeois and noble girls' socialization, that of rural and working-class girls centered less on preparation for their role as consumers than as producers and reproducers. However, this does not mean that lowerclass girls did not acquire tastes, were not receptive to aesthetic experiences, and did not try to embellish their surroundings and their dress. Members of all social groups increasingly used consumer goods, and especially dress, to mark social position and to express notions of respectability and allure. The material means for doing so have increased enormously over the last 250 years. While eighteenth-century textile workers in Europe's protoindustrial regions might have brought a couple more dresses into marriage than other lower-class girls, and could afford to dress up their appearance with the help of silk scarves, girls of the late nineteenth and early twentieth centuries, and especially of the affluent period following the 1950s, could draw on a huge array of material goods for their self-representation.[32]

Furthermore, the possibilities for girls to shape their personal appearance and consumer choices in an age-specific manner also increased tremendously. During the eighteenth century many items of clothing owned by ordinary people had been inherited or bought secondhand and the stock of clothes brought into a marriage was meant to last a lifetime. Under such conditions, generational conflicts could hardly focus on questions of hairstyle or dress. Changes in consumption, especially the new fashions girls adopted, met with considerable criticism inspired by moral and religious beliefs. Changing styles of dress increasingly served to distinguish among generations as fashions changed more frequently and youth in particular sought to follow fashion. With the erosion of traditional forms of patriarchal control and increasing mobility and visibility of young people, the consumption habits of male and female youth were frequently viewed as a social problem. Examining girls' consumption practices thus reveals another side of girls as historical actors whose social position changed with new employment opportunities, changing family practices, or new opportunities for participation in public life. While changes in consumption patterns can be understood as mirroring fundamental changes in the social fabric, some girls' individual acts of "cross-dressing"—using dress to transgress class or gender lines—can be interpreted as a significant challenge to class and gender hierarchies.

While youth of all social classes were targeted as consumers, cultural critics lamented their tastes and wasteful habits. Campaigns against cheap literature and, eventually, films, focused on the problems caused when young people had money of their own, and, increasingly, leisure time to spend as well. Girls were often portrayed as especially vulnerable to the temptations of modern consumerism and the dangers of urban places of leisure. As early as the 1790s, when "factory girls" were just beginning to appear on the scene, English mill girls were warned in stark morality tales about the ruin that threatened those who spent too much on finery they could not afford. Later, office workers and shop assistants were criticized for modeling themselves after heroines of novels and films and for aspiring to a life of luxury and idleness as their boss's wife. Dressed in feathered hats and artificial silk and ready-made clothes, these young working women seemed to transgress class lines and make it difficult to distinguish between the daughters of laborers and those from better circles.[33]

Part of the increased attention paid to girls' dress and leisure activities has to be attributed to larger concerns that surfaced toward the end of the nineteenth century about changing gender ideals, female assertiveness, and the falling birthrate. New forms of and places for dancing, cycling, and wearing short skirts and high-heeled shoes—almost every novelty that girls pursued—was seen in some circles as immoral or damaging to their reproductive health. The discourse about girls' new ways of spending time and money not only reflects contemporary concerns but also points to the pleasures girls derived from consumption and new forms of commercial leisure. Novels, magazines, and films provided entertainment that was often shared with female and male friends. Advertisements and stories confronted girls with an increasing variety of female models. More so than in earlier generations, girls growing up in the early decades of the twentieth century began to use fashion to define their personality both in relation to adults and to peers. Thus many girls experienced resistance when they decided to have their hair cut, to wear short dresses, or to use makeup. Parents, teachers, and employers reacted to what they felt was provocative dress, but questions of dress and propriety also caused controversies among youth. Members of socialist youth movements, for example, often criticized commercial culture as an expression of capitalist temptations. Religious and bourgeois youth movements were equally eager to provide youth of both sexes with spaces and codes of behavior that were untinged by consumer culture.[34] Some members of the German youth movement rejected fashionable clothes and chose styles of dress that expressed a nostalgic quest for "natural" as opposed to artificially produced notions of beauty.

With the formation of modern European consumer society between the eighteenth and the twentieth centuries, consumption and commercial forms of leisure became increasingly important sources of pleasure and means of self-expression. The power to consume, with all of its limitations, was a particularly feminine form of power. The sites of modern pleasure seeking became increasingly feminine by the twentieth century. The spaces of modern leisure and consumption cannot be overlooked as a site of girls' agency, however limited, and as a locus of gender and class anxieties that swirled around them.

Finding Female Youth History:
The Problem of the Sources

As is true for all histories "at the margins," the study of the history of female youth brings a number of methodological challenges. Central among these is the problem of silences in the historical record. The sources documenting the history of female youth are at best scattered, often sketchy, occasionally inconsistent, and typically incomplete. Not surprisingly, sources from the twentieth century are more plentiful than those from the eighteenth century, and some aspects of girls' history have left more records than others, but in general, the evidence is limited and piecemeal.

One glaring characteristic of the documentary sources, a problem shared more broadly among historians of childhood and youth, is that almost all of the available evidence has been produced by adults. Even autobiographies and memoirs, a category of sources that promises recollections of lived experience, typically provide us only with accounts of female youth as recalled by adult narrators. With the exceptions of letters, diaries, and school essays, girls have left few written records.

Girls' lives have typically left even fewer records than have boys' lives. Until the twentieth century, formal education beyond primary school was, for example, largely the preserve of boys and young men, and the few girls from affluent families who did acquire some education beyond the most basic literacy often did so at home with the help of private tutors. Educational records thus tend to tell the story of boys rather than girls. Similarly, sons of middling and poor families were far more likely to be placed in formal apprenticeship than were daughters. Apprenticeship contracts for girls are thus much rarer than those for boys, depriving us of the kinds of knowledge and insight that such contracts have provided about the history of male youth.

Other social institutions have also generated a wealth of information about young men generally not available about young women. Nineteenth-century medical records of thousands of military recruits, for example, provide important evidence about the health and physical characteristics of lower-class male youths. In comparison, we know very little about the height and weight, or the general physical condition, of these young men's female counterparts. The penal system has also produced important records chronicling the background and life course of those boys and young men who ended up in trouble with the law. Unfortunately, at least for historians, the clientele of the penal system has always been largely male.

In general, then, boys and young men have typically constituted a much greater presence in institutions that have produced central evidence for the study of youth history. Conversely, the more private social and cultural sites dominated by girls and young women have typically yielded fewer written records. Domestic service, for instance, has rarely been systematically registered or subjected to written labor agreements. Thus it is easier to investigate interactions in a workshop or a factory than relationships between masters and servant girls in the home.

Moreover, throughout the time period under investigation here, boys generally seem to have been much more culturally "visible" than have girls, and they have tended to attract more public attention and concern. Reform schools for boys, for example, have consistently outnumbered similar institutions for girls. So have the number of clubs and other leisure organizations catering to male youth. Similarly, boys' endeavors and accomplishments have been touted more frequently than those of girls. In contrast, girls have typically been warned against attracting public attention of any kind, and many seem to have taken seriously the old adage that the virtuous girl, like the virtuous woman, is the one about whom nothing is known. Public attention paid to a girl was a sign of her failure to maintain privacy and respectability.

These caveats must influence our reading of the historical evidence about girls that we do have. Some of the evidence originates in state activities that shape the record of much of European history. Basic demographic information, for example, has been collected by practically all European states (and churches as well), making it possible to determine the answers to key questions such as the average age of marriage for women, the frequency of out-of-wedlock births, and the proportion of women who never married. But of course, the categories and the terms of the state then function to contain and shape our histories.

Equally well documented are the legal and political institutions that have circumscribed the lives of girls and young women. The rights of parents over children, for example, are stipulated in legal records. So are the changing definitions of the legal age of majority. Sexual consent laws and the political controversies that usually accompanied their passage have also been carefully recorded. Educational policy debates and the implementation of public schooling have left an abundance of relevant records. The same is true with regards to labor legislation, much of which affected young female workers. Public health policies provide yet another important source of information.

Many of the authors represented in this book also rely on evidence produced by a diverse group of not always officially authorized "experts," ranging from church officials, medical professionals, and social scientists to advice columnists, fashion critics, and sex counselors. Much of this evidence is normative and prescriptive and often driven by particular ideological agendas pertaining to female youth. Yet it nevertheless reveals the shifting understandings, expectations, and boundaries of female youth.

Other authors draw more heavily on records that document social practices. Employers of all kinds frequently left records outlining workplace practices and problems. Teachers and other school officials recorded daily activities in and outside the classroom. Institutions such as orphanages, reform schools, and homes for unwed mothers have also left invaluable records. For the twentieth century in particular, we also have a wealth of records from organizations for girls and young women, such as the Girl Scouts and the YWCA.

Obviously, then, much of the history presented in this book is necessarily, because of the nature of the sources, not the history of girls but rather of the ways in which adults tried to shape young women through laws, schools, apprenticeship, sermons, advice, and other means. The discourses and definitions of authorities and other dominant players are of course invaluable. Yet at the same time these discourses are profoundly problematic, tied as they are to particular forms of definition, particular (and highly gendered) notions of private and public concerns, and so on. In early modern Europe, to offer an example of the problem, the socialization of boys was regarded as a public concern, whether in the form of apprenticeship or schooling, while girls were generally supposed to be educated at home. As in the nineteenth and twentieth centuries, lower-class girls more frequently became the target of the state and public institutions, and they become more visible in the sources. Girls' increasing visibility is both the cause and result of their being regarded as a "social problem," in contrast to the more normal and respectable girls who kept to the private realm. Thus, historical documentation, or the lack thereof, is a product of the very historical processes under examination and reflects dimensions of the history of girlhood itself, with its regional, chronological, and class variations. The very source materials on which we depend bring the risk of our simply reproducing the visions of girlhood and its problems that drove this documentation.

The wide variation among the book's chapters in the approach taken to the study of girlhood, and in the associated documentary base, are symptomatic of the particular methodological challenges confronting historians of girlhood. These problems are, of course, just a special case of a far larger problem of understanding history through always inadequate records created for other purposes than the historian's. Nevertheless, the historical study of girls presents these challenges in their extreme form because of girls' marginal position vis-à-vis centers of power and record keeping.

Girls' History, Girls as Agents of History

Despite girls' marginality with respect to centers of power and the processes of record keeping, the chapters of this book point to the ways in which taking girls into account pushes toward a revision of many aspects of modern European history. Girls' labor helps to explain Europe's particular path toward economic development before and during the Industrial Revolution. Girls played a large role in the modernization of Europe's economy again at the turn of the twentieth century. Though often not explicitly, girls were on the agenda of European states in varied and changing ways: they were, for example, taken for granted as a source of labor in economic policies and they later became the focus of pronatalist and nationalist projects by dint of their centrality to reproduction. As cultural emblems, girls have stood variously for national purity or for the excitement of modernity but also for pollution, political oppression, and exploitation. In the era of imperialism, many Europeans saw "their" young women as emblems of racial superiority, in contrast with young women in colonized areas who were dismissed as oppressed child brides. Girls as actors and as icons are at the center of much of Europe's modernity between the mid-eighteenth and the mid-twentieth centuries.

Still, by most usual criteria, girls have acted from positions of relative powerlessness, marginality, and invisibility. How, then, are we to understand the role of girls in history? And how does a focus on girls' roles in history push us to reconsider how we understand historical agency, the ability of even relatively powerless people to make a difference? Clearly, many ordinary understandings of agency and power simply do not apply. What historians of women discovered in their earliest forays into writing women into the past—that it was impossible to do so without changing the story—is even more true for girls. Prodding at historical agency through the history of girls underscores the inadequacy of prevailing notions of historical agency.

For a start, there is a problem with the usual understanding of the individual as historical actor. The history of girlhood challenges the very models of psychological development that, as it emerged along with modern notions of adolescence, underlay modern European notions of the individual, the "great man," who is able to leave an imprint on the world. The idea of adolescence as a stage of struggle and breakthrough from dependent child to the autonomous adult is both highly gendered (masculinist) and class specific (bourgeois). The paradox of thinking about girls as agents thus goes right to the heart of contradictions in modern conceptualizations of individualism and agency as epitomized by the rational (male) adult acting autonomously to further his individual visions and interests.

Even many critical notions of historical agency, such as "transformative agency" that "changes the rules," structuring historical narratives around moments of political rebellion, are difficult to reconcile with the sorts of actions and choices girls mostly have been able to take and have taken. The search for heroic behavior that so often has characterized projects of recovering agency of marginal or oppressed groups seems misplaced here. The model of subaltern studies, with its emphasis on writing history from the margins of power, of trying to hear the voices unrecorded by mainstream histories, is perhaps closer to the point.[35] Attention to more subtle forms of everyday resistance—the "weapons of the weak" that some postcolonial approaches to agency have emphasized—also may be helpful in thinking about the historical agency of girls. But even these interpretations are silent about many of the everyday activities of girls.[36] Thinking about girls in history, in short, presents in a more extreme form the problem of thinking about how women's ordinary activities embody agency. The world would not be as it is without them. They have an ongoing history. And yet the usual ways of talking about change over time do not take them into account. In the end, the effort to address the contributions of girls to modern European history brings us to question the usual notion of historical agency itself.

Notes

1. Throughout the book we use the terms "girl" and "young woman" interchangeably when referring to unmarried female youth. While "young woman" may seem the most appropriate term when speaking of postpubescent females, "girl" has, at least since the late nineteenth century, been the most popular and commonly used term in English. In *The New Girl: Girls' Culture in England, 1880–1915* (New York: Columbia University Press, 1995), Sally Mitchell argues that in England the term "girl" first emerged in popular literature and came into popular usage in the 1880s. As opposed to "young lady," it was an inclusive term, applicable across class lines. The "young lady" was a middle- or upper-class woman on the marriage market. As work became part of the experience of most young women, "girlhood" was increasingly conceptualized as an age class without reference to economic status.

2. The classic article pointing out the western European marriage pattern is John Hajnal, "European Marriage Patterns in Perspective," in *Population in History: Essays in Historical Demography*, ed. D. V. Glass and D. V. Eversly (Chicago: Aldine Publishing, 1965), 101–140. Hajnal points out the relatively late marriage in the region north and west of a line drawn from St. Petersburg, in Russia, to Trieste, on the Adriatic.

3.   James Z. Lee and Wang Feng, *One Quarter of Humanity: Malthusian My-thology and Chinese Realities, 1700–2000* (Cambridge, Mass.: Harvard University Press, 1999), 65. There were some regions of Japan, in contrast, where patterns were more similar to those of western Europe. See, for example, Mary Louise Nagata, "Labour Migration, Family and Community in Early Modern Japan," in *Women, Gender and Labour Migration*, ed. Pamela Sharpe (London: Routledge, 2001), 60–84.

4.   Erik Erikson, *Childhood and Society* (New York: Norton, 1950); Philippe Ariès, *Centuries of Childhood: A Social History of Family Life*, trans. Robert Baldick (New York: Random House, 1962); and John R. Gillis, *Youth and History: Tradition and Change in European Age Relations, 1770 to the Present* (New York: Academic Press, 1981). Other "gender blind" analyses of European youth history include Stephen Humphries, *Hooligans or Rebels? An Oral History of Working-Class Childhood and Youth, 1889–1939* (Oxford: B. Blackwell, 1981); and John Springhall, *Coming of Age: Adolescence in Britain, 1860–1960* (Dublin: Gill and Macmillan, 1986).

5.   Frances Burney, *EVELINA or, The History of a Young Lady's Entrance into the World*, ed. Stewart J. Cooke (New York: W. W. Morton, 1998).

6.   See Rebecca Rogers's chapter in this book.

7.   On gardens, see the chapter by Céline Grasser.

8.   From an interview conducted by Claire Langhamer for the project that is the basis of her chapter in this book.

9.   See, for instance, Mary Jo Maynes, *Schooling in Western Europe* (Albany: State University of New York Press, 1985); June Purvis, *A History of Women's Education in England* (Philadelphia: Open University Press, 1991); June Purvis. *Hard Lessons: The Lives and Education of Working-Class Women in Nineteenth-Century England* (Minneapolis: University of Minnesota Press, 1989); and Meg Gomersall, *Working-Class Girls in Nineteenth-Century England: Life, Work and Schooling* (New York: St. Martin's Press, 1997).

10.   On the history of menstruation, see Peter Laslett, "Age at Menarche in Europe Since the Eighteenth Century," *Journal of Interdisciplinary History* 2 (1971–72): 221–236; Joan Jacobs Brumberg, *The Body Project: An Intimate History of American Girls* (New York: Random House, 1997), 1–25; and Sabine Hering and Gudrun Maierhof, *Die unpässliche Frau: Sozialgeschichte der Menstruation und Hygiene* (Pfaffenweiler: Centaurus-Verlagsgesellschaft, 1991).

11.   Of course the gradual and uneven elimination of full-time child labor over the course of the nineteenth century played a huge role as well. On the uneven "normalization" of lower-class youth in the nineteenth century, see Mary Jo Maynes, *Taking the Hard Road: Life Course in French and German Workers' Autobiographies in the Era of Industrialization* (Chapel Hill: University of North Carolina Press, 1995). For a discussion of changing popular perceptions about youth and its entitlements, see Birgitte Søland's and Langhamer's chapters in this book.

12.   In her introduction to a special issue of the *Journal of Family History,* 17 (1992), focused on the history of youth, Barbara Hanawalt argues that adolescence was identified and acknowledged as a life stage in the Middle Ages. However, although the medieval world recognized, defined, and structured

this life stage, this particular understanding differed from the more modern concept of adolescence. For an account of key debates on adolescence at the turn of the twentieth century, see John Neubauer, *The Fin-de-Siecle Culture of Adolescence* (New Haven, Conn.: Yale University Press, 1992); Kathleen Alaimo, "Shaping Adolescence in the Popular Milieu: Social Policy, Reformers, and French Youth, 1870–1920," *Journal of Family History* 17 (1992): 419–438; and Alaimo's chapter in this book.

13. See Sterling Fishman, "Suicide, Sex, and the Discovery of the German Adolescent," *History of Education Quarterly* 10 (1970): 170–188; Tom Taylor, "Images of Youth and the Family in Wilhelmine Germany: Toward a Reconsideration of the German Sonderweg," *German Studies Review,* winter 1992, 55–74; Lenard R. Berlanstein, "Vagrants, Beggars, and Thieves: Delinquent Boys in Mid-Nineteenth Century Paris," *Journal of Social History* 12 (1979): 531–552; and W. Scott Haine, "The Development of Leisure and the Transformation of Working-Classes Adolescence, Paris 1830–1940," *Journal of Family History* 17 (1992): 451–476.

14. Carol Dyhouse, *Girls Growing Up in Late Victorian and Edwardian England* (Boston: Routledge & Kegan Paul, 1981); Felicity Hunt, ed., *Lessons for Life: The Schooling of Girls and Women, 1850–1950* (Oxford: B. Blackwell, 1987); and Martha Vicinus, *Independent Women: Women and Community for Single Women, 1850–1920* (Chicago: University of Chicago Press, 1985). On state interest in children, female youth, and unmarried mothers, see: Rachel G. Fuchs, *Poor and Pregnant in Paris* (New Brunswick, N.J.: Rutgers University Press, 1992); Valerie Fildes et al., eds., *Women and Children First: International Maternal and Child Welfare, 1870–1945* (New York: Routledge & Kegan Paul, 1992); and Sylvia Schafer, *Children in Moral Danger and the Problem of Government in Third Republic France* (Princeton, N.J.: Princeton University Press, 1997). See also Pamela Cox's chapter.

15. For an argument on the differentiated impact of these discourses on girls themselves, see Christina Benninghaus's chapter.

16. For a discussion of the new jobs for girls see also Anna Davin's chapter. On popular perceptions of girls' changing behavior in the post–World War I era, see Mary Louise Roberts, *Civilization without Sexes: Reconstructing Gender on Postwar France, 1917–1927* (Chicago: University of Chicago Press, 1994); Susan Kingsley Kent, *Making Peace: The Reconstruction of Gender in Interwar Britain* (Princeton, N.J.: Princeton University Press, 1993); and Birgitte Søland, *Becoming Modern: Young Women and the Reconstruction of Womanhood in the 1920s* (Princeton, N.J.: Princeton University Press, 2000).

17. For a discussion of this point, see the chapters by Søland and Langhamer.

18. On female youth cultures, see Mitchell; Penny Tinkler, *Constructing Girlhood: Popular Magazines for Girls Growing Up in England, 1920–1950* (London: Taylor & Francis, 1995); Sally Alexander, *Becoming a Woman and Other Essays in 19th and 20th Century Feminist History* (New York: NYU Press, 1995); D. Fowler, *The First Teenagers: The Lifestyles of Young Wage-earners in Interwar Britain* (London: Woburn Press, 1995); and Claire Langhamer, *Women's Leisure in England 1920–60* (Manchester: Manchester University Press, 2000), as well as the chapters here by Andreas Gestrich, Grasser, Langhamer, Tammy Proctor, and Karin Schmidlechner.

19.   Cited in Benninghaus's chapter in this volume.

20.   Women's work has of course been the focus of much innovative and important scholarship in European history, but the emphasis has been on connections between women's work and family and gender relations rather than
on the role of the female labor forces in economic change or on girls' labor
as such. For an excellent summary of this historical literature, see Louise
Tilly, *Industrialization and Gender Inequality* (Washington, D.C.: American
Historical Association, n.d., originally Philadelphia: Temple University Press,
1993). Important exceptions include Maxine Berg's *The Age of Manufactures, 1700–1820: Industry, Innovation, and Work in Britain* (London and
New York: Routledge & Kegan Paul, 1994); and Clare Crowston, *Fabricating
Women: The Seamstresses of Old Regime France, 1675–1791* (Durham, N.C.,
and London: Duke University Press, 2001), which take women's economic
impact as a major problem. For recent general histories of women's labor,
see Deborah Simonton, *A History of European Women's Work: 1700 to the
Present* (London: Routledge & Kegan Paul, 1998); and Colin Haywood, "Age
and Gender at the Workplace: The Historical Experiences of Young People
in Western Europe and North America," in *Working Out Gender: Perspectives
from Labor History*, ed. Margaret Walsh (Aldershot, England: Ashgate, 1999),
48–65. See also the chapters by Simonton, Mary Jo Maynes, Carol E. Morgan, and Elizabeth Jones in this volume.

21.   Studies of young women's entry into these new types of employment include Kirsten Geertsen, *Dannet Ung Pige Søges: Kvinder paa Kontor 1900–
1940* (Holme Olstrup, Denmark: Akademisk forlag, 1990); Meta Zimmeck,
"Jobs for the Girls: The Expansion of Clerical Work for Women, 1850–
1914," in *Unequal Opportunities*, ed. Angela John (Oxford: Oxford University Press, 1986), 153–177; D. Thom, "Better a Teacher than a Hairdresser?"
in *Lessons for Life: The Schooling of Girls and Women, 1850–1950*, ed. Felicity
Hunt (Oxford: Oxford University Press, 1987); T. Davy, "'A Sissy Job for
Men: A Nice Job for Girls': Women Shorthand Typists in London, 1900–
1939," in *Our Work, Our Lives, Our Words*, ed. Leonora Davidoff et al.
(Totowa, N.J.: Barnes & Noble Books, 1986), 124–144; and Theresa McBride,
"A Woman's World: Department Stores and the Evolution of Women's Employment, 1870–1920," *French Historical Studies* 10 (1978): 664–683. See
also Davin's chapter in this book.

22.   See Crowston, *Fabricating Women*, as well as Crowston's chapter in this
volume.

23.   Claire Pic's unpublished diary is cited in Rogers's chapter in this book.

24.   For an analysis of this phenomenon in the American context, see Constance
A. Nathanson, *Dangerous Passage: The Social Control of Sexuality in Women's
Adolescence* (Philadelphia: Temple University Press, 1991).

25.   For descriptions of and sources about marriage customs and youth cul-
tures in Europe, see Ingeborg Weber-Kellermann, *Die Familie: Geschichte,
Geschichten und Bilder* (Frankfurt am Main: Insel Verlag, 1976); Michael
Mitterauer, *Sozialgeschichte der Jugend* (Frankfurt: Suhrkamp, 1986);
and Andreas Gestrich, *Traditionelle Jugendkultur und Industrialisierung.
Sozialgeschichte der Jugend in einer ländlichen Arbeitergemeinde Württem-
bergs, 1800–1920* (Göttingen: Vandehoeck & Ruprecht, 1986), as well as
Gestrich's chapter in this volume. The very different situation in middle-

and upper-class milieus is documented in this book in the chapters by Irene Hardach-Pinke and Mary Lynn Stewart.

26. On this point, see Hardach-Pinke's and Langhamer's chapters in this volume. See also Gunilla-Friederike Budde, *Auf dem Weg ins Bürgerleben* (Göttingen: Vandenhoeck & Ruprecht, 1994).

27. See, for instance, Jill Harsin, *Policing Prostitution in Nineteenth-Century Paris* (Princeton, N.J.: Princeton University Press, 1985); Pamela Cox, *Bad Girls: Gender, Justice, and Welfare in Britain, 1900–1950* (London: Palgrave Macmillan, 2003); Linda Mahood, *Policing Gender: Class and Family in Britain, 1800–1945* (Alberta: University of Alberta Press, 1995); and Pamela Cox and H. Shore, eds., *Becoming Delinquent: British and European Youth, 1650–1950* (Aldershot, England: Ashgate, 2002). For a study of similar developments in the United States, see Mary Odem, *Delinquent Daughters: Protecting and Policing Adolescent Female Sexuality in the United States, 1885–1920* (Chapel Hill, N.C.: Duke University Press, 1995); Ruth M. Alexander, *The "Girl Problem": Female Sexual Delinquency in New York, 1900–1930* (Ithaca, N.Y.: Cornell University Press, 1995); and Anne McGillivray, ed., *Governing Childhood* (Brookfield, Vt.: Dartmouth University Press, 1997). See also the chapter by Cox in this volume.

28. For more on this, see Stewart's and Schmidlechner's chapters here. See also Roy Porter and Leslie Hall, *The Facts of Life: The Creation of Sexual Knowledge in Britain, 1650–1950* (New Haven, Conn., and London: Yale University Press, 1995), esp. chapter 11 (247–270).

29. For the full reference, see the chapter by Maynes.

30. Pierre Bourdieu, *La distinction. Critique sociale du jugement* (Paris, Éditions de Minuit, 1979).

31. On the expectations of middle-class women, see Gunilla-Friederike Budde, "Des Haushalts 'schönster Schmuck.' Die Hausfrau als Konsumexpertin des deutschen und englischen Bürgertums im 19. und 20. Jahrhundert" in *Europäische Konsumgeschichte. Zur Gesellschafts-und Kulturgeschichte des Konsums,* ed. Hannes Siegrist, Hartmut Kaelble, and Jürgen Kocka (Frankfurt am Main: Campus Verlag, 1997), 411–440. On women, gender, and consumption more generally, see Victoria deGrazia, *The Sex of Things: Gender and Consumption in Historical Perspective* (Berkeley: University of California Press, 1996); and Lisa Tiersten, *Marianne in the Market. Envisioning the Consumer Society in Fin-de-Siècle France* (Berkeley: University of California Press, 2001).

32. For a discussion of the quest for aesthetic experiences among the lower classes, see Kaspar Maase, " . . . ein unwiderstehlicher Drang nach Freude. Ästhetische Erfahrung als Gegenstand historischer Kulturforschung," *Historische Anthropologie* 8 (2000): 432–444. See also Hans Medick, *Weben und Überleben in Laichingen, 1650–1900. Lokalgeschichte als allgemeine Geschichte* (Göttingen: Vandenhoeck & Ruprecht, 1997).

33. See Tinkler. For a discussion of the Danish controversies about the new style, see Søland, *Becoming Modern,* 22–45.

34. Ironically, these youth movements created a market for goods connected to the movement—like badges, flags, etc.—or necessary for group activities—like backpacks and camping equipment. See Proctor's chapter in this volume.

35.   A pioneering statement of this problem appeared in Gayatri Chakravorty Spivak's "Can the Subaltern Speak? Speculations on Widow Sacrifice," *Wedge* 7/8 (winter/spring 1985): 120–130.

36.   The phrase is from James C. Scott's book *Weapons of the Weak: Everyday Forms of Peasant Resistance* (New Haven, Conn.: Yale University Press, 1985).

Part One: Working Girls' Labor
and Lives in the
Preindustrial and
Early Industrial Eras

1 Bringing Up Girls: Work in Preindustrial Europe

Deborah Simonton

Part One looks at the role of girls in Europe's preindustrial economy, gender dimensions of youth experiences, and girls' particular contributions to protoindustrial and early industrial growth. In this first chapter, Deborah Simonton discusses the various forms of work and training that were a routine part of girlhood in much of Europe in the preindustrial era. She argues that learning skills and working—whether in the parental home, as a contracted servant in the home of others, as an apprentice, or as a waged employee—were fundamental to an eighteenth-century girl's experience of growing up.

> I have heard and believe that my father and mothers names were Thomas and Dorothy Way and that they lived over against St Andrews Church in Holbourn and that I was born there and that they dyed in my infancy and that by the care of my aunt Sarah Pauling I was nursed and put to [the Charity] School in the parish. . . . About sixteen years since Jane Lilling-ston took me out of the Charity School in order to be a servant to her and Henry Rhodes. . . . I lived with them for ten years without any wages and from that time I have had four pounds per annum.[1]

In this deposition, Ann Way described her particular route into work as a servant in early modern England. Most girls of the laboring and artisanal strata in Europe before 1800 worked "in service" as domestics, farm workers, or apprentices for some period of their life before marriage. This chapter explores this life cycle stage, so significant for girls and their families in preindustrial Europe. It argues that during their youth girls were engaged in earning and learning in what was a recognized period of transition.[2]

Patterns and Structures of Girlhood

In eighteenth-century Europe, the "ladder of life" was often used as a metaphor to represent the female life cycle. Each step represented a stage—from infant to girl, and then to betrothed maiden, bride, mother, and finally grandmother, thus identifying females according to an *idealized* reproductive cycle. (See Figure 1.) However, girlhood, the relatively long period between infancy and marriage, involved the twin projects of learning a set of work skills and earning or producing a dowry for marriage. Throughout Europe, earning was a feature of girlhood for all but the most privileged young women.

Apprenticeship and schooling were the more formal ways of structuring girlhood, although this would have been the experience of the minority of girls. Apprenticeship tied a master and a young person by a written contract for a period of years and under stipulated conditions. Apprentices, or their parents or guardians, paid a master for their apprenticeship training. Parallel to this were less formal structures, such as work at home and contractual labor as a farm or town servant. Servants were generally engaged by verbal or tacit contracts, typically for one year. However, it is important to note that these structural distinctions were often blurred and changed over time. The term "service" was used widely, even to refer to apprenticeship. By the end of the eighteenth century, new forms of work such as factory labor might be termed "apprenticeship" by analogy with the familiar form of youth training.

Children's early years were usually spent in the parental home. They began to leave from the age of eight or nine, and departures accelerated around age fourteen. Thus in 1757, Jane Cook from Abbots Bromley, Staffordshire, was apprenticed to a husbandman at age eight, while in 1798 Mary Bentley, age seven, from Cannock, went to the household of a minister and landowner. These girls are representative of the large number of girls from the poorest families who were put into service by poor-law officials at very young ages.[3] This was not a uniquely English experience. On the continent, there are also examples of girls who left home at a very young age. In Germany, Margarete Hermann went to service at age nine, as did a small minority of girls in Bayeux, France, where 3 percent of servants were under age fifteen in 1796.[4]

More typically, rural children first entered farm service between twelve and fifteen and urban service somewhat later. In Terling, Essex, for example, 16 percent of boys and 9 percent of girls aged ten to fourteen had left home for service, and the percentage increased with age.[5] In eighteenth-century England, between a half and three-quarters of fifteen- to nineteen-year-old boys and girls were living at home; "there was no sudden rush . . . to leave the parental home." One-third to a half probably remained until marriage. In some areas, boys left earlier than girls or were more likely to leave. For example, in Cardington in 1782, 78 percent of boys were away, though 71 percent of girls remained at home. Some who went to service at very young ages may have had no home to

Fig. 1. "The Life & Age of Woman: Stages of Woman's Life from the Cradle to the Grave," ca. 1850. Images such as this one were well known in early modern Europe. Courtesy Library of Congress.

leave, having been abandoned or orphaned. Indeed, the death of a parent, especially fathers, was a decisive factor in leaving home.[6]

Research on England illustrates typical life cycle routes for children of laboring families. (See Table 1.) Girls were more likely to follow the patterns shown in columns A, D, and E while all six patterns represented typical avenues for boys. Probably most girls followed the route described in column E, spending their early years and much of their early working life in the familial home. Many would have left home temporarily or permanently by age fourteen for service, apprenticeship, or work, a pattern that also characterized many other regions of Europe in the eighteenth century. On the whole, girls were subject to less formal and less institutionalized forms of work and socialization than boys.

Girls at Home

In the eighteenth century, families, particularly mothers, were increasingly regarded as the major influence in childrearing and character development. Mothering took on new prominence throughout Europe and attracted the attention of philosophers and pedagogues alike. While new Enlightenment ideals about motherhood may not have dictated action, the importance of so-

Table 1.   Life Cycles, Birth to Marriage

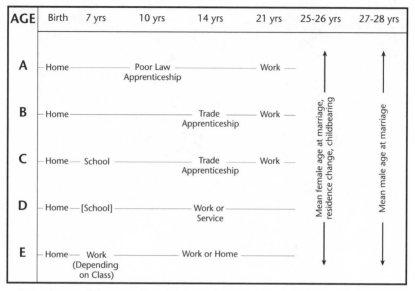

Source: Simonton, "Education and Training," 266.

cialization during the early years of life was widely recognized. However, as several historians have argued, the "move towards a more child-oriented society was challenged at every stage, and never completed. Both in attitudes . . . and behavior . . . we are confronted at every turn by ambivalence and contradictions."[7] Moreover, this ideology did not apply equally to all classes: the cultural and economic nexus of laboring life meant that the image of the child-oriented mother remained alien among the lower classes. Thus the experiences and expectations of middle- and upper-class girls were significantly different from those of poor, artisan, or laboring girls.

Studies of middle-class girls show that large numbers were educated at home, often by mothers or other women.[8] This evidence of a central role for the home suggests one important way of looking at girls' formative years. Daughters of tradesmen and craftsmen learned "female" jobs, helped in family shops, and may well have been systematically trained at home. They assisted their mothers, who sometimes carried on separate trades. Thus "laundress produced laundresses; seamstress generated seamstresses. Chocolate-maker mothers and aunts trained daughters and cousins. Tavern and café keepers' daughters helped their mothers run the business."[9] Often daughters learned a trade alongside apprentices or were taught by parents or others in an informal arrangement. For example, Ann Taylor in Colchester learned engraving and Crescentia Höss in Kaufbeuren learned weaving from their fathers. Daughters in the French book trade could receive training in technical, legal, financial, and managerial skills within family businesses. Marie Madeleine Musier, sixteen-year-old daughter of a bookstore owner, demonstrated when questioned by police in 1759 that she clearly understood the family business, through knowledge and experience gained at home. Daughters of middle-class burghers who would later support husbands' businesses and run a household usually prepared for their role in the parental home. In Edinburgh, Ann Gellately worked in her father's shop; Mary Cummy learned shopkeeping in her brother's shop. Elizabeth Rattray, a surgeon's daughter, learned to make gravecloths from her mother. Daughters were unlikely to receive wages, and so their skill and knowledge had to serve as a dowry, though sometimes fathers provided them with furnishings or tools.[10] Because girls and women could easily get work in domestic industries, training or informal service at home might suffer because of the lure of immediate earnings. For example, in Scotland, "the income from spinning, knitting and especially the embroidering of muslins discouraged young girls from going into service, allowing them to remain at home and contribute to family's income or to set up on their own."[11] Because many girls could be usefully employed in industry at home, it undoubtedly often prevented their departure.

Many girls were also expected to assist around the house, and, like their mothers, to balance "domestic" chores with field or industrial work. Moreover, schools regularly taught specifically "female" work for girls, such as needlework, laundering, and cleaning, but this was not usually the case in boys' schooling.[12] Girls were expected to learn the work roles and attitudes needed to manage their own future households. The importance of "housewifery" in English apprenticeship records bears witness to the fact that it was considered normal, and that girls were expected to learn how to carry out these essential tasks.

In eighteenth-century Europe, passing along traditions and skills from generation to generation played a key role in youth socialization. For most people in villages, and many in towns, their understanding of the world was still local, and their knowledge of the way things were done rested on verbal communication and custom. In this context, women established and maintained their own networks. Much of what girls learned about adult life was acquired from older women around them. Girls were expected, from an early age, to assist mothers by performing simple but necessary tasks. As they grew older, more able, and more experienced, tasks could grow more complex. It was effectively a girl's "apprenticeship" in domestic, agricultural, or technical skills that she would need as a woman with her own household. Food preparation, keeping of animals, needlework, and clothes production ranked high in the list. Work practices were passed down from mother to daughter, as well as an understanding of the strategies for organizing work, life, and knowledge of a woman's place in the cultural nexus in which she expected to live. Some girls, of course, became responsible for managing their family home at an early age, substituting for mothers who were unwell or dead.[13] In this way, girls' roles, knowledge, and status were transmitted through instruction and emulation of other women in the household.

Maidservants, Rural and Urban

The most frequent reason for girls to leave home in early modern Europe was to become servants. A very high proportion of young women in many regions of Europe in the eighteenth century spent at least part of their youth "in service." Learning and working was a hallmark of girlhood, and girls in service learned vocational skills and had an opportunity to save for a dowry. Importantly, service was temporary, acting as a transition from the child to the woman who would have her own household to oversee. Many entered service out of the simple need for work and accommodation; for others, service was a first step into town, and they moved on to other work once they became more established. Many went away to service initially because there was little or no work locally, while others were placed in service as part of poor-law policy. Thus in Terling in 1792 Mary Edwards was put out to Mr. Ely with this agreement:

> I do hereby agree to take Mary Edwards aged about 15 years as my servant from Michaelmas Day next for three years and do engage to find her with sufficient Victuals and Drink with washing, Lodging, Cloathing & and all other necessaries during the said term and at the expiration of the three years I do further engage to provide her with sufficient cloathing for another service. And I also acknowledge to have received of the overseer of the poor Two pounds towards cloathing the said Mary Edwards.[14]

Others left home for service when destitution was the only alternative. Some, like Claire Martelly, left because of repeated beatings at home, or like Anne Auvray "because of her sister's behavior."[15] Others went into service for more positive reasons, such as the opportunities it could provide by opening up new avenues and connections, perhaps enhancing marriage and dowry prospects. London examples show how difficult that could be in practice, but evidence from France shows that some French girls compiled dowries of 500–600 livres in the 1780s through domestic service.[16] Some of these girls married other servants and ended up running an inn or similar trade. Some stayed their whole life in one situation, becoming part of the family, often remembered in wills; others were highly mobile.

Girls going into service migrated to nearby villages, towns, and sometimes to distant regions or metropolises, usually following well-traveled routes, building on contacts with friends and family. At the age of sixteen, Sarah Jackson, for example, lodged in the house where her sister was a servant and hired herself for three weeks for bed and board. Few servants working in Europe's towns and cities had been born there, and country girls were usually preferred over town girls as domestics. Mistresses looking for servants went to coaching inns to meet girls from the country, and it was common to write to friends and relatives asking for servants. Some girls worked for local people with homes in London, such as Sarah Weston from Bocking, who hired herself to two spinsters with homes in Black Notley and in Marylebone.[17] Many traveled only twenty or thirty miles; others migrated from as far as Brittany to Paris. About a quarter of London's servants were from London, 30.8 percent from the southeast of England, and the rest from further afield.[18]

Servants often stayed relatively short periods of time in one position and were willing and able to move frequently. Mary Welbeck served in Essex and in her home county of Kent before taking employment in London. Eleanor Ashwood described the interchange between farm and domestic service, explaining that in addition to various places in London, "she has lodged at several places in the country within the said time upon haymaking and harvest work."[19] Susanna Whatman, author of a book of instructions, probably wrote it precisely because she had to replace servants so frequently. Of the six maids employed by Susanna in 1778, two at most still remained in 1779, and of their successors two, and possibly four, had gone by 1780.[20] Her experience is consistent with evidence from elsewhere. Over half of household servants in London stayed in a position less than a year. Female servants, on average, stayed in their first place about eight months and in their second about ten.[21] Sixty-eight percent of farm servants hired at Tetney, Lincolnshire, between 1780 and 1830 stayed only one year.[22] The mobility of servant girls suggests that they found it easy to get a place, although at any one time, many were out of service, looking for a new position.

The rapid growth of European cities and the urban middle classes beginning in the second half of the eighteenth century created an increasing demand for domestic servants that only subsided toward the end of the nineteenth century. The destinations of pupils departing from schools in Essex in this era show a clear rise in the proportion of girls going into service, many in commercial towns like Colchester, Chelmsford, and Romford; others went to London. Far more girls went into service than apprenticeship from Essex charity schools; boys were evenly split. Many girls who "stayed their full time" in school also went into service. Parents who removed children probably needed them for work at home or intended to hire them out. Also, records suggest that governors thought service was an appropriate route for girls.[23]

Few of these servants were "domestics" in the narrow sense that they only did housework. Many spent time in industrial employment; farm servants were primarily engaged in agricultural labor. The integration of servants into families shifted; as wages were paid periodically rather than at the end of a year, the relationship became more contractual than familial. On the one hand, the servant's position was clearly inferior, dependent entirely on the family she served, subject to its vagaries and reliant on it to honor her wages. She was also sexually vulnerable. If she complained of advances by males in the household, she was as likely to be out of a position as not, and her chances of saving for marriage were effectively thwarted. On the other hand, domestic service was the ideal female job, performed in private, and adhering to the feminine ideology of service and dependence.

A girl's experience of domestic service depended on numerous factors, including the wealth and standing of the household and the work expected of her. The number of servants was a key factor. Most households that employed servants had only one or two. Fifty-six percent of households in one London sample had only one; 96 percent were female. A further 21 percent had two; 84 percent were female.[24] Thus most girls were "maids of all work," responsible for all housework, cleaning rooms, cooking, washing up, laundering, and ironing. Simultaneously, they served the household as nanny, lady's maid, and valet to family members. They carried heavy loads of wood, coal, laundry, or food; emptied and washed chamber pots; and boiled clothes, menstrual rags, diapers, and sheets before washing them. An Essex servant wrote home in 1783, describing her workload and loneliness:

> I wish you would write a Littel ofenr for I have no body to speak to and I can not wright so often as i would because my place is so heavy and I have not time to wright I have nobody to do nothing for Me and I have not mended but three pairs of stockings since I have been at my place I hope these Lins will meat you alle in good health as I am at present bless God for it for I conclude with my duty to you my Love to brothers, sisters.[25]

In larger households, girls could work their way up, but it required experience and imitation of those seen as above them. Household practices had to be acquired in addition to the mechanics of tasks. Chambermaids and housemaids required few skills to start, usually built on knowledge gained at home. Laundry or dairymaids' work was more specialized, but contemporaries believed that it too was easily acquired, usually at home.[26] Preferment could be the result of specific training. Nancy Bere was taken from the Lymington poorhouse by the Hackmans to weed their garden. They moved her to the kitchen and eventually to lady's maid, after Mrs. Hackman "had her carefully instructed in all the elementary branches of education."[27] Employers encouraged a modicum of emulation in dress, cleanliness, and manners, because it reflected favorably on their household. Relationships even developed whereby employers took an interest in improving servants' prospects.

In rural communities, farm service was a routine life cycle stage. Evidence indicates that "[servants] left their parents as children and departed from service as adults," having acquired the skills needed to be farmers themselves. Agricultural tasks, from field labor to dairy work, were acquired early because farm servants usually were sons and daughters of small farmers and cottagers. In England around 1770, 12.7 percent of farm servants were "maids" on arable farms, and an additional 28.6 percent on grassland farms with dairy work. Resident servants (as opposed to day laborers) accounted for half the farm labor force.[28] Living conditions varied widely due to the difference in the relative wealth of families and of regions where girls went to service. In early nineteenth-century Scotland, according to one memoir,

> A holding of one hundred acres would generally employ as unmarried servants two young men as assistant ploughmen, a boy for a cow-herd, a thresher (at least in winter) and two or three maid-servants, all living permanently with the gudeman's family. The men and the grown sons on the tenant slept in the loft above the ben (if there happened to be one) or more often with the horses in the stable.

The girls slept in the kitchen with the tenant's daughters, though if a strong wind made the lum smoke all the women would spend the night with the cows.[29]

Farm servants were usually hired annually, starting at Michaelmas, Martinmas, or May Day, when, according to nineteenth-century observer William Marshall, "the roads were crowded with farm servants leaving their places and hying to the fair. It was a complete holiday: not a team to be seen, or a stroke of work going forward."[30] Female farm apprentices in Essex and Staffordshire were primarily put to "husbandry," "yeomanry," and "farming," where they were probably involved in fieldwork on the same basis as other women on the farm. In the last half of the eighteenth century, farm service was declining, but it still was the most likely destination after housewifery, mantua making, and millinery for girls placed in service.[31]

A hierarchy also operated among farm servants: upward mobility meant moving to a more responsible position or to a larger or better-run farm. The *Commercial and Agricultural Magazine* counseled young people to move from place to place to learn a wide variety of farming skills in a variety of geographical settings.[32] Like most rural women, servants expected to take up any task, including the heaviest. Mary Puddicombe, who went to farm service when she was nine, reported:

> I used to be employed when I was apprenticed in driving bullocks to field and fetching them in again; cleaning out their houses, and bedding them up; washing potatoes and boiling them for pigs; milking; in the field leading horses or bullocks to plough; maidens would not like that work now. Then I was employed in mixing lime to spread, digging potatoes, digging and pulling turnips, and anything that came to hand like a boy. I reaped a little, not much; loaded pack horses; went out with horses for furze. I got up at five or six, except on market mornings twice a week then at three. I went to bed at half-past nine. I worked more in the fields than in the house.[33]

Servant girls on farms often worked alongside their mistress with their range of work activities mirroring hers. Although maidservants were hired on all types of holdings, women's fieldwork varied quite dramatically depending on whether the farm raised animals or crops. Landowning patterns also had implications for women, particularly the way the labor service was demanded from tenants. In England live-in farm service was in decline by the latter years of the eighteenth century, increasingly replaced by day labor, as new agricultural practices altered the seasonality of labor requirements. There was apparently no similar decline across Europe. In fact, in many areas there was an increase in the demand for female farm servants.[34] But there was also more recourse to hired day labor, particularly female, which was rare before the development of intensive and commercial farming. Still, girls were a much higher proportion of farm servants than of farm day laborers. That so many women were farm servants is notable because they were to lose this option in some of Europe's regions as farm service declined.[35]

Girls as Apprentices

Girls as well as boys were apprenticed, though in smaller numbers and not consistently across Europe. To work in certain trades, guilds expected the same compliance from girls as boys. Nevertheless, girls usually could not attain full status in guilds. Men often saw women as threats to their position and honor. English and French guilds sharply curtailed women's trading opportunities, diminishing the value of apprenticeship. In Germany, girls were no longer formally apprenticed in the eighteenth century, although that had been the case earlier. The tendency of urban families to absorb girls' labor informally might explain the relatively small number of recorded apprenticeships, but exclusionary practices played a decided role. Still, the evidence demonstrates that some girls did enter trades through apprenticeship. Girls comprised 19 percent of apprentices in Geneva between 1701 and 1710, 9 percent in Staffordshire and Essex between 1750 and 1799, about 2 percent in Warwickshire, and 5 percent in Wiltshire. A third of English poor-law apprentices were girls, accounting for more than two-thirds of female apprentices in Essex and Staffordshire.[36] So while not as prominent as boys' apprenticeship, apprenticeship was a recognized mode of training for girls. As Clare Crowston will argue in chapter 4, evidence suggests that despite formal restrictions and jealousies, there was increasing interest in all forms of training for girls, including apprenticeship, in Paris beginning at the end of the seventeenth century.

Apprenticeship taught work skills, but it also integrated young workers into gender and social status hierarchies. Whereas skill and training for occupations were explicitly the function of apprenticeship, the apprenticeship period implicitly served to transmit and perpetuate work cultures and status distinctions. Corporate notions of status attached to work roles reflected male conceptualizations, particularly in corporate communities where guilds were closely linked to political power and where guilds derived influence from their roles as organizers of the town economy. Corporations deliberately restricted competing organizations, thus often affecting women in trades. For example, women in Kingston upon Thames operating in regulated trades such as chandlery were required to pay for permission to trade, just as men who had not served an apprenticeship.[37] Within the corporate community, male apprenticeship frequently led to "freeman" status with civic rights and responsibilities. Throughout Europe, guild members appeared on town councils and the guild system "with all its ways penetrated . . . political institutions through and through." In Aberdeen, the link between burgesses and the "Companies" is clear: the dean of guild, merchant-councillors, and trades-councillors were elected city positions.[38]

Apprenticeship could promote a daughter's social mobility because training in a respectable female trade could enhance her options. Families who could afford the premium used apprenticeships to improve a daughter's status and prospects, possibly with an eye to marriage within the trade or at least at a

Table 2. Distribution of Trades by Sex, for private apprentices in Staffordshire and Essex, 1750-99

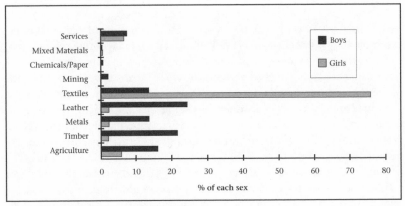

Source: Simonton, "Education and Training," 252.

comparable social level. There were economic and political reasons for apprenticing poor girls, but advice literature made it clear that socialization was often the focus in the middle classes. Education in demeanor, propriety, and sobriety, as well as technical training, could be derived through apprenticeship. Thus, the system was sometimes used to raise children in an appropriate environment. Ultimately, social education in values and behavior was an important element of female apprenticeship.

Specific examples of girls' apprenticeship patterns can be gleaned from English school records and apprenticeship contracts. This evidence suggests that parents and authorities in Essex and Staffordshire were less concerned with the nature of trades and the training component of the period of apprenticeship for girls than for boys.[39] Girls' shorter apprenticeships suggest that less training was likely to be provided, while boys' apprenticeships more clearly matched the expectations of the guild tradition. Sexual differentiation of trades meant that girls, even those whose parents were willing and able to pay high premiums, went to "female" work, while apprenticeships in more profitable trades were restricted to boys. Boys also dominated the "respectable" trades while girls were involved in those associated with less skill, training, and prestige. Girls were, for example, poorly represented in trades like cutlery or the manufacture of mechanical devices, which were believed to require substantial skills. Although the girls' opportunities were not limited to female trades, they did not appear across trades in equal numbers with boys (Table 2).

The overwhelming impression is that girls' opportunities through apprenticeship were sharply limited compared to boys'. They usually trained in low-status occupations with modest future prospects. The construction of female apprenticeship owed less to any feminine ideal and more to a status evaluation that described them as subordinate and their work, albeit economically valuable, as inferior in status to male work. Prospects of setting up on their own were slim, since they were unlikely to have access to necessary capital. Instead, they were more likely to work with husbands. Some girls were no doubt as carefully taught as boys. Others were apprenticed on the same conditions as brothers, enabling them to set up as independent mistresses and take apprentices. Nevertheless, apprenticeship opened new horizons for girls, if less systematically than for boys.

Female apprentices thus operated in a somewhat ambivalent context. Central to the idea of apprenticeship was the expectation that apprentices should receive training in a craft. Indentures in England usually stipulated that the master or mistress would teach the apprentice "in the Art of [trade] which s/he now useth . . . and Instruct or Cause to be taught and Instructed in the best way and Manner that s/he can." Within this construction there existed a regulated method of social advancement; access to apprenticeship, particularly in "good" trades was seen as enhancing children's opportunities. Children were to be instructed "in such things as may qualify them best to enter upon the world, and act for themselves when they are so enter'd."[40] Thus, the system specifically served as an initiation to the responsibility of citizenship and adulthood. Girls, however, were expected to acquire their adult status primarily through marriage. Acquisition of status through apprenticeship was less relevant for girls than for boys, leading to relatively short terms of apprenticeship for girls and an emphasis on immediate earning power rather than long-term opportunities and skills. Though available for work earlier than boys, girls' prospects of becoming financially and socially independent women diminished accordingly. In many ways the system prepared girls for a married future, as helpers to husbands, and reflected society's view of women as valued in relation to men.

From as early as the sixteenth century, the concept and practice of apprenticeship altered. For example, the Tudor practice of pauper "apprenticeship" designed to alleviate the burden of poor children on parishes blurred the original purposes and rules of apprenticeship. Because children were indentured to remove them from parish support, they were more prevalent in poorer trades, often as a disguised form of cheap labor. In husbandry or housewifery, the line between training and work was obscured by the nature of the task. By the end of the eighteenth century, the situation of apprenticeship would alter dramatically throughout Europe. Guild claims to monopoly were abolished in France during the Revolution and elsewhere either during the Napoleonic era or in the decades that followed. In England new forms of labor were challenging corporate prerogatives long before the Revolution.

In many new trades and unregulated areas, simple hiring agreements replaced apprenticeship, but the term was sometimes preserved for young workers. Josiah Wedgwood's pottery, employing two hundred to four hundred workers, provides a good example of the new kinds of training that a girl could acquire. His introduction of specialization and division of labor into pottery manufacture is often associated with de-skilling, yet each worker was expected to become expert in one process, and new designs, glazes, and refined techniques required training. Some hiring agreements, such as Ann Keeling's, 1781, are similar to apprenticeship. Wedgwood promised to feed, clothe, and house her and paid wages of £3, £4, and £5 per year, respectively, for three years. In 1784, Keeling was paid 15 shillings a week, the piece rate for journeymen painters.[41] Children were brought into the works, trained, and as they grew up and gained experience, moved into adult processes as skilled workers. Contemporaries expected young workers of both sexes to imitate their superiors and to gain experience. They recognized this as a useful and important aspect of growing up. Once involved in the world of work, learning was not necessarily finished. Where it was necessary, or possible, specific work-related training was given, ranging from mechanical skills to business practices, accounts, and organization. Despite formal restrictions on girls' work opportunities, there is substantial evidence that the range of girls' labor was expanding tremendously by the end of the eighteenth century.[42]

Girlhood was a recognized and significant stage in the female life cycle in eighteenth-century Europe. Family members and other elders "brought up" girls to provide them with the knowledge and skills required for self-support in youth and for eventual adulthood. For most, marriage marked the end of girlhood; the skills, knowledge, customs, and dowries they had acquired during youth were necessary perquisites to set them up as married women. Girls followed many routes to adult womanhood, but learning work practices and working were the mainstay of this phase of life for all but the most privileged girls. Whether she worked in the parental home, as a contracted servant in the homes of others, as an apprentice, or as a waged employee, the importance of the transmission of skills and culture were fundamental to an eighteenth-century girl's experience of growing up. Also girls often hired themselves out, especially as servants who were highly mobile, so while girlhood had significance within the social constructions of eighteenth-century Europe, it also had meaning for the girls themselves. And this special nature of girlhood, with its typical period of service, wage earning, or apprenticeship, often outside the parental home, was also a key characteristic distinguishing Europe's family and gender system.

Notes

1.   Jane Lillingston was the housekeeper; quoted in Peter Earle, *A City Full of People* (London: Methuen, 1994), 188–189. I would like to thank Elaine Chalus, Nicola Pullin, and the editors and contributors to this volume for their comments.
2.   On the stages of youth and childhood, see John Gillis, *Youth and History, Tradition and Change Childhood* (Harmondsworth: Penguin, 1973), 23–30; Philippe Ariès, *Centuries of Childhood* (Harmondsworth: Penguin, 1973),

pp. 23–30; and Joseph F. Kett, "The Stages of Life," in *The Family in Social-Historical Perspective,* ed. Michael Gordon (New York: St Martin's Press, 1978), 166–191.

3. Staffordshire Record Office (hereafter cited as SRO) D120/A/PO/1264–1400, SRO D1054/7/20, Essex Record Office (hereafter cited as ERO) D/P 264/13/4.

4. Heide Wunder, *He Is the Sun, She Is the Moon* (Cambridge, Mass.: Harvard University Press, 1998), 27; Sarah C. Maza, *Servants and Masters in Eighteenth-Century France* (Princeton, N.J.: Princeton University Press, 1983), 63.

5. ERO T/P 87, 5 May 1775 and 7 July 1778.

6. Richard Wall, "Age at Leaving Home," *Journal of Family History* 3 (1978): 190–191; Maza, 43; Tim Meldrum, *Domestic Service and Gender* (Harlow, Essex: Pearson, 2000), 19.

7. Hugh Cunningham, *Children and Childhood in Western Society Since 1500* (London: Longman, 1995), 62. These ideas were extended to the lower classes through schools, schoolbooks, and sermons such as John Burton, *Religious Education of Poor Children Recommended* (London, 1793); and John Chapman, *Ends and Uses of Charity Schools* (London, 1752).

8. Nicholas Hans, *New Trends in Education in the Eighteenth Century* (London: Routledge & Kegan Paul, 1951); and Deborah Simonton, "Education and Training of Eighteenth-Century English Girls" (Ph.D. diss., Essex, 1988), 284–297. For example, Ann Taylor Gilbert, *Autobiography and Other Memorials of Mrs. Gilbert, Formerly Ann Taylor,* 2 vols., ed. Josiah Gilbert (London: Henry S. King and Co., 1874), 41.

9. Olwen Hufton, *The Prospect Before Her* (London: Fontana Press, 1995), 94.

10. Gilbert, 103; Wunder, 87; Hufton, *The Prospect,* 92, 94; Geraldine Sheridan, "Women in the Booktrade in Eighteenth-Century France," *British Journal for Eighteenth-Century Studies* 15, no. 1 (1992): 54, 56–57; and Elizabeth C. Sanderson, *Women and Work in Eighteenth-Century Edinburgh* (London: Macmillan, 1996), 92.

11. Ian Whyte, "Protoindustrialisation in Scotland," in *Regions and Industries: A Perspective on the Industrial Revolution in Britain,* ed. Pat Hudson (Cambridge: Cambridge University Press, 1989), 240; Old Statistical Account of Scotland, 13, 293.

12. Simonton, "Education and Training," 144–148. See also Simonton, "Schooling the Poor: Gender and Class in Eighteenth-Century England," *British Journal for Eighteenth-Century Studies* 23 (autumn 2000): 183–202.

13. Wunder, 23–24.

14. ERO D/P 299/8/2 2/8/1784. For domestic service in Essex, see Pamela Sharpe, *Adapting to Capitalism* (London: Macmillan, 1996).

15. Maza, 41.

16. Olwen Hufton, *The Poor of Eighteenth-Century France, 1750–1789* (Oxford: Oxford University Press, 1974), 64.

17. ERO D/P 264/13/4, 1792.

18. Maza, 38, 41; Hufton, *Poor of Eighteenth-Century France,* 28; Meldrum, 19.

19. Meldrum, 20, 21.

20. Christina Hardyment, introduction to *The Housekeeping Book of Susanna Whatman* (1774; reprint, London: National Trust, 2000) 4, 56.

21. Meldrum, 24; also Earle, 128–129; and D. A. Kent, "Ubiquitous but Invisible: Female Domestic Servants in Mid-Eighteenth-Century London," *History Workshop* 28 (autumn 1989): 120–121.

22. Ann Kussmaul, *Servants in Husbandry in Early Modern England* (Cambridge: Cambridge University Press, 1981), 51–52, 57.

23. Simonton, "Education and Training," 169–174; ERO D/Q 24/2.

24. Earle, 125.

25. ERO D/P 245/18/6.

26. J. Jean Hecht, *The Domestic Servant in Eighteenth-Century England* (1956; reprint, London: Routledge & Kegan Paul, 1980), 35, 60–69; and Meldrum, 84–88.

27. Hecht, 183–184.

28. Alan Armstrong, *Farmworkers in England and Wales, 1770–1980* (London: Batsford, 1988), 20–23.

29. T. C. Smout, *A History of the Scottish People, 1560–1830* (London: Fontana, 1969), 285, from George Robertson, *Rural Recollections* (1827). A "ben" is the inner room of a cottage, usually called a "but and ben" where the "but" is the outer room or kitchen. A "lum" is a chimney.

30. William Marshall, *The Rural Economy of the Southern Counties*, vol. 2 (London: Nicol, 1798), 233.

31. Simonton, "Education and Training," 174, 343–349.

32. Kussmaul, 55–56.

33. Parliamentary Papers, *Women and Children in Agriculture*, vol. 12 (1843), 109.

34. Jerome Blum, *The End of the Old Order in Europe* (Princeton, N.J.: Princeton University Press, 1978), 105–106.

35. Kussmaul, 15.

36. Hufton, *The Prospect*, 94; Sheridan, 52–53; Léon Abensour, *La femme et la féminisme en France avant la Révolution* (1923; reprint, Geneva: Slatkine-Maganotis, 1966), 205; Joan Lane, "Apprenticeship in Warwickshire, 1700–1834" (Ph.D. diss., Birmingham, 1977), 122; Christabel Dale, *Wiltshire Apprentices and Their Masters* (Devizes, UK: Wiltshire Archaeology and Natural History Society, 1961), xv; and Deborah Simonton, "Apprenticeship: Training and Gender in Eighteenth-Century England," in *Markets and Manufacture in Early Industrial Europe*, ed. Maxine Berg (London: Routledge & Kegan Paul, 1991), 244–246. For a more detailed study of French apprenticeship, focused on Paris at the end of the eighteenth century, see Clare Crowston's chapter.

37. Kingston upon Thames Borough Archives, "Court of Assembly Minutes, 1725–1776," KB 1/2.

38. Mack Walker, *German Home Towns* (Ithaca, N.Y.: Cornell University Press, 1971), 98–100; *Aberdeen Journal*, 3 October 1758.

39. Simonton, "Apprenticeship," and "Education and Training," 241–263.

40. Daniel Defoe, *The Complete English Tradesman* (1726; reprint, London: Augustus M. Kelly, 1969), I, 6.

41. Wedgwood Archives, nos. 133-26816, 133-26818.

42. See chapters by Crowston, Mary Jo Maynes, and Carol E. Morgan for elaboration of this point.

2   In Search of Arachne's Daughters: European Girls, Economic Development, and the Textile Trade, 1750–1880

Mary Jo Maynes

In this chapter, Mary Jo Maynes shows how the work of young unmarried young women was crucial to Europe's particular patterns of economic development, especially in the textile sector, from the late seventeenth through the nineteenth century. Girls' textile work was initially rooted in the type of life-cyclic full-time labor documented in chapter 1; girls' mobility, and the length of time they typically worked before marriage, gave them a central place in development schemes. Maynes also recounts evidence that girls' industrial paid labor was in turn related to shifting patterns of consumption that reflected the earning power of young women.

In an essay published in 1720, Jonathan Swift suggested that the Irish House of Commons pass a resolution against the wearing of any cloth that was not produced in Ireland. He lashed out against English colonial trade policies that discouraged the manufacture of woolen cloth in Ireland and pushed Irish landlords to produce raw wool for export to England. "The fable in Ovid, of Arachne and Pallas," wrote Swift, "is to this purpose."

> The Goddess had heard of one Arachne, a young Virgin, very famous for spinning and weaving. They both set upon a trial of skill; and Pallas finding herself almost equalled in her own art, stung with rage and envy, knocked her rival down, turned her into a spider, enjoining her to spin and weave forever, out of her own bowels, and in a very narrow compass. I confess, that from a boy I always pitied poor Arachne, and could never heartily love the goddess, on account of so cruel and unjust a sentence; which, however, is fully executed on us by England, with further

addition of rigour and severity; for the greatest part of our bowel and vitals is extracted, without allowing us the liberty of spinning and weaving them.[1]

Swift's target was English trade policy in the world of colonialism and nascent capitalism. The same policy also aimed to cripple the flourishing textile industry of India and to prevent the growth of manufacture in North America. For Swift, the young virgin spinster was a powerful political metaphor. My aim in this chapter is to seek her out—not only in treatises on economic development but also in the cottages and factories where spinning took place.

Spinning was a female occupation in much of the world, but central and western Europe's pattern of late marriage enhanced the significance of young women's labor in this and other economic sectors. Married women did spin in Europe. But young unmarried women had the potential to spin full-time into their twenties, uninterrupted by the increased family responsibilities brought by marriage and childbearing. Moreover, the established practice whereby young people of both sexes typically left home for a period of service between childhood and marriage made European girls uniquely available as a mobile labor force. This mobility really mattered when the reorganization of spinning in the early stages of Europe's industrialization required spinners to move away from home—to another household in a protoindustrial region, to a handicraft shop, or to a mechanized mill. Girls' extensive participation in spinning and other aspects of textile work was essential to the economic, political, moral, and cultural construction of Europe's industrial capitalist economy between 1750 and 1850. Thereafter, the labor of girls continued to be crucial to Europe's place in global textile markets.

Protoindustrial Textile Production in Europe

Europe's textiles industries underwent dramatic change long before factories and mechanization. Beginning in the late seventeenth century, dramatic growth in the demand for fabric revolutionized these industries; merchant entrepreneurs took increasing control over small-scale handicraft production of thread and cloth and reorganized it for large and distant markets. (Historians usually call this system *protoindustry* to distinguish it from later mass production in mechanized factories.) State policymakers were also interested in textile industries, since "economic development" was increasingly seen as a determinant of a regime's success and stability. State economic advisers appreciated the potential of textile industries to encourage prosperity in both agriculture and industry. Textile workers thus played a key role in the projects of both entrepreneurs and policymakers.

Although textiles were important industries throughout most of central and western Europe, local conditions varied. In eighteenth-century Ireland, for example, the focus was on linen production, which was encouraged by the English rulers of Ireland to replace the small Irish woolen industry that had threatened to compete with England's own. By the 1780s, linen accounted for two-thirds of Irish exports, having apparently increased more than a hundredfold during the eighteenth century.[2] Irish women soon gained a reputation as expert flax spinners, whereas men initially did much of the weaving.[3]

Southern Germany offers a somewhat different example, although it also produced linen in a protoindustrial system that was flourishing in the late eighteenth century. Despite government monopolies granted to merchants for the sale of linen, rural weavers often produced directly for an international market.[4] Despite the predominance of men in weaving, women played a key role in spinning. Still, the direct domination over the industry by patriarchal male weaver-merchants may well have limited the autonomy and wage-earning capacity of spinners.

In southern France, the late eighteenth-century growth sector was silk. The industry had been introduced there in the fifteenth century. State encouragement intensified at the beginning of the seventeenth century. On the eve of the French Revolution, silk production was worth 130 million livres a year, or roughly 15 percent of the total industrial product of France. The skilled female workers who unwound silk strands from silkworm cocoons and spun it were crucial to the profitability of raw silk filatures and to the quality of the eventual woven fabric.[5]

By the early eighteenth century, all of these textile industries were feeling the impact of the "cotton craze." Cotton textiles, mainly from India, entered European markets in appreciable amounts beginning in the seventeenth century. Indian cottons soon threatened British woolens and were banned by Parliament in acts passed between 1701 and 1721.[6] Growth in the demand for cotton, along with European governments' fear of Indian imports, eventually encouraged the establishment of a European cotton industry that also relied heavily on the labor of young women. These acts of Parliament, like the Irish trade policies criticized by Swift, attest to the long tradition of entanglement between geopolitics and textiles that shaped and was shaped by the work of girls.

Girls' Labor in the Plans of Economic Theorists, Entrepreneurs, and Statesmen

State intervention into the textile trade was noticeable everywhere in Europe by the eighteenth century. The recruitment and training of spinners was one early focus of state policy. Domestic spinning was a skill that could pass from mother to daughter or mistress to servant. But rapid growth in production meant that the demand for skilled spinners often exceeded the supply. In an industry like silk, where raw materials were expensive, a badly trained spinner spelled disaster. In 1773, a French entrepreneur addressed the concerns of French silk manufacturers in a petition calling for government regulation of silk filatures, as practiced in Italy:

> The (mill) owner, sure of selling his silk . . . hurries to have it spun . . . his mill . . . is operated by an inexperienced spinner. Instead of sorting the cocoons according

to quality, the spinner throws them indiscriminately into the basin. . . . Failing to perform regular and constant twists, she forms the thread from a varying number of strands. This produces defective silk for which the mill owner, the manufacturer, and the weaver must alone carry the loss.[7]

This petition was circulated at a time when monarchs throughout Europe were establishing schools to disseminate the skills that protoindustry required. One of the earliest programs of the Irish Linen Board doled out government subsidies for schools to teach girls how to spin. More deliberate and persistent efforts to teach industrial skills were undertaken in central Europe. "Industry schools" were founded during the last third of the eighteenth century in many German states. The goal of these schools was to teach "industry" understood in both its older and its newer meanings—that is, disciplined work habits and particular manufacturing skills. The work skills that the pupils learned were most often related to textile production. And while all of the children of the lower classes were targeted for industrial training, girls were the special focus of efforts to disseminate the skills necessary for spinning, sewing, and knitting.

In Germany, the dissemination of industrial skills remained on the state agenda through the early nineteenth-century crisis of mechanization, as is apparent in the records of Württemberg's Ministry of the Interior. The ministry was interested in the best means of strengthening the state's linen industry against British machine-produced textiles. Between 1817 and 1827, the ministry considered several proposals to establish state-run spinneries and to subsidize private ventures. One proposal requested a subsidy to build a flax spinning machine like the one "recently invented" in Munich, which was "operated by one person who requires the assistance of 8 twelve-year-old girls; they then do the work of 72 people, in that 72 threads flow out of the machine from the prepared flax." The proposal's author added, "if the flax is long and fine, four of the above 8 girls can be spared."[8] In the end, the ministry decided to invest instead in schools throughout the state to teach Württemberg's girls to spin more quickly by hand using a new "double spinning" technique. With or without machines, girls' labor was at the center of the calculus of enhanced productivity and economic competitiveness.

In Great Britain, state interventions into the textile trade also shaped industrial development and contributed to the recruitment and training of a young female labor force during the eighteenth century. The history of the Irish textile industry offers especially clear evidence of the entanglement between politics and markets, and of the ways in which political-economic calculations emphasized the payoff from young female labor.[9] Thomas Prior's "Essay to Encourage and Extend the Linen-Manufacture in Ireland," published in 1749, for example, spells out how profits and economic growth would flow from state subsidies to encourage linen production. Prior's logic makes clear the shared presumption that Ireland's economic development, in advance of any notable technological changes, entailed an "industrious revolution"[10]—an increased level of market-oriented work by all available hands:

> It is in the Interest, and should be the Business, of every Gentleman, to take care that all the Women and Children on his estate should be constantly employed in Spinning . . . (this) would answer more than the Expence of maintaining a Child; and the Children of poor People would be so far from being an Incumbrance, that they would become a new Fund of Wealth to them by being employed in Spinning; which would turn also to the Advantage of the Landlord, whose rents are always paid by the Labour of the Poor.[11]

Similar proposals continued to surface until the mid-nineteenth century. What remained constant in the reckoning of political economists from the early eighteenth to the mid-nineteenth century was a calculus based on the large numbers of Irish poor, the cheapness of their labor, and a global market in which Irish prosperity and British profit lay in getting the Irish—particularly the young and the female—to spin more flax to supply the linen industry.

Girls and Their Labor in Protoindustrial and Early Industrial Textile Industries

Girls' labor was central not just in the imaginations of economic theorists and state policymakers but also in practice.[12] In regions of intensive protoindustrial activity, levels of employment among the young and the female populations were astonishingly high.[13] Girls were prominent in Ireland's protoindustrial linen industry.[14] According to one eighteenth-century report,

> Around Lisburn "a skilled spinster could earn up to 8d. per day but for the coarser yarns 4d. to 6d. was more likely, while a girl of 12 could earn 1 ½d. or 2d. per day, and a girl of seven might get a penny. In these cases, however, the spinster had to provide her own board and lodging."[15]

Later testimony from one spinner to a Parliamentary Commission of the 1830s adds some nuance about the life-cyclic dimension of spinning work and the reasoning behind the rising demand for girl laborers: "Some women earn by spinning 3 ½ d a day, if they are good spinners, and devote their whole time to it. . . . When a woman has a family to take care of, she cannot earn more than 1d a day—she will not spin more than two or three hanks in the week."[16] Older women were no doubt the most skilled spinsters, but once they married they devoted less time to spinning. Unmarried older girls were thus the most reliable spinsters. Scattered census evidence backs this up. A sample of sixteen settlements drawn from the census of Castleraghan Parish in County Cavan included just over 2,500 individuals. Among the enumerated 947 women and girls over the age of ten, fully 674 were identified as "spinning," "spinners," or "flax spinners." Of these, 310 (46 percent) were unmarried; 282 of these (42 percent) were unmarried and between the ages of ten and thirty.[17]

In central Europe, evidence on the gender division of labor in the protoindustrial linen production in the village of Laichingen in Württemberg suggests a slight variation on the Irish pattern. Rural weavers could contract for yarn with "male and female spinners in cottage industry," suggesting that the gender division of labor was not as absolute as it was in Ireland.[18] Still, spinning was a largely female occupation in Laichingen during the boom years of the mid-to-late eighteenth century, and weaving a male one. This division of labor changed during the crisis that hit Laichingen in the early nineteenth century. While women were "already previously involved in the preparatory stages of work such as spinning, reeling and hackling, in the 1820s, for the first time . . . there was mention of direct involvement of married women in weaving."[19] In protoindustrial spinning areas nearby in Switzerland, the role of girls is spelled out clearly in village censuses. In 1762, 72 percent of the spinners of the proto-industrial village of Hausen were girls or women; 39 percent were unmarried. Following the western European pattern, fully two-thirds of women in their twenties remained unmarried.[20]

In raw silk-producing areas of southern France, families relied on a similar combination of male agricultural work and female spinning to that found in other protoindustrial regions. An 1839 household budget analysis featured a household that combined agricultural production with work in silk. Fully 44 percent of the family's income came from the labor of the wife and two "post-pubescent" daughters who were engaged in spinning silk.[21] The feminine character of the silk spinning labor force was implicit in the very words employed in contemporary accounts: a "female worker (*ouvrière*), called a *fileuse*, would detach the (silk) strand (from the worm) with a marvelous dexterity. . . . A second female worker turned the reel, and bore the title of *tourneuse*." (See Figure 2.) Women and girls who worked at raw silk spinning did so both in small domestic shops and "vast sheds" where fifty spinning teams worked, already "a sort of manufactory or handicraft factory, in a rudimentary state."[22] Young women could not spin straw into gold except in fairytales, but spinning worms into silk must have seemed like a kind of magic in these regions during the years of the silk boom.

As textile production moved gradually, and at a regionally varied pace, from rural cottages to large spinneries in towns, young unmarried women played an even more marked and dramatic role. Put simply, they dominated Europe's earliest modern factory labor force. The new technologies that revolutionized textile production beginning in the eighteenth century were developed with a workforce in mind that was young and female. According to Maxine Berg,

> In calico printing, processes were broken down into a series of operations performed particularly well by teenage girls who contributed manual dexterity (learned at home) with high labour intensity. The spinning jenny was first invented for use by a young girl, its horizontal wheel making it uncomfortable for an adult worker to use for any length of time.[23]

The age and gender division of labor in protoindustrial textile production had not distinguished Europe from the rest of the world, for girls and women spun at home and in small shops in much of the world. What was more unusual was the presumed mobility of the young, female labor force of Europe. Those who were as yet unmarried could, in a pattern that was not so different from

Fig. 2. Unwinding silk, 18th century France. This illustration shows the *fileuse* (spinner) on the right, and the *tourneuse* (turner) on the left.
Courtesy James Ford Bell Library, University of Minnesota.

entering domestic service, leave home for larger and more distance workplaces. Some young women entered domestic service as spinners in protoindustrial household operations. Some moved into nearby towns to work in handicraft manufactories or silk reeling sheds for a few months of the year or longer. Eventually, they moved into factories whose spinning and weaving machines were powered by water or steam. And this pattern of labor market participation by young, unmarried women remained a key distinction between central and western Europe and much of the rest of the world until the end of the nineteenth or beginning of the twentieth century.

Europe's new mill towns were filled with young women. Mechanization came later to flax than to cotton spinning, but by the late 1820s and 1830s mechanical spinneries increasingly dominated Irish spinning, causing economic contraction in protoindustrial yarn regions. The factories feminized weaving as well as spinning, creating an even stronger demand for mobile female labor. By the end of the nineteenth century, female workers held most of the factory jobs involving the preparation, spinning, and reeling of linen and most of the factory weaving. Around 1900, northern Ireland's linen mill girls, like their grandmothers in protoindustrial spinning, started work around age twelve or thirteen.[24]

The major mechanized cotton spinnery of nineteenth-century Ireland—the

Portlaw mill near Waterford on the south coast—also filled its demand for labor by hiring girls and young women. When it was built in the 1830s, the plant was huge and thoroughly modern. In 1835, 64 percent of the mill's workers were female; fully 42 percent were females under the age of twenty-one. As the plant grew and added machine divisions, the number of adult males employed rose, but among the textile workers, young women remained dominant through the 1870s. Female mill hands, mostly between the ages of thirteen and twenty-one, comprised between 48 and 60 percent of the mill's spinners and weavers until the 1870s.[25]

As in Ireland, the modern textile mills of southern Germany also attracted a labor force that was young and female. There were over sixteen thousand female textile operatives in Bavaria by the time of the first industrial census of 1875; the female textile labor force continued to expand thereafter. By 1895, the state's twenty-eight thousand female textile operatives comprised 30 percent of the female wage labor force as recorded by the census. Roughly three-quarters of that labor force were single women; 61 percent of recorded wage-earning women were unmarried and under the age of thirty.[26]

Mechanization affected silk spinning far less than other fibers, but the invention of steam taps to adjust the temperature of the water in the basins where silk thread was unwound encouraged the concentration of spinning into larger filatures in the early nineteenth century. The labor force in some four hundred silk reeling filatures and spinning mills of the Midi totaled more than twenty thousand workers in 1840, 90 percent of whom were women and children.[27] Moreover, the *fileuse* maintained her centrality to the quality of silk yarn. According to Eduard Perris, director in the 1840s of the state-subsidized model filature of the Department of Landes, despite the introduction of steam and the growth in scale of silk reeling operations, "of all the influences affecting the filature, that exercised by the *fileuse* is the most powerful and noticeable . . . she holds in her hands both the fortune of the mill owner and the reputation of the business."[28]

Girls in Factories and Factory Towns

Accounts of protoindustrial and early factory textile production treat the labor of young women as largely unproblematic, as taken for granted. However, certain moral and political qualms did begin to surface in the changing atmosphere of the nineteenth century and with the move into larger workplaces and communities. The "sordid" associations evoked by the word *ouvrière* (female worker), found in the discourse of French political economy by the 1860s, had certainly begun to creep into rhetoric earlier.[29] For example, the economist François-Félix de La Farelle, writing in the early 1850s, admitted that he had initially greeted the arrival of silk factories in southern France "with horror" because of their size, their noise, and their intrusion upon the scenery of the countryside. He also had feared for "our mothers, our young girls until then modest, reserved, chaste . . . ready to transform themselves into factory girls!

Into factory girls! Oh! This word alone was enough to waken in me terrible recollections and cruel warnings!" Still, he argued, thirty years of experience with the factory system had brought prosperity to the silk regions. "The silk producers took that which is good from industrialization . . . without succumbing to its evils."[30] Apparently the association between female factory work and moral degradation was not automatic.

Still, as they recruited increasing numbers of girls and young women for their large spinning enterprises, factory owners sought to dispel moral anxieties through paternalism. The so-called "convent-factory" appeared toward the middle of the nineteenth century in the towns that sprang up around the silk mills of southern France. In 1879 an English journalist, in accounting for the spectacular triumph of the French silk industry, singled out two factors: "first, technical education; and, secondly, the employment of women under new conditions and arrangements." His highest praise was reserved for Jean Bonnet, a self-made man who owned silk mills near Lyon. Bonnet recruited girls from the poorer agricultural families of the region "under promise to give them board, lodging, clothes, and all that they required, together with small wages, and to teach them not only the art of silk making, but to give them a general education." Bonnet's establishment boasted dormitories staffed by members of religious orders who maintained strict discipline, a useful weapon in the struggle "to tame these little savages into order."[31]

Portlaw, site of Ireland's largest textile mill, was also organized to accommodate young women workers. The village grew from just under four hundred in 1821 to over forty-three hundred in 1851. Migration was disproportionately young and female, like the mill's labor force. Many of the immigrants came on their own and were listed in the census as "visitors" because they typically boarded in the homes of other mill hands. By 1861, there were 567 female and 342 male visitors in a population of 3,852.[32] Factory discipline was very severe and reinforced by fines and piece rates. Inside and outside of the mill, "the strictest morality was preserved and it was the rule to dismiss any girl who was guilty of the slightest impropriety."[33] This was not a "convent factory" like Jujurieux; but as a "model industrial village," Portlaw imposed paternalistic supervision of its labor force of young women on their own.

These "model" factories were the exception, however. Most young women factory workers were more truly on their own. With the expansion of industrial capitalism and the factory system, an increasing number of writings lamented the deployment of female and child labor by entrepreneurs eager to enhance their competitive position on the international market. While these laments questioned the place of female labor, and especially the labor of married women, to an extent that was not common earlier, it is important not to overlook the key role that young single women continued to play in textile production. Comparatively speaking, the presence of Europe's single young women in mobile textile labor pools was considerable and distinctive throughout the protoindustrial and early industrial periods. Similar wage labor pools would begin to be constructed elsewhere in the world, for example in Japan and China,

Fig. 3. C. J. Bonnet Company silkworkers, Jujurieux, France ca. 1900. The silk factory at Jujurieux was founded in the 1830s as a model factory where hundreds of young girls, recruited from the surrounding countryside, were housed and schooled on the factory premises.
Collections Musées des pays de l'Ain, photo by Cl. Corne.

only in the last few decades of the nineteenth century, when textile production began to be reorganized along factory models.

Girl Power?

What difference did it make to girls that their labor was of increasing interest and value to entrepreneurs and to the state? It needs to be said first that, despite the demand, the low wages that girls earned, along with their lack of control over their earnings, did preclude their economic independence. Nevertheless, there are tantalizing shreds of evidence that suggest that participation in wage labor may have translated into resources.

Some of the evidence concerns clothing and fashion—that is, the very products that spinsters helped to produce. Expanding textile markets and the "democratization" of fashion opened up new possibilities for using dress as a strategy for social mobility. Status "cross-dressing" by young women on the marriage market eroded the social boundaries previously demarcated more clearly by dress. The existence of sumptuary laws in European cities since the late Middle Ages makes it clear that dressing above status was not new in the eighteenth century. But the dimension of the problem was greatly exacerbated by the availability of low-cost fashions based on the protoindustrial and industrial production of textiles.[34]

Interest in fashion, and ownership of clothing made from the new fabrics, was hardly restricted to the upper classes; scattered historical evidence links textile work, in particular, with dressing "above rank." In Laichingen, the proto-industrial weavers' pursuit of material improvement represented a challenge to older notions of status. The old order was asserted through sumptuary laws re-iterated as late as 1712. According to one such law in Württemberg "the 'common citizens' of the cities were forbidden to wear certain new fabrics, 'cotton and *Indienne*.'" But by the end of the eighteenth century "it appears that there was a partial breakdown of the rules according to which the culture of appearance based on wealth and dress reinforced a hierarchical social ranking."[35] Inventories indicate that the value of the clothing that the village's poorest young women brought into marriage increased more rapidly than that of men, although those of wealthier brides rose even more dramatically. In fact, in all social categories, the bride's clothing was worth more on the average than the groom's, a reversal of early century gender patterns, although women's overall wealth was not increasing relative to men's.[36]

Young women's wardrobes still reflected their relative wealth and status, but consumption of particular items and fabrics was clearly "democratized" over the course of the eighteenth century. Items of apparel made of luxury fabrics like silk and cotton became more common and were increasingly worn by the poorer classes, especially the women.[37] For example, when Anna Riek, who was the daughter of a gravedigger, married the day laborer Johann Georg Autenrieth in 1799, she owned a wardrobe worth fifty-nine florins. What especially distinguished it from that of others of her class, or even of wealthier girls, was her "rich collection of silk, half-silk, 'cotton' and 'crepe' kerchiefs. . . . Her large number of silk, half-silk and cotton bonnets was rivaled in this place and time only by the pastor's daughter, the wife of the wealthy merchant Nestel." She also possessed decorative items of foreign origin, including a lace bodice in the red, white, and blue of the French Revolution, which, according to a note in the inventory, Anna claimed to have brought "herself" to the marriage, not as part of her dowry from her parents.[38]

Similar indications exist for the silk-producing regions of southern France. When La Farelle was comparing budgets of such households in 1852 with their predecessors of ten or fifteen years earlier, he attributed their greater prosperity to the contributions of "the feminine sex." Moreover, allocations for clothing had gone up "if not for the father and mother, at least for the daughters, who retain a more-or-less considerable portion of their earnings from the filature for this purpose."[39] In fact, he observed, "we have been able to observe these young craftswomen, for some time now, wearing on Sunday this precious thread that they spin on the other six days."[40]

Finally, in a similar vein, an observer describing the Irish linen district in the early 1830s complained that

The people dress in a style far superior to the line of life in which they are placed, particularly the females, who are fond of show, and comply with modern fashions

Fig. 4. Irish linen factory spinners, ca. 1917.
Courtesy Mrs. Theresa Grimley. Reproduced from Betty Messenger, *Picking Up the Linen Thread: A Study in Industrial Folklore* (Austin and London: University of Texas Press, 1978).

as far as they can afford it. They are able to indulge in this propensity by their industry in spinning and weaving coarse linens; these they bring to market, and when disposed of, they purchase ornamented clothing with a part of the profit.[41]

These observations about young women workers as consumers of fashion are hardly definitive. Still, they suggest that, even as Europe's girls played a distinctive role as producers of textiles, their participation in the labor market may in turn have enhanced their relative power as consumers. The power to consume is a limited form of power, to be sure; nevertheless, it points to a slow altering of the gender and generational distribution of resources in some regions of Europe apparent by the middle of the nineteenth century.

My focus on young women in Europe's developing textile industries between the mid-eighteenth and the mid-nineteenth centuries demonstrates their important, and from a world-historical point of view, unusual, participation in the textile labor force—not only in home industries but in large manufactories and mechanized mills as well. Historical evidence suggests that taking girls' labor for granted encouraged entrepreneurs to move toward the types of organization of production, and the technologies, that would distinguish European textile production in the international market until the end of the nineteenth century. Despite the eventual emergence of a moral critique of married women's labor and child labor toward the middle of the nineteenth century, the work of young unmarried women remained significant and critical to Europe's industrial development throughout the nineteenth century. There is also suggestive evidence that this labor pattern was in turn related to shifting patterns of consumption that reflected the increased earning power of young women, perhaps contributing to the disruption of older patriarchal relations within families.

Still, the long-term consequences of these new labor patterns for young women are far from clear. Certainly the relatively low wages they commanded precluded economic independence, a situation that both parents and employers could exploit. Moreover, in each of the regions discussed here, the late eighteenth-century promise of prosperity was darkened or interrupted by subsequent crises. As was already mentioned, a protracted depression in Württemberg's linen industry in the first half of the nineteenth century revealed the vulnerabilities that involvement with the international market could bring. In Ireland, the catastrophe that followed the boom was immense. After the Great Famine of the 1840s, Ireland's unmarried young women began crossing the ocean by the thousands in search of employment in the United States and elsewhere. They set another world-historical precedent in so doing: no previous migratory stream had included so large a proportion of unmarried young women crossing the ocean on their own. The crisis in southern France was as particular as its reliance on silk. Silkworm disease devastated cocoon production beginning in 1853. By the time the region recovered, world trade in silk cocoons was dominated by Japan. Even though Lyon continued to hold on to its position as a major center of silk production, its looms and filatures were increasingly fed by imported raw silk or imported cocoons. In all three regions, then, the young woman spinner was a crucial but transient historical figure. If early market shifts promised her prosperity, and even a modicum of bargaining power, later ones brought her ruin. As if, to continue Swift's metaphor, Arachne's web were simply torn away.

Notes

This project has benefited immensely from the work of several research assistants: Barbara Drescher, Katja Guenther, Anne Heubel, Jamie McCarthy, and Marynel Ryan. I want to thank them for their enthusiastic help. I also want to thank the University of Minnesota Graduate School and the Center for German and European Studies for support.

1. Jonathan Swift, "A Proposal for the Universal Use of Irish Manufacture," in *The Irish Confederation: Irish Political Economy,* ed. John Mitchell (1720; reprint, Dublin, 1847), 20–21.
2. Phillip Ollerenshaw, "Der Übergang von der Heim-zur Fabrikarbeit in der Leinenindustrie Ulsters (1680–1870)," in *Von der Heimarbeit in die Fabrik. Industrialisierung und Arbeiterschaft in Leinen- und Baumwollregionen Westeuropas während des 18. und 19. Jahrhunderts,* ed. Karl Ditt and Sidney Pollard (Paderborn: Ferdinand Schöningh, 1992), 57; and W. H. Crawford, "Women in the Domestic Linen Industry," in *Women in Early Modern Ireland,* ed. Margaret MacCurtain and Mary O'Dowd (Edinburgh: Edinburgh University Press, 1991), 255.
3. See Brenda Collins, "The Loom, the Land, and the Marketplace: Women Weavers and the Family Economy in Late Nineteenth- and Early Twentieth-Century Ireland," in *The Warp of Ulster's Past,* ed. Marilyn Cohen (New York: St. Martin's Press, 1997), 229–252.
4. Evidence on Laichingen is from Hans Medick, *Weben und Überleben in Laichingen. Lokalgeschichte als Allgemeine Geschichte* (Göttingen: Vandenhoeck & Ruprecht, 1996).
5. François-Félix de La Farelle, *Études Économiques sur l'industrie de la soie dans le midi de la France* (Paris: Guillaumin, 1852–1854), *premier etude,* 4–5.
6. Beverly Lemire, *Fashion's Favourite: The Cotton Trade and the Consumer in Britain, 1660–1800* (Oxford: Oxford University Press, 1991).
7. Du Perron, *Nouveau règlement pour la filature des soies* (n.p., 1773), 7.
8. Württemberg Staatsarchiv E 14/Bü 1170 (3–5).
9. For a discussion of Irish economic and population history, especially of the role of English policy in bringing about the famine, see Cormac Ó Gráda, *Ireland: A New Economic History, 1780–1939* (Oxford: Clarendon Press, 1994).
10. Jan de Vries, "Between Purchasing Power and the World of Goods: Understanding the Household Economy in Early Modern Europe," in *Women's Work: The English Experience, 1650–1914,* ed. Pamela Sharpe (London: Arnold, 1998), 214–231. According to de Vries, "truly regular, continuous, supervised labor was with few exceptions a product of the factory system, and was rare before the nineteenth century . . . However . . . a major inten-

sification of labor measurable in labor force participation rates, days worked per year, and effort per unit of labor occurred in many areas in the course of the early modern era. . . . The labor of women and children played a prominent role in this process of peasant self-exploitation: the putting-out industries made intensive use of their winter and evening labor" (218–221). See Clare Crowston's chapter for a related argument on the "industrious revolution."

11. Thomas Esq. Prior, "An Essay to Encourage and Extend the Linen-Manufacture in Ireland by Praemium and Other Means" (Dublin, 1749).

12. For a fuller discussion see Mary Jo Maynes, "Gender, Labor, and Globalization in Historical Perspective: European Spinsters in the International Textile Industry, 1750–1900," *Journal of Women's History* (winter 2004).

13. Deborah Simonton, *A History of European Women's Work* (London: Routledge & Kegan Paul, 1998), 40.

14. See Brenda Collins, "Die Heimarbeiterschaft im Leinengewerbe Ulsters während des 18. und 19. Jahrhunderts," in *Von der Heimarbeit in die Fabrik. Industrialisierung und Arbeiterschaft in Leinen- und Baumwollregionen Westeuropas während des 18. und 19. Jahrhunderts,* ed. Karl Ditt and Sidney Pollard (Paderborn: Ferdinand Schöningh, 1992), 241–242.

15. Crawford, 260.

16. Parliamentary Record, "Report from His Majesty's Commissioners for Inquiring into the Conditions of the poorer Classes in Ireland, 1836," in *Women in Ireland, 1800–1914: A Documentary History,* ed. Maria Luddy (Cork: Cork University Press, 1995), 171.

17. Dublin. National Archives. Census registers, 1821. County Cavan, Parish of Castleraghan. In a different sample drawn from the parishes of County Cavan, Jane Gray found that just over 40 percent of women aged fifteen years and older reported themselves as spinners. In a subsample that included only those parishes where everyone reported an occupation, nearly 80 percent of these women were listed as spinners. Gray also suggests that census figures may disguise underlying variations in the involvement of spinners in protoindustrial activity. See Jane Gray, "Spinners and Spinning in the Political Economy of Pre-Famine Ireland: Evidence from County Cavan in 1821," in *Reclaiming Gender: Transgressive Identities in Modern Ireland,* ed. M. Cohen and N. Curtin (New York: St. Martin's Press, 1999), 240–266.

18. Medick, 69.

19. Ibid., 271.

20. Ulrich Pfister, "Work Roles and Family Structure in Proto-Industrial Zurich," *Journal of Interdisciplinary History* 20, no. 1 (1990): 95, 100.

21. de La Farelle, *premier etude* (1852), 9.

22. Ibid., *seconde etude* (1854), 2.

23. Maxine Berg, "What Difference Did Women's Work Make to the Industrial Revolution?" in *Women's Work: The English Experience, 1650–1914,* ed. Pamela Sharpe (London: Arnold, 1998), 149–171.

24. Betty Messenger, *Picking Up the Linen Threads: A Study of Industrial Folklore* (Austin: University of Texas Press, 1975), 20–23 and appendix A.

25. Tom Hunt, *Portrait of an Industrial Village and Its Cotton Industry* (Dublin, Portland: Irish Academic Press, 2000), 59–61.

26.   Elisabeth Plössl, *Weibliche Arbeit in Familie und Betrieb. Bayerische Arbeiter-frauen, 1870–1914* (Munich: Neue Schriftenreihe des Stadtarchivs München, 1983), 165.

27.   de La Farelle, *seconde etude,* 15–18.

28.   Édouard Perris, *Traité de la culture du mûrier, de l'établissement des mag-naneries et de l'éducation des vers à soie, suivi de quelques considérations sur la filature et l'emploi de la soie, ainsi que de la filoselle* (Mont-de-Marsan: P.-V. Leclercq, 1840), 445.

29.   Joan Scott, "'L'ouvriere! Mot impie, sordide . . .': Women Workers in the Discourse of French Political Economy, 1840–1860," in *Gender and the Politics of History,* ed. Joan Scott, (New York: Columbia University Press, 1988), 139–166.

30.   de La Farelle, *seconde etude,* 5.

31.   Edward J. Watherston, "French Silk Manufactures, and the Industrial Employment of Women," *Good Words,* 1879, 107.

32.   Hunt, 58.

33.   Ibid., 56.

34.   For an excellent history of the growth of the market in cotton clothing in England, see Lemire.

35.   Medick, 387–388, 427.

36.   Ibid., 399–405.

37.   Ibid., 406.

38.   Ibid., 429.

39.   de La Farelle, *seconde etude,* 9–10.

40.   de La Farelle, *seconde etude,* 4.

41.   Mary E. Daly, "Women in the Irish Workforce from Pre-industrial to Modern Times," in *The Irish Women's History Reader,* ed. Alan Hayes and Diane Urquhart (London and New York: Routledge & Kegan Paul, 2001), 193.

3 After Dark: Girls' Leisure, Work, and Sexuality in Eighteenth- and Nineteenth-Century Rural Southwest Germany

Andreas Gestrich

Andreas Gestrich focuses on Lichtstuben, *evening gathering places for young people in rural areas of Central Europe. Young men were truly "at leisure" in the evening, whereas young women were expected to work; their* Lichtstuben *featured work as well as conviviality. Gestrich also finds that whereas boys'* Lichtstuben *tended to include all village boys of the same age, the girls' gatherings were more family and neighborhood oriented. This was consistent with a gendered socialization that pushed boys toward future "public" roles and girls more toward the "private" networks.*

Research into the history of youth has uncovered youth leisure activities from past eras.[1] This research has centered on male urban bourgeois or working-class youth; comparatively little is known about rural youth, especially female youth in rural areas prior to the twentieth century.[2] This uneven knowledge stems in part from the fact that young men were more often involved in conflict with local authorities than girls were and therefore left more archival evidence. Another reason, however, is the fact that the existing sources about young women have not been studied with the same interest and intensity as those for young men.

Was there organized leisure activity for girls in preindustrial Europe? If so, how did female peer groups compare to their male counterparts? Did girls enjoy similar freedom? What were the functions of organized female peer groups? This chapter will look at girls' peer organizations and leisure in traditional rural youth culture in villages in Württemberg in southwestern Germany. The evidence comes mainly from Walddorf and Ohmenhausen. Walddorf, a rural community situated between Tübingen and Stuttgart, had about 1,200 inhabitants in 1850 who were supported by a mixed economy of agriculture and cottage industry. There was a severe economic crisis in the first half of the nineteenth century. Factory work within the village and nearby became an important source of income toward the century's end. Many inhabitants were very pious, highly influenced by the wave of the evangelical awakening movement of pietism that swept over Württemberg in the late eighteenth and early nineteenth centuries.[3] Ohmenhausen is situated about twenty kilometers southeast of Walddorf. After the food crisis of 1846–1847 its impoverished population started to turn to the growing industry of the nearby town of Reutlingen for work. Yet Ohmenhausen's industrial workers still tried hard to maintain their small farms, partly as a form of security against industrial crises, partly as a sign of integration in the village community, where land was still the main source of social esteem. The Pietist awakening did not influence the people of Ohmenhausen. On the contrary, in the late nineteenth century many of them joined or at least voted for socialist parties. Nevertheless, traditional forms of rural youth culture were preserved longer in Ohmenhausen than in Walddorf.

The Background: Male Peer Groups in Rural Württemberg

Modern youth peer groups tend to be informal organizations; they have inner hierarchies but not the formal structures and official status of clubs or societies. In early modern Europe, and in some areas as recently as the early twentieth century, male peer group organizations took more institutionalized forms. Participation in these rural youth groups normally started at the time of school leaving. Often groups were organized according to age—young people leaving school together stayed together as a group and organized their own entertainment. These peer groups followed local traditions, which were passed down from generation to generation of young people, who defended their practices against parental or community efforts to suppress or control them.[4] In Ohmenhausen each age group of boys rented the living room of some family where they could meet in the winter months. In Walddorf in the eighteenth and early nineteenth centuries the traditional meeting places for the boys were the local bakeries; later, meeting in private homes seems also to have become common.[5] Everywhere the right to participate in youth group activities ended, regardless of age, on the day of marriage. In rural southern Germany the term "youth" implied "unmarried." This was symbolically demonstrated every Sunday in church by the fact that all unmarried men and women had to sit in separate pews.[6]

Like their more informal modern counterparts, traditional peer groups in rural areas had various purposes.[7] However, their main task was the regulation of the local marriage market. Male peer groups devoted the majority of their time and energy to keeping young men from other villages away from the local girls and to preventing widowers from marrying young women. These traditional male peer group organizations thus found their raison d'être in the western European system of late marriages, with its high quota of permanently single men and women and tradition of youth working as servants in non-parental households.[8] It is in regions where late marriage predominated that we find ample evidence for long traditions of youth group activities.[9]

Traditional rural peer groups were thus linked to European family structures in which parents tried to postpone the marriage of their children as long as possible in order to keep control over the household. However, they also typified communities in which married men as heads of their households enjoyed a considerable amount of individual and collective power to regulate their affairs and village life. In regulating the marriage market amongst themselves young men copied adult male forms of participation in village politics. At the same time, however, the organized youth groups posed a threat to parental strategies for securing family status or providing for old age through their children's marriages. From the sixteenth to the mid-nineteenth century, therefore, peer group activities were counteracted by community, church, and state attempts (generally unsuccessful) to strengthen parental influence on the choice of marriage partners.[10]

Girls' Leisure: Its Forms and Institutions in Rural Württemberg

What about peer groups activities involving girls? One of the characteristics of female leisure time in rural areas was that it was hardly ever completely free from work. Whereas for young men there was a clear division between the daily duties and the time after dark when work had stopped, girls had to justify any sort of social gatherings by carrying out some kind of useful activity such as spinning or sewing. This is why the central institutions for girls' leisure activities in southwest Germany and other areas were called *Spinnstuben* or *Lichtstuben* (literally, "spinning rooms" or "lighted rooms") because they centered on spinning in the evening and on saving lighting costs by many people working in one room.

How did these South German *Spinn-* or *Lichtstuben* work? First, they were restricted to rural areas and took place during the winter months when agricultural work was less intense and work outside had to stop earlier because of the lack of light.[11] People would gather in private houses on winter evenings to work together and to chat or gossip. The various groups chose one house where they met every winter evening. A small sum of money was paid to the landlord who provided them with the room, light, and heating.[12]

The custom of the *Lichtstuben* can be traced back into the late Middle Ages. They originally appear to have been open to both sexes. Mixed *Lichtstuben* had provided girls not only with a framework to combine textile work with social entertainment alongside other girls, but also brought them into regular contact with young unmarried men and served as an important opportunity for courtship. This roused the suspicion and opposition of both parents and authorities and caused the *Lichtstuben* to be subjected to regulation by the church and state at an early date. In Württemberg control over the *Lichtstuben* was intensified in the sixteenth and seventeenth centuries.[13] Duke Eberhard of Württemberg ruled in 1642 that he wanted "to see any gathering of married or single, engaged or unattached men and women which is suspicious or a public nuisance banned and completely abolished, since these are a true hotbed of inchastity, fornication and adultery, of which daily experience offers more than sufficient proof, especially in the case of the *Lichtstuben*. Therefore all the *Lichtstuben*, with the exception of those gatherings of women in reputable places to save light and to spin or do other useful things while conversing devoutly—all the *Lichtstuben* are to be ruthlessly abolished immediately and on no account will they be tolerated in the slightest from now on."[14] This law clearly differentiated between two different types of *Lichtstuben:* those where the women met to work and converse devoutly and those where young people of both sexes met socially. The mixed *Lichtstuben* were to be abolished, while the others were to be controlled in a way that young unmarried women were not on their own but worked in the company of married women. *Lichtstuben* became, as one historian has put it, "de-sexualized" and "domesticated."[15]

Laws rarely have their intended effects. In Württemberg control of the *Lichtstuben* remained a field of permanent struggle among church, local authorities, and young people. The Protestant church wanted to abolish them altogether, whereas local authorities often showed some understanding for the desire to save lighting costs, and sometimes they even tried to understand the needs of young people for entertainment.[16] For the young people the *Lichtstuben* incorporated three things for which they fought: a sphere of social interaction more or less uncontrolled by parents, a sphere of independent work, and a self-regulated marriage market. To what extent did they succeed? What ways were there for girls to keep a sphere of autonomous work and leisure? Were they more or less successful than their male contemporaries? The following will attempt to answer these three questions.

Controlling the *Lichtstuben* as Girls' Leisure Spaces

Evidence from these villages suggests that the various attempts by church and state to control the *Lichtstuben* were relatively successful; sex segregation of the *Lichtstuben* was imposed as a general principle in all these villages. Local custom allowed boys and girls to spend an evening together only on certain restricted days of the year. Even at the beginning of the twentieth century it was still tradition in the village of Ohmenhausen for boys to visit the *Lichtstuben* only on 6 January (the festival of the Three Kings) and celebrate with the girls with sausages and cider. All other attempts to visit the girls in their meeting places were illegal, which of course does not mean that they did not take place.

However, if boys were caught in a *Lichtstube* by the local police both they and the landlord had to pay a fine. Household heads were made responsible for what happened in their *Lichtstuben* and had to "observe as true Christians in case something illegal should happen during these evenings."[17]

Another means of controlling the *Lichtstuben* was requiring the mixing of girls and adult women. Whereas no one attempted to control boys' peer groups in this way, laws stated that girls should not attend *Lichtstuben* without adult women present. Household heads who wanted to have a *Lichtstube* in their house during the winter months not only had to ask the parish priest and parish council for approval but also had to hand in the names of the girls and women who would assemble in their houses. Only after 1871, when local laws had to be adapted to the more liberal legal framework of the new German Empire, did this form of supervision of the *Lichtstuben* gradually come to an end.

These attempts to control the *Lichtstuben* created a fascinating historical source that enables us to have a closer look at who gathered where. The female *Lichtstuben* are particularly well documented for Walddorf. Here the yearly lists of names survived without major interruption from 1780 to 1871. Detailed study of them shows that the authorities were not entirely successful in their attempts to control the *Lichtstuben*, for the policy of maintaining adult women's supervision was not always vigorously applied by the authorities.[18] In winter 1844, for example, there were seven *Lichtstuben* registered in Walddorf. The one at Joseph Lauxmann's house followed the official model of mixed age groups. Here we find

Jacob Armbruster's daughter with her mother
[unmarried] daughter of forest warden Kurz
[unmarried] Jacobine Lauxmann
Dorothea Löffler, maidservant
Maidservant of the notary
3 [married] women[19]

Some of the other *Lichtstuben* were composed of a similar mixture of local daughters, servants, and married women. However, there were also several *Lichtstuben* where only unmarried girls and servants were enrolled. Three out of the seven *Lichtstuben* seem to have been assemblies of unmarried girls only.[20]

Did girls have a "right" to participate in these activities, such as their brothers held? This seems to have been the case in Ohmenhausen in the years before World War I.[21] Still, from looking at these lists for Walddorf, it seems that not all girls attended *Lichtstuben*. Moreover, it seems clear that school-leaving age groups were by no means as strong a bond for female peer groups as they were for male ones.[22] However, it is possible to recognize other patterns of social bonds for women. If one examines the Walddorf *Lichtstuben* lists over a period of time a pattern appears that allows us to differentiate between three different types of *Lichtstuben* in this village. One is clearly a family or neighborhood-oriented type: a household head with daughters of his own hosts the daughters, wives, and servants of relatives or friends.[23] A second type tended to be more age specific and restricted to unmarried girls. Even the landlord's family seems not to have taken part in the *Lichtstube* or at least was not registered. Only more detailed analysis can show whether there was perhaps some kind of class aspect behind these uncontrolled *Lichtstuben* and whether they were reconcilable with female respectability. Finally, the third type of the *Lichtstuben* was in effect a pious evangelical prayer group. This is an interesting phenomenon that is probably specific to Walddorf. In the early nineteenth century revivalist movements became very strong here and found many followers. Members of this movement were the most prominent opponents of traditional youth culture in the village and tried for a long time to suppress it. After the mid-nineteenth century they seem to have attempted to control it by taking the *Lichtstuben* over and molding them according to their own principles, replacing courtship and local gossip with Christian edification. In 1871 the biggest *Lichtstube* in Walddorf, with nine participants, was in the house of Maria Agnes Wurster, a sixty-seven-year-old spinster and a prominent member of the most influential Pietist circle in the village.[24] However, by this time the number of *Lichtstuben* was stagnating and the number of participants declining; in this year only thirty-three village girls and women spent their winter evenings in a *Lichtstube.*

Revealing as these lists may be, they do not tell us what actually happened in or outside the *Lichtstuben* on winter nights. To what extent was the policy of "domesticating" and "de-sexualizing" the *Lichtstuben* successful? Was the presence of adult women a guarantee that there would be no boys? And what did all those girls who did not attend these regulated meetings do during the winter evenings? There is very little evidence to shed light on these questions, but the few sources we have are revealing.

In November 1827 the Walddorf parish council decided that every holder of a *Lichtstube* where the local police found young unmarried men was to be fined three guilders, and also that so-called "getting-up-nights" or "spinning through nights" were to be strictly forbidden.[25] On Saturday and Sunday evenings or on other church holidays *Lichtstuben* were not permitted for religious reasons. Nevertheless, in order to respect the Sunday and still have some pleasure, the girls in Walddorf sometimes got up after midnight to spin through the night until dawn.[26] It is unlikely that adult women took part in these events—but the documentation of conflicts shows that young men were keen to join the girls and that local police intervention could meet with a violent reaction. In 1821 young men thus attacked the village police officer who was patrolling the village at two o'clock on Monday morning in search of trespassers in the *Lichtstuben.*[27] Police reports on other conflicts among boys also show that an important part of youth activities must have taken place after the *Lichtstuben* curfew at 10 or 11 P.M. and that these also involved girls. Thus an autonomous sphere of entertainment and courting seems to have existed in Walddorf at least on certain nights.

The historian can only draw tentative conclusions as to what happened these nights. Nevertheless, sources on conflicts from the late eighteenth and early nineteenth centuries indicate that the *Lichtstuben* were still very much part of the local marriage market and provided an important opportunity for court-ship. In many cases young men were reported to have been in the *Lichtstuben* with the girls, and girls to have moved from one *Lichtstube* to another during the night—and to have met boys on the way. There are also cases that indicate that talk and behavior within the *Lichtstuben* could be highly sexualized. Catharina Heim, for example, was reported in 1797 not only to have used indecent lan-guage in the *Lichtstube* but also to have touched a boy's genitals.[28]

The 1820s and 1830s in particular seem to have been a time when young people claimed a great deal of freedom without the authorities being able to check them.[29] Even when police control of their nightly activities was tightened by the village council, youth continued to spend their time in peer groups af-ter the official closing of the *Lichtstuben*. It was only with the decline of the *Lichtstuben* in Walddorf after the middle of the nineteenth century that the number of complaints about them decreased. Subsequently, other less-regulated youth activities annoyed the local authorities. In the year 1867, the parish coun-cil formulated an official complaint stating that in Walddorf female youth had become so immoral and shameless that older people felt ashamed of them. It was said that girls between the ages of sixteen and eighteen were leaving their homes at midnight in order to "hang around on the roads and in secluded places to do mischief without interference."[30]

Returning to the question of whether the authorities succeeded in domesti-cating and de-sexualizing the *Lichtstuben* in Walddorf, the answer for the first half of the nineteenth century would appear to be positive only as far as the official procedure of licensing the *Lichtstuben* was concerned. Otherwise at least some of the girls seem to have claimed more freedom and autonomous lei-sure than previously. It is hard to know if the fact that a girl did not attend a *Lichtstube* in the early nineteenth century meant that she was not allowed to go or did not want to. By the mid-nineteenth century not attending the *Lichtstuben* was definitely no longer a guarantee that evenings were spent at home. It was more likely that the girls were elsewhere, "on the roads and in secluded places."

However, this is only half of the story. The other half is that of the consid-erable success of the Pietist religious offensive. When official control over the *Lichtstuben* was abandoned in 1871, there seems to have been a revival of the *Lichtstuben* as more autonomous meeting places for girls in many villages such Ohmenhausen. They persisted well into the twentieth century in some villages, and the autonomy of the girls to choose their mates and meeting places in-creased rather than decreased.[31] As demonstrated previously, in Walddorf, on the other hand, by the 1870s evening gatherings seem to have changed under the influence of Pietist circles. As a consequence, *Lichtstuben* ceased to be an integral part of local youth culture in Walddorf. There is no archival evidence for *Lichtstuben* to be found in Walddorf after the 1870s and, in contrast with Ohmenhausen, elderly women interviewed in Walddorf in the early 1980s could not remember them as part of their youth. Moreover, the more religiously in-clined girls of Walddorf did not seek to meet the boys on the streets at night and accepted church initiatives for alternative entertainment. The number of girls involved was by no means few—partly because of the influence of a young charismatic preacher whom many of them followed even after he had been dismissed from his post by the Lutheran church.[32] Thus, by the end of the nineteenth century the girls in Walddorf did not experience youth culture in a single coherent group any longer; rather, youth divided along religious lines.

Working in the *Lichtstuben*

Girls' leisure in the *Lichtstuben* was closely connected to the production of textiles. But did girls' work in the *Lichtstuben* form an integral part of family cottage industry, or was it independent and a source of private income for girls or a means of meeting personal needs? According to elderly women interviewed in Ohmenhausen in the early 1980s, the winter evenings spent in the *Lichtstuben* were the only times when they did not have to toil for their parents but were allowed to work for themselves especially preparing their dowry. In this respect the Ohmenhausen girls were equal to the boys, who were free from family obligations when they were out at night. However, in an analysis of eighteenth-century protoindustrial society in the Zurich Highlands a different analysis of the *Spinnstuben* tradition is given.[33] Here a differentiation was made between older types of *Lichtstuben*, which were a privilege of the unmarried youth dating back to the Middle Ages, and the more modern *Spinnstuben*, which were fully integrated into protoindustrial textile production and where the girls' evening work produced yarn that their families needed for their daytime weaving.

No clear evidence for either of these options can be found for Walddorf. However, of the girls born in 1827 there were seven whose fathers were weavers; of these only three went to the *Lichtstuben* in 1843. The other girls came from families of farmers, bakers, and others. This can be taken as an indication that, unlike in the Zurich case, female work in the *Lichtstuben* in Walddorf was not an important part of local protoindustrial textile production.[34] By the mid-nineteenth century linen weaving was in any case in crisis in Walddorf. Although in 1861 the mayor counted 66 looms, they were only used for occasional weaving as supplementary income; linen weaving was by this time clearly in decline.[35] The parish council tried to establish a spinnery with two teachers in 1853, but this institution did not survive for very long.[36] Then local authorities tried to promote cotton weaving by offering special courses with government help to young weavers.[37] The figures show that this was reasonably successful: in 1861 there were twenty-six young cotton weavers employed in Walddorf.[38] Cotton weaving made hand spinning obsolete, as machine-spun cotton was cheaper and better. Thus, it is perhaps not unlikely that, even if it was different before, with the decline of flax spinning at least some of the *Lichtstuben* girls were allowed to work on their dowries.

What about the girls who did not attend the *Lichtstuben*? Within the context of the changing structure of textile work in the village it can be assumed that they probably had to work for and with their families in the evening. The decline of traditional linen weaving was accompanied by the rise of the new cotton industry and also by the introduction of sewing, knitting, and crochet work as new forms of female cottage industry. From the middle of the nineteenth century local authorities tried to attract new forms of textile industry to the village. They found entrepreneurs who were willing to employ Walddorf girls and women in home-industry needlework, and in the late 1890s a small textile factory opened up in Walddorf. This meant that female textile work became more permanent and more commercialized and independent of the male weaving industry. It very often constituted the most important source of cash income for families. Female textile work may well have been drawn back into the family. Older girls brought pieces home from the factory to sew buttons on, and younger girls were required to help. Crochet work was done by girls after school and in the evening. The income from this work was handed over to the parents.[39] Thus, pressure on girls to earn cash from their textile work seems to have increased toward the end of the century. The *Lichtstuben* may have been an integral part of this new system of female work initially, at least for some of those families who did not object to them for religious reasons. For others their daughters' time would have been too precious to be spent at a place where other interests could distract them from their lucrative work.

Lichtstuben and the Marriage Market

Work was definitely not the only purpose of the *Lichtstuben* from the young people's point of view. As indicated above, these meetings on winter evenings were also part of courtship rituals and an important institution of the local marriage market. That is why the official policy of separating the sexes in the *Lichtstuben* met with considerable resistance from the youth, and why conflicts over young men coming into the female *Lichtstuben* can be found in the records of the village courts for more or less every winter from the early modern time into the late nineteenth century. Local language had a specific term for what boys were expected to do when they went to the girls' *Lichtstuben*. The phrase was "*auf den Vorsitz gehen*," which means "to go and sit in front of" the girl.[40] The custom was that the boy sat opposite the girl and entertained her while she was spinning. In a context where marriage partners were chosen mainly according to economic convenience and family power politics, this opens up a completely different perspective. Neither property nor male physical strength was tested here, but social competence. It was a way of discovering to what extent the couple could talk to each other and enjoy each other's company.

The *Vorsitz*, although illegal, was part of larger set of courtship customs that allowed gradually increasing intimacy between the partners. There is no clear evidence boys assumed the traditional right to visit girlfriends at night (as occurred in some European regions).[41] However, there are countless cases in the Walddorf court records where a young man was fined because he had entered a girl's bedroom to sleep with her, a fact that was usually discovered in the course of an investigation into the parentage of illegitimate children. Unmarried mothers were regularly asked where intercourse had taken place. The normal answer was that the boy had visited the girl in her father's or, more often, her master's house.[42]

It is difficult to judge whether the parents of a girl knew of and tolerated such visits. Although the general assumption is that in rural areas engagement provided young couples with a license to be sexually active, this is not a fully convincing explanation here. The very detailed inquiries into illegitimate births in Walddorf suggest that girls frequently slept with boys without any official promise of marriage.[43] Whether the daughters' parents still accepted or (in the case of socially advantageous love affairs) even supported these nightly escapades or whether they were simply unable to prevent them remains an open question. However, it is noteworthy that they did not usually report the boys' visits to the police. If they were reported, it was often only when a pregnancy ensued or as a result of a quarrel between potential rivals, especially when boys from other villages were involved. In the 1820s and 1830s there are several reports of Walddorf boys pulling a boy from another village out of the bed of a Walddorf girl.[44]

Cases like these provide us with some idea of what nightlife was like in Walddorf and how strong the tradition of clearly defined courtship rules was within the local youth culture. The *Lichtstuben* were clearly part of a wider system of youth control over matchmaking and premarital sexuality. They were normally supplemented by dances at the parish fair and at weddings as well as by regulated walks of the village youth into the fields or the nearby woods. In Ohmenhausen all these elements still operated in the early twentieth century, whereas in Walddorf dances had been forbidden since the mid-nineteenth century with very few exceptions.[45] The desire of local authorities, parents, and Pietist groups to control autonomous matchmaking clearly disturbed this system as a whole, even though some parts could obviously not be suppressed.

However, in Walddorf the evangelical revival movement of the nineteenth century was not only effective through stricter police supervision of the young people. It also affected a reasonable number of them "internally." This was of great importance for social change in the village in general and for youth culture in particular, as the Pietists tended to choose their marriage partners not necessarily from the village but rather from like-minded families elsewhere; moreover, it was considered particularly saintly to remain unmarried. In the second half of the nineteenth century we even find in Walddorf a type of miniature Protestant monastery with several unmarried men and one or two unmarried women living together in one house as religious "brothers" and "sisters." Walddorf's youth thus seem to have been very divided.[46] On the one hand we have complaints about the shamelessness of youth in the 1860s, and on the other hand we find this new type of "Protestant saints" among the young men and women.

One of the main differences between male and female leisure time in eighteenth- and nineteenth-century villages in southern Germany was how it related to work. Young men at leisure were free from work; they were also free to drink, smoke, read the newspapers, and talk about village politics in their assemblies. These were generally things they were not allowed to do at home until they were married.[47] Young women, on the other hand, were expected to work, whether it was economically necessary or not. This unequal workload continued for the women for the rest of their lives. The *Lichtstuben* may have provided them with good training in bearing this burden.

Connected to this difference in the work relatedness of leisure it is interesting to note that whereas boys' *Lichtstuben* tended to be organized strictly according to school-leaving years, the meetings of the girls legally had to be more family and neighborhood oriented. Male organized peer groups in these villages made no social distinctions between rich and poor. In this they prefigured future participation in the community of household heads representing the village as a political body. Without wanting to exaggerate the importance of the public-private dichotomy in relation to gender roles, it is clear that there was considerable pressure on girls to spend their leisure within a smaller circle of people more or less connected with their own household. While girls often tried successfully to escape this pressure and find times and places to be amongst themselves, their groups never developed the same corporative structures as their male counterparts.

Finally, another interesting phenomenon that requires further detailed study is the importance of generational relations for rural youth. For Walddorf, the period of the French Revolution and after was a time of severe internal tension and strife that was reflected in the unruliness of young people, but even then some of them formulated their protest within the context of religious movements. The same is true for the 1830s, when it was the young girls in particular in Walddorf who supported the charismatic evangelical leader Gustav Werner. At least for a considerable proportion of the young generation of that time this new type of Christianity seems to have exercised some attraction, so that the pressure for moral behavior came not only from outside—from parents and state and local authorities—but from "within."

Nonetheless, there was always a part of Walddorf youth, male and female, that was secular minded and often unruly and that tried to defend their sphere of autonomous leisure and their traditional ways of getting to know and choose possible marriage partners. When these became subject to official surveillance to a degree that they ceased to be attractive, as in the case of the *Lichtstuben,* this part of Walddorf's youth simply created their own opportunities by meeting on the roads at night, preferably outside the village. However, they did not permit their independence to be curtailed without fighting back. The antagonism between young people and the section of village society that tried to impose a new order on youth life is probably best summed up by an event that took place in the early hours of New Year's Day 1817. The parish council sent a group of twenty people out to catch the boys who, as was the custom, wanted to fire guns in front of their girlfriends' windows. On seeing the councilors approaching, one young man shouted out of the window: "Come in and kiss my backside!" and his sister added: "You ought to be ashamed of yourselves; you were young and single once!"[48]

Notes

1. The most comprehensive overview in European perspective is Michael Mitterauer, *Sozialgeschichte der Jugend* (Frankfurt a.M.: Suhrkamp, 1986) (Engl. trans.: *A History of Youth* [London: Blackwell, 1992]); see also Giovanni Levi and Jean-Claude Schmitt, eds., *A History of Young People in the West*, vol. 1, *Ancient and Medieval Rites of Passage*, trans. Camille Naish; vol. 2, *Stormy Evolution to Modern Times*, trans. Carol Volk (Cambridge, Mass., and London: Belknap Press, 1997); and Andreas Gestrich, *Einführung in die Historische Sozialisationsforschung* (Tübingen: edition diskord, 1999), 109ff.

2. For example, see Christina Benninghaus and Kerstin Kohtz, eds., *"Sag mir, wo die Mädchen sind—": Beiträge zur Geschlechtergeschichte der Jugend* (Köln, Weimar, and Wien: Böhlau, 1999), which gives a very good introduction to the "gender history of youth" but also concentrates entirely on female youth in urban contexts.

3. On the religious history of Walddorf, see Andreas Gestrich, "'Neue Menschen' in traditionaler Gesellschaft. Alltagsleben in einem Pietistischen Dorf Württembergs im 19. Jahrhundert," in *FS Geschichtsverein Leinfelden-Echterdingen* (Stuttgart: Scheufele, 1995), 75–90; Gestrich, "Pietismus und Aberglaube. Zum Zusammenhang von popularem Pietismus und dem Ende der Hexenverfolgung im 18. Jahrhundert," in *Das Ende der Hexenverfolgung*, ed. Sönke Lorenz and Dieter Bauer (Stuttgart: Steiner, 1995), 269–286; and Gestrich, "Pietismus und ländliche Frömmigkeit in Württemberg im 18. und frühen 19. Jahrhundert," in *Ländliche Frömmigkeit. Konfessionskulturen und Lebenswelten 1500–1850*, ed. Norbert Haag, Sabine Holtz and Wolfgang Zimmermann (Sigmaringen: Thorbecke, 2002), 343–357.

4. One of the earliest social histories of youth is John R. Gillis, *Youth and History: Tradition and Change in European Age Relations, 1770–Present* (New York and London: Academic Press, 1974).

5. For Ohmenhausen, see Andreas Gestrich, *Traditionelle Jugendkultur und Industrialisierung. Sozialgeschichte der Jugend in einer ländlichen Arbeitergemeinde Württembergs, 1800–1920* (Göttingen: Vandehoeck & Ruprecht, 1986), 92ff. For Walddorf, see Gemeindearchiv Walddorf (hereafter cited as GAW), A 213, Polizei 1856–1871, 7./8.12.1858.

6. It is telling that in 1845 several unmarried men came to the mayor in Walddorf asking for full recognition as citizens. They were mostly between fifty and sixty years old. Only shortly beforehand they had been allowed to sit with the adult married men in church. GAW, Gemeinderatsprotokoll, 1843–1847, 264f., 12 December 1845. Cf. Gestrich, "'Neue Menschen,'" 86.

7. On the socialization functions of "old type" peer groups, see Gestrich, *Jugendkultur*, 167–182, and Mitterauer, 10ff. and 163ff.

8. For the European marriage system, see John Hajnal, "European Marriage Patterns in Perspective," in *Population in History: Essays in Historical Demography,* ed. D. V. Glass and D. E. C. Eversley (London: Arnold, 1965), 101–143; for its relevance for the history of youth and youth groups, see Mitterauer, 28ff. For a recent discussion of Hajnal's theory, see Karl Kaser, *Macht und Erbe. Männerherrschaft, Besitz und Familie im östlichen Europa (1500–1900)* (Wien: Böhlau, 2000).

9. See Mitterauer, 168–169. No traces of peer organizations can be found in those areas of the Balkans, where large and complex households were dominant. Here couples married considerably earlier and often moved into the male parental household.

10. On these Malthusian politics especially, see Klaus-Jürgen Matz, *Pauperismus und Bevölkerung. Die gesetzlichen Ehebeschränkungen in den süddeutschen Staaten während des 19. Jahrhunderts* (Stuttgart: Klett, 1980).

11. The traditional dates were St. Martin's Day in November for the opening of the *Lichtstuben* and Candlemas in February for their closing. See Gestrich, *Jugendkultur,* 93–94.

12. Gestrich, *Jugendkultur,* 92ff.

13. See Hans Medick, "Spinnstuben auf dem Dorf. Jugendliche Sexualkultur und Feierabendbrauch in der ländlichen Gesellschaft der frühen Neuzeit," in *Sozialgeschichte der Freizeit. Untersuchungen zum Wandel der Alltagskultur in Deutschland,* ed. Gerhard Huck (Wuppertal: Hammer, 1980): 19–50; Andreas Gestrich, "Protestant Religion, the State and the Suppression of Traditional Youth Culture in Southwest Germany," *History of European Ideas* 11 (1989): 629–636; and A. L. Reyscher, *Vollständige Sammlung der württembergischen Gesetze,* 19 vols. (Stuttgart, 1828–1852). See vol. 8, part 1, 458 for the restriction of 1672.

14. Reyscher, vol. 7, part 2, 425–426. This is also quoted in Gestrich, "Protestant Religion," 629–630.

15. Medick.

16. Gestrich, *Jugendkultur,* 92.

17. Pfarrarchiv Walddorf (hereafter cited as PfAW), Kirchen-Censur-Protokoll 1778–1814, Eintrag vom 10.11.1804.

18. In Walddorf mothers were reminded occasionally that when they wanted to attend a *Lichtstube* they had to go to the same ones as their daughters. Cf. GAW, A 213 Policeisachen 1819–1835, 20.11.1822.

19. PfAW, Kirchenkonventsprotokoll 1830–1863: 238f., 2 December 1844.

20. PfAW, Kirchenkonventsprotokoll 1830–1863: 224–225, 238–239.

21. For the *Lichtstuben* and male meeting places in Ohmenhausen, see Gestrich, *Jugendkultur,* 92ff.

22. Pfarrarchiv Walddorf, Birthregister 1827; Kirchenkonventsprotokolle 1843–1852.

23. See PfAW, Kirchenkonventsprotokoll 1830–1863: 255–257, 8.12.1845. The analysis of the composition of the *Lichtstuben* could provide interesting material for testing David Sabeans's hypothesis of a change from clientele to family orientation in the nineteenth century in the south German village of Neckarhausen, which is only a few kilometers away from Walddorf. See David Warren Sabean, *Kinship in Neckarhausen, 1700–1870* (Cambridge: Cambridge University Press, 1998), and "Die Ästhetik der Heiratsallianzen.

Klassencodes und endogame Eheschließung im Bürgertum des 19. Jahrhunderts," in *Historische Familienforschung. Ergebnisse und Kontroversen,* ed. Josef Ehmer, Tamara Hareven, and Richrad Wall (Frankfurt a.M. and New York: Campus, 1997): 157–170.

24. See PfAW, Kirchenkonventsprotokoll 1863–1891, 8.12.1871: 99–101. This case was novel in the fact that a woman applied for housing in a *Lichtstube*. Traditionally, it was strictly forbidden for widows to live in a *Lichtstube*. See, for example, PfAW Kirchenkonventsprotokoll 1830–1863: 322–323, 18.11.1848. Maria Agnes Wurster was a spinster, and in her religious group staying unmarried was a sign of religious zeal. See my two general essays on Walddorf, "'Neue Menschen'" and "Pietismus und ländliche Frömmigkeit in Württemberg im 18. und frühen 19. Jahrhundert."

25. PfAW, Kirchenkonventsprotokoll 1814–1829: 192, 18.11.1827.

26. GAW, A 7, Protokoll der Beamtung in Rechts- und Strafsachen 1817–1823, 31.12.1821.

27. Ibid.

28. PfAW, Kirchenzensurprotokoll, 1778–1814, 6.6.1797: 290–291.

29. There were several interventions by the county (*Oberamt*) and other administrative bodies because of the unruliness of youth in Walddorf and elsewhere in these years. See, for example, complaints about the increase in violent conflicts among the young people in GAW, A 213, Policeisachen 1819–1835, 13.5.1830.

30. PfAW, Kirchenkonventsprotokoll 1863–1891, 24.8.1867.

31. In Ohmenhausen in the late 1970s, I interviewed elderly people who had participated as young people in these traditions before World War I. Girls seemed then to have been free to choose their *Lichtstuben* mates, whereas for boys it was still the tradition to stick strictly to their age group.

32. On the various religious groups in Walddorf, see Gestrich, "Pietismus und ländliche Frömmigkeit in Württemberg im 18. und frühen 19. Jahrhundert."

33. Rudolf Braun, *Industrialisierung und Volksleben. Veränderungen der Lebensformen unter Einwirkung der verlagsindustriellen Heimarbeit in einem ländlichen Industriegebiet (Zürcher Oberland) vor 1800,* 2d ed. (Göttingen: Vandenhoeck & Ruprecht, 1979).

34. This clearly needs further investigation, especially for the eighteenth century. Unfortunately, the most detailed investigation into the protoindustrial textile industry in Württemberg does not mention *Lichtstuben* at all. See Hans Medick, *Weben und Überleben in Laichingen, 1650–1900. Lokalgeschichte als Allgemeine Geschichte* (Göttingen: Vandenhoeck & Ruprecht, 1996).

35. GAW, A 205, Gewerbe-Sachen, Allgemeines 1855–1872. 3.12.1861.

36. GAW, B 20, Gemeinderatsprotokoll 1851–1854: 121, 7.1.1853.

37. GAW, B 21, Gemeinderatsprotokoll 1854–1859: 122, 29.1.1856.

38. GAW, A 205, Gewerbe-Sachen, Allgemeines 1855–1872. 3.12.1861.

39. In 1983 I conducted several interviews with senior citizens from Walddorf. Two women born in the 1890s reported on this system of textile work for schoolgirls.

40. See, for example, Gemeindearchiv Hülben (GAH), Gemeinderatsprotokoll 1838–1843, 29.12.1841.

41. The classic example for this custom comes from Sweden. See K. R. V.

Wikman, *Die Einleitung der Ehe. Eine vergleichende ethno-soziologische Untersuchung über die Vorstufen der Ehe in den Sitten und Gebräuchen des schwedischen Volkstum* (Abo, Finland: Abo Akademi, 1937).

42. PfAW, *Kirchen-Censur-Protokolle* 1778–1814: 24–25; for some concrete cases, see Gestrich, "'Neue Menschen,'" 87.

43. See GAW, Scortationsstrafprotokolle 1807–1844. Apart from the questions about parentage, the authorities wanted detailed information on when and where "it" had happened, as there were heavier fines for intercourse on Sundays.

44. Gestrich, "'Neue Menschen,'" 87.

45. Gestrich, *Jugendkultur,* 103ff.; PfAW, Kirchenkonventsprotokoll 1830–1863: 251, 12 October 1845, stating that dances on holidays had been forbidden in the village for a long time.

46. Gestrich, "Pietismus und ländliche Frömmigkeit in Württemberg im 18. und frühen 19. Jahrhundert," 352.

47. Gestrich, *Jugendkultur,* 96–97.

48. GAW, A 7, Protokoll der Beamtung in Rechts- und. Strafsachen 1817–1823, o.p., 2 January 1817.

4 An Industrious Revolution in Late Seventeenth-Century Paris: New Vocational Training for Adolescent Girls and the Creation of Female Labor Markets

Clare Crowston

Clare Crowston focuses on one city—Paris—to argue that there was a significant growth in vocational training opportunities for girls from the late seventeenth through the mid-eighteenth century. Many Parisian girls entered more or less formal training in adolescence. Once they had acquired necessary skills, they continued to work in workshops within and outside of the guild system. These girls' experiences belie usual claims that female workers were marginal to the early modern Parisian economy and also suggest the need to look beyond guild sources to understand the preindustrial economy and labor force and the centrality of women and girls to Europe's "industrious revolution."

In 1660, the Parisian tailors' guild drafted a set of revised statutes that allowed masters' daughters to make children's clothing but explicitly prohibited all other women and girls from working in their trade.[1] In April 1692, the Parisian embroiderers' guild successfully prosecuted a group of its own masters for having hired women because master embroiderers were not supposed to employ female workers except their own wives and daughters or the daughters of poor masters.[2] In writing the history of work, historians have been strongly influenced by records left by guilds like these tailors and embroiderers (such as statutes, apprenticeship contracts, guild reception records, royal economic legislation, and legal proceedings). The richness of guild-related sources—and the relative scarcity of sources regarding non-guild labor—has had important consequences for our understanding of the world of work in early modern Europe, and in particular for the place of women and girls within it.

Guild records portray a world of work dominated by men who held guild membership and negotiated work on behalf of their wives and children. The sources suggest that women's work was limited to the ancillary roles of helpers in the family business and providers of necessary domestic labor to free men for productive work. Even when historians paid attention to women's work, the imprint of guild-based sources continued to dominate historical writing. Historians emphasized once more the importance of the family unit in economic production, focusing on the contributions women and girls made to family workshops. They also emphasized women's exclusion from public labor markets as a result of guilds' dominance of economic production. As a logical conclusion, women's historians argued that women's situation worsened as the guilds' grip on the economy tightened in the seventeenth and eighteenth centuries.[3]

These conclusions profoundly shaped our understanding of women's labor, of the place of girls and women within families, and of girls' perceptions of their place in the world and their future possibilities. According to this model, girls' activities were directed first by their father and later by their husbands, while the female career consisted solely of negotiating the transition from daughter to wife and mother. A young woman's marriage choices were dictated by the fit between her father and her groom's social or economic preoccupations. She and her mother had little say or autonomous interests at stake in forming and maintaining families.

Recent historical investigations of early modern France have demonstrated the limitations of this understanding of women, work, and family. Studies of women's place in the guild world have demonstrated that female labor in incorporated trades by far surpassed the role of helpmeet. A small but vibrant group of exclusively female guilds (including seamstresses, linen drapers, and flower sellers) existed in Paris and Rouen. These female guilds were complemented by the presence of women in mixed corporations such as midwives in the Parisian surgeons' guild or female painters and sculptors in the Academy of Saint-Luke. Widows and daughters occupied a more independent and assertive place in business than we imagined.[4] Apart from the guild world, historians have also devised innovative methods for uncovering female entrepreneurship in non-guild trades and have found that women's economic activities belied dour legal and prescriptive restrictions. Women worked in textile production, preparing and selling food and drink, and in service trades.[5]

These revisionist studies have revealed a much more complex situation for female work in France. Many aspects of the female world of work, however, remain to be elucidated. Relatively little work has been done on how women gained access to skills or on the processes of production and re-production in female trades. These topics are the focus of this chapter. My sources reveal a significant growth in vocational training for female youth in Paris in the late seventeenth century. This growth occurred in needle trades long associated with women—but in some cases dominated by male guilds—such as sewing, embroidery, and tapestry making. Within the guild world, an exclusively female seam-stresses' guild was created in 1675 in response to the royal government's attempts to expand the corporate system. By the beginning of the eighteenth century, apprentice seamstresses outnumbered apprentices in many male trades, creating a large pool of young women possessing craft skill and a claim to independent corporate privilege. In the same years, the Catholic reform movement sparked the creation of a number of female lay communities to educate poor girls. The schools they created disseminated religious indoctrination but also practical trade skills, and their students numbered in the hundreds in Paris. Although this chapter will focus on Paris, seamstresses acquired corporate privileges either independently or within tailors' guilds in numerous cities and towns across France, leading to a similar rise in female apprenticeship. And female lay communities were equally or even more active in the provinces than they were in Paris.

The last decades of the seventeenth century thus witnessed the introduction of girls to the skilled labor market on a new scale. This evidence provides additional support for the notion of an "industrious revolution" proposed by Jan de Vries. According to his argument, over the seventeenth and early eighteenth centuries families reoriented their labor resources toward external labor markets in a conscious effort to maximize income and allow greater purchase of finished goods. A key element of this redeployment of household labor was the entry of women and children to wage or protoindustrial labor markets. De Vries concludes that the "industrious revolution" was a necessary precursor to the Industrial Revolution; the initial intense growth in demand for consumer products—and the labor forces to generate them—were thus only made possible by the work of women and children. As limited as the individual female training programs just discussed may seem to modern eyes or may have seemed to contemporary observers, together they contributed to the creation of a new economic model, with all its social and cultural consequences.[6]

Girls' Apprenticeship in Parisian Guilds

Until 1675, male tailors' guilds dominated the production of made-to-measure clothing in France. Their statutes endowed them with exclusive control over the production of garments for both men and women. Despite this monopoly, female needleworkers existed in many cities and towns, specializing in making dresses, skirts, and other outer garments for women and children. Their work was illegal and subject to prosecution by tailors' guilds. This situation changed in large part because of a 1673 edict whereby Controller General Jean-Baptiste Colbert required all unincorporated trades to form guilds. The government was motivated by several factors, including a desire to provide female artisans for elite women, to obtain revenue from membership fees, and to encourage an outlet for French textile production. The Parisian seamstresses responded eagerly to this opportunity, writing to the king to request guild status. In 1675, the Parisian seamstresses obtained an independent, exclusively female guild, with the right to produce made-to-measure clothing for women and children but not for men.[7]

This guild quickly grew to become one of the largest in Paris. With a population of 1,700 mistresses in the 1720s, it was estimated to be the fourth largest of the 124 trade corporations in the city. Each year roughly 130 new mistresses entered the guild. With some 10 percent of all guild entries, the guild enjoyed the highest entry levels of all Parisian guilds. Once they achieved mistress status, most seamstresses conducted autonomous careers. A large proportion (around 40 percent) remained unmarried. Through work in the trade, women could earn enough to support themselves independently or to supplement family income.

The guild attracted even more apprentices than it did mistresses. In 1716, the first date for which figures are available, at least 403 girls signed a notarized apprenticeship contract with a guild mistress.[8] Between 1746 and 1759, the guild recorded a yearly average of 419 new apprentices. Together, apprentice seamstresses probably constituted the largest group of apprentices in the city of Paris, some 15 percent of the total in the early 1760s.[9] At any given time there were approximately 1,250 apprentices engaged in learning this trade. Because only 130 women entered the guild as mistresses each year, finished apprentices comprised a large pool of surplus labor. They would have worked as dependent laborers for mistress seamstresses or transferred their skills to work for tailors, fashion merchants, or other craftsmen.

Like male apprentices, these girls appeared before a notary accompanied by their families and future mistresses to sign a formal contract outlining the terms of their training. Guild officials were also present to authorize the contract in the name of the guild and to collect fees for this service. A sample of contracts reveals that apprentice seamstresses began training at around fourteen years old and usually engaged themselves for a three-year training period. In comparison to male apprentices, seamstresses were slightly younger and trained for shorter periods; boys in Paris were usually close to age sixteen when they apprenticed for an average period of nearly five years.[10]

In most cases, a girl's parents took the initiative to place her in training with a seamstress. A sample of 646 apprenticeship contracts indicates that almost three-quarters of girls were represented in negotiations by both parents or by a parent's appointed representative. A substantial minority of girls appeared with a non-parental family member, uncles and aunts, siblings, grandparents, and, less frequently, cousins. These figures suggest that parents usually chose apprenticeship for their daughters and undertook the actions and expenses necessary to obtain it. Fathers were the most important figures in this process, but mothers played a significant role as well when their husbands were incapacitated. The numbers of girls involved, and the fact that their fathers chose apprenticeship for them, suggests that far from subsuming their daughters' labor under their own, many fathers actively sought formal training for their daughters in an autonomous trade. These fathers planned for a trade that the girls could learn outside the home and practice as live-in or live-out workers.

Demand for entry to the Paris seamstresses' trade was an urban and predominantly Parisian phenomenon. Over 90 percent of apprentices' parents declared a residence in the capital. Those from outside Paris rarely came from very far away. Moreover, of 339 living fathers who declared a profession, the largest group belonged to the world of artisanal crafts and commerce. With a strong foothold in the Parisian trades, we may surmise that the girls' fathers chose the trade for practical economic purposes. These were not marginal or desperate families but solid members of the working and shop-keeping classes who sought professional training for their daughters with skilled mistresses. Apprentices' families not only chose the path of formal apprenticeship; they also made significant investments to obtain it. In our sample, no apprentice received a salary from her mistress; instead, most paid for apprenticeship, on the average ninety-four livres. This sum represented almost a year's wages for a skilled female worker on a yearly contract. Although this was a heavy investment, it could pay off with ten years of income before marriage at age twenty-six or -seven.

Far from discouraging girls from receiving vocational training, government and religious authorities were eager to support and extend this training. We have already seen that the guild's creation was sponsored by the royal government, which approved the guild's statutes, including the article requiring three years of apprenticeship for each potential mistress. For their part, parish-based charity foundations expressed their support of female apprenticeship by paying for poor girls' training. According to surviving documents, the charity foundation of Saint-Jean-en-Grève parish paid for the apprenticeship of at least twenty-five girls from 1711 to 1717 and seventy-five girls from 1774 to 1787. Surprisingly, girls benefited from training subventions as much as or more than boys: from 1711 to 1717, girls equaled boys on the charity list; from 1774 to 1787, fifty-one boys received support for apprenticeship versus seventy-five girls.

Other parishes also supported female apprenticeship, albeit on a smaller scale. For example, in 1720 Sieur Descourtieux, merchant goldsmith and a former director of the parish charity foundation of Saint-Etienne-du-Mont, left the foundation a legacy to pay apprenticeship fees or dowries for the parish's poor. The legacy paid for three boys between 1732 and 1750, but also set up fifteen-year-old Opportune Bausse with a mistress seamstress in 1751, and twenty-one-year-old Marie Louise Noblet with another in 1752. In 1736, the foundation also paid for the entry of Anne François Malherbe to the seamstresses' guild.[11] As these cases suggest, lay and religious authorities took an active interest in sponsoring female training. Indeed, given the additional opportunities the guild system offered to boys, some sought to favor girls over boys for charitable subventions.

Female Vocational Training in Charity Schools

Apart from formal apprenticeship, poor girls also received vocational training in charitable schools. Most Parisian parishes established one or more free charity schools in the second half of the seventeenth century. In many parishes, the schools were established and supervised by charity companies distinct from the parish foundations that administered and distributed the charitable bequests just discussed.[12] Students entered these schools around age eight for approximately two years of education. As might be expected, the most important element of the schools' curriculum was religious instruction. Morning and afternoon prayers, as well as attendance at mass in the parish church, were integral parts of the daily routine. The schools were segregated by sex, with a female mistress for the girls and a male master for the boys.

Girls' and boys' schools were also distinguished by their curriculum. Boys generally studied religion, reading, writing, and some arithmetic. Girls received religious instruction as well, but their intellectual training sometimes consisted of lessons in reading only. By the end of the seventeenth century, to give one example, the parish of Saint-Paul operated eight charity schools for girls and four for boys. The children learned reading, writing, and arithmetic as well as "trades suitable for their sex and situation, like knitting, lace, sewing, linen work, embroidery, tapestries, etc." While the latter skills were certainly intended only for girls, instruction in "drawing, or the principles of Architecture and Sculpture" was undoubtedly offered only for boys.[13]

In the second half of the seventeenth century, these parish schools were supplemented by a number of new female religious communities whose purpose was to continue poor girls' education after they left elementary school. The motivations behind these communities were mixed. For the sisters who joined them, the communities served to satisfy desires for a religious life among pious laywomen. For their pupils, the schools were intended to enrich the vocational skills girls acquired in school and thus render them capable of earning a living from their work. Equally important was the desire to keep young girls off the streets and to ensure that the religious and moral indoctrination offered by the charity schools was not lost during the period between childhood and marriage. These schools were usually loosely tied to a parish and placed under the authority of its curé but were run by a female superior.

The most important religious community was perhaps the Filles de Sainte-Agnès. Created in 1678 in Saint-Eustache parish, the community received a new set of regulations in 1682 and royal letters patent in the following year. Later accounts suggest that the reason for the foundation was that the curé of Saint-Eustache had become concerned about the dangers poor girls faced once they left school around age twelve or thirteen. If they were too weak to perform manual labor and too poor to be trained in a trade, they would be left at home alone all day:

> Unable to put them in apprenticeship, their parents leave them to watch their homes, which they leave at daybreak and to which they only return at night.
> These young girls, bored from being alone for whole weeks, without work, without occupation, descend from their attics to dissipate themselves, make and receive visits that are always dangerous [. . .]: left to themselves at the most dangerous age without being restrained or supervised, one sees them run and scatter in the

streets, the squares, the public markets, where they corrupt themselves with bad examples.[14]

The Filles de Sainte-Agnès started out with four members and forty or fifty students. The original sisters were an English Catholic tapestry maker, two linen drapers, and a seamstress. The 1682 regulations laid out a rigid schedule of daily activities. Sisters were to rise at five o'clock for prayers, followed by breakfast. They began work with their students at seven o'clock with a collective prayer. They ceased working at eleven o'clock for lunch, recommencing at twelve-thirty and continuing until six o'clock in the evening. The morning included time set aside for spiritual reading, while the afternoon contained a half-hour break for learning the Catechism, prayers, and spiritual reading. Once the girls had left the premises at six o'clock—or before dark in the winter—the sisters' evening consisted of more prayers, spiritual reflection, and dinner. They were to be in bed with all candles extinguished by nine-thirty.

By 1729, the community numbered forty-five sisters, forty adult boarders, thirty-five child boarders, and almost 450 "poor children and external students for instruction and work." The school was divided into seven classes, two for religious education and five for vocational instruction, with one for linen work, one for embroidery, another for lace making, and two for tapestry making. Each student selected the trade in which she would train, presumably assisted and influenced by the sisters. The community possessed all the tools necessary for these trades, including looms for tapestry weaving. Instruction and work must have taken place in large classes. With a number of sisters devoting their time to administration and housekeeping, there would have been less than one mistress for every ten students. Although this was far from the guild model of apprenticeship, the sisters called their charges "apprentices" and seem to have believed they were imparting a form of apprenticeship that led from inexperience toward mastery of a trade.

The training program depended on orders from paying customers. Sales to outside customers offset the costs of tools and raw materials and, it was hoped, would eventually produce revenue for the operating budget. In 1715, a summary of the community's financial accounts for the previous years stated that the workshops had earned a total of 103,562 livres in that period, or an annual average of 3,340 livres.[15] In 1766 the sisters reported on their finances over the preceding eleven years. The tapestry, lace, linen, and embroidery classes earned an average of around two thousand livres a year. Although these seem like considerable sums, the sisters reported that they were barely enough to meet expenses.

The workshops were plagued by a number of related problems: the apprentices' inexperience, the low prices they could charge for their goods, and the need to pay wages to more experienced workers. As the account explained,

> It is true that the pieces of work this community is obliged to undertake for the
> instruction of this youth is more an expense than a profit . . . the work of these
> youths cannot be as assiduous as would be that of mature people . . . but since

these trades can only be learned by practice and not by theory we thus cannot dispense with undertaking this work to be able to instruct them and form their hands; because of these apprentices, able to do only that which is within their means, we are again obliged, so that their work will sell so as to at least recover the price of the materials that must be used in them . . . to keep on students who are fully skilled and whom therefore we must pay, both to finish the hardest parts, and to secure for them at the same time something to live on until they have found work elsewhere or until they have been placed [in service].[16]

As this document attests, the sisters' religious mission did not outweigh their commitment to training pupils. They invested more money than they could afford in their apprenticeship program, emphasizing hands-on, practical experience over abstract explanation. Indeed, their training was efficacious enough that they were required to pay wages to the most experienced pupils. Despite their emphasis on religion, the sisters were determined to impart a real "apprenticeship" to the girls. Their determination was not sufficient to overcome the financial precariousness of their community. By the time of the French Revolution, mounting inflation and dwindling income from annuities had succeeded in destroying its already precarious financial stability. These problems were compounded by a steady decline in income from the workshops.[17] Enthusiasm for the austere lifestyle of the sisters had also apparently diminished. Compared to forty-one sisters in 1766, the community numbered only twenty-seven at the time of the Revolution, with an average age of almost fifty-four years old. The sisters struggled to continue their work until their house was taken over by a national saltpeter manufacturer in 1793.

Several additional communities of this sort existed in Paris and many more were found in the provinces.[18] This example demonstrates the increasing emphasis on imparting vocational skills to girls among female educational institutions in the late seventeenth century, a desire that would persist throughout the eighteenth and nineteenth centuries. In most cases, those responsible for the training did not aim to integrate girls into the guild system. Indeed, the community of Sainte-Geneviève—which ran another charitable educational and vocational training program in Paris—specified that the trades taught should be ones where no guild existed.[19] Entry to the seamstresses' or the linen-drapers' guilds was intended for a relatively privileged few; the vast majority of girls should be content to possess the skills necessary to support themselves. They acquired these skills in large classrooms, while their brothers spent their time learning to read, write, and do mathematics and later entered small-scale training in artisanal workshops. However degraded this training may appear in comparison to the guild model, the sisters clearly believed that they succeeded in forming "apprentices" who mastered their chosen trade and would be able to earn a modest living from it after leaving the community. There was also apparent agreement between the two systems that a girl's apprenticeship should begin around age fourteen, after she had completed preliminary instruction in reading and needlework at a parish school.

Girls' Labor and French Economic Development

An impressive number of girls received training as a result of these initiatives. By the beginning of the eighteenth century, mistress seamstresses in Paris were accepting some 400 apprentices a year. The Filles de Sainte-Agnès also claimed to instruct more than 400 girls at a time. To these girls, we could add those trained by the other female communities, another hundred or so apprentice midwives and linen drapers, and the girls who entered informal training agreements with male and female workers. If we continued this list, we might arrive at a figure close to or greater than the 1,800 boys who entered guild-based apprenticeship in 1761. In eighteenth-century Paris, many poor girls did not learn trades at home from their mothers or sisters. The older women went out to wage work or small vending stands, sometimes leaving the younger ones idle and ignorant, but often entrusting them to organized forms of vocational training. Far from declining, as some historians have suggested, the possibilities for female "apprenticeship" rose significantly from 1650 to 1789. Female training was often far removed from what the guilds would recognize as apprenticeship, yet it did not exist in opposition to the guilds or even in isolation from the guild system. On the contrary, the development of female training in needlework occurred in tandem within the guilds and outside the corporate system.

The royal government took an active part in fostering this simultaneous development. The seamstresses drew on Colbert's 1673 edict to claim guild status and could only have succeeded with his approval. The community of Sainte-Agnès also benefited from Colbert's patronage. He helped the sisters obtain official letters patent in 1682 and left the community 10,000 livres in his will. Apart from sponsoring a formal guild and a charitable school, Colbert also established training programs for girls in lace making in several provincial cities, as part of his project to launch a high-quality domestic lace industry.[20] These examples point to the existence of a multifaceted movement, undertaken by the centralized administration of Louis XIV, to increase opportunities for female training. This effort was intended not only to prevent idleness among poor girls but also to create a new, skilled labor force to enhance the industries the French government was so eager to promote. After all, the mercantilist project of replacing foreign imports with high-quality domestic production could only be achieved with the contribution of a larger force of skilled hands. Seamstresses would thus provide the labor necessary to finish and distribute products from the textile industries, the most important source of economic production in France and a particular target of Colbert's energies. Lace making, embroidery, and tapestry making belonged to the luxury trades that were seen as a particular strength of French production. Viewed on an individual basis, female communities like the Filles de Sainte-Agnès appear to be small-scale efforts at religious indoctrination of poor girls, barely justified by the pretext of vocational training. Placed in the larger context, they were part of a movement of national dimensions sponsored by the highest authorities of the royal government.[21]

Over the eighteenth century, the trades available for female vocational training increased as the expansion and diversification of the Parisian economy created new opportunities for female labor. The parish of Saint-Jean-en-Grève supplies testimony to this effect. This parish, as we have seen, was active in sponsoring vocational training for orphaned children. Two sets of registers survive from the parish's charitable foundation. The first set of registers records the years 1710, 1713, and 1715–1717. They list fifty youths, divided evenly by sex, whom the parish foundation placed in apprenticeship during these years. Twenty-four of the twenty-five girls received training from a mistress seamstress, the twenty-fifth from a linen worker. By contrast, the twenty-five boys entered a total of fourteen different trades, ranging from humble cobblers to high-status textile merchant-manufacturers. Six boys undertook training with master cobblers and five with master shoemakers. Richer trades, including gilders and cloth makers, received only one or two boys each.[22]

At the other end of the century, the record lists 126 apprentices for scattered years between 1774 and 1787. In these years, girls outnumbered boys seventy-five to fifty-one. While the seamstresses remained the most important trade for girls, attracting forty-three of the seventy-five girls, the parish also turned to a host of new crafts, including fashion work, linen work, lace making, embroidery, and stocking making. Artisans involved in the contracts included men and women, members of incorporated and unincorporated trades.[23]

The example of this parish suggests that a range of new occupations opened up for girls and women across the eighteenth century, primarily in the garment and fashion trades. Where the seamstresses had been pioneers in facilitating new forms of consumption at the beginning of the eighteenth century, by its last decades they had been joined and partially displaced by practitioners of new commercial and productive specialties aimed at a wider and more acquisitive market. Training opportunities for girls accordingly grew more varied. One can witness the results of this diversification in the engravings of the *Encyclopédie*, which show women in the workshops of stocking makers, embroiderers, fan makers, enamelers, artificial flower makers, paper makers, wigmaker-barbers, saddlers, and other ostensibly "male" trades.[24]

Despite guild prohibitions, women were employed in large numbers in all needle trades and many other urban, artisanal trades. When they hired female workers, employers did not train them from scratch, nor did they rely on an informal system of mother-daughter transmission of skill. Instead, they drew from the workshops and schoolrooms of Parisian parishes and religious communities. Women thus composed an important, if hitherto largely unrecognized, component of the trained and skilled labor force in eighteenth-century Paris. Their labor—and the wages they derived from it—provided much of the impetus behind the substantial growth of production and consumption in this period. Innovations in female vocational training were crucial to French economic development, a fact wholly obscured by a focus on the guild-based apprenticeship system as the only source of training.

A significant growth in vocational training opportunities for girls occurred in late seventeenth-century Paris. The ramifications of this finding are far reaching. First, it offers insight into the means of production and re-production of a female labor market whose size, skill, and economic efficacy we are only beginning to appreciate. These female training programs offer clues as to where we could expect to find the legions of women workers hidden in guild sources and helps to explain how they acquired skill. This finding also underlines the limitations of the guilds' control over the economy and the labor force. Guild masters employed and trained a large portion of the Parisian labor market, but not all of it. They worked in competition with non-guild sectors, including a large group of female youth and adult women. The embroiderers' guild's prohibition of female labor should thus be read not as excluding women from the labor market but as trying to control and limit the existing practice of hiring female workers.

This finding also challenges our notions of the female career. Many Parisian girls did not learn from their mothers at home but entered training in adolescence with women—and sometimes men—to whom they were not related. Once they had acquired necessary skills, around age seventeen, they continued to work outside their family homes in employers' workshops. Within households, parents invested considerable time, money, and thought in acquiring skills for their daughters. Female training did not conflict with the family economy but was part of a wider strategy to maximize household earnings. When these girls left home and married, they brought their skills into new families. They could use them to further a family business, operate an autonomous career, or set aside their skills to help a husband start a new enterprise. All of these possibilities might be realized in the lifetime of an individual woman as she married, bore children, and experienced widowhood. Female skill must have been a significant factor in the marriage calculations of both bride and groom and their families.

More broadly, uncovering the entry of girls to the labor market in large numbers in the late seventeenth century helps us understand the intertwined history of production and consumption and the significant growth historians have noted in both during the eighteenth century. Women entering the garment, linen, and other needle trades on a large scale provided the cheap, skilled labor to foster a takeoff in these industries. With the income they gained from their labor—as small as it was relative to the male income—women become the most important consumers of the clothing and accessories they helped to produce. The results of these female training programs can thus be seen in the tremendous increase in the amount and variety of clothing consumed by Parisians that Daniel Roche has documented.[25]

In this "industrious revolution," the labor and purchasing power of female youth were key factors in a crucial turning point in economic production and consumption, with all its social and cultural ramifications. In addition to new levels of personal comfort and hygiene, the spread of finished goods offered new possibilities for expressions of individuality and a blurring of class distinctions. Working girls were eager and precocious beneficiaries of these innovations.[26]

Notes

1. "Statuts et ordonnances des marchands-maîtres Tailleurs d'Habits, Pourpointiers-Chaussetiers de la Ville, Fauxbourgs & Banlieue de Paris" (Paris, 1742).

2. Letter from the royal procurator at the Châtelet of Paris to the controller general, 4 April 1692, Boislisle, *Correspondance des controlleurs generaux,* t.II, #1069.

3. On France, see Olwen Hufton, *The Prospect Before Her: A History of Women in Western Europe,* vol. 1 (New York: Vintage Books, 1998), 62–101; Hufton, "Women and the Family Economy in Eighteenth-Century France," *French Historical Studies* 9 (spring 1975): 1–22; and Hufton, "Women, Work and Marriage in Eighteenth-Century France," in *Marriage and Society,* ed. R. B. Outhwaite (New York: St. Martin's Press, 1981), 186–203. See also Louise Tilly and Joan Scott, *Women, Work and Family* (New York: Holt, Rinehart and Wilson, 1978); and Natalie Zemon Davis, "Women in the Crafts in Sixteenth-Century Lyon," in *Women and Work in Preindustrial Europe,* ed. Barbara Hanawalt (Bloomington: Indiana University Press, 1986). For other European countries, see Merry Wiesner, *Working Women in Renaissance Germany* (New Brunswick, N.J.: Rutgers University Press, 1986); Wiesner, *Gender, Church and State in Early Modern Germany* (London and New York: Longman, 1998); Martha Howell, *Production and Patriarchy in Late Medieval Cities* (Chicago and London: University of Chicago Press, 1986); Howell, *The Marriage Exchange: Property, Social Place, and Gender in Cities of the Low Countries, 1300–1550* (Chicago and London: University of Chicago Press, 1998); Jean H. Quataert, "The Shaping of Women's Work in Manufacturing: Guilds, Households, and the State in Central Europe, 1648–1870," *American Historical Review* 90 (December 1985): 1122–1148; and Lindsey Charles and Lorna Duffin, eds., *Women and Work in Preindustrial England,* (London: Croom Helm, 1985).

4. On women in male guild trades, see Daryl Hafter, "Female Masters in the Ribbonmaking Guild of Eighteenth-Century Rouen," in The Forum on Women and Work (special section), *French Historical Studies* 20, no. 1 (winter 1997): 1–14; and Elizabeth C. Musgrave, "Women in the Male World of Work: The Building Industries of Eighteenth-Century Brittany," *French History* 7, no. 1 (1989): 30–52. See also Daryl Hafter, "Women Who Wove in the Eighteenth-Century Silk Industry of Lyon," in *European Women and Preindustrial Craft,* ed. Daryl Hafter (Bloomington and Indianapolis: Indiana University Press, 1995); Hafter, "Gender Formation from a Working-Class Viewpoint," *Proceedings of the Annual Meeting of the Western Society for French History* (1988) 16 (1989): 415–422. On female guilds, see Clare

Haru Crowston, *Fabricating Women: The Seamstresses of Old Regime France,
1675–1791* (Durham, N.C.: Duke University Press, 2001); Cynthia Truant,
"Parisian Guildswomen and the (Sexual) Politics of Privilege: Defending
Their Patrimonies in Print," in *Going Public: Women and Publishing in Early
Modern France,* ed. Elizabeth Goldsmith and Dena Goodman (Ithaca, N.Y.,
and London: Cornell University Press, 1995); Truant, "The Guildswomen of
Paris: Gender, Power, and Sociability in the Old Regime," *Proceedings of the
Annual Meeting of the Western Society for French History* (1987) 15 (1988):
130–138; Truant, "La maîtrise d'une identité? Corporations féminines à
Paris aux XVIIe et XVIIIé siècles," *Clio, Histoire, Femmes et Sociétés* 3
(1996): 55–69; and Judith G. Coffin, "Gender and the Guild Order: The
Garment Trades in Eighteenth-Century Paris," *Journal of Economic History*
54, no. 4 (December 1994): 768–793.

5. James B. Collins, "The Economic Role of Women in Seventeenth Century
    France," *French Historical Studies* 16 (fall 1989): 436–470.

6. Jan de Vries, "Between Purchasing Power and the World of Goods: Under-
    standing the Household Economy in Early Modern Europe," in *Consump-
    tion and the World of Goods,* ed. John Brewer and Roy Porter (London:
    Routledge & Kegan Paul, 1993), 85–132.

7. On the seamstresses' guild and apprenticeship among seamstresses, see
    Crowston, *Fabricating Women.*

8. See France, *Archives Nationales* (hereafter cited as *AN*) MC Etude CVIII 324
    for these contracts.

9. *AN* V7 428. An exhaustive survey of notarial contracts for 1761 revealed
    1,800 apprenticeship contracts for the city of Paris in that year.

10. Steven L. Kaplan, "L'Apprentissage au XVIIIe siècle: Le cas de Paris," *Revue
    d'histoire moderne et contemporarine* 40 (juillet–septembre 1993): 450–452.

11. *AN* L 637.

12. On these companies, see Marcel Fosseyeux, *Les écoles de charité à Paris
    sous l'ancien régime et dans la première partie du XIX siècle* (Paris: Daupeley-
    Gouverneur, 1912); Harvey Chisick, "French Charity Schools in the Seven-
    teenth and Eighteenth Centuries with Special Reference to Amiens," *Histoire
    Sociale* 16 (1983): 241–277; and Léon Cahen, "Les Idées charitables à Paris
    au XVIIe et au XVIIIe siècles d'après les règlements des compagnies parois-
    siales," *Revue d'histoire moderne et contemporaine* 2 (1900–1901): 5–22.
    On charity at the end of the eighteenth century, see Isser Woloch, "From
    Charity to Welfare in Revolutionary Paris," *Journal of Modern History* 58,
    no. 4 (1986): 779–812.

13. *AN* L 716, "Etat présent des bonnes œuvres et Ecoles charitables de la
    Paroisse de Saint Sulpice du 1. Decembre 1698."

14. *AN* S 7047. Hugh Cunningham reports similar concerns in England in
    "The Employment and Unemployment of Children in England c. 1680–
    1851," *Past and Present* 126 (1990): 126–131.

15. *AN* LL 1659, f. 15.

16. *AN* S 4615.

17. *AN* S 4615.

18. For example, the Soeurs de la Communauté de Sainte-Geneviève were
    founded in 1677 to "work and instruct young girls both in Christian
    doctrine and to read, write and do work appropriate for their sex." *AN*

S 7048–50, "Contrat de fondation des Soeurs de la Communauté de Sainte-Geneviève." See also *AN* L 775 for the Filles de Saint-Joseph and *AN* S 7047 for the Filles de l'Instruction Chrétienne.

19.   *AN* S 7048–50.

20.   For evidence of these activities, see Pierre Clément, *Lettres, instructions et mémoires de Colbert,* vol. 3, *Commerce et industrie* (Paris: Imprimerie impériale, 1861–1870). See also Paul-M. Bondois, *Colbert et l'industrie de la dentelle* (Paris: M. Riviere, 1926).

21.   For a related discussion, see the chapter by Mary Jo Maynes.

22.   *AN* LL 801.

23.   *AN* H5 3782.

24.   *Encyclopédie ou Dictionnaire raisonné des sciences des arts et des métiers,* vols. 23–26, 29–32 (1751–1780) (Stuttgart-Bad Cannstatt: Edition Cantz, 1967). The opportunities for obtaining training in these trades may have offset the losses represented by the decline of the charitable institutions described previously.

25.   Daniel Roche, *The Culture of Clothing,* trans. Jean Birrell (Cambridge: Cambridge University Press, 1994).

26.   Neil McKendrick makes a similar argument for English girls and women in the Industrial Revolution. I am arguing that we can see the roots of an "industrious revolution" in France in the late seventeenth century. The crucial development was not, as in McKendrick's case, new technology and mechanization but an expansion of vocational programs for girls in the needle trades. See Neil McKendrick, "Home Demand and Economic Growth: A New View of the Role of Women and Children in the Industrial Revolution," in *Historical Perspectives: Studies in English Thought and Society,* ed. Neil McKendrick (London: Europa Publications, 1974).

5 Work for Girls? The Small Metal Industries in England, 1840–1915

Carol E. Morgan

Carol Morgan looks at girls' labor in a somewhat surprising sector—the small metal industries of industrializing England. She argues that girls' contributions were of immeasurable value to families and communities alike. While some people raised concerns regarding the femininity of girl metalworkers, such concerns were largely confined to moral issues such as the need to control girls' sexuality. Otherwise, Morgan argues, despite the harsh conditions under which they labored, girl metalworkers managed to reconcile their life and labor with their own conceptions of responsibility, respectability, and femininity.

During early industrialization, female labor was vital to the expansion of European production. This was true, of course, in textile sectors, which had been traditionally defined as "women's work." Perhaps more surprisingly, women also played a key role in metal manufacture. This chapter examines the role of female youth in small metal industries centered in the West Midlands of England.[1] From the late eighteenth century and earlier, this area was home to the production of a great diversity of metal goods, from swords and guns to agricultural implements, domestic items, nails and chains, and buckles and buttons, as well as a variety of small brass articles.[2] During the nineteenth century, new products were added such as metal bedsteads, steel pens, wire ropes, steam engines, railway rolling stock, sewing machines, hydraulic machinery, and wrought iron. Taken together, such metalwares became England's largest export commodity after textiles.[3] And female labor continued to be critical as mechanization progressed. The paid labor of girls from the time they left school until marriage was vital to household survival, largely taken for granted, and wholly acceptable in most working-class milieus. Yet the work itself varied considerably, as did perceptions of it. This chapter will then consider the following questions: How was girls' metalwork perceived in the community? Although their labor was expected and necessary, under what conditions was it deemed unsuitable? How was femininity perceived and defined in relation to girls and their paid labor?

Ideals regarding femininity often clashed sharply with the labor in which girls and women in metalworking were engaged. Laments were frequent regarding female labor in general, particularly that of married women, as well as that of girls, although less commonly. Yet the concerns raised, particularly in relation to girls, were limited in scope, being largely confined to issues of morality rather than conditions of labor. Moreover, presumptions about femininity were sometimes used to justify the employment of girls, thereby serving to reconcile work with ideas of young womanhood. Conceptions of femininity were also thoroughly intertwined with employers' desires for a cheap and compliant workforce. For the most part, however, girls' labor was non-controversial, being regarded as simply necessary and acceptable to families and communities, as well as employers, under a variety of conditions.

Work and Female Youth

The labor of female youth was particularly predominant in a number of the Birmingham small metal industries such as pin, screw, and button making, as well as in such finishing processes as lacquering.[4] In the button trade, the work was said to be "carried on principally by women and children"; by the mid-nineteenth century their numbers outpaced men's by ten to one in at least one establishment.[5] In pin manufacturing, "big girls" were generally hired for the final process of sticking the pins on paper to be sold, while in screw manufacturing they worked at such laborious processes as notching the head of the screw, labor that required considerable bending and stooping. In some of these manufactories it was a rule not to admit children under the age of fourteen, leading to the widespread employment of girls and young women between the ages of fifteen and twenty-four or so.[6]

As the pin and screw industries mechanized, female youth were increasingly employed as machine minders. In the manufacture of pins, wire was wound into a machine that, as described in 1864, "cuts it into pin lengths, forms the heads by means of hammers, the points by revolving files, and throws out the pins complete, in a continuous stream, at the rate, without stoppage, of 220 in a minute, or in the day of eleven hours 145,200."[7] On average, a single woman or girl watched about four of these machines, turning out nearly 600,000 pins in a day and, in a week, 3,000,000. In screw manufacturing, one girl reported to the Royal Commission on Children's Employment in 1864 that she attended as many as fifteen machines.[8] Girls often worked continuously in these industries from childhood to perhaps their mid-twenties: they generally labored from 8 A.M. to 7 P.M. with an hour for dinner and, if allowed, twenty minutes for tea, earning on average five shillings per week.[9] Parliamentary investigations showed that dangerous conditions prevailed in these industries.[10]

Conditions in the jewelry trade, where 1,000 girls and women were employed in the 1850s in the manufacture of gold and silver chains, were also found wanting. Here workers used pliers to form the links of the delicate chains or soldered the links by means of a gas jet. Typically, they worked in small groups, sitting close together at a semicircular table, each with their own jet of gas in addition to the central large jet used for light. One woman, who had begun work as a girl and had been employed in the same establishment for twenty years, told the commission of 1863 that it was "very unhealthy work" and she was "never very well." A girl of fourteen testified that she was "not near sighted, but my work wants looking at close and my stool is rather too high, so I have to stoop a good deal. My chest hurts me sometimes, and I am not strong."[11]

In electroplate manufacture, girls were widely engaged in polishing or buffing small metal articles, resulting in dust "settling plentifully on the heads and dresses of the workpeople," which led to "very bad health" after years of employment.[12] In lacquering as well, a process nearly universally applied to brassware, the shops were often poorly ventilated. One girl of fourteen testified that she and the other girls were seldom without a cold, adding, "Am subject to sore throats, and can't speak very well."[13] Despite such conditions of work, the extent to which the labor of girls was considered non-controversial and, indeed, welcomed in both Birmingham and the Black Country, is striking. J. S. Wright, a major manufacturer, writing in 1857, maintained that the city

> owes its position to the ready supply of cheap labour afforded by women and girls, the suspension of whose industry, as at present carried on, would annihilate many of those trades for which Birmingham has been celebrated.[14]

Fathers generally arranged for the labor of children and younger workers who turned over their wages to their mothers. Older girls, as well as boys, contributed board from their wages, while retaining a portion for themselves.[15] This contribution was undoubtedly often responsible for enabling families to survive as long as they remained at home. Employers often specifically preferred female youth in comparison both to children and to men because they produced high-quality work and they kept wages low.[16] A manager of an electroplate manufactory indicated that he considered it

> a pity that females should work in factories at all, as it interferes so much with their proper life, the domestic. They are, however . . . very useful, and it may not be possible to do without them. Indeed we have employed them upon a branch of work which was formerly done by men, because the latter were so much more difficult to keep steady to their work.[17]

In general, employers and social commentators, remarking on hours of labor, evinced no concern regarding the long hours of labor of youth, including girls. Button and pen manufacturers alike thus did not consider the hours of work by "the young in Birmingham" to be excessive. Regarding possible improvements in the situation of young people, the commissioner J. E. White of the Children's Employment Commission of 1864 suggested only a prohibition on the labor of children before a certain age, without suggesting any changes in relation to female youth specifically.[18]

In the community of Darlaston in the Black Country, where some girls were employed in lock making, screw making, and other kinds of smiths' work, a similar approach was taken by one manufacturer who suggested that children not be employed before the age of ten. By that time, Samuel Wilks maintained, "they have acquired more strength, and a mind more fit, and would in most cases do far more work and better in the next eleven years than they would have done in twelve years by going to work a year earlier." That he was referring to both boys and girls with these comments is clear as he continued, saying, "If the work be of a kind to require one position and action of body and limbs during the whole day . . . no boy or girl ought to be allowed to do it till they are of the age of 14 years."[19]

Girls were clearly viewed as young workers with the strength, endurance, and ability to carry out all kinds of labor, often equally with boys, suggesting little gender distinction at this stage of the life cycle among working-class youth. Yet a discourse expressing concern for the femininity of young women laborers did emerge. In certain instances, such concerns actually served to uphold the labor of girls while in others their labor appeared to be contested. Yet in all instances it appears that concern was limited indeed.

Femininity and Girls' Work

Comments made by a number of medical men and other observers to the Children's Employment Commission of 1843 often lamented the fact that "females are from necessity bred up from their youth in the workshops." As a result, they contended, "The minds and morals of the girls become debased, and they marry totally ignorant of all those habits of domestic economy which tend to render a husband's home comfortable and happy."[20] A skilled workman, employed as a button burnisher at a major manufactory, voiced a concern that would be frequently repeated regarding the employment of female youth—the problem of working alongside men:

> It is not difficult to imagine a young female, of pleasing face and person . . . exposed by being placed in a manufactory, to the lewd remarks and familiarities of the coarse and dissipated of the other sex. Perhaps not one idea of virtue was ever established in the mind of this susceptible and credulous creature. . . . She is now put in the certain path to ruin and seduction.[21]

Girls, and women, many believed, should be employed only at a "well-conducted factory" and apart from men, as the latter's presence would be "very bad for their morals."[22] A jeweler thus reported to the Children's Employment Commission of 1864 that "The girl whom I [employ] now I keep at work near me, and when I have more I keep them separate or under some trustworthy man, and never allow any improper language."[23] Others attempted to ascertain the girls' "previous character" and to impose a moral code upon the girls them-

Fig. 5. Girl making nails, late 19th century.
Reproduced from *The English Illustrated Magazine*, 1890.

selves. Thus George Ireland indicated that in his electroplate manufactory they discharged unmarried women who gave birth, even while acknowledging the "hardship and temptation" to which the girls would be exposed by such action![24] Although their logic might often be questionable, these examples suggest that some employers in Birmingham saw themselves as upholding feminine ideals by encouraging proper behavior on the part of their female employees. The pen-making industry was particularly noteworthy for its attention to its female employees.

The report of the Children's Employment Commission of 1864 noted that "the greater number of women and girls in Birmingham" were employed in press work. Operated by fly handles or treadles, presses were "used for cutting out, shaping, or fitting together thin metal" and other materials to make buttons, jewelry, clasps, fastenings, "in fact an endless variety of miscellaneous useful or ornamental productions." With Joseph Gillott's inventions adapting the press to the making of pens, girls from the age of fifteen or sixteen were frequently hired at such labor due to the quality of work they produced. In a single day, they cut out 36,000 pens, a process requiring "72,000 distinct motions of the arm, or two motions in each second."[25] In such factories, markings of the various manufacturers were impressed by a stamp. In 1880, a reporter for the *British Mail* provided a word picture of this process "for which the nimble and delicate fingers of women [were] found of inestimable service." According to this description, the marker

> takes a handful of pens all lying confusedly from a heap at her left hand, and with a dexterous palming motion, marshals a little procession of them between the thumb and forefinger in parallel order, presenting the foremost in a convenient position to be seized. The right hand travels backwards and forwards to the stamp about twice in a second, each time taking a pen, turning it over point foremost and right side up, and placing [it] exactly under the descending punch, which she causes by the motion of her foot to give a constant succession of blows in regular beat, almost as quick as they could be counted. The nimble fingers play in and out under the heavy stamp hammer with an airy indifference to danger . . . which quite reassures the spectator, though it is evident that the slightest miscalculation of time or distance would make a case for the nearest hospital.[26]

Injuries were not uncommon and, White reported, could be "extremely painful" for the girls "though not actually incapacitating them from labour." As Elizabeth Steward, a marker of three years at age seventeen, said, "Have pinched my fingers . . . three times, once from my foot slipping from the loop, but have not hurt myself badly. They all of them pinch their fingers," she mused.[27]

Some employers in pen manufacturing became known for their well-run establishments and the safety measures they adopted. Located in sections of town where employers could take advantage of the labor of wives and daughters of gun and jewelry workers, such establishments as Josiah Mason's took care to provide adequate ventilation and guards around the moving machinery.[28] At Gillott's, work rooms were noted for their isolation from one another, each being "lofty, cleanly, and well lighted." The *British Mail* reporter quoted previously thus declared "the perfect order in which every department of their extensive manufactory is kept, and the cheerful and respectable appearance which the workpeople present . . . a treat to see." Accordingly, he considered the labor at Gillott's steel-pen works to be as "as suitable for women as any mechanical art can be said to be."[29]

Paternalistic measures and clean conditions of work could serve to reconcile female labor with what it meant to be feminine.[30] A light and airy atmosphere was indicative not only of a respectable workplace, but the workers themselves were then said to take on the characteristics of the establishment, projecting a "cheerful and respectable appearance." Girls and women employed in a pleasant atmosphere, where the work was well organized, were associated with order, discipline, and cleanliness, and their labor was accordingly deemed suitable.[31] In pen making, where the factories were often noted for such characteristics, the labor itself was also considered fit for girls and women, requiring nimbleness, delicacy, and dexterity, all considered female attributes.

An additional concern was clearly present regarding the labor of female

Fig. 6. Young women workers at a modern pen factory, on the occasion of a royal visit, 1874. Reproduced from *The Graphic*, 1874.

youth. An individual wage represented a degree of independence that was considered a potential threat to young women's propriety. The manufacturer Wright argued that, "The more direct control of their wages, the opportunity afforded for gossip, and, above all, the liberty a shop-girl has to spend time after work in the evening as she chooses, are allurements that cannot be resisted."[32] At least when they were in the workplace and under the control of employers, the latter considered it their responsibility to protect the girls from their own naturally untamed and sensual nature, which, it was believed, made them constantly vulnerable to temptation. Declared Wright,

The nature of the trades have . . . much to do with the matter: Those which are cleanly will give a higher moral tone to the hands, and a large number of young women working together seem to have a protective interest over each other's conduct; where trades are dirty, and it is impossible to preserve the person or dress clean, or when women work in small numbers promiscuously with men, we shall almost be sure to find low and depraved habits.[33]

A rigidly sex-segregated workforce was maintained in Birmingham, upheld in some instances by employers who instituted favorable conditions, considered appropriate for girls and women. At the same time it is clear that these employers took such steps in order to create a steady, cheap, and docile workforce. In other settings in the metal trades, similar concerns regarding female labor were voiced, and again those concerns proved to be somewhat limited, centering on issues of morality, as the labor of female youth in particular was generally deemed desirable.

Nails and Chains: Opposition to Girls' Labor?

By the mid-nineteenth century, there was considerable employment of female labor in the manufacture of nails and chains throughout the Black Country. A "positive explosion of young people employed in nailing" occurred, with the increase in the number of young females so employed described as "astounding." In Staffordshire alone, girls and young women accounted for 80 percent of the approximately twenty-five hundred employees in the fifteen-to-twenty-five-year-old age group.[34] In the chain-making region around Cradley Heath in the 1860s and 1870s, girls and women accounted for about one-quarter to one-third of those employed in the trade.[35]

Throughout the Black Country, the landscape was dotted by small workshops and "hovels" located to the back of many cottages where the manufacture of nails and chains took place. "Looking in upon one of them when the fire is not lighted," the inspector R. H. Horne commented in 1843, it "presents the appearance of a dilapidated coal-hole or little black den."[36] Over fifty years later, Sylvia Pankhurst echoed these sentiments, describing the chain shops she visited in the Cradley Heath region as "mean and miserable."[37] Here whole families would be employed together, possibly including several generations, with a grandmother, mother, daughters, and sons working beside a couple of unrelated workers, often girls.[38] Working between the hours of 6 A.M. and 9 P.M., a girl might earn five to six shillings per week, of which, by the age of fourteen or sixteen, she would pay her parents for board or get her own lodgings. In the mid-1880s, a girl working in the chain trade would earn as little as four shillings per week for making over two thousand links, due to overcrowding in the trade.[39]

The work itself in both nails and chains required "a great deal of expertness," according to a writer for the *Labour Tribune* who visited the chain-making district in the late 1880s:

The proper heat has to be maintained . . . and then since the iron is very light in the small chain it must be manipulated with great rapidity and dexterity. From the moment of cutting off the bit of iron that is to form the link until it is properly heated, bent, linked, and welded, less than half a minute is occupied in the case of what is known as No. 1. And in this brief space of time the worker has to take the iron out of the fire, and put it back again, and use the anvil twice.[40]

The writer concluded that it was "simply astonishing what a degree of dexterity is required and attained in the handling of the tools," suggesting that "the labour is of a very exacting nature."[41] In 1890, Rev. Harold Rylett similarly marveled at the speed and dexterity required to make a nail, using a small hammer to make the point and a heavy hammer operated with a foot lever to form the head. "The iron is heated and the nail made," he concluded, "in much less time than will be occupied in reading [a] description of the process." He estimated that "a strong and clever girl of sixteen or eighteen" who worked the full ten hours at such labor would make twenty-five hundred small nails in a day.[42]

Rylett's description of what he considered to be "the cruellest occupation in which women and young girls" were employed, the making of spike nails, is particularly striking. Here two people worked together, most commonly an adult man and a girl aged between fourteen and eighteen. After the iron rods were placed in the appropriate position, "The girl then gets close behind the man," Rylett reported, "generally holding him by the waist, and they both jump together upon the treadle which works the oliver [or sledgehammer], and with one, two, or three blows, according to the thickness of the iron, the required length is cut off." When this operation was completed, the man headed the spike and flung it to the girl on the other side of the hearth, who proceeded to place it in the fire, blow the bellows, snatch the heated spike from the fire, and rapidly pound it with the oliver and hand hammer, drawing the iron to a point, the spike then being completed. "A more brutal and loathsome spectacle I never witnessed in my life," Rylett concluded, adding that it was "humiliating to see a girl thus occupied."[43]

Rylett voiced a common view when he expressed moral concerns about female labor. Following a tour of the nail and chain manufacturing centers in the Black Country in 1875, the government subinspector Brewer concluded in his report that he was "more and more convinced that this woman's labour is the bane of this place." Indeed, "idle, lazy young lads," according to Brewer, "look[ed] out for skilled industrious wives in order to obtain 'an easy life.'"[44] A notable effect of this trend was an overcrowding of the trade and a consequent lowering of wages particularly resented by the organized male laborers of Walsall. When female competition served to threaten the wages and status of these skilled male laborers, they were able to launch a significant campaign against it, proposing to prohibit by legislation the labor of girls prior to the age of sixteen.[45]

During the course of this campaign, which later sought to set the age at which girls could enter the trade at fourteen, the purportedly unfeminine nature of nail and chain making became a major issue. Particular concerns were raised regarding the moral danger associated with young female laborers. Referring to the nail-making community of Sedgley, which the inspector Horne described as "the district of female blacksmiths" because their number considerably exceeded that of boys, he declared that the girls' appearance, manners, habits, and moral natures (so far as the word *moral* can be applied to them), are in accordance with their half-civilised condition. Constantly associating with ignorant and depraved adults and young persons of the opposite sex, they naturally fall into all their ways; and drink, smoke, swear, throw off all restraint in word and act, and become as bad as a man.[46]

With the men and boys "usually naked" except for trousers and an open shirt, and the women and girls wearing only "a thin ragged petticoat, and an open shirt without sleeves," Horne concluded that in such circumstances, "it is but too evident that the efforts of the Sunday-schools can only be productive of a very limited good."[47] Richard Juggins of the Nut and Bolt Makers, and the leading figure in Black Country trade unionism in this period, similarly bemoaned the girls' lives being so "brutalised and debased," referring to such labor on the part of women as "unnatural" and "a disgrace to civilization."[48]

Still, perhaps more striking than this discourse itself are the challenges raised against it. In the chain-making district of Cradley Heath, where, in contrast to Walsall, domestic labor prevailed, widespread opposition emerged to the proposed restrictive legislation, in large part due to that area's economic dependence on female labor. Chain makers and their defenders in this district saw the Walsall men as protecting their own narrow interests, simply desiring to maintain their earning power.[49] Of most significance to the discussion here is the solid defense within the nail- and chain-making areas of the labor of female youth. In response to the charges of immorality at the workplace, affecting girls in particular, defenders of their labor, including community leaders, feminists, and male union leaders, indicated that they often worked in the presence of their mothers and fathers and were generally under sufficient, often meaning older male, supervision.[50] In several instances, women workers voiced opposition to the suggested age restrictions, indicating in relation to their daughters that they could not "keep them" until the age proposed for their starting work without the contribution of their earnings to the family income. The significance of that contribution was perhaps brought out most clearly by a comment made at a meeting of female nail and rivet makers. Here a woman declared that, if female labor was abolished, as feared, "There would be no marriages." The comment was naturally met with laughter, but it also served to bring out the importance of female labor to the district, suggesting again that skilled young women were particularly valued as brides.[51]

Older women attested to the value placed on the labor of female youth, in terms of both skill and earning power, when they reflected on their own experiences. The women recalled their youth with pride in the skills they had attained and the financial contribution they had made during that period of their lives. When Sylvia Pankhurst visited the chain-making area in 1907, a woman told her "that she had worked most of her life at the chain and had made the finest quality and smallest sizes." Now, however "her sight was not good & she thought that she had done her share."[52] Another woman, working alongside her husband, contrasted her own situation with that of a "young woman" whose earning power was greater because she did not have "the young ones and the washin' to see to, which I has to give up a day every week to."[53]

Girls themselves were apparently well aware of the value placed on their contributions and generally chose labor at the forge in preference to domestic work. Visiting a mother and two girls laboring at the nail trade, a *Sunday Chronicle* reporter, accompanied by Richard Juggins, noted that the older daughter was "quite domesticated, a good washer, can bake a loaf, clean a house, and make a bed with anybody." Juggins then asked the mother why the girl did not work as a domestic. When she replied, "Her'd rather stay home," the girl nodded in agreement, indicating she was best employed "helping mother."[54]

In all likelihood, the girl had learned the trade from her mother, a point that serves to bring out a significant aspect of the culture of the area, the training of daughters by their mothers in their craft. Sylvia Pankhurst, during her 1907 visit, talked to a "big strongly built woman" who was making "common" or "slap chain." She indicated that she should be making "best" chain but that she had "'slap' for the children to learn on."[55] Having been trained by and worked closely with their mothers, who were in need of their contributions, the girls were not inclined to go off to Birmingham to work for another family. The proposed legislation, prohibiting the labor of girls, would similarly disrupt the bond between mother and daughter and thus the tradition and culture of the area. Besides, the mothers were all too aware of how important it was for their daughters, later in life, to be able to support themselves by working in the only trade open to them. The issue of femininity really only emerged as a major concern at a later stage of the life cycle: when girls faced marriage and motherhood.

Morality, Female Employment, and the Life Cycle

Concerns regarding girl laborers ultimately rested on such moral tenets as the need to protect girls, to keep them separate from their male counterparts, and to keep them under male supervision, although the actual conditions of labor and the strength and endurance required were typically of less concern. The need to control girls' sexuality was of utmost importance, but the sexual division of labor or, at least, the separation of the sexes in the workplace, served to meet this need.[56] For married women, on the other hand, work itself was often seen to undermine femininity by interfering with domestic duties. Where "change is most to be desired," stated the button manufacturer J. P. Turner with reference to legislation regarding hours of labor, "is in the employment of married women. . . . It makes them neglect their homes and families," he continued, "and they have often to pay large sums weekly for putting out their children to strangers."[57] Thomas Homer of the Cradley Heath chain makers concurred, complaining that, "when the man goes in to his little place, his little castle as it should be, there is nothing clean and tidy . . . which would not be if the women were better domesticated."[58]

The seemingly unfeminine nature of the work in which they were engaged was also a concern when it came to married women, in contrast to female youth.

In Birmingham, for example, the contrast is evident.[59] Here, by the turn of the century, female employment in the small metal industries had expanded considerably, extending particularly to all kinds of lathe work, often formerly a male preserve."[60] In the controversy over sweated, meaning generally low-wage, non-factory, labor, the conditions under which thousands of women labored became a major focus of attention. In using an emery wheel to polish brass items, the *Sunday Chronicle* reported, the arms of the workers were "bared from the shoulder and the grime and grit eat their way into the skin, fly into the eyes, and are drawn in into the lungs." Interviewed by the *Chronicle* reporter, the brassworkers' leader W. J. Davis concluded that as a result, "These women are absolutely unfit to be wives and mothers, and yet hundreds of married women are employed and no questions asked."[61] Davis's further comments are particularly revealing and instructive for the distinction he made between the effects of labor on women and on girls, particularly as these observations came from a most vociferous critic of female labor. Even while working under the conditions described above, prevailing in the brass industry, Davis declared:

> The young girls still retained the advantages and characteristics of their sex. In spite of the dirt, the coarse clothing, and the hard, mis-shaped hands, they possessed the airs, graces, and attractions of the eternal feminine. The work had not had time to disfigure their bodies, the brass had not entered into their souls.[62]

"But about the older women," he continued, "there was nothing feminine but their clothes." They had "pride only in their strength and endurance," having apparently lost their feminine qualities.[63] Only the Birmingham union organizer Julia Varley pointed out how this contradiction may have served the interests of male trade unionists attempting to exclude adult women from certain trades while they "allowed their children to work for pocket money."[64]

The girls themselves, however, were not indifferent to their working conditions. Finding it imperative to produce an income immediately upon leaving school, they often "drift[ed] into the first work suggested," according to Edward Cadbury in his important study of Birmingham.[65] Yet the girls also had a sense of the significance of this step, as noted by Kathleen Dayus, who wrote about her "yearn[ing] to leave school and be a grown-up woman, earning [her] own living." She and others had definite ideas about what this implied as they continually sought better wages and conditions, attempting to satisfy their desire for respectability. They thus "flitted from one job to another" while expressing particular pride in working at an establishment where certain rules were instituted, such as not allowing the wearing of hair curlers and requiring boots to be clean. They were also known to rebel when proper washing facilities were not provided, "deplor[ing] the roughened conditions of their hands."[66]

A collectivity emerged among female youth, as it was often "the next girl" who trained those just entering the workforce. Some trades took a matter of weeks or months to learn thoroughly, making the new worker dependent on the experienced for her success. With the work engendering such close ties, it is hardly surprising that girls often went on to form their own clubs at the workplace, contributing to funds for the purchase of clothing as well as for parties, the latter allowing them to end work early one day for a party of cake and tea, often mixed with rum or gin.[67]

Despite such camaraderie, girls were also intensely aware of their standing in relation to one another, as a social hierarchy emerged among them. Among girls working at the press and other employments, for instance, those engaged in lacquering were considered "ladies," "quite apart from the rest."[68] The lacquerers clearly accepted such status distinctions, even refusing to dine with others on occasion. Cadbury argued that such action "must not be put down to simple snobbishness" but was "only natural" as the girls were "so well aware how easily a girl or family is dragged down by the pressure of want or ill-luck."[69] It was indeed often the young laborer's contribution that made the difference in this regard.[70] In a similar vein, the girls deployed their independent status as wage earners in their relationships with their parents, as Kathleen Dayus recalled, relating an incident between her older sister, Mary, and her mother. In response to her mother asking Mary to borrow some money, Dayus reported, "Mary was adamant. 'No!' she declared, claiming, 'You've had the last off me. I never get it back.'"[71]

For working-class girls associated with the metal trades in Birmingham and the Black Country, the period of youth between school and marriage was clearly a significant stage in the life cycle. Their labor was often arranged for them, they worked for low wages, and they often lived at home where they were expected to offer assistance to their mothers. In this respect, their status can most accurately be described as semi-independent.[72] Yet, when possible and within definite parameters, they made choices regarding their labor, set their own standards, established their own culture, and expressed pride in what they did. Their lives were shaped by paid labor and at times they looked back to this period of their lives as one of accomplishment in this respect. Clearly their contributions were of immeasurable value to families and communities alike. While concerns were raised regarding their femininity, these were largely confined to the question of morality, meaning the need to control girls' sexuality and to prevent them from forming "depraved habits" that would carry over into marriage and motherhood, the next stage of the life cycle. Otherwise, despite the harsh conditions under which they labored, the girls managed to reconcile their life and labor and the independence they so achieved with their own conceptions of responsibility, respectability, and femininity.

Notes

1. Maxine Berg, *The Age of Manufactures: Industry, Innovation and Work in Britain 1700–1820* (Totowa, N.J.: Barnes & Noble Books, 1985), 134–151 and 268–282.

2.　　G. C. Allen, *The Industrial Development of Birmingham and the Black Country 1860–1927* (London: George Allen and Unwin, 1929), 14–20; and Marie B. Rowlands, *Masters and Men in the West Midland Metalware Trades before the Industrial Revolution* (Manchester: Manchester University Press, 1975), 125–127 and 34–35.

3.　　Allen, 35–6; Rowlands, 126–127.

4.　　Berg, 288–312.

5.　　Great Britain, Parliamentary Papers, Commons (B.P.P.), *Royal Commission on Children's Employment* (hereafter cited as *RCCE*), x, 1843, 140.

6.　　Ibid., 119–126 and 153–157.

7.　　B.P.P., *Third Report of the RCCE*, xiv, 1864,108.

8.　　Ibid., 108–110.

9.　　Ibid., 57–58 and 110.

10.　　B.P.P., *Children's Employment Commission* (hereafter cited as *CEC*), x, 1843, 153–157; B.P.P., *CEC*, 1864, 110.

11.　　B.P.P., *CEC*, 1864, 118–119.

12.　　Ibid., 124.

13.　　"Brassfounding: Messrs. Tonks, Limited," *Tinsley's Magazine* 6 (November 1889): 685; B.P.P., *CEC*, 1864, 117.

14.　　J. S. Wright, "On the Employment of Women in Factories in Birmingham," *Transactions of the National Association for the Promotion of Social Science* (1857): 538.

15.　　B.P.P., *CEC*, 1864, 117.

16.　　Ibid., 90.

17.　　Ibid., 123.

18.　　Ibid., 90–95 and 63.

19.　　B.P.P., *RCCE*, xi, 1843, 44.

20.　　B.P.P., *RCCE*, x, 1843, 179.

21.　　Ibid., 132.

22.　　B.P.P., *CEC*, 1864, 119.

23.　　B.P.P., *CEC*, 1864, 62.

24.　　Ibid., 123. See also testimony of a button manufacturer, 91.

25.　　Ibid., 55; and Wright, 540.

26.　　"Messrs. Joseph Gillott & Sons' Steel Pen Manufactory, Birmingham," *British Mail*, 2 August 1880, 2–3, London, British Library of Political and Economic Science, British Association for the Advancement of Science, Misc. 486.

27.　　B.P.P., *CEC*, 1864, 58.

28.　　B.P.P., *CEC*, 1864, 87.

29.　　"Messrs. Joseph Gillot & Sons' Manufactory," 3.

30.　　See Judy Lown, *Women and Industrialization: Gender at Work in Nineteenth-Century England* (Minneapolis: University of Minnesota Press, 1980).

31.　　See Jane Long's discussion of female lead workers in *Conversations in Cold Rooms: Women, Work and Poverty in Nineteenth-Century Northumberland* (Rochester, N.Y.: Boydell Press, 1999).

32.　　Wright, 542. Their "love of dress" was also commented upon by commissioners. See B.P.P., *CEC*, 1864, 112.

33.　　Ibid., 544.

34. Bill Kings and Margaret Cooper, *Glory Gone: The Story of Nailing in Bromsgrove* (Bromsgrove: Halfshire Books, 1989), 58–64.

35. R. H. Tawney, *The Establishment of Minimum Rates in the Chain-Making Industry under the Trade Boards Act of 1909* (London: G. Bell & Sons, 1914), 2.

36. B.P.P., *CEC*, xi, 1843, 76–78.

37. Women, Suffrage and Politics: The Papers of Sylvia Pankhurst, 1882–1960, Part 1, Reel 2, File 27. Amsterdam, International Instituut voor Sociale Geschiedemis.

38. Rev. Harold Rylett, "Nails and Chains," *English Illustrated Magazine* (1890): 163.

39. B.P.P., *CEC*, xi, 1843, 57; and Tawney, 20–21 and 6. Tawney and Sheila Blackburn have emphasized that, with little capital required to supply the few necessary tools, middlemen came to dominate the trade, which was soon overcrowded. See Sheila Blackburn, "Working-Class Attitudes to Social Reform: Black Country Chainmakers and Anti-sweating Legislation, 1880–1930," *International Review of Social History* 33 (1988): 42–69; and B.P.P., *CEC*, 1864, 136.

40. "The Small Chain Makers of Cradley Heath," *Labour Tribune*, 1 September 1888.

41. Ibid.

42. Rylett, 163–164.

43. Ibid., 168.

44. B.P.P., *Report under the Laws Relating to Factories and Workshops by Robert Baker, Esq., for the Half-year Ended April 30, 1875*.

45. See B.P.P., *Report of the Commissioners Appointed to Inquire into the Working of the Factory and Workshops Acts*, 1876, xxix; and *County Advertiser* for 1883. For a fuller discussion of the general issues, see Carol E. Morgan, *Women Workers and Gender Identities, 1835–1913: The Cotton and Metal Industries in England* (London and New York: Routledge & Kegan Paul, 2001).

46. B.P.P., *CEC*, xi, 1843, 78.

47. Ibid.

48. "'Chains and Slavery.' A Visit to the Strikers at Cradley-Heath," *Sunday Chronicle*, 7 November 1886. Richard Juggins, Letter to editor, *Sunday Chronicle*, 5 December 1886. Juggins was also mindful of the role of low wages in such brutalization.

49. See *County Advertiser*, 1883; and Morgan.

50. B.P.P., *Report of Commissioners*, 1876, 298.

51. See *County Advertiser*, January–May 1883.

52. Papers of Sylvia Pankhurst, 9.

53. "'Chains and Slavery,'" *Sunday Chronicle*, 7 November 1886.

54. "Non-unionism and the Nailmakers," *Sunday Chronicle*, 25 October 1891.

55. Papers of Sylvia Pankhurst, 15.

56. Jane Humphries, "'. . . The Most Free from Objection . . .': The Sexual Division of Labor and Women's Work in Nineteenth-Century England," *Journal of Economic History* 47 (December 1987): 929–949.

57. B.P.P., *CEC*, 1864, 95.

58. B.P.P., *Commission on Labour,* 439.

59. For a richly textured account of working-class women in Birmingham, the extent of their labor, and their strength and abilities in difficult conditions, see Carl Chinn, *They Worked All Their Lives: Women of the Urban Poor in England, 1880–1939* (Manchester: Manchester University Press, 1988).

60. Edward Cadbury, M. Cecile Matheson, and George Shann, *Women's Work and Wages,* (London: T. Fisher Unwin, 1906), 50–56.

61. "The Dangerous and Labouring Life of Birmingham's Women Metal Workers," *Sunday Chronicle,* 21 September 1908, Gertrude Tuckwell Collection, 504a/1.

62. Ibid.

63. Ibid.

64. Trades Union Congress, *Report of Proceedings at the Forty-Second Annual Trades Union Congress,* 1909, 168.

65. Cadbury, Matheson, and Shann, 46–47.

66. Kathleen Dayus, *All My Days* (London: Virago Press, 1989), 40–41; and Cadbury, Matheson, and Shann.

67. Cadbury, Matheson, and Shann, 196–197.

68. Ibid., 70–71.

69. Ibid., 71.

70. Paul Thompson, *The Edwardians: The Remaking of British Society* (Bloomington: Indiana University Press, 1975), 125–127.

71. Dayus, 19.

72. Elizabeth Roberts, *A Woman's Place: An Oral History of Working-Class Women, 1890–1940* (Oxford: Basil Blackwell, 1984), 39.

Part Two: Spaces of Socialization
of Middle- and
Upper-Class Girls
in the Eighteenth and
Nineteenth Centuries

6   Managing Girls' Sexuality among the German Upper Classes

Irene Hardach-Pinke

*Part Two turns to the very different spaces inhabited by middle-
and upper-class girls—their homes, convent schools, and gardens. Assuring a proper match was the focus of parental strategy
for girls of this class. For young women from the German upper
classes, as Irene Hardach-Pinke suggests in this chapter, deviating from the correct path to adulthood could bring social disaster. Among German Protestant pedagogues, theologians, physicians, and upper-class parents, an argument had emerged by the
late eighteenth and early nineteenth centuries that girls could
look after themselves if they received the right education. Young
women had to learn to form judgments and make decisions
in order to fend off seducers once they moved into mixed-sex
society for courtship. German authors saw this to be a better
approach to instilling sexual morality than the "French" practice
of secluding girls in convent schools.*

According to German novels and advice books of the eighteenth and nineteenth
centuries, seducers lurked everywhere, eager to lead girls astray. The fate of
fictional victims warned parents and daughters to watch out and to make themselves familiar with the personality and the methods of seducers. Respectable
female youth was understood as a period of chastity. If a girl was enticed to
ignore prohibitions and to leave the proper path to marriage and motherhood,
she risked her health, happiness, and future. Daughters and their parents were
repeatedly warned: "one step away from the path of virtue, and everything,
everything is gone!"[1]

This chapter examines German literary discourses about sexuality and seduction between 1750 and 1850. What was considered to be the "normal path"
to adult female status and what indicated that a girl had been led astray? I focus
on the situation of upper-class girls, because the advice literature and educa-

tional novels were mostly concerned with daughters of the nobility and the higher bourgeoisie. The paper asks, furthermore, to what extent the consequences of a seduction were really as dramatic and irreversible in everyday life as the prescriptive literature suggested. Was there no way out of the "horrible vortices" and back to normal life?[2]

The sources used here include advice literature, legal texts, letters, autobiographies, and diaries. Advice books had become very popular by the eighteenth century and addressed themselves to parents, to parents and daughters, daughters alone, and occasionally to young people of both sexes.[3] Books of medical advice were written by men, generally doctors, while educational advice books and novels were written by both men and women, including former governesses, women who ran schools or boarding houses, and educated society ladies. Though the majority of German authors came from a Protestant background, they tried to reach the Catholic public as well. Advice books with a distinct Catholic perspective were mostly French imports and appeared on the German market either in the original version or in a translation that adapted the content to local conditions.[4]

Prescriptive literature for young girls dealt mainly with questions of health, psychology, education, finding a husband, pastimes, and manners. Their advice was to a large extent based on what authors took to be prevailing practices, which were either criticized or recommended. But if a girl wanted to know how to deal with the consequences of seduction, she had to turn to other sources for information.

Rites of Passage

Girls who had reached puberty were fortunate. Having survived childhood and not yet being confronted with the hazards of pregnancy and childbirth, their risk of a premature death was comparatively low.[5] For most of them a new stage of life began between the ages of fourteen and eighteen with a more or less formalized rite of passage defined by religion, social class, and gender, but only loosely connected with sexual maturation. By the second half of the eighteenth century almost all Protestant communities in Germany had ritualized confirmation, which took place between the ages of thirteen and eighteen. Girls and boys attended classes to prepare for the public examination that preceded the ceremony, as this rite of passage marked intellectual, not physical, development. Some girls who were already sexually mature had to wait several years before they were confirmed, while others were allowed to participate in the social life of adults even though their menstruation had not yet started. For Catholic upper-class girls the transition from childhood to youth was in Germany less ritualized by religion than for their Protestant counterparts. In almost all autobiographies by Protestant women, confirmation appeared as a decisive point in their lives, while First Communion and confirmation were rarely mentioned in the recollections of German Catholic authors.

A common rite of passage for both Catholic and Protestant upper-class girls was the entrée. Confirmation being a prerequisite for Protestant girls' entrée, this introduction into polite society occurred generally between fourteen and eighteen years of age. The occasion was often very expensive, especially if held at court or at an elegant ball. Less affluent parents tried to cut down costs by introducing their daughters at less formal occasions like local dances, dinners, or tea parties. While the theological meaning of confirmation stressed the importance of acquiring judgment, responsibility, and individual independence, the entrée emphasized the importance of being attractive to the opposite sex. The number of men who wanted to dance with her measured a girl's social success. Parents therefore made sure in advance that their daughters had enough partners and did not become wallflowers, but sometimes this sad fate could not be avoided. Despite the fear of being left to sit out while the others danced, and although some very pious girls refused to dance, for most girls the first ball was the subject of dreams and great expectations. In family stories handed down from grandmother to granddaughter, from mother to daughter, it played a large role in shaping an upper-class woman's identity. What a girl wore and how she felt on this occasion was recalled in many autobiographies and became the subject of novels and fairy tales. The entrée was a gender-specific rite of transition; men cherished quite different collective memories of the passage to adulthood.

Youth neither began nor ended for all women at the same age. Women usually gained adult status by marrying but sometimes also by entering a convent nunnery or taking a position such as that of lady-in-waiting, governess, or schoolteacher.[6] Most people married in their twenties; age of first marriage was lowest in the aristocracy and highest in the peasantry. But the age of first marriage also varied within social classes. Some daughters of noble or bourgeois families got married at fourteen, the minimum legal age, others not until thirty. A woman who was still single when she turned thirty was considered an old maid, because by that age most women were married. With no attractive prospects for the future, this long period of youth could become burdensome. Conversely, girls who married right after confirmation had to step too abruptly from childhood into adult status. Mostly, though, youth lasted five to ten years for women of the upper classes, two to three years less than for their brothers, who tended to marry later.

Educators, theologians, and medical experts were convinced that the period between childhood and adulthood should be spent in preparing for a healthy and happy life, though they also held that it had a value in itself. Youth rather than childhood was increasingly considered the happiest time of life: "A time of love and merriment."[7] Observers claimed that young people often possessed a carefree, cheerful, and optimistic disposition, and parents were encouraged to leave them room to enjoy themselves: "At this age we can endow our whole life with a joyful tenor; from these days of first bloom we must carry our cheerfulness on into our future lives."[8] But young people could only profit from youth as a happy time if they respected certain rules and followed a certain path.

Programs for Female Youth

By the end of the eighteenth century, for men in the upper classes, youth had become a time of preparation and training for a career; young men generally spent these years away from home as officers, students, or trainees in merchant houses. In the meantime, their sisters were supposed to get ready for the responsibilities of a wife and mother.[9] However, they had also to acquire the knowledge, habits, and abilities needed to maintain their social status and distinguish themselves from members of the lower strata. Therefore they continued to take lessons after the end of childhood in such subjects as French, literature, music, dance, needlework, painting, history, nature study, and religion. And though many pedagogues and theologians questioned the usefulness of this plan of instruction, most upper-class parents followed it if they had the means. Upper-class daughters who did not speak French, play an instrument, and know how to dance were regarded by the end of the eighteenth century as culturally deficient.

Female youth was considered a time not only for instruction but also for amusement. Young girls' enjoyments helped to develop a pleasant, optimistic personality and accumulate happy memories for the difficult times ahead, when they had to fulfill the responsibilities of wives and mothers. The natural cheerfulness young people presumably possessed should be strengthened, so that it could counteract melancholy and fearfulness. "Certainly a girl needs a time of innocent pleasures; she must have been a daughter of paradise, before she can become an industrious wife in the humble abode. Only when she has enjoyed youth, the time of the poets, can she acquire the life, the flexibility and the joyful, harmless disposition which are necessary for her job vocation."[10] Advice books made various practical suggestions for appropriate youthful entertainments and discussed controversial issues such as whether dancing with young men and playing cards should be permitted or not.[11] Letters, diaries, and autobiographies show that upper-class parents provided their daughters with opportunities to dance, travel, play games, perform plays and music, arrange *tableaux vivants,* paint, and meet other young people at outings, picnics, or sleigh rides. By the end of the eighteenth century the so-called *Backfisch* had emerged as a social type—the cheerful, carefree girl aged fourteen to seventeen with time and money to spare.[12] The *Backfische* organized distinct social gatherings, kept diaries, read books especially written for them, shared crushes on certain men or women, and giggled a lot. Their innocent gender-specific pastimes lasted well into the twentieth century.

The third and last item on the agenda of female youth was the choice of a husband. Parents felt responsible for preventing an unsuitable match, but it was considered cruel to force a daughter to marry somebody she did not want. Girls themselves thus had to learn to judge a man by his character and not fall for outer appearances or succumb to flattery.[13] In order to find a suitable husband they had to be attractive to men, but at the same time they had to be careful not to overstep the boundaries of propriety.

Prescriptive literature thus defined the "right path" to female adulthood. But as the medical and educational experts pointed out, these very same programs could also lead girls astray. Learning French might encourage reading unsuitable books. And the entrée ball could become the first step on a dangerous road because in dance, as Lord Byron put it, youth and pleasure met.[14] Balls brought girls into close physical contact with men who might turn out to be unscrupulous seducers. For this reason a few authors of advice books went so far as to ask girls to dance only among themselves or with members of their families.[15] But like the well-meant warnings against learning French and reading novels, this advice was widely ignored in everyday life.

The Problem of Enforced Chastity

Though the influential *Backfischkultur* was based on the stereotype of young girls as cheerful and innocent, the dark side of their growing up years was not ignored.[16] Melancholy, changeability, willfulness, and turmoil were also regarded as typical attributes of youth. The symptoms of what would later come to be called *adolescence* were already noted in eighteenth-century sources.[17] Parents complained that after childhood their daughters and sons turned into "*furiosi*" who behaved strangely and often were rebellious and moody.[18] Girls rebelled, especially against their mothers, and often made their lives hell.[19] The program for female youth aimed at counteracting the dark side of growing up by keeping young girls occupied and by directing their aims toward marriage. The cheerful *Backfisch* was not supposed to turn into an old maid or a nun but into a happy wife and mother. Until then she had to live a life of chastity, understood to be no easy task.

Sexual maturity was indicated by the onset of menstruation, but the relationship between the two phenomena was not yet understood. After Karl-Ernst von Baer discovered the female reproductive cell in 1827, the ovaries rather than the uterus gradually came to be perceived as the main organs involved in sexual maturation.[20] But for some time physicians continued to debate whether the monthly blood came from the uterus, the vagina, the arteries, or the veins. Some saw menstruation as a form of degeneration, others as a method of detoxification, and still others as the result of repressed sexuality. Some physicians considered emotional turmoil as the cause of menstruation; others considered it to be a side effect. The theory that prevailed in Germany until the mid-nineteenth century suggested that women who were not pregnant lost the superfluous blood that the body had produced since childhood for the nourishment of a fetus. If the surplus blood (plethora) did not flow off monthly, it could clog the veins and become the cause of countless ailments. Thus a regular and normal blood flow was regarded as the most important symptom of a woman's good health, and this positive perception influenced everyday life much more than any negative interpretations of the monthly blood as a poisonous and foul substance.

When a daughter started to have her period, her parents welcomed this sign of sexual maturation because menstruation indicated the girl's potential to become a wife and mother one day. While families preferred early sexual maturation in their daughters, physicians and educators found late development less problematic for both sexes. They were unanimous, though, in believing that puberty put more stress on girls, who frequently suffered from psychological conflicts and physical ailments.[21] Physicians warned families to be patient and not to try and hasten the onset of menstruation by giving their daughters dubious herbal medicines and forcing hot baths on them.[22] Parents were encouraged instead to prepare the girls for what was to come and to teach them a healthy lifestyle: "When a girl has reached mature years, that is her 15th or 16th year or sometimes her 12th, she has, if she is healthy, a bloody discharge through the sexual organs every month for a few days; this discharge, which is called purification, is of greatest importance, because on it depends the health, the strength, the life of the girl. Disorders in purification bring about the most horrible illnesses, chlorosis, swelling of the whole body, cramps, madness and rage."[23] Girls who were about to start menstruation or just had started it needed a well-balanced diet, exercise, entertainment to cheer them up, and careful hygiene. They should avoid heavy meals, too much dancing, anger, and getting too hot or catching cold.[24] If they neglected this advice, they had themselves to blame "that the flower, which has only just started to bloom, wilts and falls off."[25]

Daughters of the upper classes, who did not have to work hard and were well nourished, menstruated earlier than peasant girls. Leading physicians of their time assumed that the first period started between the age of twelve and twenty, but mostly between fourteen and sixteen. Many girls had to wait another few years after the onset of their period for the development of breasts and other so-called secondary sex characteristics. Physicians warned against using corsets and other tricks in order to look more womanly. Though menstruation was by no means a general taboo, as it was treated openly not only in medical and educational advice books but also in letters, it nevertheless filled some women in the higher classes with social uneasiness and even shame. Since the eighteenth century, doctors and educators had emphasized the delicacy surrounding menstruation and encouraged upper-class girls to hide the symptoms with cloths and bandages. After 1800, some physicians advocated wearing drawers for comfort and propriety, but this new fashion did not catch on until the second part of the nineteenth century.[26] The majority of ordinary women, though, just continued to let the blood flow until well into the twentieth century.

Physicians, educators, and theologians argued against early marriages, which were legally allowed for women at fourteen and men at eighteen, because they did not leave young people enough time to develop body and mind. Medical experts regarded heterosexual intercourse, if it took place too early and too often, as a very dangerous activity for men. The loss of fluids that could not be replaced was supposed to harm male health and reduce life expectancy. For women, by contrast, sexual intercourse was considered a healthy activity once menstruation had been established for two or three years.[27] Thus physicians advised a shorter period of chastity following sexual maturation for women than for men. They told young people how to avoid sexual urges and asked them to ignore novels, talk, and situations that might excite erotic interest. Instead, young women and men were told to watch their diet, take cold baths, and lead an ascetic life. Renowned German physicians like Johann Peter Frank, Christoph Wilhelm Hufeland, and Ludwig Vogel even wanted to raise the legal age of marriage to secure a healthier population. Frank, for example, advised lawmakers to fix the minimum age of marriage in rural areas at eighteen for women and twenty-five for men, but in town, where it was more difficult to stay chaste, at sixteen and twenty-two, respectively.[28] These suggestions for reform are curious given that most people married well after the ages suggested. The early marriages the experts feared were not at all common in practice.

The experts also claimed that the loss of chastity before marriage was a great hazard for men, but in practice this was not true. Young men who visited brothels or got involved with women of the lower classes generally did not ruin their prospects for the future, whereas a young girl whose good reputation was damaged or who got pregnant faced very serious consequences. In the lower classes a pregnancy outside marriage often led to the quick foundation of a family through marriage or cohabitation. In the upper classes a single mother had no social status and even the mistresses of princes and mothers of their illegitimate offspring had to be married to somebody. Though this double standard was considered unfair by many pedagogues, theologians, and the educated public, it did not seem possible to change it.[29] Instead, young girls were requested to conform.[30]

The number of illegitimate pregnancies was low among the German upper classes, which meant that most girls must have obeyed the prescription of chastity until marriage because information on birth control and on abortion was difficult to get, and prevailing methods were not reliable or safe. Though there was a double standard, many men also refrained from sexual intercourse before marriage.[31] Pedagogues and physicians held conflicting views on whether young women or young men found it more difficult to resist their sexual drives. Some were convinced that men had the stronger sexual urges; others thought girls did. But they were unanimous that girls typically lacked useful occupations and were thereby encouraged to daydream about love and romance, which made them susceptible to seduction.

Preventing Seduction

Joachim Heinrich Campe's *Fatherly Advice for My Daughter* (published first in 1789), which became the most widely read advice book on girls in Germany in the first half of the nineteenth century, described sexual intercourse as a "sensual pleasure for the man as well as for the woman."[32] However, Campe also warned his daughter through terrible examples that this pleasure was not to be experienced before marriage. The famous educator preached continence and pointed out that masturbation was also to be avoided, because sexual desires should be kept dormant until marriage. He thus participated in the debate about masturbation among male authors who warned that their children might be seduced into this "vice" by servants or friends and thus depart from the path to happiness and longevity.[33] The discourse mainly concerned boys. In everyday life, parents of daughters worried more about pregnancy than masturbation; forms of sexual behavior that could not result in an illegitimate birth appeared as minor issues.[34] In the same vein, homosexual relations among girls did not seem to worry educators or physicians, while homosexual relations among boys did.[35]

Seduction was generally regarded as a legal offense but was only prosecuted, if at all, when a pregnancy resulted. In the lower classes, lovers might denounce each other in court as the party responsible for the seduction and thus for the resulting illegitimate birth. The law regarded women as well as men as possible seducers in most German states. But in the upper classes a girl who got pregnant was almost uniformly considered the victim of seduction and thereby pitied by her family and her community. Her lack of experience or judgment, her desire to please, her romantic illusions, her sexual weakness, or her strong sexual drive were offered as explanations for her fall. It was presumed that no upper-class girl in her right mind would risk pregnancy out of wedlock and thereby ruin the chances to marry and lead an honorable life.

Two approaches to protecting girls from seduction and its unhappy consequences were compared in Germany by the educated public during the eighteenth and first half of the nineteenth century. The Catholic or French method relied on the seclusion of young girls symbolized by a convent wall. Secluding young women until marriage was associated with parental choice of a husband; the couple only met shortly before the wedding. Under such arrangements there was no opportunity for premarital intimacy. In France itself this approach was much criticized during the eighteenth century. Jean-Jacques Rousseau pointed out the benefits of the Protestant model, which allowed girls to enter mixed society before marriage and thus get to know the ways of the world.[36] And in his novel *Les Liaisons Dangereuses,* Choderlos de Laclos vividly described the negative consequences of seclusion, which did not teach upper-class girls to protect themselves and recognize a seducer if he approached them.[37]

German pedagogues and physicians, not only Protestants but also Catholics like Johann Peter Frank, rejected the so-called Catholic approach, as they were convinced that women and men should get to know each other before marriage. Though they recognized that letting young people meet, dance, and talk together always presented a risk of illicit sexual encounters and that the wall made the fear of seduction superfluous, they preferred the German approach, which was based on self-control and self-protection.[38] Advice books stated that girls did not need to be protected by walls because they could look after themselves, although only if they had received the right education and developed the necessary self-control. These two different approaches to bringing up daughters help to clarify the social values embedded in existing practices. In 1829, Ottilie von Goethe, daughter-in-law of the poet, took up the subject in the journal she edited in Weimar. Here the French custom of introducing young women to male society only after marriage was criticized because it kept them from knowing and shaping their emotions vis-à-vis men from youth on. No wonder that French wives took lovers out of frustration! A German mother who was anxious about her daughter moving in the society of men, the author concluded, had only minor grounds for fear in comparison with her French equivalent.[39]

Advice books expected young women to protect themselves from seduction, but while some authors advocated sex education, others claimed that innocence was the best protection.[40] Parents generally found it difficult to explain the facts of life to their children and often contented themselves with general warnings and vague hints. Some avoided the topic altogether, but a girl without any sexual knowledge was the exception, and advice books mostly presumed that the majority learned about sexuality from servants, elder siblings, or friends. Educators and physicians deplored this fact, as these unofficial sources could not be relied upon to stress that marriage was the only place for sexual pleasure.

But even when girls understood what seduction meant in practice, they often could not distinguish a potential seducer from a well-meaning suitor. Every man who flirted with a woman whom he would not or could not marry, either because he was already engaged or because his status was too high or too low, was considered a seducer.[41] How was a girl to know? She had to rely on information from her family and watch a man's behavior cautiously. Advice books warned that some men tried to win her by false promises, ardent compliments, and declarations of passionate love. To resist them, it was important to decipher their speeches. A girl had to listen carefully and form a judgment. On the one hand, in order not to encourage potential seducers, she was warned to refrain from being too open or too flirtatious. On the other hand, she had to attract suitors if she did not want to leave the choice of a husband to her family, and therefore she should not appear prudish or shy in the society of men. Only a self-assured woman could handle these conflicting messages. Though advice books provided many useful hints on how to behave in mixed gendered society, everyday life sources show that even well-educated girls of conscientious parents could get into trouble.

Dealing with the Worst Case

Illegitimate births were highest in the vicinity of universities and barracks, but these concerned mostly the daughters of the lower classes.[42] Seducers of upper-class girls were often stereotyped in German novels as vile noblemen or dashing officers who had the means to impress a young heart but would leave before a betrothal took place. Advice books gave a much more differentiated picture and were not blind to the fact that often a girl could take the initiative to attract the wrong man. They also pointed out that danger came not only from outside the house but also from within. Although there was no allusion to incest, they cautioned parents not to leave their daughters alone with a tutor during lessons at home. Nevertheless, several women recall in their autobiographies how a tutor tried to make love to them, with or without their consent, under their parents' roof.[43]

What happened when an unmarried upper-class girl got pregnant? As advice books did not deal with such problems, she had to turn to other sources for help. Most girls in trouble were apparently rescued by adults who knew how to save the situation. Hermann von Egloffstein tells the story of the daughter of noble Catholic parents in southern Germany at the end of the eighteenth century who had an affair with a priest and became pregnant. Marriage, of course, was out of the question. The young woman confessed to her mother, who asked a prelate for help. He approached the Countess von Egloffstein, as she had the reputation of being a kindhearted Christian, and persuaded her to invite the young woman to her estate and present her as a widow under a false name. After the child was born, it was handed over to a foster mother and died soon after. The young woman returned to her family, got married, and became a happy and respected wife. The priest who had seduced her remained, with good reason, forever grateful to the prelate.[44] The story was recorded in the von Egloffstein family sources as evidence of the good sense and social competence of their ancestor. It was a typical case of seduction, as the priest made love to a girl whom he could not marry and then left her to her destiny. The consequences were also typical: the pregnant daughter turned to family and friends, was sent away and gave birth under a false identity, and the child was handed over to foster parents and died. Everybody acted in the greatest secrecy, thereby saving the status and respectability of the girl.

Another example is that of Marianne von der Lahr, daughter of the respected Huguenot widow of a parson who ran a boarding school in Pomerania. Her brothers were at university and two older sisters worked as governesses in noble families. Marianne was the youngest daughter; she took lessons every afternoon from the teacher Poulet. In May 1770, it became apparent that she was pregnant by her teacher, who was married and had several children. Her mother was too overwhelmed to keep the daughter's pregnancy secret and was therefore reproached by the Huguenot community for her lack of delicacy. Parents took their daughters out of the now disgraced school. In church, nobody talked to the widow any more. The two older sisters tried to help their mother and younger sister. One wrote to the Huguenot parson Formey for advice and help.[45] Formey took matters into his own hands. The teacher Poulet was forced to leave Stettin. Young Marianne delivered her child, a boy, and was sent to the Russian province of Kurland to work as a governess. The boy went to the orphanage of the Huguenot community in Berlin. The good reputation of the family was reestablished and eventually the pupils returned to the school. In Kurland, young Marianne became a successful governess, was respected, and earned a very good salary. To the great disappointment of her mother, however, she returned to Pomerania ten years later to marry Poulet after his wife had died. Her mother understood her motive (to provide a home for her son) but was heartbroken that her intelligent and successful daughter should end up with such a detestable husband.[46] In the upper classes a pregnancy out of wedlock was supposed to be hidden; the delivery had to take place far away from community, family, and neighbors and the baby disposed of. There was no place in the upper classes for a single mother with a child.

The correct path from childhood to adulthood was very clearly laid out for young women from the upper classes. Deviating from it could bring failure. Without instruction in French, music, and dance, girls were not able to reproduce the habits of their social class; without the merriment of youth they could not equip themselves with happy memories for the future; without a healthy lifestyle they risked irregular menstruation, chlorosis, and cramps; and without respecting the rules of chastity they could lose their social status.

Becoming pregnant out of wedlock was the greatest hazard of female youth and many pedagogues, theologians, physicians, and elite women gave advice on how to prevent it. Following prevailing assumptions about gender, they regarded men as active and women as passive, but they increasingly argued that girls could look after themselves if they received the right education. Young women had to learn to form judgments and make decisions in order to fend off seducers when they moved in mixed-gender society. It was thus a girl's own responsibility to stay on the path of virtue until marriage. They could even ignore supposedly feminine attributes and become quite energetic and active if the circumstances demanded it: "A girl who defends her honour, is allowed everything."[47]

Notes

1. Wilhelmine Christiane Charlotte Gensel, *Elisens von Honau und ihrer Erzieherin Eulalia Waller Unterredung in Briefen. Allen gefühlvollen Mädchen bei ihrem Eintritt in die große Welt gewidmet* (Berlin: Maurer, 1803), 189.
2. Joachim Heinrich Campe, *Väterlicher Rath für meine Tochter. Der erwachsenen Jugend gewidmet* [Braunschweig 1796] (Paderborn: Verlag für historische Publikationen und Reprints, 1988), 5.
3. Advice books for girls and their parents had a long tradition. See, for instance, Cornelia Niekus Moore, "The Maiden's Mirror. Reading Material for German Girls in the Sixteenth and Seventeenth Centuries," in *Wolfenbüttler Forschungen*, Bd. 36 (Wiesbaden: Harrassowitz, 1987); Susanne Barth, *Jungfrauenzucht. Literaturwissenschaftliche und pädagogische Studien zur Mädchenerziehungsliteratur zwischen 1200 und 1600* (Stuttgart: M&P, Verlag für Wissenschaft und Forschung, 1994); Irene Hardach-Pinke, *Bleichsucht und Blütenträume. Junge Mädchen 1750–1850* (Frankfurt/Main: Campus, 2000); and Susanne Barth, *Mädchenlektüren, Lesediskurse im 18. und 19. Jahrhundert* (Frankfurt/Main: Campus, 2002).
4. See, for example, the interesting adaptations of works by Jeanne-Marie Le Prince de Beaumont by Johann Joachim Schwab: *Der Frau Maria le*

Prince de Beaumont lehrreiches Magazin für junge Leute, besonders jungen Frauenzimmern nach deutscher Art eingerichtet von Johann Joachim Schwab (Wien, 1767).

5. Only about half of all infants reached the age of fifteen, the percentage of boys being even lower than that of girls. See Peter Marschalk, *Bevölkerungsgeschichte Deutschlands im 19. und 20. Jahrhundert* (Frankfurt/Main: Suhrkamp, 1984), 39 and 19ff.

6. Irene Hardach-Pinke, *Die Gouvernante. Geschichte eines Frauenberufs* (Frankfurt/Main: Campus, 1993).

7. J. G. D. Schmiedgen, *Theobalds Morgengabe für seine Enkeltochter Pauline. Ein Buch für deutsche Töchter, aus den mittlern und höhern Ständen, zur Beherzigung in der Zeit der Liebe und des Frohsinns* (Leipzig: Fleischer, 1798).

8. Christian August Struve, *Der Gesundheitsfreund der Jugend oder praktische Anweisung, wie man in der Jugend den Grund zu einer dauerhaften Gesundheit legen und sich bis ins späteste Alter erhalten könne* (Hannover: Hahn, 1803), 81.

9. Elisabeth Eleonore Bernhardi, *Ein Wort zu seiner Zeit. Für verständige Mütter und erwachsene Töchter. In Briefen einer Mutter,* ed. Karl Gottlob Sonntag (Freyberg: Craz, 1798), 33.

10. Johann Ludwig Ewald, *Die Kunst ein gutes Mädchen, eine gute Gattin, Mutter und Hausfrau zu werden. Ein Handbuch für erwachsene Töchter, Gattinnen und Mütte,* Erster Band (Frankfurt a. M.: Wilmans, 1804), 103.

11. Betty Gleim, *Ueber die Bildung der Frauen und die Behauptung ihrer Würde in den wichtigsten Verhältnissen ihres Lebens. Ein Buch für Jungfrauen, Gattinnen und Mütter* (Bremen und Leipzig: Comptoir für Literatur, 1814), 74ff.; and Christian Wilhelm Hufeland, *Anleitung zur physischen und moralischen Erziehung des weiblichen Geschlechts. Nach d. Engl. von E. Darwin* (Leipzig: Brockhaus, 1822), 98ff.

12. *Backfische* were literally fish that were still too small for consumption and had to be thrown back into the water to keep on growing. Before the end of the eighteenth century, young men had also sometimes been called *Backfische,* but this practice disappeared completely.

13. Johanna von Bültzingsloewen, *Briefe über weibliche Bildung gewechselt zwischen Tante und Nichte* (Berlin: Neue Berlinische Buchhandlung, 1819), 62–63.

14. Lord Byron, *Childe Harold's Pilgrimage,* Canto III, st. 22.

15. Gleim, 74ff.

16. Hardach-Pinke, *Bleichsucht,* 95ff.

17. Janet Oppenheim, *"Shattered Nerves": Doctors, Patients and Depression in Victorian England* (New York and Oxford: Oxford University Press, 1991), 250ff.

18. Johann Heinrich Zedler, *Grossess Universal Lexicon aller Wissenschaften und Künste,* Erster Band (Halle and Leipzig, 1732), 538. Zedler speaks of "Adolescence" as between fourteen and twenty-five years of age.

19. Bernhardi, 14.

20. Friedrich Ludwig Meissner, *Die Frauenzimmerkrankheiten nach den neuesten Ansichten und Erfahrungen zum Unterricht für praktische Ärzte* (Leipzig: Wigand, 1846); Hans Georg Müller-Hess, "Die Lehre von der Menstruation vom Beginn der Neuzeit bis zur Begründung der Zellenlehre," in *Abhandlun-*

gen zur Geschichte der Medinzin und der Naturwissenschaften, Heft 27 (Berlin: Ebering, 1938); and Esther Fischer-Homberger, *Krankheit Frau: Zur Geschichte der Einbildungen* (Darmstadt: Luchterhand, 1988). See also Maryanne Cline Horowitz, "The 'Science' of Embryology before the Discovery of the Ovum," in *Connecting Spheres: Women in the Western World, 1500 to the Present,* ed. Marilyn J. Boxer and Jean H. Quataert (Oxford: Oxford University Press, 1987), 86–94

21. Meissner, 575.

22. Johann Peter Frank, *System einer vollständigen medicinischen Polizei,* Erster Band (Mannheim: Schwan, 1779), 75.

23. Peter Villaume, "Ueber die Unzuchtssünden in der Jugend. Eine gekrönte Preisschrift," in *Allgemeine revision des gesamten Schul- und Erziehungswesens,* VII Theil, ed J. H. Campe (Hamburg: Bohn, 1787), 282.

24. *Geschenk für meine Kinder, am Tage ihrer Verlobung oder Vollständiger Unterricht über die Erziehung der Jugend vom Keime an, bis in das mannbare Alter von einem Menschenfreunde,* Fünfter Theil (Wien: Strauß, 1814), 233ff.

25. *Geschenk für meine Kinder,* 234.

26. J. E. Aronsson, *Die Kunst das Leben des schönen Geschlechts zu verlängern, seine Schönheit zu erhalten, und es in seinen eigenthümlichen Krankheiten vor Mißgriffen zu bewahren. Ein Handbuch für Mütter und erwachsene Töchter* (Berlin: J. W. Schmidt, 1807), 69; and Johann Ludwig Andreas Vogel, *Diätetisches Lexikon oder theoretisch-praktischer Unterricht über Nahrungsmittel und die mannichfaltigen Zubereitungen derselben. Ein Familienbuch, zu einem Ratgeber in allen, die Erhaltung des Lebens und der Gesundheit betreffenden Angelegenheiten bestimmt,* Erster Band (Erfurt: Keyser, 1800), 51–52.

27. Frank, 237ff.

28. Ibid., 258–259.

29. Friedrich Heinrich Christian Schwarz, *Grundriß einer Theorie der Mädchenerziehung in Hinsicht auf die mittleren Stände* (Jena: Cröke, 1792), 280–281.

30. Bültzingsloewen, 58ff.

31. Anne-Charlott Trepp, *Sanfte Männlichkeit und selbständige Weiblichkeit. Frauen und Männer im Hamburger Bürgertum zwischen 1770 und 1840* (Göttingen: Vandenhoeck & Ruprecht, 1996), 79ff.

32. Campe, 152.

33. On the anti-masturbation campaign in Germany, see: Isabel V. Hull, *Sexuality, State, and Civil Society in Germany, 1700–1815* (Ithaca, N.Y., and London: Cornell University Press, 1996), 258ff.

34. Gensel, 189.

35. *Geschenk für meine Kinder,* 243–244. This advice book deals with young people of both sexes but only treats homosexual relations of boys as a problem. For a similar comparison between France and England, see the chapter by Céline Grasser.

36. Jean-Jacques Rousseau, *Emil oder über die Erziehung,* Fifth Book (1762; reprint, München: Schöningh, 1981), 509–510.

37. Choderlos de Laclos, *Die gefährlichen Bekanntschaften oder Briefe gesammelt in einer Gesellschaft und zur Belehrung einiger anderer bekanntgemacht* [1782] (1782; reprint, Leipzig: Insel-Verlag, 1987).

38. B. S. Walther, *Ueber die Erziehung junger Frauenzimmer aus mittlern und höhern Ständen* (Berlin: Hesse, 1781), 38.

39.   "Briefpost," *Chaos* 35 (1829), in *Chaos*, ed. Ottilie von Goethe (Bern: H. Lang, 1968), 139.

40.   Rudolf Wilhelm Zobel, *Briefe über die Erziehung der Frauenzimmer* (Berlin and Stralsund, 1773), 218–219; and Gleim, 100.

41.   Ewald, 73–74.

42.   Arthur E. Imhof and Helmut Schumacher, "Todesursachen," in *Historische Demographie als Sozialgeschichte. Gießen und Umgebung vom 17. zum 19. Jahrhundert*, Teil I (Darmstadt und Marburg: Selbstverlag der Hessischen Historischen Kommission Darmstadt und der Historischen Kommission für Hessen, 1975), 538.

43.   Hardach-Pinke, *Bleichsucht*, 90–91.

44.   Hermann Freiherr von Egloffstein, ed., "Zeugnisse über Altweimar in Briefen der Familie von Egloffstein an einen fränkischen Prälaten," in *Jahrbuch der Goethe-Gesellschaft*, vol. 13, ed. Max Hecke (Weimar: Verlag der Goethe-Gesellschaft, 1927), 205–206.

45.   Louise von der Lahr (7.6.1770), Deutsche Staatsbibliothek Berlin, Nachlass Formey.

46.   Marianne von der Lahr (17.12.1781), Deutsche Staatsbibliothek Berlin, Nachlass Formey.

47.   *Mutterlehren der Frau Hofräthin von H*** an ihre sechzehnjährige Tochter* (Erfurt: G. A. Keyser, 1782), 47.

7 Porous Walls and Prying Eyes: Control, Discipline, and Morality in Boarding Schools for Girls in Mid-Nineteenth-Century France

Rebecca Rogers

Rebecca Rogers looks into those schools so derided by German pedagogical reformers. She points to a paradox regarding the aims and outcomes of girls' boarding-school education in nineteenth-century France. This education provided middle-class girls in France with few opportunities for independence and autonomy. French boarding schools were secluded from the outside, but within their walls, individuals lived a life under surveillance. As a result, girls forged their identity in constant contact with others, learning to "perform" within an institutional world whose rules they learned how to evade.

> A Romish school is a building with porous walls, a hollow
> floor, a false ceiling; every room in this house . . . has eye-holes
> and ear-holes, and what the house is, the inhabitants are, very
> treacherous; they all think it lawful to tell lies, they all call
> it politeness to profess friendship where they feel hatred.
> (Charlotte Brontë, 1845–1846)[1]

Enclosed female spaces have exerted considerable fascination in French society since the seventeenth century. Seen alternatively as prisons or sites of debauchery, the history of such spaces is intimately tied up with perceptions of female sexuality.[2] Were the walls that surrounded women permeable? Were these walls a rampart that allowed those within to engage in practices that went against prevailing sexual mores? In the early modern period the speculation and fantasy generated by such female spaces generally focused on adult women. Charlotte Brontë's comment reminds us that Catholic girls' schools in the nineteenth century were also seen as spaces whose walls were far less solid than they appeared. Her emphasis on deceit and stratagems encourages us to explore the practices within these walled spaces. In turning my gaze to the boarding schools that sheltered adolescent girls in the mid-nineteenth century, I examine the vision of female youth and womanhood that underlay and structured the emerging system of girls' secondary education, whose repercussions extended far beyond the school.[3]

The revolutionary period largely destroyed existing girls' schools, so the period from 1800 was one of institutional reconstruction and cultural experimentation. Both lay and religious women opened schools; for the middle classes boarding schools prevailed. In Paris, in particular, such schools proliferated: in 1800 some forty-five *maisons d'éducation* run by women were noted; by 1830 this figure had jumped to 190. In 1864 the city of Paris harbored 316 boarding schools with almost 12,000 students.[4] These Parisian schools were mostly run by lay women, although religious institutions constituted the majority elsewhere in France.[5] Unlike in England, where middle-class families sent their boys to boarding schools but kept their daughters at home, French middle-class women frequently sent their daughters off to school to prepare their First Communion or to finish their education.

Within these schools, girls were the object of a whole range of disciplinary strategies. These strategies were a response to increasingly vocal representations of female sexuality, but they also mimicked existing arrangements within boys' schools and religious convents.[6] How did students respond to the highly regulated and controlled environment in which they lived? Drawing on private writings and memoirs, this chapter explores how the spatial and disciplinary politics of boarding-school life affected and influenced schoolgirls' perception of themselves and their relationship with men and other women. My arguments contribute to the history of French gender relations whose specificities emerge most clearly in comparison with other countries.

Visions of Schoolgirls' Sexuality in Mid-Nineteenth-Century France

Medical attitudes toward women influenced both prescriptive literature and romantic fiction in the nineteenth century, contributing to a general discourse about female youth with widespread cultural ramifications. The onslaught of puberty was often believed to leave girls in a fragile mental and physical state.[7] Pedagogue Nathalie de Lajolais put it this way: "As young girls approach the nubile years, they require extreme attention . . . having arrived at that period [menstruation], a well-built and plethoric adolescent is tormented by dizziness, severe and repeated head aches, sleeplessness, gushing nosebleeds . . . she needs to follow carefully a light, calming and refreshing regime, accompanied by physical exercise."[8] Under these conditions, special attention needed to be paid to girls' surrounding environment. Collective educational settings came under closer scrutiny by both doctors and the educated public, who all assumed that adolescent girls had passions requiring some form of control. Medical experts marshaled physiological arguments to criticize boarding schools, insisting that they coarsened and overstimulated girls, often bringing on hysteria. Jean-Louis Brachet wrote in 1847 "Most women become hysterical, more from the vices of their education than from those of their constitution." This opinion circulated as well among writers and intellectuals whose texts reinforced negative stereotypes about the sexual consequences of boarding-school education.[9]

Outsiders' descriptions of girls' schools commonly portrayed them as sites of lost innocence. Balzac's statement that "A girl may leave her boarding school a virgin, but never chaste" offers the most famous claim about what occurred when girls were raised together under the same roof. The constant association with other girls led to secret sessions "where honor is lost in advance."[10] Brachet echoed the Balzacian viewpoint when he argued, "In spite of the most active surveillance, girls teach each other things of which they should long remain ignorant [...] Their little secret chats, their caresses so naive in appearance, those Balzacian virginal nibbles, this pussying about excites their senses, fills them with anticipation, and leads almost always to the knowledge of illicit pleasures which is the beginning of depravity."[11] For these men, the boarding-school environment with its cloying promiscuity nourished youthful sensuality and introduced girls to sensations and ideas that could be avoided in homes. Erotic literature, in particular, frequently used the convent setting as the background for sapphic adventures, following an enduring tradition that assumed the existence of female passions.

Promiscuity among girls was not the only concern about life in schools; the presence of male professors also became problematic in the 1840s.[12] Countless humorous portraits suggested the inevitable result: male teachers would lust after or inspire lust in young girls. Or alternatively, writers and lithographers depicted schools with porous walls that enabled a lively and sensuous exchange between young men and women (see Figures 7 and 8).[13] Finally, doctors as well as contemporary writers criticized schools for their excessive attention to such activities as music, dancing, or acting, which were perceived as heightening girls' sensitivity and even hastening their physical development. Ecarnot emphasized, in particular, the negative effects of the vibration of musical instrument strings upon a young girl's constitution, while Henri Duval warned that boarding-school education "developed the germs of vanity and coquetry and other vices which trouble the body's health and the purity of the soul."[14]

Both the humorous and the more serious criticisms of collective education fashioned a vision of female youth as a stage of life during which girls needed protection to preserve feminine innocence. Pedagogical literature responded to these anxieties about the potential dangers of maturing girlhood, though generally without the same wealth of graphic details. Instead, countless writers advocated the cultivation of serious qualities and particularly piety as a way to counter the stormy influence of feminine passions.[15] Most frequently, pedagogical and advice literature recommended directing girls' emotional energy toward

Mettez donc vos filles dans un Pensionnat !

Fig. 7. "Place your girls in boarding schools!" 1831 comic French image suggesting that boarding-school walls were not impenetrable.
Courtesy Bibliothèque Nationale de France. Original source: Frédéric Bouchot, "Mettez donc vos filles dans un pensionnat!" *Le Voisinage,* series of 9 plates published by Aubert in 1832.

spiritual outlets, redirecting their capacity for love toward God. Marie Curo, for example, in her *Etudes morales et religieuses* (1860) repeatedly stressed the importance of suppressing desire and promoting temperance.[16] Educational programs insisted on the need to harness, control, and repress feminine biological instincts. Lajolais stated, "The goal of a proper education is to train the soul to tame the body, to vanquish desires, to suppress guilty affections, and to allow enlightened reason, along with religious sentiment to guide one toward what is best."[17] Many believed with the influential pedagogue Louis Aimé-Martin that boarding-school education did not elevate the soul but rather produced young

Fig. 8. "A boarding-school girl's dreams," 1831 comic French image about schoolgirls'
fantasies.
Courtesy Bibliothèque Nationale de France. Original source: Frédéric Bouchot, *Rêve
d'une pensionnaire,* series of 5 plates published by Aubert in Paris, and Tilt in London,
in 1831.

women attentive to "small-minded devotions, with a boarding-school morality, mechanical talents, a love of pleasures, an ignorance of all things serious and a need to love and be loved."[18]

By the middle decades of the century, girls' boarding schools had nonetheless burgeoned in the French urban landscape, and they represented a common educational experience for daughters of the middle classes. In response, educational authorities established guidelines for their operation involving both a certification process for teachers and an inspection procedure for all lay schools that aspired to secondary status. The concerns underlying the new administrative rulings were both professional and moral; teachers had to have adequate knowledge but also impeccable moral standards in order to open a school.[19] The effort to codify and control the growing number of girls' schools reflected a new concern on the part of municipal and educational officials to ensure that girls were raised in an appropriately "safe" environment.

Control, Discipline, and Morality within the Boarding-School Setting

Efforts to reform secondary girls' schools in the middle decades of the century focused on providing serious Christian education, without the frills associated with aristocratic manners. Ornamental accomplishments such as singing and painting or the speaking of certain foreign languages, notably Italian, were seen as incompatible with an emerging domestic ideology. Both the theatrical productions and the elaborate prize-giving ceremonies associated with elite institutions came under attack as they were seen to encourage girls' vanity. The criticisms directed against the superficiality of girls' education represented, on the one hand, an effort to promulgate a specifically bourgeois vision of serious domestic women. On the other hand, it also clearly responded to anxieties about stimulating girls' passions at an age where emotions were ready to surface.[20]

Headmistresses responded to these criticisms through efforts to present their institutions as secure and moral environments where young girls would thrive in relative isolation from the outside world. Boarding-school advertisements offer an interesting way to explore how teachers during this period represented their institutions, while also revealing cultural assumptions about the necessary environment for raising girls. Most advertisements began by stating that religion and morality were at the heart of the education provided and then went on to note the presence of a garden, the hygienic quality of the air, and the healthy and varied quality of the food served. When male teachers were mentioned, they were always presented as "distinguished," both for their abilities and their morals. Implicitly, these documents suggest that moral and health concerns prevailed over the quality of learning. Finally, frequent mention was made of the quality of surveillance exerted at all moments of the day and night.[21]

The rules and programs elaborated within boarding-school environments testify even more strongly to the French concern to regulate and control every minute of the student's day. From the moment girls were awakened until their final prayer before going to sleep, institutions sought to provide a daily regimen that would keep girls occupied, both mentally and physically, in order to prevent the flights of imagination that educators feared in their young pupils. According to Nathalie de Lajolais, "this uniformity of days and weeks, not to say monotony, is a useful corrective for youth's ardent and capricious spirit. It prevents the internal overexcitement which inevitably occurs in the outside world." She also argued that discipline provided the most important benefit of boarding-school life: "That invariable daily rule with its appropriate balance of work, meals, and fasting, offers a very salutary moral and physical influence."[22]

Pedagogical methods reinforced the control evident in the organization of everyday life. The emphasis on memorization that characterized the French educational system was obviously one way to rein in overactive imaginations. The famous English educator Dorothy Beale responded negatively to her experience as a sixteen year old in a fashionable Parisian school: "imagine our disgust at being required to read English history in Mrs. Trimmer, to learn by heart all Murray's Grammar, to learn even lists of prepositions by heart, in order that we might parse without the trouble of thinking. I learned them with such anger that the list was burnt into my brain, and I can say it now . . . I felt oppressed with the routine life; I, who had been able to moon, grub, alone for hours, to live in a world of dreams and thoughts of my own, was now put into a cage and had to walk round and round like a squirrel. I felt thought was killed."[23] French girls were less critical of memorization in their writings, their complaints focused more often on what they were not allowed to read.

Girls' institutions carefully supervised the reading matter available to their students. Novels were, of course, strictly forbidden, but even the writing of accepted classical authors was often presented only in excerpts. Eugénie Servant expressed her frustration in her diary about reading only selected passages: "I discover a passage from Chateaubriand, Xavier de Maistre or Bernardin de Saint-Pierre, I stop, I read with pleasure, and then at the most interesting moment, crack . . . several periods, the selection goes on no further and I am left with my regrets. When will I be able to read all those books whose names alone make me dream!"[24] In addition, headmistresses monitored students' private correspondence and confiscated or censored all suspect writings, while students' daily activities were also the object of constant surveillance.

The surveillance of girls extended to nighttime as well as daytime. Architectural plans reveal the presence of strategically placed beds for monitors who ensured that students slept during the night. In most institutions, dormitories prevailed over single rooms; the latter were the privilege of older or wealthier students. At times curtains separated one bed from another, but even this encouraged little privacy. The Countess Puliga specified that a *glass* door separate the dormitory of the older and younger students. Still, girls' descriptions of their beds, like that of the garden, reveal that these were among the few spaces where they felt unburdened from the weight of constant discipline. Numerous diaries describe weeping in bed, be it from homesickness, a sense of loneliness, or because of the frustrations of daily life. Some of Pauline Weill's better memories are of playing with friends in her bed, while Eugénie Servant describes pranks played at night within the dormitory.[25] The careful policing of dormitories was part of the general disciplinary program, but it is not clear whether this stemmed from concerns about sexuality. As late as the 1880s most monitors were clearly not looking for lesbian behavior. When three female couples were found in bed together at one of the schools of the Legion of Honor, the report indicates that the night inspectors initially thought nothing of this behavior; only when they heard the girls expressing their desire for each other did the authorities intervene.[26]

The efforts to regulate boarding-school life and provide a moral and hygienic environment involved limiting contact with the outside world. Increasingly, officials urged headmistresses to avoid the public nature of prize-giving ceremonies, while visiting days became more restricted. Indeed families were often perceived as a bad influence on their daughters, too apt to humor girls' passions at an age when these needed to be carefully redirected in appropriate directions. Educators' and pedagogues' frequent mention of female passions and emotions suggests that girls of this age were indeed considered vulnerable; a serious moral and religious education was the necessary safeguard. Excessive religiosity, however, was also viewed as potentially dangerous. Mme Octave Feuillet describes how her family pulled her out of a religious convent in Caen because she threw herself too passionately into religious practices: "They decided they would try to stifle this ardent soul. The list of books was examined; some were burnt. The harp was hidden within a *garde meuble*."[27] Books, music, and even religion required careful surveillance.

Women inspectors' reports reveal how anxiety about morality structured reform efforts. The presence of older women boarders within boarding schools increasingly generated criticism because of the example they might offer to young girls. In the early 1840s, demoiselle Hacault's school came under criticism because of the presence of older girls who wanted to take the teaching exams: "These young women have separate rooms, receive whom they wish, go out when they want without telling the director; they enjoy an improper and dangerous liberty, and recently five of them were expelled for establishing communication with the young men in the vicinity." Headmistress Desbrières was criticized for letting her students exchange love letters with the neighboring male boarders.[28] Other problems arose because of the presence of the headmistress' husband. In 1840, inspectress Molé protested: "One cannot allow a girl of twelve or thirteen, at the age when one silently notices everything, when one is all eyes and ears, to sleep under the same roof as this community [a couple in the prime of life], her parents may indeed have placed her in a boarding school to avoid this problem."[29] Concern about the influence of adult women on adolescent girls can also be found in the debates surrounding the efforts to develop institutional rules for boarding schools. In 1838, departmental authorities insisted that the morality of teacher's aides should also come under close supervision:

"The presence of young women whose passions are already developed amidst young girls whose inclinations and passions are just emerging . . . is frequently the cause of disorders against which the headmistress can do little."[30]

The most alarming reports emphasized that schools were not hermetically sealed from the outside. In the Clipet boarding school, for example, girls encountered the male visitors of older women boarders in the stairwell. The inspectress noted that these encounters "undoubtedly planted unfortunate messages in their hearts."[31] More troubling yet was the evidence that one headmistress, Mme Lebreton, took her boarders and her teacher's aides to dance and strip before a wealthy bachelor, M. Carter, who was described in the report as being afflicted with a "monomania of lechery." Although no physical intimacy resulted, the resemblance here between the prostitute's *maison close* and the *pensionnat de demoiselle* would undoubtedly have struck contemporaries. Not surprisingly, the school was quickly closed down.[32]

These reports certainly suggest that educators, like medical experts, saw both biological and environmental factors combining within the boarding school to produce a particularly volatile situation. The pedagogical concern to control and monitor schoolgirls' thoughts and actions by providing an increasingly regulated school setting naturally had implications for the students within these schools. The following section explores how girls experienced these constraints by focusing in particular on how they expressed feelings and emotions about themselves and others.

On Intimacy, Bodies, and Relationships

Within English boarding schools for girls, pervasive control broke down the barriers between public and private and encouraged an emotional life dependent on discipline and distance. This discipline, however, seems to have been far more internalized among English girls than French.[33] In French boarding schools, discipline operated in a more external fashion and was imposed from above. The nature of institutional life gave little scope for privacy or introspection. In a very material sense these private institutions were wholly public spaces. In classrooms, dining rooms, gardens, and dormitories girls studied, ate, played, and slept collectively with no space, much less a room, of their own. The pedagogical intent behind this organization of daily life was to emphasize and develop a sense of group identity where the individual and the private had little place. Moral preoccupations also factored into this insistence on the group: by preventing the development of intimate relationships, teachers sought to distance or circumvent the undisciplined character of schoolgirl passions. Not surprisingly, however, these efforts encountered resistance.[34]

Private writings and memoirs repeatedly emphasize the burdensome nature of school rules and express resentment toward the walls that cut boarding-school girls off from the outside world, in particular their families. Like boys, girls characterized their schools as "prisons," and in their memoirs described how the school's door closing signaled the end of their childhood: "The large door of the boarding school, of the prison! opened. It closed behind us with a thunderous noise."[35] Boarding-school life meant adjusting to a universe where bells marked off the different activities of the day and where private thoughts and moments were stolen from the imposed daily regime.

Schoolgirls' aspirations for privacy and intimacy were expressed most commonly through friendships. These friendships generally involved violating the rule about always being in groups and were expressed through the exchange of small objects, through letters and poems, and, at times, by escaping surveillance in order to spend time together. In a setting where speaking was controlled and limited and where girls' actions were carefully watched, friends sought to establish intimacy in very material ways: for example, intertwining their initials in books and notebooks in order to mark themselves off as special friends.[36]

These efforts to establish relationships based on personal affinities were systematically discouraged as a result of widespread anxiety in Catholic culture about "particular friendships." Naturally schoolgirls did not use this expression in their own writings; instead they described a variety of attachments that did indeed often detract from the pedagogical project. Certain "perverse" friends introduced girls to forbidden ideas and concepts. In girls' schools "perversion" was less obviously sexual than in boys' schools, but involved more frequently the introduction of improper books or efforts to implant irreligious thoughts.[37] George Sand insisted, however, that the efforts to preserve innocence were themselves insidious: "The major problem in convent education is the exaggeration of chastity. We were not allowed to walk as pairs, we were obliged always to be three, we were not allowed to embrace each other; our innocent correspondences came under scrutiny, and all this would have made us ponder if we had had even the slightest of those tendencies toward bad instincts which we were supposed to harbor."[38]

Schoolgirls' writings contain relatively few direct allusions to their sexuality; Daniel Stern's statement that she stopped menstruating while a student at the Sacred Heart convent is highly unusual, possibly explained by the fact that she wrote this as a mature woman in her memoirs, not in her youthful writings.[39] Catholic culture inspired a general distrust of the body that manifested itself within boarding schools through a concern to keep the body covered at all times, even when washing. Girls rarely mentioned their own physique, except at times their face or hair coloring. Henriette Berthoud, for example, described herself at age nineteen as being in good health and "my cheeks are round and fresh."[40] References to their own sensuality and physical longings remained highly allusive and were expressed in the language they encountered in their readings. At times this emerged in discussions about nature, but it also seems likely that the intense mystic experiences, which many young girls describe in their adolescence, had very real sensual underpinnings. George Sand, in particular, describes her religious conversion in physical terms, using a rhetoric of passion and longing to describe her ecstatic devotions.[41]

Intense romantic friendships do not appear to have flourished, probably because teachers' surveillance prevented such effusions in practice or writing.

Instead, girls wrote about distant worship of women teachers and older girls in the schools. A student at the collège Sévigné in the 1880s, Jeanne Crouzet-Benaben described such youthful friendships as being "exclusive, stormy and full of jealousies." And yet at the same time she insisted these friendships were pure.[42] Schoolgirls expressed their affection through small gestures, like gathering flowers, or by aiding in small tasks, but these "flames" were certainly not encouraged. The diary of a teacher training school student in Le Mans appears quite exceptional in the writer's frankness about her physical longing, perhaps in part because she was somewhat older than the average boarding-school student. In 1883, she expressed her longing for two people in her diary: Miss, one of her teachers, and a nameless "he." The former was a daily presence in her life, a woman toward whom she directed much love and affection and from whom she constantly sought approval. When, for example, she was able to hug and kiss this teacher, her days went better. Her affection for "him" was clearly more sensual but also more abstract, because their contact was more episodic.[43] This young woman's sense of her own sexuality and desires was far more developed than that of the average girl. Not surprisingly, she ended up dropping out of the school.

Despite attempts to seal girls off from contact with the opposite sex, interest in men or in boys appears to have flourished within the boarding-school setting. Curiosity about men was often sparked by the presence of male teachers or the husband of the headmistress within the school; their physical appearance and mannerisms are frequently dissected in personal writings. Mme Leroy Allais, for example, described her mother's boarding school where the writing master M. Courtois had acquired the nickname M. Du Mollet (Mister Calves) because of his leggings: "His tightly stretched stockings and his bow shoes impressed the young girls at least as much as the solemn manner he adopted to teach."[44] The memoir of the Countess Puliga also highlights the physical features of one of her male teachers; M. Dantier, the history and literature professor, is described as an "*ancien beau*" who dressed like a dandy and curled his hair.[45]

These men did not leave schoolgirls indifferent, although evidence for schoolgirl crushes is relatively piecemeal. Amélie Weiler describes one teacher who taught in a school in Strasbourg: "all the girls were fascinated by him. One day he left behind a pair of gloves that were then covered in kisses and hotly disputed."[46] More frequently, girls recorded their physical revulsions. Fanny Kemble described her master for French and Latin as "a clever, ugly, impudent, stuffy, dirty little man, who wrote vaudevilles for the minor theatres and made love to his pupils," while Pauline Weill in her diary expressed her disgust with a male inspector who held her hands while speaking with her.[47] More unusual are this same diarist's frequent allusions in her writings to her future husband, whom she is prepared to love and cherish before having met him. She even wrote him love letters, provoking the mockery of her friends. Her directness in evoking her future married state may be the result of her considerable liberty within the Jewish school where at age sixteen and seventeen she helped out as a teacher's aide. Certainly her diary distinguishes itself from Catholic diaries in its frankness, and her schooling experience distinguishes itself as well in its absence of rules and constraining timetables.

Advertisements to the contrary, boarding schools were not hermetically sealed spaces. Personal writings contain countless references to events and people beyond school walls. Leroy Allais, for example, noted in her memoirs that her brother's *collège* was next to her own boarding school and that windows in both buildings opened onto the courtyard. While the girls were never allowed to linger at these windows, the boys were, "since the authorities considered with reason that the sight of girl boarders and nuns following a cross and banners was unlikely to inspire bad thoughts among male youth." Nonetheless, the author admitted that baby passions (*passionnettes*) were born of such encounters, although they never developed into anything more serious.[48]

Like schoolboys, schoolgirls found ways to escape the control exercised over their movements, generally by seeking out secluded areas of their school such as attics, gardens, and basements. Fifteen-year-old Mathilde Savarin relates one such escapade that reveals how thoroughly she had internalized the messages concerning her body: "Oh how curious and disobedient are the daughters of Eve! We had been forbidden to go into the garden before the castle because of the presence of statues. I decided to go there with a few other girls, I looked at two statues which were not indecent, but at the end of the garden there was an Amphitrite [Goddess of the ocean] that was almost nude; I didn't look at it and I left."[49]

Girls obviously resisted the pedagogical project through daydreaming or romantic longings whose historical traces are unfortunately rare, but as the preceding example shows they also internalized many constraints. Students learned to negotiate the lines between what was acceptable, tolerated, and forbidden behavior; in the latter category went expression of personal affection. As a result, the nature of boarding-school life encouraged forms of dissimulation that may well have left its traces in the lives of adult women.

British and American visitors to France frequently commented on the contrast between the education of Anglo-Saxon and French girls. The relative freedom and autonomy granted in Protestant countries bore little relationship to the cloistered upbringing of the daughters of Marianne. And yet French adult women were often judged superficial, flirtatious, coquettish, and, above all, sexual in a way that English and American women were not; the discipline, order, and modesty of their upbringing appeared to leave few traces. What does this national cultural stereotype tell us about gender relations in France, and what might this reveal about the relationship between cultural representations of sexuality and the lived experiences of French women?

The emphasis on rules, surveillance, and discipline within nineteenth-century girls' boarding schools were in part a response to attitudes about female adolescent sexuality, although the logic underlying these rules was not solely linked to representations of girls' sexuality. Instead teachers and headmistresses used these rules to encourage a sense of group identity, thus stifling girls' individual and sexual identities. Even though the boarding-school experience remained limited to a short period in a girl's life, pedagogues still hoped that the habits acquired at this age would last into adulthood. By the last quarter of the century, the justification for such discipline was increasingly under attack, in part no doubt because of the spread of democratic ideals. Louis Legrand, for example, believed that collective education was a form of aberration since it "robbed girls of all that more or less characterizes them: the spontaneity of sentiment and the happy ignorance of ingenuity. I do not wish to examine or suspect the secrets and dreams of the boarding school; all I know is that one scabby sheep is enough to taint the entire flock and one can never guarantee that such a sheep does not exist."[50]

Girls learned about passions secondhand, through lessons about religion, for example, but they also learned more directly about such matters though their experiences as boarders. Foreign observers were very critical of what these experiences involved. In the 1830s, Emma Willard argued that the discipline underlying girls' boarding schools produced a system that failed to prepare girls "for the duties of life. It keeps them in a state of perpetual infancy; —or rather it makes them like the parts of a great machine. . . . The will revolting at this unremitting surveillance, artifice is practiced to elude its dictates, and habits of deceit thus formed, fretfulness is engendered, and the temper ruined: and when at length the period of escape arrives, it is hailed as the dawn of a brighter world."[51] Schoolgirls' writings offer a more nuanced picture of this process, but one that also emphasizes bending rules and concealing thoughts. Compared to Protestant England and the United States, formal education for middle-class girls in France provided fewer lessons in independence and autonomy, in part at least, because of cultural representations concerning female sexuality. Paradoxically, boarding schools were both secluded and public spaces, secluded from the outside world but public for the individuals within. As a result, girls forged a sense of their identity in contact with others, learning to perform within a universe whose constraints they also learned to negotiate and circumvent. That such learned behavior was later viewed as coquetry and flirtatiousness speaks eloquently to the paradoxes within the disciplinary project. Claiming a sense of self involved drawing attention to oneself through small gestures directed toward others such as poems, letters, and handholding. By both recognizing and seeking to stifle what was perceived as natural female sexuality, boarding schools and their teachers inadvertently helped to produce the sensual women foreigners commented upon so abundantly.

Notes

This chapter greatly benefited from our discussions in Columbus and Bielefeld. My particular thanks go to the editors of the book for their expert organization and sense of collegiality and to Céline Grasser for her apt suggestions and bibliographic guidance.

1. Charlotte Brontë, *The Professor,* ed. Margaret Smith and Herbert Rosengarten (Oxford: Oxford University Press, 1991).
2. See Michel Delon, *Le savoir-vivre libertin* (Paris: Hachette, 2000).
3. Agnès Thiercé maintains that the concept of adolescence did not exist for middle-class girls prior to the end of the century. See her *Histoire de l'adolescence (1850–1914)* (Paris: Belin, 1999).
4. Louis Grimaud, *Histoire de la liberté d'enseignement en France,* vols. 4 and 5 (Paris: Apostolat de la Presse, 1954). For Paris, see Isabelle Bricard, *Saintes et pouliches. L'éducation des jeunes filles au XIXe siècle* (Paris: Albin Michel, 1985), 64; and the *Almanacs de commerce.*
5. A national survey of boarding schools in 1864 revealed the presence of 2,338 religious schools and 1,142 lay schools. Archives Nationales (hereafter cited as AN), F^{17} 6843–6849.
6. See André Rauch, *Le premier sexe. Mutations et crises de l'identité masculine* (Paris: Hachette, 2000), 177–210. For medical attitudes toward women's bodies in France, see Linda Schiebinger, *The Mind Has No Sex? Women in the Origins of Modern Science* (Cambridge, Mass.: Harvard University Press, 1989); and Yvonne Knibiehler and Catherine Fouquet, *La femme et les médecins* (Paris: Hachette, 1983).
7. See chapters by Irene Hardach-Pinke, Céline Grasser, Kathleen Alaimo, and Mary Lynn Stewart.
8. Nathalie de Lajolais, *Le livre des mères de famille et des institutrices sur l'éducation pratique des femmes,* 2d ed. (Paris: Didier, 1843), 181–182.
9. Jean-Louis Brachet, *Traité de l'hystérie* (Paris: Baillère, 1847), cited in Jann Matlock, *Scenes of Seduction: Prostitution, Hysteria, and Reading Difference in Nineteenth-Century France* (New York: Columbia University Press, 1993), 176–177. See, as well, the influential writings of Etienne-Jean Georget, *De la physiologie du système nerveux et spécialement du cerveau* (Paris: J. B. Baillère, 1821).
10. Balzac, *Physiologie du mariage* (1829; reprint, Paris: Garnier-Flammarion, 1968), 94.
11. Matlock, 168–169. See also Ecarnot, "The Country School for Young Ladies," translated from the French in *Pictures of the French: A Series of Literary and Graphic Delineations of French Character* (London: W. S. Orr and Company, 1840), 219. On gendered space, see Sharon Marcus, *Apartment Stories: City and Home in Nineteenth-Century Paris and London* (Berkeley: University of California Press, 1999).
12. Rebecca Rogers, "Le professeur a-t-il un sexe?: les débats autour de la présence d'hommes dans l'enseignement secondaire féminin, 1840–1880," *Clio: Histoire, Femmes et Société* 4 (1996): 221–239.
13. See Gabrielle Houbre, *La discipline de l'amour. Education sentimentale des filles et des garçons à l'âge du romantisme* (Paris: Plon, 1997), 170–185.
14. Henri Duval, *Conseils aux mères de famille* (Paris: Jouhanneau, 1840), cited in Houbre, 26.
15. See, for example, Fanny de Mongellaz, *De l'Influence des femmes sur les moeurs et les destinées des nations, sur leurs familles et la société, et de l'influence des moeurs sur le bonheur de la vie* (Paris: Michaud, 1831); and Claire Rémusat, *Essai sur l'éducation des femmes* (Paris: Ladvocat, 1824).

16. See Yvonne Fumat, "La socialisation des filles au XIXe siècle," *Revue française de sociologie* 52 (1980): 36.

17. de Lajolais, 2.

18. Louis Aimé-Martin, *De l'éducation des mères de famille ou de la civilisation du genre humain par les femmes,* vol. 1 (Brussels: Meline, 1837), 83.

19. See Rebecca Rogers, "Boarding Schools, Women Teachers and Domesticity: Reforming Girls' Secondary Education in the First Half of the Nineteenth Century," *French Historical Studies* 19 (1995): 153–181.

20. Madame Necker de Saussure, *L'éducation progressive ou étude du cours de la vie,* vol. 3 (Brussels: Meline, 1840), 129.

21. For Paris, see Archives départementales de la Seine (hereafter cited as AD Seine) VD^6 158.

22. de Lajolais, 24–27.

23. Cited from Beale's autobiography in Josephine Kamm, *How Different from Us: A Biography of Miss Buss and Miss Beale* (London: Bodley Head, 1958), 24.

24. Eugénie Servant, fall 1879, quoted in Rebecca Rogers, *Les demoiselles de la Légion d'honneur, Les maisons d'éducation de la Légion d'honneur au XIXe siècle* (Paris: Plon, 1992), 216.

25. See the diaries of Eugénie Servant (private archives of the congrégation de la Mère de Dieu) and Pauline Weill (private archives of Philippe Lejeune). The Countess Puliga specified that she slept in a "white flannel bag that closed with a string tied under the arms." Brada (pseudonym for the Countess Puliga), *Souvenirs d'une petite Second Empire* (Paris: Calmann-Lévy, 1921), 41.

26. Rogers, *Les demoiselles,* 138–139.

27. Valérie Feuillet, *Quelques années de ma vie,* 4th ed. (Paris: Calmann Lévy, 1894), 15.

28. AN, F^{17} 12431. For Desbrières, see AD Seine, VD^6 142, n°2. No date is specified.

29. AD Seine, D^{2}T^{1}110 dossier Bournier-Beaulieu, inspection report of 24 August 1840. For other cases revolving around headmistresses' husbands, see AN, F^{17} 12431, dossier Mme Colon, June 1839, and F^{17} 12448, Affaire Millet, summer and fall of 1843.

30. Archives départementales de l'Eure-et Loire, 1 T 72, letter of 5 October 1838.

31. AN, F^{17} 12431, dossier Clipet.

32. Ibid., dossier Lebreton.

33. See Martha Vicinus, *Independent Women, Work and Community for Single Women, 1850–1920* (Chicago: University of Chicago Press, 1985), 165; and Vicinus, "Distance and Desire: English Boarding-School Friendships," *Signs* 9 (1984): 600–622.

34. See Rebecca Rogers, "Schools, Discipline and Community: Diary-Writing and Schoolgirl Culture in Late Nineteenth-Century France," *Women's History Review* 4 (1995): 525–554.

35. Juliette Adam (pseudonym for Juliette Lambert), *Le roman de mon enfance et de ma jeunesse,* 3d ed. (Paris: A. Lemerre, 1902), 68.

36. Examples can be found in George Sand, *Histoire de ma vie,* vol.1 (Paris: Gallimard, 1970), and in the diary of Eugénie Servant (1875–1881).

37.   For an example, see Adam, 236–237.

38.   Sand, 939.

39.   Daniel Stern, *Mes souvenirs* (Paris: Calmann Lévy, 1877). See the new biography, Phyllis Stock-Morton, *The Life of Marie d'Agoult, alias Daniel Stern* (Baltimore: Johns Hopkins University Press, 2000).

40.   Henriette Picanon, *Mon frère et moi. Souvenirs de jeunesse accompagnés de poésies d'E. Berthoud* (Paris: J. Bonhoux, 1876), 51.

41.   Sand, 959–1010.

42.   Jeanne Crouzet-Benaben, *Souvenirs d'une jeune fille bête. Souvenirs autobiographiques d'une des premières agrégées de France* (Paris: Nouvelles Editions Debresse, 1971), 287–298.

43.   Sharif Germie, *Women and Schooling in France, 1815–1914. Gender, Authority and Identity in the Female Schooling Sector* (Keele, England: Keele University Press, 1995), 181–196.

44.   Leroy Allais, *Alphonse Allais, Souvenirs d'enfance et de jeunesse* (Paris: Flammarion, n.d.).

45.   Brada, 88.

46.   Amélie Weiler, *Journal d'une jeune fille mal dans son siècle, 1840–1859* (Strasbourg: La Nuée Bleue, 1994), 180.

47.   Fanny Kemble, *Record of a Girlhood*, vol. 1 (London: Bentley, 1878), 99.

48.   Allais, 138–142.

49.   Private archives of Philippe Lejeune, diary of M. Savarin, 23 June 1881.

50.   Louis Legrand, *Le mariage et les moeurs en France* (Paris: Hachette, 1879), 71.

51.   Emma Willard, *Journal and Letters from France and Great Britain* (Troy, N.Y.: N. Tuttle, printer, 1833), 245.

8 Good Girls versus Blooming Maidens: The Building of Female Middle- and Upper-Class Identities in the Garden, England and France, 1820–1870

Céline Grasser

Picking up on some of the same themes introduced in the two previous chapters, Céline Grasser examines English and French cultural representations of the garden as a site of socialization for middle-class girls. She argues that similar garden activities of girls held different meanings in these two cultural contexts. While the "good girl" of Protestant England worked in the garden toward becoming a rational woman, an efficient organizer, and a clear-sighted educator, in France gardens produced "blooming maidens," biological mothers with a great capacity for emotion, as sensual women. Grasser suggests that these representations of girls in gardens echoed other cultural differences in gender relations as well.

> Rose at 4. After breakfast worked in my Flower garden. Took the dead Snow-drops up. (Adela Capel, Cassiobury Park, 10 March 1842)[1]

> I love you, beloved flowers. When one of your leaves is withered, I watch it fall with sadness; it feels as if one of your joys was going away. (Caroline Normand, Rennes, December 1859)[2]

These two garden stories, concerned with dead flowers, capture a national difference in girls' attitudes about gardens and in girls' identities. Diaries, letters, novels, and paintings are the basis of this chapter's examination of female identity formation and the building of the self as evident in French and English discourses surrounding middle- and upper-class girls in the garden.[3] Girls in their late teens and early twenties in both countries related to the landscape of the garden; they interpreted it by reading, dreaming, gardening, observing, and sharing. The previous chapter showed the more repressive aspects of the construction of French female identity within boarding-school walls; I am interested in the other, more ambiguous, side of the same story. If a girl's ability to control her feelings and desires was indispensable, so was her capacity to use these same feelings to assume a woman's role as wife and mother. Although this woman's role appeared natural, it was nonetheless the product of education, a cultural construction in which the garden—itself a combination of nature and culture—played an instrumental role as an enclosed space where public issues could be dealt with in private and intimate ways.

At once connected to the home and open to the world, the garden was in both countries an intermediate space where girls could indulge in a narcissistic quest for self, a place where they could build the most secret part of their personality, as well as female middle-class identities. The garden not only played a socializing role and conveyed middle-class values and moral virtues by teaching girls to become good wives and mothers, it was also a place associated with sexuality, love, and courtship; as such, it was a setting where girls could express potentially disruptive feelings. Despite similarities between France and England, however, experiences and the understandings of sexual roles and identities took on national cultural forms and meanings: the "good girl" of Protestant England who can be discerned through her discourse on the garden was not Catholic France's "blooming maiden."[4] Becoming a wife, a mother, and, more generally, a woman did not have exactly the same meaning in France and in England, and I will explore the content of these notions comparatively.[5] By contrasting the two national discourses through an analysis of the more intimate aspects of female middle-class identity and cultural practices, I shall try and shed light on what it meant to grow up female in these two countries in the nineteenth century.[6]

The Narcissistic Garden of the Blooming Maiden

In both countries, the garden, in contrast with world and home, was a free zone where girls could indulge in a narcissistic quest for self. This quest, however, took nationally specific forms and meanings. In Catholic France, much more than in Protestant England, girls tended to live secluded lives while waiting for marriage. Often isolated, and chaperoned when in company, the aristocratic or bourgeois French girl would wait for her future to be decided, while pursuing education and practicing domestic as well as more intellectual activities, such as reading and writing. In this context, the garden functioned as a free space where her secret self could expand. As the sixteen-year-old Aurore Dupin, later George Sand, wrote to a school friend of hers: "I spend my life in the garden, only outside can I breathe freely."[7] In the garden, the French girl became part of the natural world, a "blooming maiden" among the flowers, her "daughters"

Fig. 9. *Woman Reading or Springtime,* Claude Monet, 1872.
Courtesy the Walters Art Gallery, Baltimore.

and "sisters," as horticulture and botany guides for women put it.[8] *A Woman Reading or Springtime,* painted by Claude Monet in 1872 (Figure 9), is a typical representation of this "blooming maiden": all in white, pure, modest, and virginal, she sits on the grass in the shade of a shrub and reads. Her dress looks like a whorl of petals. Specks of light extend the little flowers of the foreground onto it, associating the young woman with the natural world. She is a flower among the flowers.

Condemned to while away their solitude in the garden, French middle-class girls were prone to muse over themselves, their future, their feelings, and their sensations. Lacking an opportunity for action, they exercised their imagination, as well as a great capacity for emotion, using the garden and its changes as a metaphor for their fate. Two recurrent and conflicting attitudes organized their musings: between spring and winter, dawn and dusk, French girls would hope and despair. They hesitated constantly between optimism and faith in the future on the one hand, and pessimism and uncertainty regarding what was to come on the other. In the garden by moonlight, French girls assumed a contemplative attitude and gave way to meditations lulled by the song of the nightingale. "Are you trying, by your melancholy warbling, to soothe the soul of those kept awake by their sufferings?" Caroline Normand asked the "gentle musician" (14 August 1857), while even a girl as full of life as Lucile Le Verrier, the daughter of a famous Parisian astronomer, admitted that she "always ended up crying" when listening to the nightingale by the cypresses in the evening. "It is so exquisite," she added, "and at the same time it leaves me with a feeling of emptiness."[9] Melancholy, sadness, and death, perceived quite complacently as an alternative to choosing a life path, filled these evening meditations: "Night has come, death will come" reads as a litany in Catholic girls' diaries.[10]

In stark contrast with the melancholy of the night, the "smiling spring morning" stood as a metaphor for all that was bright and cheerful in French girls' lives. Its evocation implied a wide-ranging use of the senses; smell, sight, hearing, and touch combined to create a moment of harmony. As Caroline Normand wrote in her diary, "The half-open roses exhale their sweetest perfume, this breath of the flowers; the flexible stems swing softly under the gentle breeze; birds flitting gaily from branch to branch sing their hymns of love which carry the aspirations of a pure heart; bright dewdrops clinging to flowers' petals add glitter to freshness, while reflecting the colors of the prism under the first kisses of the sun."[11] The emotion that followed was an unmistakable call for sensuality and, in the garden, French girls sometimes gave way to the voice of nature. One June morning, Marie-Edmée Pau, a young bourgeois girl from Nancy, confided to her diary: "the big branches of the Virginia creeper . . . , flexible but already vigorous, caress my cheeks . . . , and I, who don't like human tenderness, have just caught myself kissing the tip of one of those festoons which brushed my lips almost like a friend." This disturbing sensual need was often diverted and sublimated into an outburst of expansive piety, especially in the second half of the nineteenth century, when religion became more emotional. After her burst of tenderness, Marie-Edmée Pau then added, "Well! Yes, I love you, O Nature, creation of my God! I admire you."[12] In French gardens the soul was touched through the senses, and the eyes turned to heaven.[13]

The emotional and physical proximity of the French girl to nature and sweet-scented flowers was an innocent outlet for a repressed sensuality.[14] It was also the means of awakening to a woman's life and role. Catholic girls were meant to serve God and become wives. They could contract a sacred union by entering religious life, but they could also choose marriage and childbearing. Girls were metaphorically taught their reproductive destiny by observing the cycle of nature in the garden. As the French historian Jules Michelet wrote in 1858 in *The Woman,* a famous and controversial book: girls who "have learnt early the generation of plants and insects," by observing and gardening, "know that, in every species, life reproduces itself by the egg, and that nature as a whole is unremittingly engaged in the process of ovulation." Girls thus "won't be surprised to follow the common rule." And, Michelet explained, "nothing is easier than the revelation of sex," or, to be more precise, of menstruation, if the mother tells the following dream to her daughter, in order to make things clear for her: "You were alone in the garden, you had pricked yourself on the rose-bush. I wanted to cure your wound, and I could not do it: you were wounded for life."[15] The association with the rosebush naturalized the event; the onset of menses, thus revealed, no doubt appeared as very simple and natural. Unmediated by religion, this direct evocation of female biology created a scandal. However, the message conveyed by Catholic education was very much the same, if more cryptic. Marie-Edmée Pau understood it very well, when she wrote in her diary: "Nature embellishes herself to become lovable; she loves in order to multiply; she multiplies to serve, and she serves to accomplish her destiny, which is to prove she loves to Him she must love."[16] More simply, French girls discovered by gardening that they were by nature biological mothers. They internalized their reproductive role, which was perceived as women's creative side, as is evidenced in the joy that bursts out of the cry of Caroline Normand: "I watch the seeds I've sown shoot: I am a gardener, at last!"[17] This understanding of French girls as natural and biological mothers, combined with their dispositions for emotions and sensuality, rendered their association with the garden highly ambivalent and even dangerous: while the garden was supposed to be an innocent educator, it could easily become a perverse initiator.[18] The French girl who followed her instincts in the garden was not only *potentially* a virgin or a mother, but also a fallen woman, as Gustave Courbet suggested in *The Hammock,* an 1844 painting with somewhat biblical overtones (Figure 10). Representing a young girl asleep in a hammock in dark shrubbery and hinting at the potential consequences of her natural sensuality, this painting is a perfect image of the ambivalence of the association of the French girl with the garden. Although the girl is asleep, and innocent, she is pictured with a most inappropriate kind of flower, luxuriant red roses, the symbol of passionate sexual love. Their scent, no doubt, pervades her dreams. She has untied the top of her dress; the viewer can discern her breasts and nipples through the thin fabric of her shirt. One of her hands rests directly over her genitals, and, following the direction it indicates, the gaze leads up a garden path to a green, bright, warm, smooth, and lush place. In woman's sensual nature lies a path to the Garden of Eden. There is, however, a darker side: the hammock—*not a very stable instrument*—hangs right above a swamp, suggesting that giving way to sensuality could lead to a fall with dire consequences. In the garden, a virgin is a potential Eve.

Much more than merely a romantic place for courtship, the garden in France was instrumental in revealing mutual attractions. It brought friends together and, more dangerously, it initiated love between a man and a woman by providing a sensual atmosphere. Romantic literature, in particular, offered a model of love in which nature, in Victor Hugo's words, "pungent, voluptuous and fragrant," hinted at physical pleasure, even if this sensual promise was often sublimated in an outburst of pure, chaste, and spiritual feelings. In a Parisian garden presented as a "temple of greenery," nature thus brought together the heroes of Hugo's *Les misérables:* sitting on a bench, Marius and Cosette followed nature's guidance and fell in love.[19] If things were often more complicated in real life, advice manuals nevertheless anxiously pointed out that girls "must avoid taking strolls in secluded walks, where one could suppose they look for a companion to fill their solitude."[20] And indeed, Lucile Le Verrier's story bears evi-

Fig. 10. Gustave Courbet, *The Hammock*, 1844.
Oskar Reinhart am Römerholz Collection, Winthertour. Reproduced in: Maria Blunden and Godfrey Blunden, *La peinture de l'impressionisme*. Geneva: Skira, 1981.

dence that this sort of advice was not entirely ill founded. In a letter to her cousin and future husband, Lucien Magne, she recalled her falling in love with him in the garden of his parents at Eaubonne: "It was there that, as a cousin, I started to feel more than affection for you. . . . Do you remember my first visit? In the evening, we played hide-and-seek, and we hid in a shrubbery where we had to huddle together. Definitely, Mr mimi, I already loved you well."[21]

While marriage was more often the result of a matrimonial strategy than of mutual attractions formed under nature's guidance, the garden was nevertheless the place where French engaged couples escaped to find some intimacy, hold hands, and kiss.[22] Being surrounded by nature enhanced physical sensations and desire; twining plants evoked other kinds of embraces and, in the second half of the nineteenth century, a French girl in the garden with her fiancé would sometimes admit to yearning for something more fulfilling. In 1866, after visiting the park of Sélignat, Claire Pic, aged eighteen, recorded in her diary the emotion she felt at the contact of an exuberant nature. She then connected this emotion with love and the presence of her future husband, Adolphe, and concluded: "I think that if I had a second home in a beautiful countryside, and the opportunity for enjoying it, waiting would become impossible for me. Love is more intense [and] more expansive . . . under the sky and the trees than in a room or a drawing-room."[23] By the 1870s, literature had become more explicit in revealing sexual fantasies. In Zola's *Faute de l'abbé Mouret*, the garden not only brought the lovers together but initiated them into lovemaking as well. In the middle of a new Eden, a tree of knowledge guided Serge and Albine through their first sexual experience, metaphorically suggested by a graphic description of the tree: "Its sap was so vigorous that it was trickling down its bark, steeping it in a fecund mist, making it the very virility of the earth. . . . At times, its loins made cracking sounds, its limbs stiffened like those of a woman giving birth; the sweat of life that trickled down its bark sprinkled the grass around, exhaling the softness of desire, swamping the air with emotion, making the glade pale with pleasure. The tree then drooped along with its shadow, its carpet of turf, its belt of thick brushwood. It was sensual delight embodied."[24] The sin was committed under the tree; sex was revealed and approved, by Zola if not generally, opening the way to sexuality and the quest for pleasure. But this is fiction, of course, and certainly not fiction for innocent girls. In contrast, the sensible girl Claire Pic added, after admitting her yearning: "Yet love is no deeper for all that, so given the present circumstances, things are quite fine as they are."[25]

The Sensible and Social Garden of the Good English Girl

As in France, in nineteenth-century England the garden was also a place where girls pursued their education and built their personality. In a Protestant context, this quest for self took the name of self-education; in the garden, girls had to cultivate and better themselves. Indeed, unlike her French counterpart, the "good girl" of Protestant England was not a sensitive flower waiting for her fate to be decided.[26] Always on the move, she combined activities and could often be seen reading while walking and exercising.[27] In the garden and beyond, she had access to a wider world; she was active and much freer to meet people of both sexes and of different classes, provided it was in a socially acceptable context. The garden gate was a filter, but by no means the boundary of a girl's horizons: English girls were sensible and could be trusted to exercise their judgment, wherever they went. They had not been educated as "heroines in romance," as Maria Edgeworth put it; from an early age, their sensitivity had been "managed with peculiar caution" and their "reasoning powers" cultivated, just like those of boys. While French female identity was built in natural and biological contrast with male identity, the construction and understanding of gender was much more subtle in England. As their biological role was not emphasized, Englishwomen differed from men not so much by their intellectual capacities as, simply, by their opportunities. "Women," as Edgeworth remarked, were "called upon for the daily exercise of quiet domestic virtues" only *from their situation and duties in society*."[28] I would argue that this construction of gender differences, which was only lightly anchored in the biological, and hence much more tenuous and questionable than in France, accounts for the earlier development of a strong feminist movement in England, as opposed to France where the perception of sharper boundaries between the sexes slowed the development of feminist perceptions.[29]

Unlike her French counterpart, the young Englishwoman was not regarded as a biological mother. She was expected to become a rational woman, aware of her rank and able to position herself within a hierarchical community, a confirmed organizer capable of housekeeping and a clear-sighted educator.[30] In the garden, she learned such a woman's role. There, rather than daydreaming in the grass, young Emily Shore looked after her siblings. She not only took them "out of doors" and botanized with them but also told them stories while "walking about the garden," thus learning to communicate her knowledge. She added: "this has been my practice ever since I was six or seven years old, and is a great amusement both to them and myself."[31] In the English garden, the older sister appeared as a "little mother" looking after her "children." Painted by Lord Leighton around 1862, *Sisters* records this ambiguity: the title of this painting set in a garden pavilion is our sole means of understanding the real nature of the relationship between the two characters (Figure 11).[32] When no sibling was around, gardening and pet keeping prepared girls for housekeeping. In combination with lessons from her governess, Adela Capel, the fourteen-year-old daughter of the Earl of Essex, recorded working in her little garden almost every day. She kept both a flower and a kitchen garden, dug, hoed, raked, weeded, reaped heartily, and produced enough vegetables to nourish an impressive number of pets. By tending these, she learned all about the practical management of a flock, although one hopes she had fewer casualties in her human nursery later on.[33]

In the garden, the English girl also learned her rank and how to relate to servants and "inferiors" by transmitting orders to the gardeners.[34] In some cases, this training extended to estate management. Anne Lister, who was to inherit her uncle's estate near Halifax, visited farms and planted trees in the garden with her aunt as a young woman in the late 1810s, before becoming an improver in her own right.[35] Even when not actually managing the estate, educated English girls had to master a reading of space and landscapes through visual codes very similar to those learned by boys, suggesting a totally different relation to land, landownership, and thus status and power than a French girl was likely to master, with her lowered gaze and her focus on garden details. While the English girl learned such a visual approach to space by drawing landscapes, her French counterpart was kept from such a masculine view of the world: drawing was good for her according to advice manuals, but she was expected to choose less ambitious topics, such as flowers, which could later be put to good use as models for embroideries. Although the English girl thus literally had better "prospects" than her French counterpart, gender difference still gave rise to different opportunities; while English girls learned through drawing landscapes and garden work, young men learned by traveling.[36]

Like her French counterpart, the good girl in England was supposed to be pious and worship God. In a largely Protestant context, however, this took a very

Fig. 11. Lord Leighton, *Sisters*, 1862.
Courtesy Julian Hartnoll.

different meaning. English girls did not indulge in devotional outbursts when contemplating nature. Because Protestantism posited that man was on earth to perform earthly works whose success was a sign of God's blessing, deeds were expected, not words.[37] Instead of focusing on self-centered garden activities, middle- and upper-class girls did a lot of visiting, learning to position both themselves and their family socially.[38] Not only did they call on neighbors of the same rank, often with vegetable gifts from their garden, they also visited the poor and did a lot of relief work on their own. While Adela Capel regularly took vegetables to poor people "out of her gardens," Clarissa Trant made quite similar resolutions.[39] On 29 March 1828, she thus wrote in her diary: "I endeavoured to spend this summer a little more profitably than the preceding ones: instead of passing hour after hour in reading or writing in my Grotto among the rocks, hoping I dare say, that when I raised my eyes I would by accident meet those of some delightful and unexpected visitor, I made myself better acquainted with our poor neighbours."[40]

Often designed for young people regardless of their sex, English natural history books reminded their readers that the study of nature was the study of God's creation.[41] However, scientific interest and a taste for daring experiments prevailed over worship in the diaries of girls who practiced botany or entomology. Emily Shore, an Anglican clergyman's daughter who was an enthusiastic naturalist, was perfectly aware that "it is particularly important not to come too hastily to conclusions, but to study facts from observation frequently and most carefully before any inference is drawn from them."[42] For the sake of science, she was not averse to experimenting on God's creation, as she recorded in her diary: "I attempted to kill [a] gnat [. . .] by severing the head from the body; I had no sooner done this than, to my astonishment, the head, legs and wings all flew off briskly together, leaving the decapitated trunk behind. This gnat, on near examination, is very beautiful and delicate."[43] Far from showing a moral interest in the fate of floral sisters like their French counterparts, English girls proved themselves keen observers with scientific minds, ready to undertake experiments, just like their brothers and often with them. The only difference between them was one of opportunities: while men could make their work public, women had to be content with serving as helpmates to male relatives.[44] This acknowledged proximity of mind, however, certainly explains the freedom of encounters between young people of both sexes in England. Indeed, intellectual sympathy and discussion, not mutual attraction based on the senses, were at the heart of friendship in the English garden. If anything forbidden were to happen, a wilder setting was required; as in Elizabeth Gaskell's *Wives and Daughters*, illicit encounters happened in the woods, not in the garden.

This construction of the English girl as a rational woman with intellectual capacities does not mean that sensuality was not part of her personality. English girls were not prone to dwell upon themselves but, upon their renewed contact with nature after long confinements, they characteristically recorded emotions and sensations in ways not dissimilar to the solitary French girl. As Emily Shore

Fig. 12. Atkinson Grimshaw, *The Rector's Garden: Queen of the Lilies,* 1877.
Courtesy Harris Museum and Art Gallery, Preston, Lancashire, UK.

wrote on 5 May 1838: "It was the first evening walk I have had for seven or eight months, and it seemed to me like Paradise. There was just breeze enough to temper the heat of the descending sun; the sky was cloudless, the birds singing joyously, the air scented with wallflowers and primroses; the shrubs were tinted with the fresh green foliage of May. And oh, the soft, soft cool green turf! I ran about it as if I was still a child; I stooped down and pressed it with my hand. . . . I rushed about hither and thither, unable to control my delight; I took off my bonnet, and stood still to let the air blow through my hair and cool my face. . . . Mary, too, could not resist the temptation of sitting down on the shady grass. I think she was as happy as I was."[45] If nearly all the senses were mentioned, the emphasis was not so much on smell and touch colored by imagination, as in France, as on sight and touch rendered by graphic descriptions. In English sources sensual delight was above all tactile and visual. This is what Atkinson Grimshaw recorded when he painted *The Rector's Garden: Queen of the Lilies,* in 1877 (Figure 12).[46] The girl, all in white and wearing a hat that looks like a halo, stands by a white lily with a dreamy air. She is pure, chaste, and innocent; the garden gate is closed, but the viewer senses that the painter fantasized her as a sensual woman in the making. She is surrounded by a highly detailed garden with exuberant green foliage, a true pleasure of the sight, and she gently holds a stem of a lily. She is an angel in the garden, prefiguring the "angel in the house" she will become, the ideal Victorian housewife perceived quite explicitly, in Coventry Patmore's poem, as both sensual and sexual.[47]

When it came to the choice of a partner, however, English girls did not let their senses guide them. Marriage was a no-nonsense business in which, because of their greater freedom, they had much more to lose than their French counterparts.[48] In both literature and life, the garden was indeed associated with love and proposal, but only as a setting, not as a means. Margaret Oliphant thus recalled the first time somebody paid her "a compliment . . . which gave [her] that bewildering happy sense of being able to touch somebody else's heart—which was half fun and infinitely amusing, yet something more." She was sixteen, and the "speaker" was a young Irish minister who had joined her and her brother on a walk. She went on: "when we were passing and looking at a very pretty cottage on the slope of the hill at Everton, embowered in gardens and shrubberies, he suddenly looked at me and said, 'It would be Elysium.' I laughed till I cried at this speech afterwards, though at the moment [I was] demure and startled. But the little incident remains to me, as so many scenes in my early life do, like a picture suffused with a soft delightful light: the glow in the young man's eyes; the lowered tone and little speech aside; the soft thrill of meaning which was nothing and yet much."[49] The romantic setting of a garden could indeed trigger a declaration, but more was needed for the good girl to surrender. Sensible English girls were expected to be able to guard themselves and choose wisely; discussion and knowledge of the other were therefore the keys to a successful match. As Emily Birchall wrote to her best friend after her engagement, "Just as we were going down the carriage drive, he proposed. . . . Instead of going in we walked about the lawn and garden talking it all over for half an hour."[50] In English gardens, potential partners walked and discussed business well before they thought of kissing.

Through an exploration of the discourses surrounding girls in the garden in both France and England, one can see the building and understanding of female middle-class identities and of sexual roles in national contexts. Similar garden activities were endowed with different meanings by middle- and upper-class girls in these two cultural contexts. While the "good girl" of Protestant England walked out of the garden as a rational woman, an efficient organizer, and a clear-sighted educator, relying on sight and touch, Catholic France's "blooming maiden" emerged as a biological mother with a great capacity for emotion, as a sensual woman privileging smell and imagination. Naturally these cultural constructions of female identities also shaped and informed both the understanding of male identities and the relations between the sexes. Although deeply rooted, they contained seeds of emancipation and of frustration and, in both countries, allowed individuals to reconfigure their meanings. In England, while the managerial and social role of the housewife, or a chosen and active spinsterhood, could be rewarding, the acknowledgement of women's intellectual capacities in the context of limits upon female ambition could lead women with a potential for public action to frustration: they became "invalids" and re-clined on their sofa waiting for better days.[51] In France, beyond happy mother-hood, faith, and a taste for emotions of all kinds could be the high road to religious life and to action, while hysteria always loomed behind unfulfilled sen-sual promises.[52]

Notes

I would like to thank the editors and the group at large for the intellectual stimulation and the fun. Special thanks to Katie Holmes for sharing with me her perceptive way of reading diaries and gardens and, most particularly, to Rebecca Rogers for her early en-thusiasm, intellectual generosity, countless readings, and for erasing the most obvious residual traces of my Frenchness.

1. Adela Capel, *Diary for the Years 1841 and 1842*, D/Z32 F1, Hertfordshire County Record Office, in Amanda Vickery, ed., *Women's Language and Experience, 1500–1940: Women's Diaries and Related Sources* (Marlborough: Adam Matthew Publications, 1996), microfilm collection, part 1, reel 16.

2. Caroline Normand, *Souvenirs et pensées d'une jeune fille, juillet 1857–avril 1861* (Rennes: Chez les principaux libraires, 1865), 111–113.

3. Girls' diaries constitute the main sources for this chapter. Philippe Lejeune, *Le Moi des demoiselles, Enquête sur le journal de jeune fille* (Paris: Seuil, 1993); and Harriet Blodgett, ed., *"Capacious Hold-All": An Anthology of Englishwomen's Diary Writings* (Charlottesville: University of Virginia Press, 1991) are both most useful. A subtle and perceptive approach of girls' diary writing in relation with the building of the self can be found in Colette Cosnier, *Le silence des filles, De l'aiguille à la plume* (Paris: Fayard, 2001). See also the introduction of Valerie Sanders, ed., *Records of Girlhood: An Anthology of Nineteenth-Century Women's Childhoods* (Aldershot, England: Ashgate, 2000), 1–21.

4. Protestantism and Catholicism are to be understood here as largely secular moral viewpoints whose influence pervades the two national cultures I study beyond the existing diversity of religious movements and denomina-tions in both countries. I am not arguing that there are no differences within these movements; there are, just as there are differences related to a more precise appreciation of social status and of urban and rural logics that I could not address here.

5. Contrasting two key studies on gender and middle-class identity formation, that of Davidoff and Hall for England and that of Smith for France, offers one way of understanding the difference between the two countries that emphasizes religion as an explanatory factor and parallels my discussion here. See Leonore Davidoff and Catherine Hall, *Family Fortunes: Men and Women of the English Middle Class 1780–1850* (London: Routledge & Kegan Paul, 1987); and Bonnie G. Smith, *Ladies of the Leisure Class: The Bour-geoises of Northern France in the Nineteenth Century* (Princeton, N.J.: Prince-ton University Press, 1981).

6. For the general framework that informs this paper, see Philippe Ariès and Georges Duby, eds., *Histoire de la vie privée,* vol. 4, *De la Révolution à la Grande Guerre* (Paris: Seuil, 1987), especially the chapter by Alain Corbin, "Coulisses," 413–611, on most of the issues I deal with. On girls' education in France, see Marie-Françoise Lévy, *De mères en filles, l'éducation des françaises 1850–1880* (Paris: Calmann-Lévy, 1984), 103–150. For England, see Joan N. Burstyn, *Victorian Education and the Ideal of Womanhood* (London: Croom Helm, 1980); and Deborah Gorham, *The Victorian Girl and the Feminine Ideal* (Bloomington: Indiana University Press, 1982). For insights on the understanding of national identities in a gendered and comparative perspective, see Michèle Cohen, *Fashioning Masculinity: National Identity and Language in the Eighteenth Century* (London: Routledge & Kegan Paul, 1996); Linda Colley, *Britons, Forging the Nation 1707–1837* (London: Vintage, 1996); and Clarissa Campbell Orr, ed., *Wollstonecraft's Daughters: Womanhood in England and France 1780–1920* (Manchester: Manchester University Press, 1996), 1–42.

7. Sand to Jane and Chérie Bazouin, October 1820, George Sand, *Correspondance,* vol. 25 (Paris: Garnier, 1991), 12.

8. See, for example, Comte de Foelix, *Botanique et horticulture des dames,* in Jean-Jacques Granville, *Les fleurs animées,* vol. 2 (Paris: G. de Gonet, 1847), 185–187 and 190.

9. Le Verrier to Mme Léonie Gavarni, 8 May 1871, Lucile Le Verrier, *Journal d'une jeune fille Second Empire (1866–1878)* (Cadeilhan: Zulma, 1994), 176. See also Sand to Chérie Bazouin, May 1821, Sand, vol. 25, 36.

10. Marie-Edmée Pau, *Journal* (Paris: Plon, 1876), 190, entry for 21 July 1863. See also Normand, 41–42, November 1858.

11. Normand, 197–198, Pensée XXIV.

12. Pau, 438, 13 June 1869

13. For a useful overview, see Gérard Cholvy, *Etre Chrétien en France au XIXe siècle, 1790–1914* (Paris: Seuil, 1997).

14. Alain Corbin, *Le miasme et la jonquille. L'odorat et l'imaginaire social XVIIIe–XIXe siècles* (Paris: Flammarion, 1986), 227–228.

15. Jules Michelet, *La femme* (1858; reprint, Paris: Flammarion, 1981), 144–146.

16. Pau, 431, 12 April 1869.

17. Normand, 144, April 1861.

18. Apart from Alain Corbin, see, on sentimental education, Gabrielle Houbre, *La discipline de l'amour, L'éducation sentimentale des filles et des garçons à l'âge du romantisme* (Paris: Plon, 1997), 154–283. On girls' bodies, see Louise Bruit Zaidman et al., *Le corps des jeunes filles de l'Antiquité à nos jours* (Paris: Perrin, 2001), especially Jean-Claude Caron, "Jeune fille, jeune corps: objet et catégorie (France, XIXe–XXe siècles)," 167–188.

19. Victor Hugo, *Les misérables* (1862; reprint, Paris: Le livre de poche, 1985), vol. 2, 460–461; vol. 3, 34–35, 53.

20. Louise d'Alq, *Le savoir-vivre en toutes les circonstances de la vie* (Paris: F. Ebhardt, c.1867), 40.

21. Le Verrier, 254, October 1873.

22. Ibid., 223 and 254, August and October 1873.

23. Claire Pic, unpublished diary [Association Pour l'Autobiographie], 21 May 1866. Claire Pic was the daughter of a physician living in Bourg-en-Bresse.

24.   Emile Zola, *La faute de l'abbé Mouret* (1875; reprint, Paris: Le livre de poche, 1985), 163–165 and 241–245.

25.   *Pic*, 21 May 1866.

26.   On the "good girl" and formative literature, see Judith Rowbotham, *Good Girls Make Good Wives: Guidance for Girls in Victorian Fiction* (Oxford: Blackwell, 1989). On man and the natural world in England, see Keith Thomas, *Dans le jardin de la nature, La mutation des sensibilités en Angleterre à l'époque moderne* (Paris: Gallimard, 1985).

27.   See, for example, Agnes Grey walking by the park, "enjoying the threefold luxury of solitude, a book, and pleasant weather," Anne Brontë, *Agnes Grey* (1847; reprint, Harmondsworth: Penguin, 1988), 144.

28.   Maria Edgeworth and Richard Lovell Edgeworth, *Essays on Practical Education*, vol. 1 (London, 1815), 380. The emphasis is mine.

29.   That could be a way of understanding the "French singularity" discussed in Mona Ozouf, *Les mots des femmes, Essai sur la singularité française* (Paris: Fayard, 1995), 323–397.

30.   On a woman's role in Georgian England, see Amanda Vickery, *The Gentleman's Daughter, Women's Lives in Georgian England* (New Haven, Conn.: Yale University Press, 1998). Robert B. Shoemaker, *Gender in English Society, 1650–1850: The Emergence of Separate Spheres?* (Harlow: Longman, 1998) provides a useful overview.

31.   *Journal of Emily Shore* (London: Kegan Paul, Trench, Trübner and Co., 1891), 33–34, 30 January and 9 February 1833.

32.   Christopher Newall, *The Art of Lord Leighton* (London: Phaidon, 1990), 39.

33.   See, for example, entries for 3 May 1841, 29 June 1841, 5 July 1841, 6 August 1841, and 11 February 1842.

34.   Capel, entries for 5 July 1841, 26 November 1841, and 21 March 1842.

35.   *I Know My Own Heart: The Diaries of Anne Lister 1791–1840*, ed. Helena Whitbread (New York: New York University Press, 1992), 68–69, 126, 130, and 229, entries for the years 1818 to 1822. See also Jill Liddington, *Female Fortune, Land, Gender and Authority: The Anne Lister Diaries and Other Writings, 1833–36* (London: Rivers Oram, 1998).

36.   See Ann Bermingham, "Elegant Females and Gentlemen Connoisseurs: The Commerce in Culture and Self-Image in Eighteenth-Century England," in *The Consumption of Culture, 1600–1800: Image, Object, Text*, ed. Ann Bermingham and John Brewer (London: Routledge & Kegan Paul, 1995), 489–513.

37.   See Max Weber, *L'éthique protestante et l'esprit du capitalisme* (1947; reprint, Paris: Pocket, 1964). On the religious context in England, see James Obelkevich, "Religion," in *The Cambridge Social History of Britain, 1750–1950*, vol. 3, *Social Agencies and Institutions*, ed. F. M. L. Thompson (Cambridge: Cambridge University Press, 1990), 311–356.

38.   On social positioning, see Leonore Davidoff, *The Best Circles: Society Etiquette and the Season* (London: Croom Helm, 1973); and Elizabeth Langland, *Nobody's Angels: Middle-Class Women and Domestic Ideology in Victorian Culture* (Ithaca, N.Y.: Cornell University Press, 1995).

39.   Capel, entries for 29 June 1841 and 3 November 1841.

40.   *The Journal of Clarissa Trant, 1800–1832* (London: John Lane, 1925), 240. See also F. K. Prochaska, "Philanthropy," in *The Cambridge Social History*

of Britain, 1750–1950, vol. 3, *Social Agencies and Institutions,* ed. F. M. L. Thompson (Cambridge: Cambridge University Press, 1990), 357–393.

41. See, for example, Priscilla Wakefield, *Domestic Recreation, or Dialogues Illustrative of Natural and Scientific Subjects* (London: Darton and Harvey, 1806), 17. On women's education in a particular non-conformist context, see Ruth Watts, *Gender, Power and the Unitarians in England, 1760–1860* (Harlow: Longman, 1998).

42. Shore, 119, 9 September 1835.

43. Ibid., 67, 17 September 1833.

44. This point is discussed in Ann B. Shteir, *Cultivating Women, Cultivating Science: Flora's Daughters and Botany in England 1760 to 1860* (Baltimore: Johns Hopkins University Press, 1996).

45. Shore, 246, 5 May 1838.

46. Alexander Robertson, *Atkinson Grimshaw* (London: Phaidon, 1988), 70.

47. On the "stratagems of sensuality," and on Patmore's poem, see Peter Gay, *The Tender Passion: The Bourgeois Experience, Victoria to Freud,* vol. 2 (Oxford: Oxford University Press, 1986), 270–312.

48. On courtship, see Vickery, *The Gentleman's Daughter,* 39–58. See also Michael Mason, *The Making of Victorian Sexuality* (Oxford: Oxford University Press, 1995), 109–133; and Houbre, *La discipline de l'amour,* 255–268. See also Rowbotham, 11–52; and Gabrielle Houbre, "Demoiselles catholiques et *misses* protestantes: deux modèles éducatifs antagonistes au XIXe siècle," *Bulletin de la Société d'histoire du protestantisme français* 146 (2000): 49–68.

49. Mrs Harry Coghill, ed., *Autobiography and Letters of Mrs. Margaret Oliphant* (Leicester: Leicester University Press, 1974), 15.

50. Letter from the future Emily Birchall, 22 October 1872, David Verey, ed., *The Diary of a Victorian Squire: Extracts from the Diaries and Letters of Dearman and Emily Birchall* (Gloucester: Alan Sutton, 1983), 48. See also, for a literary example, Charlotte Brontë, *Jane Eyre* (1847; reprint, Harmondsworth: Penguin, 1996), 278–288.

51. See, for example, Miss Williams, in Charlotte Mary Yonge, *The Clever Woman of the Family* (1865; reprint, London: Macmillan, 1902), 32–34. See also Elaine Showalter, *The Female Malady: Women, Madness, and English Culture, 1830–1980* (Harmondsworth: Penguin, 1985).

52. On religious life and the possibilities of action it offered, see Rebecca Rogers, "Retrograde or Modern? Unveiling the Teaching Nun in Nineteenth-Century France," *Social History* 23, no. 2 (1998): 146–164. Thank you, Rebecca, for pointing out the hysteric to me.

Part Three: Redefining Girlhood:
Competing Discourses
on Female Adolescence,
1880–1950

9 The Authority of Experts: The Crisis of Female Adolescence in France and England, 1880–1920

Kathleen Alaimo

Kathleen Alaimo begins Part Three, on changing discourses on girlhood, by examining the emergence of modern and highly gendered notions of adolescence in France and England. She argues that during the late nineteenth and early twentieth centuries the scientific study of female adolescence linking physiology, psychology, and pedagogy tended to make girls captives of their bodies in ways boys were not. With few exceptions, the scientific study of puberty in girls seemed to reinforce conventional moral arguments favoring limits on girls' and women's activities. Experts rooted their discourses in seemingly immutable "natural" phenomena. Through their careful tracking of the girl's passage through puberty, experts sharpened the gendered nature and experience of adolescence.

In 1900, the French education bureaucracy urged its teachers to turn their attention to adolescence. Identifying the education of adolescents as a "singular service to the nation," officials called upon teachers to educate, socialize, and moralize French youth.[1] Fortunately for teachers, they were able to draw on a substantial body of expert literature examining the nature and challenges of adolescence. Taking as its point of departure the larger debate over the meaning of adolescence in modern societies, this chapter focuses on the development of an expert discourse on female adolescence in late nineteenth-century England and France. First, I explore the emergence of a heightened concern about youth in the late nineteenth century and the increasingly professionalized nature of the discussions triggered by these concerns. Second, I investigate the particular social and cultural circumstances that shaped the discourse on female adolescence. And third, I examine the English and French discourses on female adolescence, paying particular attention to the intersection of science and gender that resulted in the blending of conventional and modern advice regarding the rearing of young girls.

The Emergence of Adolescence

The period from 1880 to 1920 witnessed the emergence of a new discourse on youth that emphasized the supposedly "universal" nature of the adolescent stage of life and its attendant challenges. This represented a break with earlier nineteenth-century discussions that tended to identify youth problems with particular socioeconomic circumstances. By the turn of the twentieth century such criteria were no longer central to contemporary understandings of troubled youth. By then, experts had established compelling physiological and psychological characteristics of adolescence, significantly expanding the field of potential intervention. Experts conceptualized adolescence as a developmental stage of life rooted in the traumatic onset of puberty and shaped by unsettling psychological confusions. While most public policy continued to express heightened worry about lower-class youths, the new ideas about adolescence that emerged at the end of the nineteenth century stimulated concern about the well-being of young people in the ever-expanding stratum of middling groups. Adolescence emerged as a terrain of troubled development, subject to tumultuous physical, mental, and emotional upheavals and requiring a therapeutic treatment of vigilant supervision.[2]

These changing understandings emerged within a greater context of social upheaval. In the course of the nineteenth century, and culminating in the decades around 1900, the roles and experiences of European youth changed significantly.[3] In the wake of democratizing revolutions and reform movements came the need to educate children and youth to be responsible future citizens. Attention to age groups marked much public policy of the nineteenth century. Through child labor regulations, juvenile corrections, and schooling, lawmakers and reformers fine-tuned the age demarcations as they rethought the role of young people in modern European societies. The movements that gradually resulted in the sending of more children and young people to school (rather than work), along with campaigns to increase the schooling of girls, created a distinct school-going population by the end of the nineteenth century. In addition, working youth became increasingly visible in urban, consumer culture. Whether strolling through municipal parks or clustered on street corners, young people attracted attention. Some of this attention contributed to heightened concerns about juvenile delinquency and an obsession with disciplining and punishing young people, as evidenced by the growth of correctional institutions.[4] Popular juvenile literature proliferated in increasingly age-graded material, while adolescent characters multiplied.[5] As the nineteenth century shaded into the twentieth, young people were becoming increasingly visible in public policy, age-graded institutions, popular culture, art and literature, and social commentary. Dislodged by profound political, economic, and social changes, young people also carried some of the cultural burden associated with late nineteenth-century anxieties about modernity.[6]

The changing nature of nineteenth-century life increased the visibility of young people and made it more likely that they would become objects of attention not only among reformers and educators but also among academics and professionals. The emergence of an active child protection movement committed to using the state to guarantee child welfare and to spreading public education at both the primary and secondary levels stimulated more rigorous research focused on young people. More and more adults devoted their time to, and earned their livings by, supervising the lives of young people. Teachers, school administrators, and child welfare inspectors produced a voluminous body of reports and studies, while developments within the academic disciplines contributed to the emergence of a more scientific discourse about the problems of young people.

The American psychologist G. Stanley Hall and his colleagues at Clark University are often credited with pioneering the new field of adolescent studies in the 1890s. Clark, a professor of psychology and pedagogy, wrote extensively on adolescence from an interdisciplinary perspective. Hall's work culminated in his two-volume study *Adolescence: Its Psychology and Its Relations to Physiology, Anthropology, Sociology, Sex, Crime, Religion and Education,* published in 1904, which was translated into several languages and enjoyed wide currency in France and England. Hall even called for a new field of medical specialization devoted to "the treatment of adolescent troubles of mind and body." He mused that "had I been a physician, I might have easily worked up a lucrative practice from such cases."[7] He and his colleagues were also active in the international school hygiene movement.

Psychologists, professors of pedagogy, and physicians were leading figures in the emerging field of adolescent studies. Joined by sociologists, teachers, school administrators, physical education instructors, psychiatrists, hygienists, physiologists, and other specialists, these experts shaped an authoritative discourse about adolescence. Unlike traditional advice manuals written by religious authorities or maternal figures, late nineteenth-century writings were more often authored by experts, that is, men and women in possession of professional credentials and writing within a structured institutional framework. Instructions and guidelines for teachers and school administrators increasingly pushed aside the genre of "advice to mothers." In comparison to the latter, the new form of writing appeared "scientific," based on observations, clinical studies, surveys, interviews, and other methods associated with the human and social sciences, and therefore endowed with more authority.

Such scientific writing about adolescence was part of an international discourse, with significant transatlantic links. The emerging "expert" literature was supported by extensive bibliographic apparatus referring readers to works in English (both British and American), French, Dutch, German, and Italian. Many works appeared in translation. This international discourse found support in the multitude of congresses, journals, and conference proceedings that mark the decades around 1900. Experts from continental Europe, the British Commonwealth, Latin America and the United States met, for example, at the International Congress on Protection of Children, the International Congress of Penitentiary and Penal Science, and the International Congress on School Hygiene.[8]

The emergence of the social sciences and their links with the biological sciences, so characteristic of the age of social Darwinism, helped to transform discussions about the problems of adolescence. By the end of the nineteenth century, the disciplines of anthropology, sociology, and psychology, as well as criminology and pedagogy, were joined to human biology and physiology in the systematic study of human beings and their behaviors. Specialization as well as interdisciplinary efforts characterized this trend. In France, the emergence in the 1880s of experimental psychology from the traditional study of moral philosophy marked a significant step.[9] The late nineteenth century also saw the emergence in Britain of "sexual science" and the growing importance of experts in the social scientific study of sex.[10]

Among those experts shaping the new field of research on adolescence were some that expressed great interest in the gender dimensions of this life phase. Several factors account for the intense interest in female adolescence and may explain the emergence of a distinctive set of ideas about female adolescence. The decades of the 1880s through the 1920s were a time of contested expansion of girls' postprimary and secondary education.[11] As girls appeared in greater numbers at schoolhouse doors, including a few who breached university doors, social commentary about the advisability of this trend escalated. Opponents claimed that girls were mentally and physically ill equipped for the rigors of academic life and argued that advanced education would denature women. Supporters responded with studies designed to demonstrate that girls could handle the challenge. As some female graduates of secondary and higher education obtained professional employment, the debate intensified and the volumes of studies multiplied.

As girls' education expanded, so did the personnel associated with these institutions; they contributed to the debates, conducted studies, presented papers, and published books and articles. Despite their vested interest in defending the proposition of expanded female education, they had to address the pervasive claims about gender differences and separate spheres. Embedded, though hardly hidden, in the discussions about education and employment for young women were explicit concerns about their health, present and future. As a result, the debates were not confined to moral, social, or economic dimensions but also revolved around the biological and physiological. Given the emergence of psychophysiological study, the debate about the nature of female adolescence and its relationship to the adult status of women took on a new look at the end of the nineteenth century.

The role of the women's movement, also contested but expanding during these same decades, added to the intensity of the discourse. Many of the scientific experts writing about female adolescence addressed implicitly or explicitly, in passing or more extensively, the influence of feminism on girls' lives. Commenting on a 1907 paper presented by Dr. Mary Scharlieb on physical training for adolescent girls, a female school administrator noted the importance of this issue, anticipating that young women in the near future would "take a position in the State of far more important character than that occupied by her now."[12] Feminists themselves also contributed to the debates, using their new positions as doctors, teachers, and administrators to anchor their authority.

The new visibility of young people also had implications for the discourse about female adolescence. The transformations in work, leisure, education, and popular culture drew larger numbers of young women into public spaces, and contemporaries debated the consequences of this. Increased female literacy and the growth of print culture sharpened concerns about the reading habits of girls. Girls on bicycles fueled debates about the consequences of mobility for female adolescent health. Contemporaries even began to worry about the rise of girl gangs as a new form of female juvenile delinquency at the end of the nineteenth century.[13] Finally, it should be noted that pronatalism in France and the eugenics movement in England, both drawing on science for reinforcement, placed the health of young women at the center of their concern.

In combination, these developments functioned to create a new world for girls and young women and shaped the discourse about female adolescence. Though part of the larger discussion about adolescence, this discourse was nonetheless distinct. While some experts undertook comparative research on boys and girls, a significant body of literature focused exclusively on girls. This work typically approached the study of female adolescence from a psychosocial and physiological perspective, focusing on the impact of puberty, menstruation, and emerging reproductive potential on girls' social, physical, and mental development. Education and physical fitness, often linked together, attracted much attention. These concerns tended to focus attention on middle-class girls. Studies of girls' labor and delinquency, often connected to concerns about working-class life and tied to legislative reform efforts, also appeared; these studies recast discussions about female youth delinquency and work by borrowing from the discourse on female adolescence, especially the psychological and physiological insights. Thus, the encounter between girls and science (including social science) distinguished the discourse about female adolescence in the decades from the 1880s to 1920s from earlier discussions about girlhood. And although the discussions about female adolescence shared many themes found in the discussions about male adolescence, the contemporary concern with gender disorder and the perception that female puberty was markedly different than male puberty gave the discourse about female adolescence a distinct content and tone. Scientific and clinical analysis was incorporated into social commentary.

Changing Understandings of Puberty

While puberty was seen as a fundamentally physiological process, the new ideas about adolescence defined it as encompassing profound mental and emotional changes. The marriage of physiology and psychology contributed to the emergence of a consensus identifying puberty as the opening stage of adolescence. Experts agreed that puberty was a time of crisis, part of the difficult transition from child to adult. Physiological maturation stood as the primary feature of puberty, most specifically and importantly manifested in the development of reproductive organs. In contrast to the regular, gradual growth during childhood, puberty seemed characterized by bursts of growth, irregular and discordant. The equilibrium achieved by older children was suddenly torn asunder by the seemingly unexpected changes of puberty. Two questions plagued experts: When did puberty begin? And how long did it last? Disagreements of a semantic nature were complicated by the difficulty of determining when sex organs had achieved their full maturity. In the case of girls, first menstruation provided experts with a useful point of reference. At the same time, the gradually declining age of menarche in western Europe (combined with the still relatively late age of marriage) heightened anxiety about the sexual changes associated with puberty.

All who studied puberty recognized its social-sexual importance, even those who focused on measuring weight gains, height increases, and voice changes. Since the end result of puberty was to produce young men and women with sex-specific characteristics and reproductive functions, most experts pointed to puberty as the beginning of a permanent divergence between boys and girls. While experts agreed on the centrality of puberty in the life cycle of both adolescent girls and boys, they emphasized the important divergences that puberty signaled in the social development of women and men. Some experts argued that prior to puberty, girls and boys were relatively undifferentiated.[14] Children of both sexes could even play at the same games and sports.[15] However, the adolescent boy or girl emerged from puberty as a "more specific being than the child."[16] Puberty marked a new beginning by establishing sex specificity.

According to experts, the crisis that surrounded boys and girls as they proceeded down their divergent paths to sexual maturity was much more profound for girls than for boys. Most believed that puberty held special hazards for girls. Armand Siredey, a French gynecologist, suggested the transformation of puberty was "more rapid and more accentuated among girls than among boys."[17] Similarly, Gabriel Compayré, an internationally recognized French psychologist and educational theorist, claimed that puberty struck girls with more force than boys.[18] According to Pierre Mendousse, another French expert on adolescence and a lycée professor whose book on female adolescence remained in print throughout the twentieth century, girls' bodies were subject to physiological repercussions considerably more serious than were boys'.[19] Experts also insisted that girls suffered more illnesses associated with puberty, such as anemia and curvature of the spine, arguing that the evolution of the ovaries played a key role in these maladies, as a "*condition prédisposante.*"[20] Dr. Marthe Francillon suggested that the mental confusion sometimes associated with puberty appeared more frequently in girls than boys.[21] While experts were also concerned about the health of adolescent boys, they tended to express this concern differently. Adolescent health problems in boys might compromise their physical fitness and academic work but not ultimately their masculine identity. Adolescent health problems in girls posed possible threats to physical appearance as well as fitness, mental stability as well as the ability to learn. Most critical of all, female adolescent health problems could undermine the healthy development of reproductive organs and thus compromise successful establishment of feminine identity.

For girls, as for boys, puberty brought a variety of physical changes. The most noted physiological changes were those related to external sex. The secondary sex characteristics for girls included enlargement of the pelvis, development of breasts, rounding out of body shape, delicacy of skeletal frame, and growth of body hair. In addition, girls experienced rapid physical growth often coinciding with the start of menstruation at an average age of fourteen. Francillon, a former intern of the Hopitaux de Paris, believed that "the rapid growth of puberty [among girls] is often accompanied by aching bones, digestive troubles, and nervous disorders (neurasthenia)." She also noted extreme fatigue among girls who grew rapidly during puberty.[22] Siredey, one of her colleagues, noted that girls' growth (height and weight) was more rapid and pronounced than that of boys.[23] Others noted the irregularity of growth and the absence of coordination between height and weight increases.[24]

The scientific methods of observation and measurement buttressed expert concern with physiology. This led to page after page of data charting the effect of puberty on girls' blood, urine, secretions, pulse rate, heartbeat, circulation, voice tone, body temperature, thyroid function, vision, and sense of touch. According to Francillon, the more rapid pulse rate of women was at its height during puberty: boys and girls showed no difference at birth, minimal difference at age seven, maximum difference at age fourteen.[25] Siredey noted that changes in the heart were more likely to produce troubles for girls than boys. Moreover, difficulties such as heart palpitations and breathlessness were, he argued, more frequent among adolescent girls.[26]

Of all the bodily changes associated with female puberty none attracted more attention than the onset of menstruation. A. Raciborski's *Treatise on Menstruation,* for example, published in 1868 and still frequently cited in the late 1890s, pronounced menstruation "one of the most significant attributes of puberty."[27] Some experts concentrated on determining the average age of menarche in different settings so as to identify factors that inhibited or accelerated first menstruation. Other researchers focused on the physiological impact and still others on psychological changes. All agreed that menstruation introduced unique challenges into the lives of girls and directly affected their behaviors.[28] The management of menstruation thus constituted a central feature of female puberty and many experts devoted significant attention to this issue.

Francillon was among the experts who devoted themselves to studying the impact of menstruation on the behavior of young women. Her research concentrated on the "malaise" that supposedly preceded the first menstruation, the physiological changes that accompanied its appearance, and the behavioral and emotional modifications that often marked it.[29] Though she believed that the onset of menstruation had an immediate and direct impact on the conduct of girls, Francillon disagreed with what she called the exaggerated claims that linked menstruation with inevitable physical and psychological disorders. Like Mary Wood-Allen, she rejected the idea that menstruation was a "sick condition" or one necessarily "pathological." Nonetheless, she conceded that the physiological condition of women was temporarily altered during menstruation as part of a "normal" function and as a result menstruation could temporarily inhibit the activities of women.[30]

While experts agreed that puberty was a time of turmoil and stress in body and mind for boys and girls alike, they took special interest in the implications of this stress for girls, and they emphasized the predominance of bodily stresses in pubescent girls. Mendousse suggested that for girls physical changes dominated adolescence, while for boys mental changes predominated.[31] At a time when increasing numbers of adolescent girls attended school, experts increasingly focused on the physical stress of schooling and linked it to concerns about sexual development. Henri Marion, a French authority on the psychology and education of women, insisted that during puberty changes in a girl's body were so profound they interfered with her intellectual development, during a "momentary predominance of physiological functions."[32] Compayré advised that during puberty girls should devote their attention to physical health, which he considered more important for the future of the race than the health of boys.[33] Siredey also focused on the stresses of the body during female adolescence, noting that good care of body was the surest way to avoid physical as well as psychological problems.[34] Marguerite Evard, a lycée professor, advised that since the physiological crisis was so great for girls, their mental efforts should be reduced during the peak of puberty.[35] Maria E. Findlay, a British authority, recommended that girls take off from school during their monthly periods to avoid health complications and suggested that during puberty girls should not sit for comprehensive examinations.[36] Yet another authority concluded that since girls experienced an earlier and faster puberty, they ended up with a less mature intelligence than did boys.[37]

Many experts agreed that the physiological transformations in pubescent girls created a "special vulnerability" to illness and several suggested that some disorders were almost exclusively present during puberty.[38] Francillon maintained that menstruation played a role in the genesis of hysteria and insisted that the role of menstruation in the appearance of epilepsy was "generally admitted." She added that when epilepsy occurred during puberty it exercised permanent damage on the intelligence and moral sentiments of girls and young women. Epileptic girls became "defiant, indifferent, lazy, even dangerous, capable of murder, arson, theft, and suicide." Chlorosis (a type of anemia), neurasthenia, hysteria, and epilepsy were considered nervous disorders brought on by puberty, though not necessarily due to physiological changes themselves but to the fatigue and weakness that supposedly often plagued many girls during puberty. This clarification left open the possibility of forestalling the onset or reducing the burdens of these disorders through proper management.

Managing Puberty

To manage the passage through puberty, experts recommended a variety of measures intended to reduce the impact of this crisis on the bodies and minds of young girls. These measures generally aimed to limit excitement and create a smoothly regulated lifestyle. The vast majority of recommendations were hygienic in nature, reflecting the emphasis on bodily changes: a healthy diet, low in fat, spices, and meat and high in legumes and vegetables; adequate sleep to pacify the nerves; physical exercise and fresh air to strengthen the body; and even clothing reform. Good hygiene, important at all ages, appeared especially vital during puberty. Experts advised adolescent girls to concentrate their energies on healthy activities. Leisurely strolls and promenades were rejected in favor of more effective physical activities. Many experts preferred Swedish gymnastics, bicycling, and swimming for adolescent girls and agreed that moderate physical activity would ward off nervous disorders. Clothing that permitted movement and allowed the body to breathe was also recommended.[39]

While concern for good health stood at the heart of these hygienic recommendations, concerns about morality abounded. Too much sleep, as well as lounging in bed after awakening, would predispose a girl to dreaming and the temptations of sensuality. Laziness would lead to "ennui," the "poison of youth." Coffee, tea, and spicy foods seemed to carry nearly as much danger as alcohol. During puberty it was important for girls to engage in exercise not only to strengthen their bodies but also to utilize surplus energy that would otherwise be expended in "sensual dreams and precocious sentimentalisms."[40] Sexual fantasy might lead to sexual "self-abuse." In recommending bicycling as an ideal sport for adolescent girls, experts emphasized its physical and moral benefits: it helped digestion, relaxed nerves, and did not have the moral inconveniences of dance. In fact, several experts specifically urged that dance be avoided during puberty as it was too great a stimulant, citing promiscuous company, overheated rooms, improper dress, and late hours. Clearly, diet and exercise were intended to purify the soul as well as the body of pubescent girls.

The debate over exercise, physical fitness, and sports reveals a number of interesting disagreements and contradictions. Confusion abounded, for example, over whether adolescents suffered from surplus energy or loss of energy, and over whether adolescents needed more activity to channel their energies or less activity to reduce inappropriate stimulation. Most experts, male and female, regarded adolescent girls as in need of more rest than boys but they also believed adolescent girls would profit from moderate exercise. Female experts appeared less concerned about the possibility of overexertion, though most of them still offered advice that took into account perceived gender differences not only in physiology but also in social expectations. Female physicians tended to have a greater interest in preventative medicine and therefore were more supportive of physical fitness programs for girls. In comparison, male experts were more likely to support programs of physical fitness for girls rather than advanced education because of the perceived reproductive benefits of exercise. British experts were more likely than their French counterparts to see vigorous physical activity, including sports, as a positive experience for adolescent girls. Although French authorities recognized the importance of physical education to the healthy development of girls' bodies and their ability later in life to have healthy pregnancies, they tended to regard sports and rigorous exercise as potentially debilitating. As late as 1928, the French doctor Boigey warned against too much athleticism among young women, seeing it as a danger for future procreation.[41]

Other recommendations for how to manage female adolescence were of a moral character. They included, for example, the recommendation that reading materials be restricted. Expert after expert decried the influence of novels on the adolescent imagination, but they worried particularly about their impact on girls. Concerned about the threat novels might pose to the nervous system, Raciborski demanded that girls be prohibited from reading novels until the age of twenty.[42] Marion recommended that reading be done in "small doses" and as a family activity rather than a private one: "To plunge alone into novels and devour them one after another" was indeed a "*grand mal.*" Furthermore, he suggested that intense reading interest, while a sign of promise in boys, was less important in girls. Instead girls might "from time to time" read a good novel for "recreation," while otherwise the habit of reading for moral uplift should be encouraged.[43] Especially in France, where young girls who had completed a course of secondary study typically returned home to lives of "idleness" that might last for years until marriage, reading habits were a matter of serious concern. Novels, diaries, and daydreams all constituted unregulated spaces in the distinctly dangerous age of female adolescence.

A matter of similarly grave concern was the issue of female education. Given the increasing availability of education for girls after 1880, most experts writing on female adolescence directly addressed this topic. As G. Stanley Hall noted in 1904, the value of education for adolescent girls was so hotly debated, with "wide divergences between doctors," that it constituted a "holy war."[44] Some experts argued that intellectual life posed grave dangers for adolescent girls, leading them away from their natural role as women, that is, as reproducers. In this view, the educated woman stood not only as an anomaly but a "biological monstrosity."[45] These writers saw pubescent girls as so dominated by physiological transformations designed to develop their procreative abilities that they insisted on minimizing all influences that might distract or excite girls. Speaking specifically to feminists who advocated that adolescent boys and girls receive the same education, Compayré warned against erasing the natural differences of sex.[46] Edouard Claparède argued that the laws of nature arranged for girls to attain physical maturity earlier than boys, thus sacrificing their intellectual development, so as to ensure the future interests of the race. Thus a girl would have less "taste for research and for those enterprises which would carry her far from the domestic hearth."[47] Eugenicists expressed heightened concern over the dangerous impact of "intellectual overload" in middle-class girls, claiming that it did more damage than the physical overload borne by working-class girls. Herbert Spencer declared that middle-class girls exhibited a "diminution of reproductive power" as a result of "overtaxing their brains." Not only were such girls more likely to be sterile or to cease childbearing at an earlier age but they also exhibited the "very frequent inability . . . to suckle their infants." Spencer concluded that "most flat-chested girls who survive their high-pressure education are unable to do this [nurse their infants]."[48]

Other experts viewed education for the adolescent girl as useful within parameters that acknowledged her feminine identity. Marion believed that some intellectual activity was essential for girls as a way of avoiding the poison of *ennui,* but he also cautioned against excessive intellectual work that would cause fatigue, disturb the nervous system, and interfere with the healthy development of the female body during puberty. In practice, Marion recommended that girls' schools operate according to "more or less elastic rules" and rejected a school regime of "implacable uniformity and mechanical rigidity."[49] Francillon advocated that girls be given an "*éducation intellectuelle bien comprise*" but was skeptical of girls' schools and recommended that girls receive their education "*en famille.*" She feared that bringing older and younger adolescent girls together in a communal environment, where an uncontrollable "literary mania" might overtake them, would exacerbate the exaltation and intemperance common among girls during puberty.[50]

Declaring that the "development of the spirit/mind ought not to be made to the detriment of the body," Siredey applauded girls' schools that had modified their schedules by increasing the morning hours of study and decreasing the afternoon hours because girls were typically "fatigued, headachy, lazy, and inattentive" in the afternoon as a result of the unavoidable demands of their organic development.[51] Janet Campbell, a medical advisor to the Board of Education in England, also argued that girls during puberty needed protection from overwork at school, recommending a decrease in subjects that caused mental strain, such as mathematics, and a substitution of subjects such as "cookery, embroidery or the handicrafts . . . as they cause comparatively little mental strain." A 1923 government report in England presented physiological evidence to argue that girls have less energy than boys and therefore should not receive an equal education.[52]

Only a few experts, usually women doctors and educators, advocated a solid education for adolescent girls.[53] Casimire Proczek, writing in 1918, concurred with her contemporaries that girls and boys differed in psychological development. This led her to a significant methodological conclusion: adolescent boys and girls must be studied separately so that an accurate scientific understanding of female development could be used to shape a scientific pedagogy. Noting that no one disputed the importance of education for boys, she rejected the idea that girls could manage on the basis of "moral instincts." Girls, she insisted, should be educated not only for their future contributions to society and their future role in the family but also for themselves. Faulty education, based on the prejudiced views of most experts, had produced generation after generation of lazy, frivolous, confused girls. In contrast, girls with a strong interest in science or "some other absorbing activity" rarely suffered the troublesome effects of puberty. Proczek asserted, "The stage of puberty is especially difficult to cross for young girls whose days are filled with petty tasks requiring no thoughtful effort and leaving their wandering imaginations free to roam." It did not surprise her that most girls questioned wished they were boys, or that many girls expressed suicidal inclinations by the age of seventeen.[54]

In general, the scientific study of female adolescence linking physiology, psychology, and pedagogy tended to make girls, and ultimately women, captives of their bodies in ways boys were not. In comparing the management techniques suggested for dealing with boys and girls, there are certainly similarities. Boys too were encouraged to adopt proper diet, exercise, clothes, and sleep routines, and experts worried about intellectual fatigue in adolescent boys. But for boys, most experts placed far less emphasis on the need for calm and reduced study. While tranquility and a flexible course of study for adolescents have much to recommend them, the arguments of many experts writing on puberty and adolescence in the decades around 1900 tended to identify these traits with the female passage through puberty. With few exceptions, the scientific study of puberty in girls seemed to reinforce conventional moral arguments favoring limits on women. At the very least, turn-of-the-century research encouraged an intensified observation of young girls, replacing, at least in the French case, the walls of early nineteenth-century convent schools with the gaze of the clinical observer. Experts rooted their discourse in seemingly immutable natural phenomena. They believed they had contributed to an advance in understanding by their recognition of the distinct physiology and psychology of adolescence. Yet, through their careful tracking of the passage through puberty, experts sharpened the gendered nature and experience of adolescence through a blending of biology and psychology.

Notes

1.   Ministère de l'Instruction Publique, Direction de l'Enseignement Primaire, *Inspection Académique de 1900* (Paris: Imprimerie Nationale, 1900), 268–269, 597.
2.   For more on the emergence of adolescence as a concept in France, see the chapters by Rebecca Rogers and Céline Grasser in this volume.
3.   For introductions to the history of youth, see Colin Heywood, "Childrearing

and Childhood," and Andrew Donson, "Youth and Adolescence," in *Encyclopedia of European Social History from 1350 to 2000*, vol. 4, ed. Peter N. Stearns et al. (New York: Charles Scribner's Sons, 2001), 175–206.

4. See Kathleen Alaimo, "Juvenile Delinquency and Hooliganism," in *Encyclopedia of European Social History from 1350 to 2000*, vol. 3, ed. Peter N. Stearns et al. (New York: Charles Scribner's Sons, 2001), 383–397.

5. See Sally R. Mitchell, *Girls' Culture in England, 1880–1915* (New York: Columbia University Press, 1996).

6. See John Neubauer, *The Fin-de-Siècle Culture of Adolescence* (New Haven, Conn.: Yale University Press, 1992).

7. G. Stanley Hall, "Adolescence: The Need for a New Field of Medical Practice," in *Monthly Cyclopedia of Practical Medicine* (June 1905), cited by Heather M. Prescott, *A Doctor of Their Own: The History of Adolescent Medicine* (Cambridge, Mass.: Harvard University Press, 1998), 7.

8. Triennial meetings of the International Congress on School Hygiene began in 1904 (Nuremberg), followed by 1907 (London), 1910 (Paris), and 1913 (Buffalo, N.Y.). Published multivolume "proceedings" included texts of all presentations and discussion commentary, as well as lists of participating individuals and organizations. Papers were printed in a variety of languages. The overwhelming majority of participants were professors, physicians, teachers, and school administrators and many of the experts whose work will be discussed later in this chapter participated in these meetings.

9. See John I. Brooks III, *The Eclectic Legacy: Academic Philosophy and the Human Sciences in Nineteenth-Century France* (Newark: University of Delaware Press, 1998).

10. Roy Porter and Lesley Hall, *The Facts of Life: The Creation of Sexual Knowledge in Britain, 1650–1950* (New Haven, Conn.: Yale University Press, 1995), 186–187.

11. See Françoise Mayeur, *L'Enseignement secondaire des jeunes filles sous la Troisième Republique* (Paris: Presses de la Fondation nationale des sciences politiques, 1978); Jo Burr Margadant, *Madame le Professeur: Women Educators in the Third Republic* (Princeton, N.J.: Princeton University Press, 1990); and Joyce Senders Pedersen, *The Reform of Girls' Secondary and Higher Education in Victorian England: A Study of Elites and Educational Change* (New York: Garland, 1987).

12. Comment by Mrs. Despard, manager of schools, England in *Second International Congress on School Hygiene 1907* (London: Royal Sanitary Institute, 1908), 265–266.

13. See Andrew Davies, " 'These Viragos are no less cruel than the lads': Young Women, Gangs, and Violence in Late Victorian Manchester and Salford," *British Journal of Criminology* 39 (1999): 72–89.

14. See, for example, Marthe Francillon, *Essaie sur la puberté chez la femme: Psychologie, physiologie, pathologie* (Paris: Felix Alcan, 1906), 1, 191; Gabriel Compayré, *L'Adolescence, etudes de psychologie et de pedagogie*, 2d ed. (Paris: Felix Alcan, 1910), 5; Eugène Apert, *La Croissance* (Paris: E. Flammarion, 1921), 247; Mary Wood-Allen, *What a Young Girl Ought to Know*, rev. ed. (Philadelphia and London: Vir Publishing, 1905), 105 (later translated into several languages, including French).

15. J. O. A. Doleris, "Les sports au point de l'hygiene chez la femme et la jeune fille," in *Second International Congress on School Hygiene 1907* (London: Royal Sanitary Institute, 1908), 22.

16. Pierre Mendousse, *L'Ame de l'adolescent* (Paris: Felix Alcan, 1909), ii, 15; also Compayré, *L'Adolescence,* 5–9.

17. Armand Siredey, "La puberté et l'éducation des jeunes filles," *Archives Internationales d'hygiene scolaire* 4 (1907): 66.

18. Compayré, *L'Adolescence,* 53.

19. Mendousse, iii.

20. Apert, 231.

21. Francillon, 202.

22. Francillon, 19–20.

23. Siredey, 67.

24. Marguerite Evard, *L'Adolescente: Essaie de psychologie experimentale* (Neuchatel: Delachaux & Niestle, 1914), 12–13.

25. Francillon, 122.

26. Siredey, 67–68.

27. A. Raciborski, *Traité de la menstruation, ses rapports avec l'ovulation, la fecondation, l'hygiene de la puberté et l'age critique, son rôle dans les differentes maladies, ses troubles et leur traitements* (Paris: J-B Baillière et Fils, 1868), 166.

28. Francillon, 192–193; Mendousse, *L'Ame de l'adolescente* (Paris: Felix Alcan, 1928), 31–34; Wood-Allen; and Hall, vol. 1, 491ff.

29. Francillon, 161–169.

30. Ibid., 197–198.

31. Mendousse, iii.

32. Henri Marion, *L'Education des jeunes filles* (Paris: A Colin, 1902), 83.

33. Gabriel Compayré, "La pedagogie de l'adolescence," *Revue Philosophique* 61 (juin 1906): 586.

34. Siredey, 71.

35. Evard, 199.

36. Cited by Carol Dyhouse, *Girls Growing Up in Late Victorian and Edwardian England* (London: Routledge & Kegan Paul, 1981), 134.

37. Francillon, 225–226; Edouard Claparède, *Experimental Pedagogy and the Psychology of the Child,* trans. Mary Louch and Henry Holman, from *Psychologie de l'enfant et pedagogie experimentale,* 4th ed. (New York: Longman, 1911), 147.

38. Francillon, 199, 217–21; Evard, 18; and Siredey, 70–71.

39. Siredey, 69–70; Casimire Proczek, *Contribution à la psychologie de l'adolescente* (Lausanne: Imprimerie Centrale, 1918), 73; Wood-Allen, 61ff.; Doleris, 23–24, 29; and *Second International Congress on School Hygiene 1907,* 239–243.

40. Proczek, 72, 96.

41. Cited by Yvonne Knibiehler et al., *De la pucelle à la minette: Les jeunes filles de l'age classique à nos jours* (Paris: Temps Actuels, 1983), 222–223.

42. Raciborski, 317–318.

43. Marion, 100.

44. Hall, vol. 2, 569.

45. M.-C. Schuyten, *L'Education de la femme* (Paris: O. Doin, 1908), 124–137.

46. Gabriel Compayré, *Histoire critique des doctrines de l'éducation en France,* 2

vols. (Paris: Hachette, 1898 [1st ed. 1877]), 386; and Compayré, *L'Adolescence,* 193–194.

47. Claparède, 148.
48. Cited by Emily Pfeiffer, *Women and Work: An Essay Treating on the Relation to Health and Physical Education of the Higher Education of Girls, and the Intellectual or More Systematized Effort of Women* (Boston: Ticknor, 1887; London: Trubner, 1888), 70.
49. Marion, 87, 91–93.
50. Francillon, 193–196.
51. Siredey, 70–71.
52. Cited by Dyhouse, 132–135.
53. For example, Marie Dugard, *De l'education moderne des jeunes filles* (Paris: A. Colin, 1900).
54. Proczek, 7–10, 19, 41, 48, 94.

10 Sex Education and Sexual Initiation of Bourgeois French Girls, 1880–1930

Mary Lynn Stewart

Despite the circulation of new scientific ideas about adolescence toward the end of the nineteenth century, Mary Lynn Stewart suggests that the largely domestic sex education of bourgeois girls in France changed relatively little before the 1920s. Several decades into the twentieth century most French parents continued to believe in sheltering their adolescent daughters and keeping them "innocent," meaning ignorant about the female body and female sexuality. Consequently, turn-of-the-century girls typically received very little information about sex and often reached puberty without any knowledge of menstruation. Like their predecessors of a century earlier, Stewart argues, they would often marry with only the vaguest of notions about heterosexual intercourse.

In the final decades of the nineteenth century, medical, physiological, and psychological understandings of adolescence were changing throughout the Western world. Yet, as this chapter will argue, these new theories seemed to have little impact on the lives of French bourgeois girls who came of age in the 1880s and 1890s. Several decades into the twentieth century, most French parents continued to believe in sheltering their adolescent daughters and keeping them "innocent," meaning ignorant about the female body and female sexuality. Consequently, turn-of-the-century girls typically received information no more helpful than the "sex education" of a century earlier.[1] Like their predecessors, they often reached puberty without any knowledge of menstruation; later in life they would often enter marriage with only the vaguest of notions about heterosexual intercourse.

Because of the emphasis on girls' innocence prior to marriage, we have little historical evidence about nineteenth-century French adolescent sexuality. Historians seeking to determine what turn-of-the-century girls knew about sex have to extrapolate from many different sources, including prescriptive literature such as pamphlets advocating sex education, medical manuals and columns addressed to women, and sex advice books. Because most of the authors of these texts were male physicians or Catholic clerics, and because most of them promoted strictly marital and reproductive sexuality, these sources offer only limited insight. They must be checked against other kinds of prescriptive literature, including health manuals for women and children written by women doctors.[2] Finally, the prescriptive literature must be compared to the rare references to sexuality in French girls' journals and in French women's memoirs and autobiographical novels.

Puberty and Menstruation

According to turn-of-the-century medical researchers, adolescence had a more obvious starting point for girls than for boys. It began with menarche, which, in 1900, arrived around age fourteen, and in the 1930s, a year earlier. At this point in their lives, instead of advice about human biology and sexuality, most pubescent girls encountered only heightened attention to, and tension about, their maturing bodies. In general, parents and girls' schools did not recognize puberty as marking a stage of life other than by beginning to call pubescent girls "big girls" and intensifying supervision over them.[3]

In many cases, girls were entirely unprepared for the onset of menstruation. Although older sisters or friends sometimes warned prepubescent girls about "the reds and the whites" (menstrual blood and a white discharge that often preceded menses), some girls repressed this knowledge or failed to apply it when they first noticed their own menstrual blood. Parents and girls' schools usually waited until a girl began to menstruate to explain it, and even then, efforts were made to keep the information confidential between a girl and her mother.

In spite of their silence about menstruation until daughters reached puberty, mothers played a central role in the lives of menstruating girls. While they generally told daughters to keep menstruation a secret, they also imposed a regimen that alerted family and friends to the girls' condition. For example, mothers tended to limit menstruating girls' physical activities, for example by asking teachers to excuse them from gymnastics classes. By the 1920s, more girls maintained normal physical activities during menstruation. The exceptions were bicycling and strenuous sports, which even the most progressive women doctors forbade because they might inhibit "normal" menstrual flow and interfere with reproductive development. If a girl had cramps, her mother prescribed rest, herbal teas, and hot foods. Mothers treated more debilitating symptoms by administering over-the-counter herbal concoctions, prescription drugs, and vaginal douches.

Popular beliefs that associated menstrual blood with various dangers, including toxicity, undoubtedly influenced young girls' experiences as well. Attempting to dispel this myth, Dr. E. A. Goupil, a Catholic gynecologist who in the 1880s operated the largest gynecological clinic in Paris, informed readers of his medical advice book that menstrual blood was "the same as normal blood except that it is mixed with mucous" expelled from the uterus, which accounted for the smell and viscosity that contributed to popular fears. Washing the pubic area during menstruation would reduce the unpleasant odor and the incidence of genital infections.[4] While Dr. Goupil may have convinced gynecologists and hygienists, he did not seem to alter popular views significantly. Through the 1930s, French doctors continued to find it necessary to denounce popular beliefs about the toxic properties of menstrual blood.[5] Other medical experts campaigned against customary practices of not changing underwear during menstruation.[6] Women's health manuals also sought to "modernize" popular attitudes toward menstruation, repeatedly criticizing the custom of using rags or old skirts to absorb menstrual blood. Yet, despite such efforts on the part of experts, the near silence about menstruation in French women's journals and memoirs suggests that girls learned not to talk about menstruation.

The Adolescent Female Body

While some experts focused on menstruation, other medical researchers investigated other aspects of the female body during puberty. Adam Raciborski, for example, the first French medical scientist to specialize in puberty, described the appearance of external genitalia "that Linnaeus so ingeniously compared to the petals of a flower."[7] Marthe Francillon, the first native Frenchwomen to get a medical degree in the twentieth century, in 1905, documented changes in bone density and the rate of skeletal growth.[8] However, girls' hygiene texts incorporated little of this research and medical manuals for mothers and doctors' columns in women's magazines only introduced this data slowly and selectively. Besides, even though these texts provided some information on internal reproductive organs, they were silent about external sex organs other than breasts, which were described as necessary for breastfeeding infants.

In addition to physiological changes, some experts devoted their research to psychological changes during puberty. Writing before theories about the ovaries as glands, Raciborski held that modifications in the ovarian system "excited" the nervous system. This excitement, he claimed, often expressed itself in excessively close friendships with other girls, coquetry and melancholy, and pathologically in hysteria and nymphomania.[9] One endocrinologist depicted the adolescent girl's personality as simultaneously reserved and flirtatious, the first due to "a natural disposition to modesty," the second to "an instinctive need to seduce."[10] Musing about "girls' nature" discouraged a sociocultural analysis of how these attitudes might be a reasonable response to a society conflicted about their sexuality, even though Marthe Francillon and another woman doctor at the turn of the century offered cultural explanations of pubescent girls' moodiness and volatile behavior.[11]

Preparing Girls for Marriage

Before the First World War, bourgeois mothers typically prepared their daughters more for courtship than for conjugal relations, which meant instilling in them an ambiguous mixture of propriety and coquetry, appropriate for attracting a spouse. For example, in the 1880s and 1890s, young single women were often forbidden to use powder or rouge, though they could apply floral perfumes, which were considered to be fresh and virginal. They were supposed to wear only chaste white or pale-colored dresses with high necklines and no jewelry to proclaim their purity. Of course, young women subverted these restrictions.[12] By 1900, respectable young ladies applied powder and donned evening gowns with modest décolleté and jewelry, all signals that that they were nearly adult and available.[13] Along the same lines, hygienists advised mothers to keep their adolescent daughters occupied to avoid "romantic fantasies," a notion that embraced erotic and sensual fantasies. Even after the First World War, hygienists recommended that girls be prevented from reading romantic literature, attending "lascivious plays," and looking at "obscene" paintings—a category that included "artistic" nudes";[14] these rules were also widely evaded.

While no longer sent routinely to convent schools, respectable French girls of 1900 still faced strict limits on their freedom to move around. Until the early twentieth century, mothers or aunts escorted young single women to balls, parties, theaters, resorts, and casinos to meet eligible men. Ideally, single women were not supposed to dance or talk with unknown men or to remain in the company of any one partner for too long unless they had an understanding about marriage. In actuality, "flirts" or more intimate conversations were permissible.[15]

Nonetheless, young bourgeois women tended to have very little physical contact of any kind with men outside their families, with the predictable result that the slightest touch could arouse much stronger feelings than the same gesture would today. At nineteen, one young woman noted in her diary how much she had enjoyed her bicycle instructor's hand on her shoulder to steady her. From the turn of the century, new kinds of social dancing increased the opportunities for physical contact. As a teenager, Clara Malraux reveled in the "swing of my body in a boy's arm during a tango, an expected or unexpected kiss." Her first kiss "filled me with disgust and [. . .] longing to experience it again."[16]

The First World War contributed decisively to breaking down older patterns of courtship. According to Clara Malraux,

> there was a continual obsession with sex, even for those whose reading was supervised; it was splashed on the walls and on the Morris pillars with their film and theater posters; it ran through the songs, . . . in our recently shortened skirts, in

our more and more exaggerated make-up. In the midst of all this girls were supposed to be chaste, though not in the least ignorant; since they were freer, so they were also more threatened.[17]

After 1918, many middle-class parents financially ruined by the war were unable to afford dowries, which reduced their control over daughters' conduct.[18] Moreover, the fact that there were over one million more marriageable women than there were eligible men weighed heavily on parents' minds. They did not consider that poor marital prospects provided some young women with an excuse to avoid unwanted alliances or marriage itself.[19] Ultimately, these changes granted young girls greater personal liberty in the postwar era, permitting them to make up, dress up, and even to flirt.

Throughout the 1920s and 1930s Catholic moralists lamented this state of affairs. In the mid-1930s, Canon Cordonnier, for example, took on flirting. Accepting the cultural consensus that coquetry was part of feminine nature, he nevertheless criticized it as cruel to a (male) partner, since sexual attraction was "very violent and imperious in young men." He faulted young women for arousing men with "naked arms and legs, cleavage, tight or short dresses in light or transparent fabrics."[20] The same year, a lay Catholic, Monique Levallet-Montal, conceded that some physical contact would be proper, though only between engaged women and men. She allowed women to kiss their fiancés on the lips if the kisses "did not provoke carnal excitement."[21] This kind of advice addresses the same anxieties that appear in letters from practicing Catholics asking Abbé Viollet, a Catholic priest who founded the Association for Christian Marriage, about appropriate premarital contact between the sexes. One letter, for example, asks if the Church forbade kisses on the lips between the affianced and if such kisses were "essentially sensual?"[22]

The Wedding-Night Surprise: Marital Sexuality

Throughout the period from 1880 to 1930, French sex experts decried female sexual ignorance. But they were generally less concerned that it might leave girls vulnerable to seductions and pregnancies than they were about its implications for the birthrate. Most placed the blame for girls' ignorance on mothers who were criticized for failing to talk to their daughters about marital sexuality until the eve of the wedding. Secular authors ascribed mothers' silence to clerical warnings about "the seductive aspects of pleasure."[23] Clerics, however, reported that mothers typically asked, "Why scandalize them, possibly filling them with disgust for marriage?" Certainly, many mothers believed that speaking to daughters about intercourse stripped them of their valued "innocence."[24]

In 1884, one medical specialist reported that mothers and aunts waited until the night before the wedding to whisper vague and disturbing things to the bride-to-be, such as: "Don't be afraid, . . . love has its duties."[25] Experts also worried about husbands who considered the wedding night a "savage rutting" and who committed "veritable rapes" that permanently scarred brides.[26] Into the 1920s, gynecologists were familiar with brutal wedding night initiations and "ballistic uterine inflammations," though few repeated the term rape.[27] The few novels that broached the subject of maternal sexual instruction agreed that mothers were remiss.

Yet, daughters often cut short their mothers' embarrassed efforts to introduce the subject of sex. Simone de Beauvoir recalled in her autobiography that as a girl of sixteen she had told her relieved mother, "I know all about that!" In reality, Beauvoir knew only what she had read in novels; she did not even understand what was happening when a male stranger fondled her. In her recollection, she interpreted her reaction as an expression of her family's confusion of nudity with indecency but also thought that adult male bodies inspired terror in virgins.[28] While terror seems an extreme emotion, repugnance may have been quite common.

Still, according to popular as well as learned opinion, it was primarily the mother's responsibility to teach girls about sex, even though they had very little scientific information about the functioning of the sex organs and such information was withheld. Natural science and hygiene texts, doctor's columns in women's magazines and women's health manuals did not describe them.[29] In 1902, a maternal feminist who designed a course to educate future mothers "according to their physiology" omitted any mention of them.[30] In the first French edition of Woman, Family Doctor, published in 1902, Dr. Anna Fischer, a German feminist, included the only illustrations of women's external sex organs to appear in French women's health literature between the 1880s and the 1930s. Fischer's manual was so popular the publishers printed 200,000 copies of the second edition, but the illustrations of female genitalia were so controversial that they were eliminated from the second and third editions, published in 1905 and 1924.[31]

Such prudery about the pubic area was not uncommon at the turn of the twentieth century. Some bourgeois mothers insisted that their daughters pull a clean slip over their used one before removing the latter, to avoid seeing their private parts. Others made girls wear slips when they bathed "for the sake of modesty and good breeding."[32] Nonetheless, according to popular medical manuals, mothers should wash their prepubescent daughters' pubic region because it was vulnerable to infections and scratching these infections could lead to masturbation.[33] When their daughters reached menarche, mothers were supposed to supervise their daughters' daily pubic ablutions to avoid "vicious practices." One need not be a Freudian to recognize that silence about, concealment of, and constant admonition to cleanse female genitalia might impair girls' sexual imagination and their health. In the late twentieth century, an older French woman recalling her youth relates the story of another woman who had never seen another adult woman naked. She "could not imagine exposing her nakedness," with the result that she died during a difficult delivery.[34] Nonetheless, from the early 1900s when the number of nurses began to expand, a growing number of women apparently began to learn more about their anatomy and physiology, and in some cases they passed some of this knowledge on to their daughters.[35]

In fact, it was precisely a mother "terrified by the ravages caused by this disastrous ignorance," who in the 1880s had inspired the Catholic gynecologist E. A. Goupil to write a book on women's reproductive functions designed for mothers to give their daughters before the wedding night.[36] Over the next fifty years, a dozen priests, almost as many medical doctors, and a handful of mothers published premarital sex guides for girls. Four women doctors included sections on the subject in their health manuals. Most of the sex guides went through several printings; three of the health manuals merited second and third editions, suggesting an audience hungry for sexual information in preparation for marriage.

To establish their authority on the subject of sex, secular authors assured readers that their approach was scientific; to distance their manuals from erotica, they explained, "Science is always chaste. Do not blush, Madame, your modesty has nothing to fear."[37] Authors also avoided charges of prurience by using Latin terminology for sex organs and describing only internal, reproductive organs. Another method of establishing respectability was avoiding the subject of sexual intercourse.

French books for fiancées did not mention foreplay or how to prepare for intercourse beyond telling wives to relax and trust their husbands. Many warned against expecting romance in the marital bed, as they might have learned from romance novels. These warnings add a layer of meaning to the strictures on girls reading romance novels: such reading material might raise expectations about marital sex.[38] Premarital guides implicitly offered negative prognoses for early conjugal relations. Before the war, only Anna Fischer among guidebook authors had asserted that women had a sexual instinct and that women had no reason to be ashamed of their desire. After the war, this argument was more widely accepted. However, only Dr. Hélina Gaboriau, a Theosophist, enthused about early marital sex. Significantly, these two exceptions appeared in women's health manuals intended for adult women, not premarital sex guides intended for fiancées.[39]

All of these works advocated virginity before the wedding and sexual initiation on the wedding night. Several authors noted the logical contradiction between on the one hand keeping girls ignorant about sexuality, and on the other hand expecting them to carry out their conjugal duties. Still, like contemporary sex experts in Germany and the United States, French experts were committed to reinforcing marriage as a "bulwark against sexual decadence."[40] Sex manuals reinforced marital sexuality in different ways for young women than for young men. With the exception of clerics, few were critical of premarital male heterosexuality. Most secular sex advisors expected that grooms would be familiar with "casual love."[41] They believed that the groom needed experience to take charge of the bride's sexual initiation. Some offered cautionary tales about inexperienced grooms "straying" after marriage.[42] Few experts recognized that it might be problematic to entrust a virgin's first penetration to a man whose experience consisted of sex with experienced women.

In the mid-1930s, a handbook finally appeared that acknowledged female sexual satisfaction in a more direct way. Nelly Nelfrand of the University of Chicago wrote *What Every Young Girl Should Know at Puberty.* The handbook was addressed to "young French working women and their mothers" and written at the suggestion of the (eugenic) Society for Sanitary and Moral Protection. Nelfrand quoted Alphonse Paré, a seventeenth-century French erotic writer, on how to arouse women. In detail comparable to erotica, she divulged arousal techniques that her readers would otherwise have learned only by clandestine reading or from experienced and considerate lovers.[43]

Programs of Sex Education for Adolescent Girls

Long after the Third French Republic introduced free public primary education for girls in 1880–1881, it remained the ideal that girls would learn about sexuality from their mothers.[44] Clerics and physicians alike published childrearing manuals assigning mothers responsibility for the physical and moral instruction of prepubescent and pubescent girls.[45] They also agreed that mothers should stress their daughters' future motherhood "from the crib" and protect them from conditions that would "compromise" their future reproductive health.[46] Although Catholic and lay hygienists clashed on some subjects, they were unanimous on the importance of preparing girls for maternity.

Around 1900, the European-wide campaign against venereal diseases put the issue of sexual education on the public agenda.[47] As early as 1890, Dr. Fournier, a French venerealogist, decried what he termed the "syphilis of the innocents," defined as the chaste bride and the nursing child.[48] In 1901, the Society for Sanitary and Moral Protection formed to fight venereal diseases. Over the next four decades, the society encouraged several female physicians to write premarital sex guides to alert mothers about the need for vigilance in detecting infection in potential fiancés.[49] During the interwar years, a successor society cooperated with feminist groups to teach young women about venereal diseases and intimate hygiene.

Socialists also promoted sex education and sometimes quite radical views about female sexuality.[50] In France, Léon Blum, a socialist lawyer and journalist, publicly criticized premarital chastity in a 1907 tract. Blum proposed that girls "give in to all instinctual demands" for ten to fifteen years before marriage. "Planned and voluntary procreation"—code words for contraception—would allow for heterosexual intercourse without pregnancies. An experienced woman would have a better introduction to marriage and a better marriage.[51] This provocative tract was reprinted many times over the next few decades, but Blum's views never became mainstream.

Along with new ideas about sex education, radical criticisms of sexual conventions, including criticisms of premarital chastity and the practice of keeping young girls ignorant about sexuality, began to circulate during and after World War I. An anarchist pamphlet, for example, blamed cultural "disdain for the body" and "horror of everything to do with sex" for making human beings seem ugly and dirty. Because the author, Jean Marestan, advocated "free love," contraception, and abortion on demand, he had less impact in France than Marie Stopes, with her more conservative rationale for contraception, had in Great Britain in the 1920s.[52] Another writer, the feminist Avril de Sainte-Croix, recommended the teaching of reproduction in the natural sciences. Unlike Catholic sex educators, she favored a positive introduction to sex as "an initiation in the good, healthy life." Yet, because the public associated her proposals with feminist opposition to the draconian anti-abortion and anti-female-controlled contraception act of 1920, her modest proposals had little impact.[53] Eager to distance themselves from such radical ideas, most secular sex experts of the postwar era continued to champion conventional ideas and practices, such as maternal responsibility for girls' sex education.[54]

Yet, even if new ideas about sexual pleasure began to permeate French culture, institutional approaches to sex education changed very slowly. At the turn of the century, many bourgeois girls still attended convent schools, where sex education continued to consist of "surveillance and silence." To discourage intimacy between students or self-exploration, girls had to sleep one to a bed, with a sister in every dormitory room. Progressive Catholic schools introduced physical education to counteract girls' sensibility, which these schools linked to their sexuality.[55]

The secular school system that educated an increasing proportion of French girls was almost as conservative. At the Third International Congress on School Hygiene in 1910, prominent French physicians endorsed proposals to "prepare" adolescent boys for sexual life.[56] Their endorsement, and postwar alarm about venereal disease, persuaded educators to introduce a unit on venereal diseases in hygiene classes for adolescent boys. For adolescent girls, the new feature was a unit on child care.[57] The innovations reflected gendered cultural priorities: the emerging sexuality of adolescent boys and the future maternity of adolescent girls.

In the postwar climate of anxiety about the birthrate, any proposal for public sex education evoked heated opposition. Accordingly, proponents reverted to the traditional panacea of maternal "tact."[58] When the Paris Medical Faculty endorsed a proposal to make sexual hygiene a branch of public education, the assembly of French cardinals and archbishops rejected "scientific initiation" because courses might promote "physiological laws [such as the dangers of sexual continence] contrary to truth as much as the moral order."[59] In the mid-1930s many teachers thought that they should teach children about sexual life at school but were reluctant to do so because of parental conviction that the subject was "dirty."[60] The Ministry of Public Education did not introduce sex education into the school system until the mid-1970s—and then provided few instructional resources.[61]

Yet, other attempts to provide sexual education were beginning to reach at least some young French women in the interwar years. In the early 1920s, Dr. Montreuil-Strauss of the French Association of Women Doctors, for example, joined with the French League against the Venereal Peril to organize a series of educational meetings for women. In 1925, the Association of Women Doctors went on to establish the Feminine Education Committee, which gained the support of the French Union for Women's Suffrage, the League for the Rights of Women, Red Cross societies, and 175 other student, nursing, and even Catholic youth groups. With subsidies from the Ministry of Health, Welfare, and Social Insurance, the committee held 644 conferences between 1925 and 1935 on subjects like maternity and venereal diseases, attracting more than 140,000 people. The committee also distributed 83,000 brochures to almost a third of all female public school teachers.[62] In talks sponsored by the Ministry of Health, Montreuil-Strauss favored "biological education for maternity" and warned about venereal diseases. Indicative of the changes, however slowly, underway in French society in the interwar years, the conservative Association for Christian Marriage printed a report by Montreuil-Strauss, documenting that young women were not shocked but rather reassured by sex education.[63]

Notes

1.   Gabrielle Houbre, *La discipline de l'amour. L'education sentimentale des filles et des garcons à l'age du romantisme* (Paris: Plon, 1997).

2.   Two early examples were Anna Fischer, *La femme, médecin du foyer,* new ed., trans. Louise Azéma (Paris: A. Posselt, 1902); and Marie Schultz, *Hygiène génitale de la femme* (Paris, 1902). Four of the eight women doctors writing such manuals were Theosophists and/or feminists who had more positive attitudes toward feminine sexuality. However, three of these manuals were written by foreign or foreign-born women.

3.   Mary Lynn Stewart, *For Health and Beauty: Physical Culture for French-women, 1880s–1930s* (Baltimore: Johns Hopkins University Press, 2001), 80–83 and 92–93.

4.   E. A. Goupil, *Les trois âges de la femme. L'age de formation* (Publications populaires de médecine et d'hygiène) (Paris: L'Auteur, 1886), 48; M. Camboulives, *L'homme et la femme à tous les âges de la vie* (Paris: Marpon and Flammarion, 1890), 187; and Germaine Montreuil-Strauss, *Tu seras mère* (Paris: Comité d'éducation féminine, 1928), 12.

5.   Dr Marthe Francillon, *Essai sur la puberté* (Paris: Thèse méd., 1906), 74–81; N. Eddé, *Hygiène des maladies de la femme* (Paris: Maloine, 1922), 59; and G. Houlnick, *La femme et la fonction menstruelle* (Paris: Thèse méd., 1926), 29.

6.   Mme A. Gensse, *Les quatre âges de la femme au point de vue physiologique* (Corbeil, 1899), 15–16; and Charlotte L. Houlton, "Questions d'hygiène spéciale de la femme," *La Dame à la Lampe* 3 (1924): 25.

7.   Adam Raciborski, *Traité de la menstruation* (Paris: Baillière, 1866), 91.

8. Francillon, 2–63; and P. Dalché, *Gynécologie médicale. La puberté chez la femme* (Paris: A. Rueff, 1906), 6–9 and 28.

9. Raciborski, 90–107.

10. H. Vignes, *Physiologie gynécologique et médecine des femmes* (Paris: Masson, 1929), 99–100.

11. Francillon, 189 and 197; and Marthe Noel Evans, *Fits and Starts: A Genealogy of Hysteria in Modern France* (Ithaca, N.Y.: Cornell University Press, 1991), 78ff.

12. Louise de Alq, *Les secrets du cabinet de toilette. Conseils et recettes* (Paris: Bureaus des Causeries familières, 1881), 71; and E. de Gramont, *Souvenirs du monde de 1890 à 1940,* vol. 1, *Au temps d'equipages* (Paris: Grasset, 1966), 145.

13. Catherine Pozzi, *Journal de Jeunesse: 1893–1906* (Paris: Claire Paulhan, 1995), 106 and 154; and Lucie Delarue-Mardrus, "Mes Mémoires," *Revue des deux mondes,* 12 mars 1938, 72–73 and 82–83.

14. Houlnick, 80–85; and A.-M. Chartier and J. Hébard, *Discours sur la lecture (1880–1980)* (Paris: Bibliothèque publique d'information, 1989), 49ff.

15. L. Duchesne and E. Michel, *Traité élémentaire d'hygiène . . . programmes des lycées de jeunes filles,* 3d ed. (Paris: Doin, 1887), 162–163; J. L. Mora and C. Vesiez, *Nouveau cours d'hygiène* (Paris: Doin, 1890), 26–30; Vicomtesse Nacla (pseud. for Mme T. Alcan), *Il! Le choisir, le garder* (Paris: Flammarion, 1897), 17–40; and E. de Gramont, "Retrospective (1900–14)," in *Souvenirs du monde de 1890 à 1940,* vol. 3, *Claire de lune et taxi-auto* (Paris: Grasset, 1966), 11–58. See also Anne-Marie Sohn, *Du Premier Baiser à l'alcove: la Sexualité des Français au Quotidian: 1850–1950* (Paris: Aubier, 1996), 207–208.

16. Julie Manet, *Journal (1893–99)* (Paris: Klincksieck, 1979), 133 and 148; and Clara Malraux, *Memoirs,* trans. P. O'Brien (New York: Farrar, Strauss and Giroux, 1967), 100–101.

17. Malraux, 138–139. See also Baronne J. Michaux, *En Marge du drame. Journal d'une Parisienne pendant la guerre 1914–1915* (Paris: Perrin, 1916), 18, 124–125, 135, 185–186, 211, and 232–233; and Gramont, vol. 3, chapters on the war and the home front.

18. Mary Louise Roberts, *Civilization without Sexes: Reconstructing Gender in Postwar France, 1917–1927* (Chicago: University of Chicago Press, 1994), 154 and 183.

19. Simone de Beauvoir, *Memoirs of a Dutiful Daughter,* trans. James Kirkup (New York: Harper and Row, 1958), 71 and 171ff.

20. Canon Cordonnier, *Causeries familiales. II. Le mariage approche . . . Etes-vous prêtes?* (Avignon: Aubenel Père, 1935), 45–85.

21. Monique Levallet-Montal, *Pour les vingt ans de Colette* (Paris: Desclée de Brouwer, 1935), 196–223.

22. Martine Sevegrand, *L'amour en toutes lettres. Questions à l'abbé Viollet sur la sexualité 1924–1943* (Paris: Albin Michel, 1997), 24.

23. H. Fischer, *Hygiène d'enfance: L'education sexuelle* (Paris: Ollier-Henry, 1903), 20; Mayoux, *L'Education des sexes* (Paris: Librairie Scientifique, 1906), 10; and Jeanne Stephani-Cherbuliez, *Le sexe a ses raisons. Instruction et éducation sexuelles* (Paris: Baillière, 1934), 20–27.

24. Abbé Charles Grimaud, *Aux mères et à leurs grandes jeunes filles, futures*

épouses, 19th ed. (Paris: P. Téqui, 1927), 24–25, 31, 140–143, 181, 186, 190–193, and 282. On beliefs about girls' innocence, see Anne Martin-Fugier, *La Bourgeoisie: Femme au temps de Paul Bourget* (Paris: Grasset, 1983), 56.

25.   A. Siredey, *L'hygiène des maladies de la femme* (Paris: Masson, 1907), 91.

26.   A. Coriveaud, *Le lendemain du mariage. Etude d'hygiène* (Paris: Baillière, 1884), 9–16.

27.   E.g., Siredey, 28–29.

28.   Beauvoir, 163–171.

29.   My evaluation of Pasteurian hygiene is less positive than that of Yvonne Knibiehler, Marcel Bernos, Elisabeth Ravoux-Rallo, and Eliane Richard, *De la pucelle à la minette. Les jeunes filles de l'age classique à nos jours* (Paris: Temps actuels, 1983), because I focus on sex organs and sexuality.

30.   Mme Augusta Moll-Weiss, *Les mères de demain. L'education de la jeune fille d'après sa physiologie* (Paris, 1902).

31.   Anna Fischer, 2d and 3d editions (1905 and 1924), preface and 268ff. Fischer's manual was one of only three women's health manuals to promote women-controlled contraception in these five decades.

32.   *Loving Picasso: The Private Journal of Fernande Olivier,* trans. C. Baker and M. Raeburn (New York: Abrams, 2001), 78; and Liane de Pougy, *My Blue Notebooks,* trans. Diana Athill (New York: Harper and Row, 1979), 100.

33.   Mlle A. Quint, *Manuel d'hygiène et d'enseignement social* (Paris: Alcan, 1914), 61; and Une Doctoresse, *Le guide médical de la femme et de la famille* (Paris: Editions du "Petite Echo de la Mode," 1933), 269.

34.   Emilie Carles as told to Robert Destanque, *A Life of Her Own: The Transformation of a Countrywoman in Twentieth-Century France,* trans. A. H. Goldberger (New York: Penguin, 1992), 52.

35.   Stewart, 58ff.

36.   Goupil, 6–7.

37.   Alexis Clerc, *Hygiène et médecine des deux sexes* (Paris: Rouff, 1885), 5; and G. M. Bessède, *L'instruction sexuelle à l'école et dans la famille* (Paris: Reinwald, n.d.), 7.

38.   Nacla, 80.

39.   Fischer, 1902, 264; and Hélina Gaboriau, *Les trois ages de la femme* (Paris: Larousse, 1923), 94.

40.   Lutz D. H. Sauerteig, "Sex Education in Germany from the Eighteenth to the Twentieth Century," in *Sexual Cultures in Europe: Themes in Sexuality,* ed. Franz X. Eder et al. (Manchester: Manchester University Press, 1999), 12; and Patricia J. Campbell, *Sex Education Books for Young Adults, 1892–1979* (New York: R. R. Bowker, 1979), 6–8.

41.   E. Stérian, *L'education sexuelle* (Paris: Belliére et fils, 1910), 77ff and 146ff; G. J. Witkowski, *La génération humaine,* 9th ed. (Paris: Maloine, 1927), 229ff.; and L.-M. Des Preaux, *L'education des sexes et la répopulation* (Paris: Imprimerie générale, 1904).

42.   Pierre de Lano, *Du coeur aux sens. A travers le mariage* (Paris: Flammarion, 1898), 25.   .

43.   N. Nelfrand, *Ce que toute jeune fille doit savoir à l'âge de la puberté. Éducation sexuelle de l'adolescence. Petite physiologie génitale de l'hygiène interne de l'homme et de la femme* (Paris: Editions Prima, 1932), 20–41.

44.   Jules Rochard, "L'Education des filles," *Revue de deux mondes* (l février 1888).

45. J.-B. Fonssagrives, *L'education physique des jeunes filles ou Avis aux mères* (Paris: Hachette, 1869), v and vii; Mme H. Meunier, *Le docteur au village. Entretiens familiers sur l'hygiène* (Paris: Hachette, 1880), 3; E. Caubet, *Hygiène de la femme* (Paris: Rueff, 1894), 1; and Bessède, 87.

46. C. Barbaud and C. Lefevre, *La puberté chez la femme* (Paris: Maloine, 1897), vi; and E. Monin, *La santé de la femme* (Paris: Michel, 1928), 9.

47. Sauerteig, 13 and 15.

48. A. Fournier, *Syphilis et mariage,* 2d ed. (Paris: Masson, 1890), 21–27 and 141–144.

49. Anne Carol, *Histoire de l'eugénisme en France. Les médecins et la procréation, XIXe–XXe siècle* (Paris: Seuil, 1995), 51–63; and Yvonne Knibiehler and Catherine Fouquet, *La femme et les médecins* (Paris: Hachette, 1983), 221.

50. Sauerteig, 14.

51. Léon Blum, "Du Mariage," in *L'Oeuvre de Léon Blum, 1905–14* (Paris: A. Michel, 1962).

52. Jean Marestan, *L'education sexuelle* (Paris: Silvette, 1916); and Roy Porter and Lesley Hall, *The Facts of Life: The Creation of Sexual Knowledge in Britain, 1650–1950* (New Haven, Conn.: Yale University Press, 1995), 203ff. On Stopes and her correspondents, see Wally Secombe, "Starting to Stop: Working-Class Fertility Decline in Britain," *Past & Present,* no. 126 (February 1990): 151–185.

53. Mme Avril de Sainte-Croix, *L'education sexuelle* (Paris: Alcan, 1918).

54. Compared to their predecessors, postwar sex experts tended to include more eugenic warnings about the dangers of marrying men with hereditary diseases like syphilis. See Michel Bourgas, *Le droit à l'amour pour la femme* (Paris: Vigot frères, 1914 and 1919), 1–4; and René Vaucaire, *Ce que toute jeune fille à marier doit savoir* (Paris: A. Michel, 1921), 15ff and 39ff.

55. Odile Arnold, *Le corps et l'âme: La vie des religieuses au XIXe siècle* (Paris: Seuil, 1984), 81, 90, 135, 156, and 195–197; Judith Gautier, *Le collier des jours. Souvenirs de ma vie* (Paris: Juven, n.d.), 154ff.; and Mère Marie du Sacré-Coeur, *La formation catholique de la femme contemporaine,* 2d ed. (Paris: X. Rodnelet, 1899), 21–32.

56. Bessède, 7ff.; L. Mathe, *L'enseignement de l'hygiene sexuelle à l'école,* 2d ed. (Paris: Vigot, 1912), 14, 21 and 98ff.; and Jablonski, *L'education sexuelle. Conférence faite à la Ligue d'Hygiène scolaire* (Poitiers, 1913).

57. M. R. Paty, "L'Enseignement de l'hygiène à l'école primaire," in *Journées médico-scolaires de l'enfance d'âge scolaire* (Paris: Office de Protection Maternelle et Infantile, 1935), 260–264; and A. Pizon, *Hygiène. Nouveaux programmes. Classe de 3me, garçons et filles* (Paris: Doin, 1927).

58. Vaucaire, 15ff. and 39ff.

59. Abrand Ganay and Abbé J. Viollet, *Les initiations nécessaires,* 26th ed. (Paris: Association du Mariage Chrétien, 1933), 5–7.

60. P. Aulaire. *La leçon d'amour: Traité d'instruction et d'éducation sexuelles* (Paris: Blanchard, 1930), 7 and 19; Stephani-Cherbuliez, 13–20, 54–55, and 171–178; and Léon Eisenstein, *Éducation sexuelle (Etude biologique et psychique du problème)* (Lyon: Thèse Méd., 1939).

61. International Planned Parenthood Federation (IPPF), *A Survey on the Status of Sex Education in European Member Countries* (London: IPPF, 1975), 6–7, 19, 22–27, and 46–47.

62.   Bibliothèque historique de la Ville de Paris, Fonds Dr. Germaine Montreuil-Straus, Dr. Aimé Gauthier, "La Femme contre le peril vénérien," *Vers la santé,* November 1925, 6 and 11; and Bibliothèque historique de la Ville de Paris, Montreuil-Straus, *L'Oeuvre accomplie par le Comité d'Éducation feminine* (1925–1935).

63.   Germaine Montreuil-Strauss, "Note relative à l'éducation sexuelle des jeunes filles" in *L'Eglise et l'éducation sexuelle* (Paris: Association du Mariage Chrétien, 1929), 142–146.

11 In Their Own Words: Girls' Representations of Growing Up in Germany in the 1920s

Christina Benninghaus

Christina Benninghaus is also interested in the reception of expert notions of adolescence—in this case by girls themselves. Looking at school essays written by German girls in the 1920s, Benninghaus argues that while the new discourses were appropriated by middle-class girls, working-class adolescents did not adopt the new rhetoric of adolescence. Working-class girls, in contrast to their middle-class peers, depicted youth as a socially determined life phase rather than as a time of significant psychological development. Furthermore, working-class girls seem to have been very reluctant to display social ambitions or articulate claims to independence. Middle-class girls, by contrast, not only had more options but also took advantage of contemporary discourses on youth as particular life phase to make more direct claims to some independence in life. The "invention" of female adolescence, Benninghaus argues, was thus a very class-specific phenomenon.

Girls born in the first two decades of the twentieth century grew up at a time when, according to much evidence and opinion, generational and gender relations were rapidly changing. As in other European countries, German women had recently gained access to higher education and to professions previously reserved for men. During World War I, they had taken on jobs and responsibilities traditionally held by men. In 1919 they won the vote. Women's private roles as wives and mothers were also transformed as new, more rational, or scientific standards of motherhood and housework were introduced.[1] Finally, many women's styles of dress and behavior altered as they ventured into new public spheres.

Simultaneously, new ideas were emerging about youth, both as a phase of life and as a social category. In part, these new ideas were prompted by the increasing visibility of young people, caused by demographic developments and by new forms of commercial culture and a thriving youth movement. In part, they derived from more general anxieties about modernity. As a result, youth became the topic of a growing number of sociological and psychological studies and the target of new laws and institutions meant to care for and to control young boys and—to a lesser extent—girls.[2] No longer the concern of churches alone, youth was increasingly the focus of a host of political and state initiatives. A "battle for youth" was launched, which eventually led to high levels of participation in youth groups.[3]

During the first decades of the twentieth century, preoccupation with youth was a general European phenomenon, but both debates about youth and its place in society and attempts to control the activities of young people seem to have been particularly intense in Germany.[4] During the Weimar Republic—the period of political and cultural experimentation sandwiched between the end of the war and the rise of the Nazis—images of the "New Woman" and the "new generation" served as focal points for anxieties and aspirations connected with modernity. Yet, the actual impact of the new ideas on the experiences and perspectives of girls growing up in the 1920s has rarely been studied. While social historians have stressed the continuities in economic structures and power relations in the Weimar years, cultural historians have pointed to the changes in the representation of gender relations and especially of young women in mass culture, art, and the sciences.[5] However, neither structural conditions nor cultural discourses directly translate into peoples' lived experiences. This chapter investigates the relationship between changing adult discourses and the experiences, self-perceptions, and expectations of girls growing up during the 1920s. By analyzing texts written by fourteen- to seventeen-year-old girls during the "golden years" of the Weimar Republic, it explores the dissemination of these new ideas among young girls of different class backgrounds. This chapter concentrates on girls' perception of generational relations, on their work experiences, and on the ways in which they linked femininity and paid employment.

Girls' Voices: Some Remarks on Sources

The social history of youth has to make use of materials written by adults—by teachers, researchers, and contemporary observers or by autobiographers writing about their earlier life. The perspective of young people themselves tends to be absent from such sources. However, while children's voices are difficult to discover, adolescents have sometimes left behind letters, diaries, pieces of art, and court statements—to name only a few sources.

In addition to these sources, twentieth-century youths produced other forms of writing as well. After 1900, writing compositions became an increasingly common part of German classes even at the elementary school level. All German children and young people under eighteen years of age were obliged to attend school. For the majority of children this meant eight years of full-time elementary school followed by three years of part-time schooling (six to eight hours a week) in vocational schools. While the actual implementation of universal postelementary schooling was incomplete during the Weimar years, urban adolescents were soon required to attend classes in academic and vocational subjects and—in the case of girls—often also in home economics.[6] As was true in elementary schools, writing compositions was part of the vocational school curriculum.

During the 1920s, school essays were often written at the request of professional researchers who considered them a particularly useful source for understanding the inner world of adolescents. Together with participant observation, the collection of diaries, and the analysis of data compiled from questionnaires, the "*Aufsatz-Methode*" (essay method) was seen as an important technique of qualitative youth studies.[7] Youth researchers requested that pupils write compositions on topics such as "My occupation," "My mother," "Sorrow and consolation," "If I had 1000 Marks . . . ," and "How I spend my leisure time."[8] These essays were written in class. They were always written anonymously and were neither corrected nor graded. After being analyzed by researchers, many of these essays were subsequently published in collections intended to give teachers, welfare workers, and other interested readers insights into the lives and thoughts of the young generation. This chapter is based on the analysis of 1,400 such compositions, originally written and published either in their entirety or in excerpted form during the 1920s and early 1930s. The analysis of these texts reveals the patterns of interpretation that were available to girls as they tried to make sense of their world.

Girls and Generational Relations

Given that "generational identity and generational conflict were concepts which exerted a powerful fascination in Weimar Germany,"[9] it is not surprising that a number of studies were undertaken to investigate the relationship between parents and children. The most comprehensive of these studies was undertaken at the end of the 1920s when 1,700 boys and girls from Berlin were asked to write essays on the topic "What my family means to me." According to the youth researcher, the study did not support contemporary fears about the disintegration of the family. On the contrary, about four out of five essays by girls and three out of four essays by boys showed that the adolescents had strong ties to their families.[10]

Among those girls belonging to the minority of adolescents, those classified as having a tense relationship with their parents or as having broken with them completely, some clearly expressed a sense of belonging to a new generation. Thus a sixteen-year-old future dressmaker wrote:

As my father is not unknown in certain circles, I will not mention his occupation. But my father has a secure, well-established position so that material problems are unheard of in my family. My father and my mother both come from the country-side. It is due to the hard work of my father that we are well-situated today. Look-ing at the way my parents were brought up, it is not surprising that they have some-what narrow-minded ideas. I am a person of modern and free ideas. Between my opinions and those of my parents there is a deep gap which I surely cannot bridge as this would require old-fashioned thinking. My parents, on the other hand, do not make any attempt to understand me. Obviously, we do not live in harmony. To me my mother is a mother but not a friend. My father is too much occupied with other things to pay attention to me.[11]

Clearly, this girl believed that generational differences in socialization were leading to generational conflict. Presenting herself as a modern metropolitan girl, she accused her parents of being old-fashioned and disinterested. While the source does not specify the social background of the girl, the language employed points to a lower-middle or middle-class background. Working-class girls would not have expected their mothers to be a "friend." When praising or criticizing their mothers, they normally referred to their mothers' domestic skills.[12]

Class-specific variations showed up in other aspects of the essays as well. Working-class girls were more reluctant than their bourgeois peers to criti-cize their mothers. Of the 3,597 anonymously written essays on "My Mother," collected by Else Schilfarth, only fifty showed a fundamental rejection of the mother and almost all of these were written by middle-class girls, who scolded their mothers for being "impractical," inconsistent in their childrearing prac-tices, or generally old-fashioned.[13] Working-class girls, by contrast, refrained from admitting to conflicts with their parents and generally did not present themselves as self-assured and ambitious but more typically as docile and obe-dient. A sixteen-year-old working-class girl who had experienced an important conflict with her parents thus described her experience in the following way:

I finished elementary school two years ago. Then I had to learn a trade. My wish was to become a seamstress. But my parents thought differently. I was supposed to become a worker and to help to earn a living since there are many siblings. When my parents proposed this, I thought, no, I won't become a worker. But soon I thought differently. I looked for a job and soon found one. I work at W. in Fichten Street. I am really happy with my work. Perhaps much happier than if I had be-come a seamstress because now I know that I support my parents.[14]

In this essay, the girl recalls her initial aversion to becoming a worker and her rejection of her parents' suggestion. However, the conflict is not described fur-ther and instead the girl depicts her experience of giving in as having led to a new sense of confidence based on her self-perception as an important source of support for her parents.

In general, working-class girls seem to have had great difficulties in present-ing themselves as engaged in conflicts with their parents. This impression is confirmed by surveys that directly questioned girls from different social back-grounds about their ideas regarding the parent-child relationship. Apparently, working-class girls were more willing to accept criticism from their parents than middle-class girls; they were also more likely to describe the parent-child relationship as one based on obedience rather than trust.[15] Consequently, girls from lower social groups—typically growing up in patriarchal families that favored authoritarian styles of upbringing sometimes linked to religious beliefs and practices—were less likely than their middle-class peers to represent themselves as engaged in generational conflict. As one youth researcher put it: "Generational conflict, which today in time of rapid mental change plays such an important role for the adolescents in middle-class families, tends to be out of the question for proletarian youth."[16]

Youth and the Life Cycle

Social differences in the use of the discourse of generational conflict generally correspond with different notions of youth as a lifecycle phase. Psychological concepts of youth as a phase of insecurity, romanticism, and daydreaming, supporting the assumption that mutual understanding between grown-ups and youths was necessarily difficult, were popular amongst middle-class girls and can be found in many contemporary diaries. However, this discourse was rarely picked up by working-class girls. In their school essays, they described youth as a distinct life phase associated with certain responsibilities, namely work, and certain privileges, especially in the realm of leisure. At the same time, they depicted life course transitions as results of external forces. Institutional events, rather than individual physical or psychological development, marked the end of childhood. As one working-class student in a postelementary class wrote, "when I left school, the difficulties started. The time came and I had to leave school, and I had to part from those I liked. Although it was very hard for me, I had to go, as the years of school were over."[17] While the end of childhood was clearly marked by leaving school, having one's confirmation, and taking up employment, even the transition to adulthood associated with marriage was depicted more as an institutional step coming quasi-automatically in the early to mid-twenties than as an intensely personal moment. Two dressmakers wrote: "I would like to get married in the countryside, but only between 21 and 25," and "At the age of 22 to 25 I want to get married, not later, as I want to be really innocent when getting married." An office worker explained that at the age of sixteen she still had "lots of aversions" against a relationship with a young man but she was sure that this was only a passing phase: "When I am 24, a decent man will approach me and propose marriage."[18]

Based on the compositions, it appears that working-class girls tended to imagine the life course as a sequence of consecutive events leaving relatively little room for individual decisions and personal development. Psychological definitions of adolescence as a time of upheaval were rather alien to them, as were corresponding ideas of a "youth front" or "youth mission," which were propagated by parts of the bourgeois youth movement and stressed the specific potentials of young people as a social group. Consequently, middle-class researchers, trying to investigate the psychology of working-class girls, sometimes seemed rather disappointed that girls from the working class did not show "the romantic feelings of the 'Backfisch-years'" and other related psychological symptoms of adolescence.[19]

Making Sense of Limited Opportunities

Girls growing up during the 1920s spent their youth somewhat differently from their mothers and grandmothers. However, while women from middle- and upper-class families took up further education, went to the university, and entered new professions like medicine, teaching, and social work, working-class girls' working lives did not change nearly as much. Certainly, hours of work were reduced and working conditions in industry, domestic service, and even in agriculture improved. However, girls continued to be paid considerably less than boys or adult workers. They often did not receive a formal training and their occupational choices were extremely limited. Despite an increase in the number of jobs as shop assistant or office worker, most girls still worked in the traditional areas of agriculture and domestic service. On the whole, girls' position in the Weimar labor market was far from favorable. Not only was the economy of the Weimar Republic crisis ridden, the demographic development also contributed to an overcrowding of the labor market.[20] But how did girls, growing up in the 1920s, make sense of this situation?

It has often been assumed that girls did not take their work or their choice of occupation all that seriously because they imagined their employment as a temporary phenomenon before marriage. However, both school essays and contemporary surveys point in a different direction. When asked about their future plans, almost none of the female school-leavers mentioned unskilled work as a desirable option.[21] Among the 130 unskilled laborers whose essays are quoted in Schilfarth's collection, none suggests that learning a trade was unnecessary or useless for girls. Apparently, girls had clear preferences regarding their employment opportunities. Although they expected to get married, they knew from experience that marriage did not exclude paid employment. More importantly, they did not think of occupational training as something that would eventually pay off in the future. Instead, they seemed to conceive of it as an immediate asset providing them social recognition and job satisfaction.

From the point of view of school-leaving girls, youth was not a short period of transition but a long phase in life, stretching from fourteen to the mid-twenties. While the women's movement and labor exchange officers argued for better education for girls, invoking the bleak picture of the poor widow and deserted wife unable to support herself and her children through her unskilled work, girls themselves were more concerned with the immediate benefits of being an apprentice. They often simply enjoyed learning. In addition, apprenticeship was seen as an avenue to better paid and less heavy and dirty work. The higher social status attached to the work of saleswomen, office workers, dressmakers, and hairdressers also meant better chances on the marriage market.[22]

A close reading of the school compositions reveals surprising silences. In contrast to what might be expected, some of the topoi used by the labor and women's movements to protest against the labor market situation of women are conspicuously absent from the texts of working-class girls. Thus, the fact that boys were far more likely than girls to receive vocational training was not criticized, and earnings were not a prominent theme in the essays. While girls mentioned being proud of contributing to the family income, a desire for higher wages was rarely expressed. If girls did indeed note that they hoped to be able to increase their earnings, they always added that they needed the money to care for their relatives. In comparison, boys were much bolder in their statements about their earnings and quite happily announced that they needed money for their own purposes.[23] The earning differential between men and women was not mentioned at all.[24] If girls compared their working conditions, their hours of work, or their wages to other people's, these "others" were always young girls in different occupations. Thus, gender inequality was not one of the common themes in girls' essays. In comparison, social inequality did receive some more attention. Though not a widespread phenomenon, at least some girls used the language of the labor movement to criticize their disadvantaged position in a capitalist labor market.

> As I am from a working class background and as only my mother, my sister and I earn, I could not do anything else but start working in a factory.

> When 14¾ years of age I started working as a laborer at J.G. Sch. . . . I don't like my job at all. . . . Only the prospect of getting paid on Friday—though only very little—stops me from chucking it in. . . . I regard this factory life as a form of slavery which we can't get rid of as it is the basis of our existence.[25]

While some of the workers used socialist rhetoric when contemplating their situation, the most explicit texts criticizing the limited opportunities for working-class girls were typically written by individuals who had managed to get some education or formal training themselves. A future printer thus wrote:

> My greatest wish would have been to become a dressmaker, but unfortunately my poor parents did not command the necessary resources to pay for my training. They always had to fight for their daily bread, which is something that hurt my parents terribly. The capitalists, the ruling classes, are able to send their daughters and sons to secondary schools to have them educated. But the worker has to be glad to earn his daily bread by the sweat of his brow with heavy work, to start working with an empty stomach and to eke out a living.[26]

Spelling out complaints about social inequality thus seems to have been a privilege of girls who belonged to the higher ranks of the working class. In contrast, gender (and generational) inequality were not even problematized by these girls. That male and female opportunities regarding earnings, occupational choices, and vocational training were fundamentally different seems to have gone without saying for girls growing up in the 1920s.

Endangered Femininity:
Negotiating Respectability and Work

Girls coming of age in the 1920s were confronted with many different images of femininity. Mother, sisters, and neighbors presumably remained important role models, but female teachers and youth leaders along with the images of women promoted by the mass media were becoming more influential. However, perhaps more important than the variety of images was the intensity of the debates on gender relations. But how did adolescent girls experience this situation? While girls could make use of new and contradictory representations of young womanhood, the school essays suggest that such conflicting notions of femininity could also produce anxiety among adolescent girls.

Many of the compositions featured unease about the relationship between work and femininity. The problem was especially marked for girls who did manual labor, who often had to fight the prejudices of contemporaries, including many trade unionists. The school compositions suggest that such girls employed a variety of discursive strategies to underline their respectability. Some girls addressed the problem directly. One young manual laborer recalled how a female acquaintance reproached her for being a worker: "You, you are a worker? Aren't you embarrassed about doing such dirty work?" and how she reacted by claiming that her job was as good a job as any other. Another girl whose desire to become a shop assistant had been thwarted, wrote: "So I became a worker and I am as happy with my job as if it was a skilled one. I know that factory life is deemed disreputable but I am not worried by this, I think there is no reason to be ashamed of doing one's job."[27] Other girls tried to present themselves or their workplace as an exception. One girl thus noted that "the others all like me, why, because I work hard and I am not as vulgar as the other girls." Another explained that "I started to work in the film department at the Bing Factory with very decent people. There I do not need to be in danger of falling in with bad company. I like doing my work so after each Sunday I like going back to work."[28]

Another way of defending one's respectability was to underline one's interest in housework and to present one's factory employment as a passing phase. Adopting this strategy, a sixteen-year-old female factory worker wrote:

How nice it is if a person can follow a profession! I want to become a good housewife. I am already preparing myself for this at home. Now I work in a factory so that I can use my wages to buy things. My father always says that once I am 18 I will be allowed to attend sewing classes so that I learn the sewing necessary for running a household. I like the factory a lot. I am an apprentice in the cardboard box department of O. During these two years of apprenticeship pay is not really to be counted. Now we make the Biller cameras. The work has to be done very carefully. Only the best workers are asked to do it. I am glad that I am one of them. I have to spread the parts with glue without smudging any. My fellow workers all treat me very well; you don't hear a bad word the entire day; from the girls and women nearby one never hears an indecent word either. I really feel at home amongst my fellow-workers, they are so motherly with me. And I also enjoy doing the work. My wish is that soon I will become a good housewife.[29]

This essay can be read as a reaction to a whole array of different prejudices often harbored against workers. The girl presented her work as clean and tidy, her fellow workers as decent women, and the atmosphere in the factory as homelike and secure. Furthermore, she described her work as a mere interlude, framing her work description with statements about her wish to become a good housewife. The essay suggests that this girl felt threatened by the de-feminization commonly associated with factory employment.

Compared to manual laborers, young girls who worked as dressmakers could be far more relaxed regarding the reputation of their work as proper for girls. They worked in an all-female environment, often in small workshops that were part of the private household of the mistress. Since the formal craft apprenticeship system had been opened to girls in 1897, many dressmakers received a formal training lasting three years, culminating with an examination by the chamber of industry and commerce. These girls took great pride in their skills. They owned their own tools and, ideally, displayed their status by ways of behavior and speech. And they generally loved their work. When writing essays on "My occupation" only 57 or 5.8 percent out of 980 dressmakers wrote that they did not find fulfillment in their work and only 27 or 2.8 percent wrote that they would have preferred a different job.[30]

When writing about their apprenticeship, some dressmakers deliberately praised the feminine character of their work. As one girl noted, "I choose this occupation because I think of it as practical and also as really feminine."[31] Other dressmakers implicitly depicted their work as a typically female occupation. They pointed to historical traditions of women making their own garments and/or represented their apprenticeship as a continuation of childhood socialization. In addition, many stressed the aesthetic character of their work and the possibilities it gave them to in turn train future apprentices. Hence, an eighteen year old exclaimed:

As I am training to become a dressmaker, and as I am enjoying it a lot, I think that I will be happiest when later in life I will be able to fulfill my job completely. Often when lost in thought, I imagine my future home. It will include a beautiful, large workshop, in which I imagine a band of young, cheerful girls who have chosen my profession, and I will have the pleasure of showing and teaching it to them.[32]

The expectation of future self-employment is here presented in an image that fit conventional visions of femininity. The mistress is not presented as an independent businesswoman managing a profitable workshop but as a motherly figure.

For office workers the situation was very different. Like their counterparts who performed manual labor, office workers, typists, stenographers, and accountants faced critics who questioned the gender appropriateness of their work, but they were fewer and generally confined to middle-class circles. For working-class girls, office work (along with dressmaking) was the most attractive form of occupation. According to the essays, the work itself, its cleanliness, the nicer dress, and the more refined manners associated with it attracted many girls to office work. Interestingly, the prospect of higher wages was not mentioned as a key reason for seeking such employment.

While manual laborers wrote a lot about their colleagues, office workers tended to focus on their boss. In a number of texts, girls expressed a desire to please their boss or to be of real help to their employer. For example, one sixteen-year-old girl wrote that she chose office work "because I wanted to find a job which satisfies me. This, however, was not the case at the beginning of my apprenticeship when I made many stupid mistakes." Fortunately, her performance improved and as a result she was rewarded a pay raise of 10 percent for her good work. "This made me so happy," she noted, "that I would rather have done without my entire wages than without those 10%. . . . I am not really ambitious, but I want to do well so that I will be of real help to my boss and he will be able to leave things to be done by me on my own."[33]

Office work was not only the occupation of working-class and lower middle-class girls who often learned the necessary skills on the job or in short-term typewriting classes. Girls from the higher ranks of society also did office work, though they tended to prepare for the work by attending trade schools. Nonetheless, office work seems to have been less appealing to bourgeois girls. When 151 middle-class girls attending the Leipzig High School for Women's Occupations were asked to write essays about their "plans and wishes for the future," half of them insisted that attending classes for office workers was not their personal preference but was presumably their parents' decision.[34] On the contrary, many were unhappy with the prospect of having to work in an office, perceiving such work as "meaningless." One of these girls even proclaimed that she would never be able to accept an office job that she believed entailed nothing but "sitting in a narrow room, from morning till evening, every day being the same as the one before."[35] Many of these girls would have preferred to become teachers, nurses, or artists. In their essays, they drew colorful images of life as a nurse who supposedly "walked lightly through the rooms of the hospital like an elf" and like "an angel" and whispered words of consolation to patients. When comparing the work of a kindergarten teacher to that of an accountant one girl asked, "Is it not a thousand times more beautiful to surround these little creatures with love, than to write empty and crazy numbers?"[36]

In general, then, girls' expectations regarding their work depended on their social background. Both working- and middle-class girls tackled the question of whether their work was suitable for women and developed discursive strategies to underline their respectability. To voice ambitions was apparently difficult for girls, as texts written by dressmakers and by office workers suggest. However, middle-class girls were more daring in their pursuit of happiness. The vision of "spiritual motherhood," promoted by many bourgeois women since the end of the nineteenth century, and the culture of the youth movement, which highlighted the specific competence of young people, provided them with arguments for claiming access to new types of occupations like nursing, teaching, or welfare work. Such arguments were not accessible for working-class girls who underlined their respectability by pointing to their moral integrity and their willingness to be of service (for their employer or their family).

Discourses on youth and generational conflict were omnipresent in German society at the beginning of the twentieth century and especially after the First World War. The very existence of the source material used for this study testifies to the enormous attention paid to adolescence. The "cult of youth" and the desire to control and organize young people combined to widen the material and discursive spheres open to adolescent girls and boys. Yet, based on a close reading of school essays written by fourteen- to seventeen-year-old girls from various social backgrounds, it appears that while the new discourses were appropriated by middle-class girls, working-class adolescents did not adopt the new rhetoric. Thus working-class girls described the parent-child relationship as based on authoritarian structures—not on friendship or camaraderie—and felt uneasy about criticizing their mothers. In contrast to their middle-class peers, they depicted youth as a socially determined life phase, not as a time of strenuous psychological development. Confronted by an extremely unfavorable labor market, they did not challenge gender inequality on the job market, nor did they aspire to occupations that were beyond what was available to them. Furthermore, working-class girls seem to have been very reluctant to display ambitions. Instead, they used representations of femininity based on notions of obedience and service. Middle-class girls, by contrast, not only had more options but also took advantage of contemporary discourses on youth as a life phase and on the specific potential of womanhood to make more direct claims to some independence in life. The "invention of adolescence" thus seems to have been of little importance for the self-perception and the ambitions of working-class girls growing up during the 1920s. While their lives might well have been far more conflict filled than the essays suggest, these girls made sense of their situation within a mental framework based on existing gender and generational hierarchies. Rebellion against these hierarchies seemed out of the question.

Notes

1.   As an introduction, see Ute Frevert, *Women in German History: From Bourgeois Emancipation to Sexual Liberation* (Oxford: Berg, 1988).

2.   As an introduction, see Winfried Speitkamp, *Jugend in der Neuzeit. Deutschland vom 16. bis zum 20. Jahrhundert* (Göttingen: Vandenhoeck & Ruprecht, 1998). See also Elizabeth Harvey, *Youth and the Welfare State in Weimar Germany* (Oxford: Clarendon Press, 1993); Derek S. Linton, *"Who has the youth, has the future": The Campaign to Save Young Workers in Imperial Ger-*

many (Cambridge: Cambridge University Press, 1991); Detlev J. K. Peukert, *Grenzen der Sozialdisziplinierung. Aufstieg und Krise der deutschen Jugendfürsorge von 1878 bis 1932* (Köln: Bund-Verlag, 1986).

3. Jürgen Reulecke, "The Battle for the Young: Mobilising Young People in Wilhelmine Germany," in *Generations in Conflict: Youth Revolt and Generation Formation in Germany, 1770–1968*, ed. Mark Roseman (Cambridge: Cambridge University Press, 1995), 92–104.

4. Mark Roseman, "Generational Conflict and German History, 1770–1968," in *Generations in Conflict: Youth Revolt and Generation Formation in Germany, 1770–1968*, ed. Mark Roseman (Cambridge: Cambridge University Press, 1995), 1–46. For a different view on the discourse of generational conflict in Germany, see Tom Taylor, "Images of Youth and the Family in Wilhelmine Germany: Toward a Reconsideration of the German Sonderweg," *German Studies Review, Special Issue: German Identity,* winter 1992, 55–74.

5. Patrice Petro, *Joyless Streets: Women and Melodramatic Representation in Weimar Germany* (Princeton, N.J.: Princeton University Press, 1989); Vibeke Rützou Petersen, *Women and Modernity in Weimar Germany: Reality and Representation in Popular Fiction* (New York: Berghahn Books, 2001); Katharina von Ankum, ed., *Women in the Metropolis: Gender and Modernity in Weimar Culture* (Berkeley: University of California Press, 1997); Marsha Meskimmon and Shearer West, eds., *Visions of the "Neue Frau": Women and the Visional Art in Weimar Germany* (Aldershot, England: Scolar Press, 1995); Petra Bock and Katja Koblitz, eds., *Neue Frauen zwischen den Zeiten* (Berlin: Edition Hentrich, 1995); and Katharina Sykora et al., eds., *Die Neue Frau. Herausforderungen für die Bildmedien der Zwanziger Jahre* (Marburg: Jonas Verlag, 1993).

6. For more details, see Christina Benninghaus, *Die anderen Jugendlichen. Arbeitermädchen in der Weimarer Republik* (Frankfurt a.M.: Campus, 1999), 24–31.

7. For the development of sociological and psychological youth research in Germany, see Peter Dudek, *Jugend als Objekt der Wissenschaften. Geschichte der Jugendforschung in Deutschland und Österreich* (Opladen: Westdeutscher Verlag, 1990); and Johannes von Bühler, *Die gesellschaftliche Konstruktion des Jugendalters. Zur Entstehung der Jugendforschung am Beginn des 20. Jahrhunderts* (Weinheim: Deutscher Studien-Verlag, 1990).

8. Else Schilfarth, *Die psychologischen Grundlagen der heutigen Mädchenbildung, Bd. 1: Berufsgestaltung* and *Bd. 2: Lebensgestaltung* (Leipzig: Klinkhardt, 1926–1927); Mathilde Kelchner, *Kummer und Trost jugendlicher Arbeiterinnen. Eine sozialpsychologische Untersuchung an Aufsätzen von Schülerinnen der Berufsschule* (Leipzig: Hirschfeld, 1929); Philipp Behler, *Psychologie des Berufsschülers. Ein Beitrag zur Industriepädagogik* (Köln: DuMont-Schauberg, 1928); and Robert Dinse, *Das Freizeitleben der Großstadtjugend. 5000 Jungen und Mädchen berichten* (Berlin: Verlagsgesellschaft R. Müller, 1932).

9. Elisabeth Harvey, "Gender, Generation and Politics: Young Protestant Women in the Final Years of the Weimar Republic," in *Generations in Conflict: Youth Revolt and Generation Formation in Germany, 1770–1968*, ed. Mark Roseman (Cambridge: Cambridge University Press, 1995), 184.

10.   Günter Krolzig, *Der Jugendliche in der Großstadtfamilie. Auf Grund von Niederschriften Berliner Berufsschüler und -schülerinnen* (Berlin: F. A. Herbig, 1930).

11.   Krolzig, 31–32.

12.   Studies based on oral history interviews with working-class women came to similar results: "In trying to explain to me why their mother was a 'good mother,' respondents often talked in terms of her skill and energy as a housekeeper: the cleanliness and order of the house, the ability to make good food from very little, her potted meat, her thrift" (Lynn Jamieson, "Limited Resources and Limiting Conventions: Working-Class Mothers and Daughters in Urban Scotland, 1890–1925," in *Labour and Love: Women's Experience of Home and Family, 1850–1940,* ed. Jane Lewis [Oxford: Blackwell, 1986], 49–69). For Germany, see Dorothee Wierling, "Vom Mädchen zum Dienstmädchen. Kindliche Sozialisation und Beruf im Kaiserreich," in *Geschichte im Alltag—Alltag in der Geschichte,* ed. Klaus Bergmann and Rolf Schörken (Berlin: Dietz, 1982), 71.

13.   Schilfarth, 1926, 89.

14.   Ibid., 73.

15.   Therese Roth, *Das Backfischalter. Erziehungsnöte und -hilfen* (Leipzig: B. G. Teubner, 1930); and Michael Ruland, *Die Entwicklung des sittlichen Bewußtseins in den Jugendjahren. Nach Erhebungen und Ausfrageversuchen an Volks- und Fortbildungsschulen und höheren Lehranstalten* (Leipzig: Nemnich, 1923), 32–34.

16.   Hildegard Jüngst, *Die jugendliche Fabrikarbeiterin. Ein Beitrag zur Industriepädagogik* (Paderborn: Schöningh, 1929), 81.

17.   Kelchner, 37.

18.   Schilfarth, 1927, 134, 140, 133.

19.   Else Croner, *Die Psyche der weiblichen Jugend, 5. Aufl. mit einem Nachtrag: Zur Psyche der Mädchen aus einfacheren Volksschichten* (Langensalza: Beyer, 1930), 63; and Helene Glaue-Bulß, *Das Schwärmen der jungen Mädchen* (Leipzig: Eger, 1914). See chapter by Irene Hardach-Pinke.

20.   For more details see Christina Benninghaus, "Stolpersteine auf dem Weg ins Leben. Die Arbeitsmarktsituation weiblicher Jugendlicher nach der Berufszählung von 1925," *Tel Aviver Jahrbuch für deutsche Geschichte* 21 (1992): 227–242.

21.   Of 4,347 girls from Cologne leaving elementary school in 1924 only 44 (1 percent) wanted to start working as an unskilled worker. For more details, see Benninghaus, *Die anderen Jugendlichen,* 155–156.

22.   For more information and references, see Benninghaus, *Die anderen Jugendlichen,* 204–292.

23.   Benninghaus, *Die anderen Jugendlichen,* 195.

24.   The only exception is an essay by an office worker who, however, does not question the earning differential but only mentions it in passing. See Schilfarth, 1926, 50; and Benninghaus, *Die anderen Jugendlichen,* 194.

25.   Schilfarth, 1926, 133, 128–129.

26.   Ibid., 84.

27.   Ibid., 170 and 148.

28.   Ibid., 59 and 88.

29.   Ibid., 225.

30. Ibid., 281. An analysis of the texts by milliners would come to similar results.
31. Ibid., 222.
32. Ibid., 60.
33. Ibid., 50.
34. Oskar Kupky, "Berufswünsche und Berufswahl junger Mädchen," *Zeitschrift für Pädagogische Psychologie* 26 (1925): 568.
35. Fritz Mascheck, "Die seelischen Einstellungen der jungen Mädchen zu den Möglichkeiten und Forderungen des Lebens, insbesondere zu Beruf und Ehe," in *Berufswünsche und Zukunftspläne der Jugend an höheren Schulen,* ed. Theodor Friedrich and Waldemar Voigt (Breslau: Hirt, 1928), 368–390, 388.
36. Kupky, 571.

12 Girls in Trouble: Defining Female Delinquency, Britain, 1900–1950

Pamela Cox

Pamela Cox examines the role of new expert discourses about female adolescence in the functioning of the twentieth-century British juvenile justice system. Such discourses clearly have an important place in the histories of delinquency and of girlhood. They attempt to account for girls' misbehavior, which was usually seen as contrary to girls' presumably "natural" tendency to obedience and conformity. Reinforcing Kathleen Alaimo's analysis, Cox notes the experts' particular emphasis on the body—the stresses of puberty or physical appearance—and on family ties. In actual practice, Cox suggests, the application of these new ideas was flexible and uneven. Still, the very discussion of girls' delinquency in terms of modern understandings of female adolescent pathology created what Cox terms "a permanent panic about such girls that ultimately functioned to keep all girls in their place."

> The girl of the present is not the girl of ten or even five years ago, and is not always responsive to influences which have proved effective in the past.
>
> —London County Council Inspector,
> "Report on Sunderland Girls' Reformatory," 1918[1]

The "girl of the present" raised many questions in early twentieth-century Britain. Her changing lifestyle was featured in novels, plays, films, and magazines, and her schooling, leisure, employment, and fitness were debated by politicians, reformers, and inspectors of various kinds.[2] Like the "New Woman," the "modern girl" was an elusive cultural character who nevertheless seemed to embody lasting social change. Though some observers found little reason to worry, others were deeply troubled by her very existence, believing it a sign of gender upheaval and rebelliousness on the part of female youth. As a result, the various incarnations of the "modern girl" attracted considerable attention both among those seeking to understand adolescence in general and among those more specifically interested in diagnosing juvenile delinquency. This chapter offers an analysis of contemporary British writing on this issue and a discussion of the wider impact of this writing.[3]

In the early twentieth century, adolescents and delinquents were usually imagined as boys—a fact that reflected both the general practice of masculine norms in many spheres of life and the very real predominance of boys within juvenile justice statistics where they accounted for over 90 percent of cases between 1900 and 1950.[4] However, some experts did focus on girls. Girls in trouble featured in investigations of delinquency and also in broader studies of adult women's crime, prostitution, adolescence, child poverty, and youth work.[5] Analyses of female delinquency generally assumed that a combination of nature and nurture led most girls to conform and kept them out of trouble. The researchers' task was thus to discover what led a minority of girls to break criminal laws and, more significantly, to flout social and gender codes. In this, they echoed Italian criminal anthropologists C. Lombroso and W. Ferrero's infamous late nineteenth-century dictum that most women conformed but those who did not were "doubly monstrous."[6]

Writings about female delinquency were thus marked by a common belief that delinquent girls were more "extreme" than delinquent boys. In their 1958 investigation of 318 girls admitted to one London institution for girls in trouble, namely one of the so-called approved schools,[7] John Cowie and his colleagues concluded, for example, that while "the behaviour of delinquent girls [was] much less obnoxious than that of delinquent boys," the girls themselves constituted "a more abnormal sample." Their research supported "the very wide consensus that girl delinquents deviate from sociological and psychological norms much more than boy delinquents." Their findings thus seemed to confirm those of early twentieth-century studies of male and female delinquency, which they summarized as follows:

> Comparing delinquent girls with delinquent boys, the girls are found to come
> from economically poorer homes, with more mental abnormality in the family,
> with poorer moral standards, worse discipline, more often a broken home, more
> frequent changes of home, more conflict at home and more disturbed intrafamilial
> relations. . . . The girls have a worse school record. . . . Pathological psychiatric de-
> viations are much more common in delinquent girls than in boys. . . . Delinquent
> girls more often than boys have other forms of impaired physical health; they are
> noticed to be oversized, lumpish, uncouth and graceless, with a raised incidence of
> minor physical defects.[8]

Two broad questions followed from this dominant formulation of girls' conformity and delinquency. What factors caused a small number of girls to swap conformity for delinquency, and were these factors increasing? Or, put another way, what lay behind girls' traditional immunity to delinquency, and was this immunity weakening? How did the girl of the present compare with the girl of the past? As this chapter shows, experts' answers to these questions mixed the pathological and the biological with the social and the cultural, and combined discussions of puberty, genetics, and natural dispositions with discussions of girls' changing uses of sex, their increasing social emancipation, and their place within "weakening" families. However, as important as these specialist texts were in creating new ways of diagnosing female delinquency, their wider influence should not be taken for granted.

Pathological Explanations for Delinquency

Despite the fact that property crimes accounted for the vast majority of girls' juvenile court appearances across this period, much diagnostic writing on girls' delinquency emphasized sexual misbehavior. The kinds of behaviors that might result in the verdict by a juvenile court magistrate, a psychologist, or a sociologist that a girl was sexually delinquent were many and varied and by no means confined to the simple act of premarital sex. In fact, a girl could be judged to be "beyond control" or "in need of care or protection" (the formal terms used by English juvenile courts in this period) simply because she had repeatedly disobeyed her parents. It could also happen if the girl was a thief, a truant, or a runaway. In other cases, a girl might end up with such a judgment against her because she had parents or guardians thought to be "unsuitable" because of their own criminal or immoral records.

If sexual delinquency could take many forms, the factors that might cause such abnormal behavior in a girl were equally varied. Psychologists such as August Aichhorn, director of an experimental Austrian juvenile training school that used psychoanalytic approaches, believed, for example, that the repression that accompanied the awakening of the adolescent libido during puberty was more powerfully experienced by girls because of the stricter social constraints they faced. According to Aichhorn and other experts, adolescent girls who were physically ready for sex but prevented by moral conventions from acting out their desires necessarily encountered difficulties.[9] Cyril Burt, Britain's first state-appointed educational psychologist, outlined three possible outcomes regarding this common sexual frustration: girls could give in to their desires and embark on sexual relationships, they could divert their desires by committing other petty crimes, or they could repress their desires, often with damaging emotional results.[10]

Medical authorities offered different explanations. Some doctors believed that bodily toxins, in particular those generated by the uterus or the ovaries, could cause delinquency in girls because they triggered a range of other physical disorders. Henry Cotton, director of a clinic serving New Jersey juvenile institutions, promoted this argument, citing as evidence the fact that all the inmates of one state home for girls suffered either dental, intestinal, cervical, or glandular problems.[11] Other medical experts highlighted genetic factors as key to explaining delinquency. Cowie and his colleagues, for example, argued that girls' immunity from delinquency and boys' propensity for it must be explained to some degree by the chromosomal differences that underlay gender differences in "[e]nergy, aggressiveness, enterprise and rebelliousness."[12] In some ways pre-empting the late twentieth-century search for "the criminal gene," they believed that future genetic research would support this claim, although they stressed that genetically based delinquent predispositions should always be considered alongside a range of other factors, particularly socialization and inferior family relationships.

Besides discussions of inherited characteristics, medical explanations for delinquency focused on the kinds of physiological problems that might inhibit children's academic and social development, thereby making it difficult for them to form good relationships with their peers. Large numbers of delinquent girls, like boys, were recorded in many studies as suffering from simple problems of hearing, speech, and sight, as well as more complex but relatively common conditions such as epilepsy. Discussion of mental defects of various degrees were also common in these texts.[13] As well as general learning difficulties, these studies observed that a number of delinquent children showed signs of psychiatric conditions ranging from neuroses and depression to hysteria and schizophrenia. Many researchers observed such conditions more commonly in girls than in boys.

Girls' ability to form good social relationships, according to many of these studies, was very dependent on their physical appearance. While not going quite as far as the American researchers Sheldon and Eleanor Glueck, who apparently described the young women they observed as a "swarm of defective, diseased, anti-social misfits," suffering "practically every imaginable defect and handicap,"[14] Cowie and his colleagues still described their sample of over three hundred girls in fairly brutal terms. According to the researchers, the girls tended to "lack . . . grace or beauty," to "be of dysplastic physique." A "large proportion of them [were] large-boned powerfully built girls, nearly all overweight, and some grossly obese," while "a smaller number [were] small, thin and poorly developed girls with pinched and sometimes shrewish faces." They concluded that it was "quite likely that physical defects and lack of physical attractiveness . . . played a part in causing delinquency" and that "[w]ith such a disadvantage, a girl will be all the more likely, one supposes, to become miserable, angry, rebellious or resentful when adolescence compels her to take notice of it."[15]

But if plain girls were prone to delinquency, then so were pretty girls. In her study undertaken in three institutions in the 1950s, Helen Richardson noted that despite the preponderance of "odd" looking girls in her sample, around one-fifth of the girls studied (86 of 500) "had qualities of physique which would have drawn notice of an agreeable kind to them in a crowd."[16] Good looks held their own hazards. Cyril Burt suggested how easily a "good-looking girl" might become a prostitute: first "petted and spoiled by kindly uncles and by munificent friends of the family" she might begin "to cultivate a coy appealing look for every visitor—a silent glance that begs, always in the most winsome and irreproachable way, for sweets, for a silver coin, or for an invitation to the pantomime or the pictures." As she grew older, she might realize that "the same feminine arts can be practised with success on the moneyed youths of the neighbourhood." From there it might be "no long step to soliciting, with dumb demureness, the passing stranger in the street."[17] Thus, if the plain girl found it hard to form relationships, the pretty girl formed only false and manipulative ones. The ideal girl, in this scenario, was the good-looking but good-living girl; in short, one who never knowingly or obviously used her sexuality to her own advantage. This was an ideal that proved as elusive within diagnostic texts as in everyday life.

In one sense, then, this brief survey of psychoanalytic, psychological, and medical opinion confirms a view that girls' misbehaviors were widely seen as rooted in the physical, the biological, and the sexual in general, and in a highly pathologized pubescence in particular. Yet expert opinion also challenged this view. All these accounts stress the *variety* of forms that girls' delinquency could take and the *variety* of physical, psychical, and emotional factors that could trigger a delinquent episode. Because most diagnostic texts emphasized girls' tendency to conform (as opposed to boys' tendency to rebel), they were concerned to identify those external factors that threatened to subvert this. In doing so, they situated discussions of the biological very firmly within the realm of the social.

Social Explanations of Delinquency

Broadly speaking, these studies tended to agree that girls who enjoyed good relationships with good parents and who went on to form an acceptable sexual relationship with an appropriate partner at an appropriate time were very unlikely to fall into delinquency. The quality of a girl's family life was seen as highly important. For Cowie and his coauthors, the range of physical and mental problems they observed in delinquent girls was "dwarfed in importance by the nearly universal evidence of grossly disturbed family life."[18] This finding seemed to confirm half a century of Western research on bad girls. Investigations carried out between the turn of the twentieth century and the late 1960s all seemed to reach the same conclusion: "The delinquent girl" was "generally an unhappy girl," and her unhappiness was "most commonly related to disturbed emotional relationships with the parents."[19] Family stability seemed to matter much more to girls than to boys. Helen Richardson found that between 50 and 60 percent of her sample of delinquent girls came from broken or disrupted homes, a proportion far exceeding that "found in any major research into male juvenile delinquency."[20] Researchers investigating this question generally ignored the fact that children from broken, disrupted, or disreputable homes were likely to be subject to differential treatment by law enforcement and social agencies, and that this was one of the key reasons why they were likely to display higher delinquency rates.[21] Instead, they set out to divine the causes of and remedies for family instability. In doing so, they greatly narrowed definitions of the proper family and girls' place within it.

The view that unstable families produced delinquent girls was based on the deeply rooted assumption that girls were more closely tied to their family than boys and therefore more seriously affected by family disruption. If a girl's family relations collapsed, her whole world collapsed. In the same circumstances, a boy, although affected, would find compensation in other parts of his more socially differentiated world. Besides, a "normal" boy was supposed to break with his parents (particularly with his mother) as a prelude to making his own way in that more differentiated world. Some writers saw these ties between girls and their families as social, others as biological, and others as a combination of the two. All, however, were preoccupied with the circumstances under which these ties were weakened or broken and the wider effects of this.

Of all the possible forms family breakdown could take, that of absent mothers came to be the most influential in mid-century British texts. A particularly striking and influential claim was that of John Bowlby, who insisted that those children separated from their mothers for any substantial length of time were more likely to develop disturbed and delinquent personalities. Moreover, the effects of separation could manifest themselves at any time after the event, making it difficult, if not impossible, to compensate for earlier absences.[22] In another study, Bowlby concluded that up to a third of prostitutes had started life as "affectionless" girls who had suffered prolonged separations from one or both parents.[23] As a result of such claims, the behavior of mothers and girls who would be future mothers came under particular scrutiny in texts exploring the links between the family and delinquency.

"Traditional" family dynamics and the gender relations therein were presented as being disrupted by a now familiar lineup of "modern" culprits in which commercial youth cultures, American cinema, and indifferent education stood alongside state benefits, working mothers, contraception, divorce reform, and others. These social developments "undermined" the family as a result of the essentially liberalizing effect they seemed to have especially upon (girl) children and women. Supposedly, they exposed children to new values and legitimized their challenges to parental authority in ways that could open the door to delinquency. Of course, both the scale of these fears and the impact of these new freedoms were exaggerated. Nevertheless, the idea that "modern" social trends would seriously undermine the family by encouraging girls to renegotiate their positions within it exerted a powerful and lasting influence in these diagnostic texts. Central to this was the view that "modern" girls were increasingly ready and able to use sex to get what they wanted.

Female Sexuality and Delinquency

William I. Thomas's position in his 1923 text *The Unadjusted Girl* might be taken as an example of this view. Thomas believed that girls and young women experienced change in dramatic ways, caught as they were between old moral values and new social practices and unable or unwilling to "adjust." While "[a]ll age levels" were "affected by the feeling that much, too much [was] being missed in life," this "unrest" was "felt most by those who have, heretofore, been most excluded from general participation in life—the mature woman and the young girl," who might express this through "despair and depression" but also "in breaking all bounds."[24] Thomas insisted that the blurring of traditional boundaries between "two types of women," the one "completely good and the other completely bad" had been caused by "the same movement": "a desire to realize their wishes under the changing social conditions" or, put another way, "the release of social energies which could not find their expression under the norms of the past."[25]

While he believed that girls, by nature, had a greater need than boys for love and affection, Thomas also believed that modern girls were increasingly using degrees of sexual persuasion to achieve material and emotional gains. As he put it, "[t]heir sex is used as a condition of the realization of other wishes. It is their *capital*."[26] In a new age of individualism, a girl knew that she "should pay something as she goes" and that "she does not pay in cash but in favors."[27] Such behavior was the mark of a society in which traditional morality was losing its bargaining power and where it no longer necessarily benefited girls to stay pure. Forty years later, British researchers Trevor Gibbens and Joyce Prince echoed these ideas, characterizing girls' sexual appeal as a form of capital activated by puberty, which "suddenly converts the [disadvantaged] girl from one who feels an underrated child to a person with *assets* which are sought after, and which supply a need for affection as well as things which money can buy." Sexual waywardness—"staying out late, running away, going with undesirable boys or being promiscuous"—could deliver both affection and material goods, whereas conventional crime was comparatively "unrewarding."[28]

Many other British writers saw this new strategic use of sex by girls and young women as a mark of modernity. For Gladys Hall, this supposed new promiscuity was a new form of prostitution, sanctioned by a new morality. As a result, a young man "had opportunities for promiscuous sexual relations with girls from among his own social group" and would "pay for his satisfaction," as he would pay a prostitute, although with a new form of payment: "a gift, or a dinner, or a motor run." The "episode appear[ed] less commercial" and therefore "infinitely more attractive" than "a similar episode with a prostitute." The fall in professional prostitution in 1930s Britain could therefore be largely explained, according to Hall, by "the increase in the number of amateurs."[29] Cecil Bishop, who claimed that modern girls were willing to sell their virginity for the price of a cinema ticket, went on to argue that "in many cases the girls do not trouble to disguise their irregularities, maintaining that it is now 'the thing' to disregard old-fashioned laws of conduct."[30]

These writers differed on the question of whether modern girls endured or enjoyed their "new" sexual bargaining power: Bishop, for example, clearly believed that they were happy to use it, while Thomas believed that they did so under sufferance, that even to the young prostitute "sexual intercourse [was] something submitted to with some reluctance and embarrassment and something she is glad to be over with."[31] To view sex as capital was not, then, to assume that young women were experiencing any kind of straightforward sexual or social emancipation. More significant, perhaps, is the fact that these early texts clearly viewed girls' sexuality as the product of social strategies rather than biological drives.

Sociological Explanations of Delinquency

William I. Thomas was one of the architects of Western sociology. His ethnographic approach inspired a later generation of researchers concerned to decode delinquent dispositions, though far less concerned with girls than with boys. From the 1930s onward, these sociologists began to develop distinct diagnoses of modern delinquency. Functionalist, subcultural, labeling, and strain theories revolutionized interpretations of social disorder but prioritized the experiences of boys and men. While the notion of social capital was central to their work, these writers tended to define this in much narrower economic terms. Girls' use of sex as a form of capital was therefore sidelined in accounts that tended to focus on boys' use of crime as a form of capital. In these readings, (working-class) boys were cast as active agents maneuvering to improve their position in an unequal world. Girls, to the extent they were studied at all, were cast as much more passive and bound by their natures.

One of the lasting effects of this approach was to fix the notion that delinquency was essentially an activity used by boys and young men as a strategy to achieve status, selfhood, and manhood. It followed from this that girls and young women had little need of similar "delinquent solutions" and therefore had little place in emerging analyses of such solutions. Girls were assumed not to be subject to the same cultural and economic pressures as boys and not encouraged or expected to achieve social status in the same terms. Their route to status, selfhood, and womanhood took a very different turn, taking girls through processes of relationship, marriage, and motherhood that were played out in very different spaces: the family, the domestic, the home. Girls' proper development, then, did not depend upon their successful public performance within peer groups so much as upon their successful private performance as daughters, partners, and parents. Those who found this process difficult might well become delinquent, but their delinquency would be far less likely to take place among groups of other girls and far more likely to be expressed sexually than criminally.

Classic sociological writings on delinquency did address the modern girl's strategic uses of personal and sexual relationships. However, because of their primary interest in the modern boy's negotiation of his class and peer-group position, this element was discussed in a very cursory and uncritical manner that continued to rely on crude assumptions about girls' "natural" dispositions.

It was only with the work of second wave feminist researchers in the 1970s and 1980s that discussions of delinquent girls' sexual and other social strategies regained the complexity hinted at in earlier diagnostic texts.[32]

The Impact of Expert Diagnoses

My focus so far has been on early twentieth-century experts' analyses of delinquency. To chart the consumption and application of these theories is more difficult. Certainly, the impact of medical, psychological, and sociological research upon British juvenile justice practice was limited. The picture of a juvenile justice system where legal judgment was increasingly based upon behavioral disorders, and where children were increasingly dealt with on the basis of the "origins of their pathological conduct" rather than on the basis of their illegal acts, is hard to reconcile with pictures painted by accounts of everyday practice.[33] Juvenile justice personnel, from magistrates to approved school managers to probation officers to social workers, did work with experts where resources allowed, but many remained skeptical, and many simply ignorant, of the new diagnostic discourses.

Nonetheless, expert discourses of delinquency did have some impact in early and mid-twentieth-century Britain. Penal reformers, radical magistrates, and education officers helped to circulate the new concepts. New institutions were established that employed experts: the Children's Branch of the Home Office, the Child Guidance Council and the Institute for the Scientific Treatment of Delinquency (ISTD) were all set up in the 1910s and 1920s. New training programs that required knowledge of the social and human sciences were developed for voluntary and statutory child welfare workers. A number of guides were published and radio series broadcast that aimed to help teachers and parents identify and deal with delinquent behavior. Expert texts were reviewed and discussed in social service and welfare journals.

Still, expert discourses also had their prominent detractors. Many juvenile court magistrates, for example, were skeptical about "fads and cranks."[34] One such magistrate considered Freudian approaches that related delinquency to sex as "both fanciful and mischievous, and even a trifle nasty . . . especially when these suggestions are passed on to the children themselves."[35] Criminologist and a founder of the ISTD, Edward Glover, recorded how his early 1920s address to magistrates on the importance of psychoanalysis in understanding crime simply "fell flat."[36] Writing in the 1930s, Dora Russell, a child welfare worker and social reformer, complained that "ideas that are commonplace to the mind of the psychologist still seem fantastic to the mind of a judge."[37]

Moreover, new institutions were not integrated into the daily running of the juvenile justice system. The Children's Branch of the Home Office was essentially concerned with the administration of the juvenile justice system but the lack of specialist clinical facilities drew all too frequent comment. Where they did exist, these facilities tended to be reserved for those delinquent children who had committed extreme offenses or whose bad behavior disrupted correctional institutions. Consequently, the work of Cyril Burt, Helen Richardson, John Cowie, Trevor Gibbens, and other British researchers who based their published work on institutional case studies was in many ways exceptional. In general, and in marked contrast to their American and continental European counterparts, British psychologists, doctors, and psychiatrists were rarely employed as permanent staff, and rarely able to conduct major research projects, in juvenile justice institutions. Of the approved schools studied by Richardson, for example, none appointed a trained psychologist until 1957.[38]

More research into the relationship between expert and lay discourses is needed. However, preliminary work clearly shows that new languages of delinquency did not displace older ones but existed alongside them. Diagnoses were certainly shaped by the emergent social sciences, but they were also shaped by other discourses, from sin to citizenship, melodrama to moral management. Often, old and new terms were put to work together. A 1938 Children's Branch publication feared that "emotionally unstable" girls might drift into "moral disaster" or "indecent or immoral habits."[39] In the late 1940s, professional social service journals featured articles exploring maternal deprivation or genetic dispositions next to articles lamenting the "decline of manners" or warning against the dangers of "eschew[ing] religion unless one has found an equally effective moral gyroscope."[40] New social work training courses at the London School of Economics were attended by students who very often had prior experience in moral welfare work and whose studies were often funded by religious charities, such as the many Church of England diocesan associations. Approved school managers might consult a doctor, or more rarely a psychologist, to help them limit the disruption caused by a girl who persisted in acting in the "wrong way at night" (most likely masturbating), or who insisted on "dwell[ing] on all the miserable things that she experienced and witnessed in her wretched home," or who continually tried to make forbidden contact with her "unfit mother."[41] However, they might also seek the advice of the local vicar, priest, or rabbi. Such school managers also continued to believe that the best cure for girls' delinquency was to be found in a combination of hard domestic work, strict discipline, managed rewards, and, ultimately, marriage and motherhood—a combination of practices and values that characterized most of these institutions into the 1950s.

Still, even those who continued to use old languages actively addressed and tried to accommodate "the modern girl." Institutional managers from the 1910s to the 1950s aimed to introduce reforms that they hoped would reflect their sensitivity to changing times, from the modernization of girls' uniforms to the liberalization of leisure activities and from the relaxation of rules governing family contact to the introduction of new work placements. Police, magistrates, and welfare workers pondered the urgency of particular cases, especially those involving girls above the school-leaving age. To what extent was a fourteen-year-old girl facing "real" moral danger? Were her attempts to exercise independence legitimate in the face of overprotective parents? Was a fifteen-year-old girl in regular employment but with an unsuitable, older boyfriend to be judged as being "in need of care or protection"? How practical or productive would it be to incarcerate a young pregnant prostitute? How inconvenient to remand a young thief infected with a sexually transmitted disease? Such questions were part of the everyday concerns of juvenile justice workers. Ultimately, the fact that only a minority of the total numbers of "wayward" girls who might have been defined as delinquent were ever brought to public attention and an even smaller number actually subjected to probation or incarceration as opposed to a warning or a fine is also testament to the existence of different views as to the most effective ways of dealing with such girls.

Ultimately, the reasons why so few girls appeared in court are many and complicated. They committed fewer reportable crimes than boys. They were very often diverted into a network of voluntary homes and voluntary supervision. Some cases against them were too difficult to prove: sometimes because of public and parental reluctance to prosecute girls, sometimes because of magistrates' unwillingness to allow sensitive sexual evidence to circulate in court, sometimes because the cases themselves were so minor or tenuous. Some girls were judged simply too "difficult" to be accommodated within the system and its institutions. Ironically, those judged to be sexually delinquent in the extreme such as those who were pregnant, working as prostitutes, infected with "venereal disease," or the victims of sexual abuse were often excluded from designated juvenile justice institutions (on the grounds that they would be too disruptive or would corrupt other girls) and left to the care of other voluntary organizations. All this suggests that there were no easy or fixed responses to the many problems posed by troublesome girls and helps to explain why different and often conflicting diagnoses of their delinquency circulated simultaneously.

Expert diagnoses may not have transformed juvenile justice practices, yet they clearly have an important place in both the histories of delinquency and histories of girlhood. Although written within different academic traditions, from psychology to medicine to sociology, the texts analyzed girls' (mis)behavior in terms more similar than might be expected: all seemed concerned to identify the factors that appeared to be eroding girls' "traditional" conformity despite the fact that this "tradition" was far more imagined than real. The factors identified seem, at first glance, to explain girls' delinquency in overly narrow terms: pathology, puberty, physical appearance, and family ties. A closer look suggests that these apparently rigid terms were actually rather flexible. In insisting on the pervasiveness and importance of, for example, emotional repression or maternal deprivation or the "increasingly" strategic use of sex, these writers effectively and often consciously promoted the view that the lived consequences of these things could be varied and even unpredictable. These things might affect "all" girls but the ways in which they did so were, necessarily, diverse. The fluidity of these diagnostic discourses could therefore be said to have worked both for and against girls themselves. On the one hand, it created spaces for deliberation of the differences between bad girls and modern girls, spaces that allowed some to break old boundaries. On the other hand, it helped to sustain a permanent panic about such girls that ultimately functioned to keep all girls in their place.

Notes

1. London Metropolitan Archive, EO/PS/12/SP/177/2.
2. For histories of British girlhood in this period, see Felicity Hunt, ed., *Lessons for Life: The Schooling of Girls and Women 1850–1950* (Oxford: Basil Blackwell, 1987); Carol Dyhouse, *Girls Growing Up in Late Victorian and Edwardian England* (London: Routledge & Kegan Paul, 1981); Penny Tinkler, *Constructing Girlhood: Popular Magazines for Girls Growing Up in England 1920–1950* (London: Taylor & Francis, 1995); Anna Davin, *Growing Up Poor: Home, School and Street in London 1870–1914* (London: Rivers Oram, 1996); and L. Johnson, *The Modern Girl: Girlhood and Growing Up* (Milton Keynes: Open University Press, 1993).
3. Because British thinking on these issues was very much influenced by researchers from continental Europe and North America, writings from these areas also feature in my discussion.
4. For example, in 1910, 1,899 girls and 31,699 boys appeared before the English and Welsh juvenile courts, which were set up in 1908. In 1946, 4,838 girls and 60,319 boys appeared. Source: Home Office, *Criminal Statistics*, 1910 and 1946.
5. For full discussion of delinquent girls in Britain in this period, see Pamela Cox, *Gender, Justice and Welfare: Bad Girls in Britain, 1900–1950* (Basingstoke: Palgrave, 2003). See also Linda Mahood, *Policing Gender: Class and Family Britain, 1800–1945* (London: UCL Press, 1995).
6. C. Lombroso and W. Ferrero, *The Female Offender* (London: T. Fisher and Unwin, 1895). For a review of some of these early texts, see Carol Smart, *Women, Crime and Criminology* (London: Routledge & Kegan Paul, 1976), chapters 2 and 3; Frances Heidensohn, *Women and Crime* (London: Macmillan, 1985; 2nd ed. 1996), chapters 6 and 7; and D. Klein, "The Aetiology of Female Crime: A Review of the Literature," in *The Female Offender*, ed. L. Crites (Lexington: D. C. Heath, 1976).
7. Approved schools were established in England and Wales in 1933. They admitted children up to the age of seventeen who had been committed to custody by a juvenile court, either because they had been found guilty of an offense or because they were judged to be "in need of care or protection." They were formed through the amalgamation of two older institutions— industrial schools and reformatory schools—that had been set up in the 1850s.
8. J. Cowie, V. Cowie, and E. Slater, *Delinquency in Girls* (London: Heinemann, 1968), 166–167.
9. August Aichhorn, *Wayward Youth*, trans. Elizabeth Bryant et al. (London: Putnam, 1936), 76–77.
10. Cyril Burt, *The Young Delinquent* (London: University of London Press, 1925), 227–228.

11. Henry Cotton, *The Defective Delinquent and Insane* (Princeton, N.J.: Princeton University Press, 1921), 174.

12. Cowie, Cowie, and Slater, 170–172; and E. Otterström and G. Dahlberg, "Delinquency and Children from Bad Homes: A Study of Their Prognosis from a Social Point of View," *Acta Pædiat* 33 (1946): 5.

13. See, for example Burt, 321; and Winifred Elkin, *English Juvenile Courts* (London: Kegan Paul, Trench, Trubner, 1938), 16.

14. S. Glueck and E. Glueck, *Five Hundred Delinquent Women* (New York: Knopf, 1934), cited in Cowie, Cowie, and Slater, 12.

15. Cowie, Cowie, and Slater, 64.

16. Ibid., 58.

17. Burt, 137.

18. Cowie, Cowie, and Slater, 162.

19. Ibid., p. 45, drawn from their summary of their survey of previous researchers' findings.

20. Helen Richardson, *Adolescent Girls in Approved Schools* (London: Routledge & Kegan Paul, 1969), 104.

21. P. M. Smith, "Broken Homes and Juvenile Delinquency," *Sociology and Social Research* 39 (1955): 307–311.

22. John Bowlby, *Maternal Care and Mental Health* (Geneva, 1951); John Bowlby et al., "The Effects of Mother-Child Separation: A Follow-up Study," *British Journal of Medical Psychology* 29 (1956): 211–247.

23. John Bowlby, *Forty-Four Juvenile Thieves: Their Characters and Home-Life* (London: Balliere, Tindall and Cox, 1946), 53.

24. William I. Thomas, *The Unadjusted Girl* (Boston: Little, Brown and Co, 1923; reprint, New York, London: Harper Torchbooks, 1967), 72.

25. Ibid., 109.

26. Ibid., my emphasis.

27. Ibid., 119.

28. Trevor C. N. Gibbens and Joyce Prince, *Shoplifting* (London: ISTD, 1962), 120, my emphasis.

29. Gladys Hall, *Prostitution: A Survey and a Challenge* (London: Williams and Norgate, 1933), 30.

30. Cecil Bishop, *Women and Crime* (London: Chatto and Windus, 1931), 14–15.

31. Thomas, 109.

32. See, for example, Smart; Heidensohn; Anne Campbell, *Girl Delinquents* (Oxford: Basil Blackwell, 1981); Campbell, *The Girls in the Gang* (Oxford: Basil Blackwell, 1984); and Loraine Gelsthorpe, *Sexism and the Female Offender* (Hants: Gower, 1989).

33. Nikolas Rose, *The Psychological Complex: Psychology, Politics and Society in England 1869–1939* (London: Routledge & Kegan Paul, 1985), 173–174. See Pamela Cox, "Girls, Deficiency and Delinquency," in *From Idiocy to Mental Deficiency: Historical Perspectives on People with Learning Disabilities,* ed. D. Wright and A. Digby (London: Routledge & Kegan Paul, 1996), for wider critique of this position.

34. D. Smith, "Juvenile Delinquency in Britain in the First World War," *Criminal Justice History* 11 (1990): 119–145.

35. Henry Waddy, *The Police Court and Its Work* (London: Butterworth, 1925), 148–149.

36. Edward Glover, *The Roots of Crime: Selected Papers on Psychoanalysis,* vol. 2 (London: Imago Publishing, 1960).
37. Dora Russell, *In Defence of Children* (London: Hamish Hamilton, 1932), 266.
38. Richardson, 221.
39. Home Office, *Fifth Report on the Work of the Children's Branch* (London: HMSO, 1938), 50.
40. D. Bardens, "The Decline of Manners," *Social Service,* December 1947, 124–127.
41. Church of England Incorporated Society for Providing Homes for Waifs and Strays case files: case 10, correspondence, 15 February 1912; case 34, correspondence, 25 August 1923, 13 September 1924; case 26, correspondence, 7 February 1921. For discussion of these and other case files, see Cox, *Gender, Justice and Welfare,* chapters 4 and 5.

Part Four: Changing Patterns of Work and Leisure, 1880–1960

13 City Girls: Young Women, New Employment, and the City, London, 1880–1910

Anna Davin

Anna Davin explores the world of the London office worker at the turn of the twentieth century and the social type of the "New Woman" who emerged in urban Europe at the very end of the nineteenth century. The young "lady clerks" on their way to and from work—on the underground, in the bus or train, and walking or even cycling in the city streets—made the presence of the New Woman apparent to many Londoners. Office jobs seemed to promise social mobility. Class distinctions among these women were to some extent obscured by the similar cloth- ing they increasingly wore—white blouse, tight belt, and dark skirt. Still, Davin argues, both gender and class status mattered to female clerks. As women they were always paid less than men, and they were always subordinate to men, even if of socially superior family origins. But they were part of a new wave of women who had won themselves more education, pushed back boundaries of employment, and made themselves a place in the modern world.

Prospects for young women broadened dramatically in late nineteenth- and early twentieth-century Britain, especially in London and other cities. Eco- nomic and technological changes were creating new jobs. Telegraph machines, typewriters, and telephone exchanges provided alternatives to kitchens, fields, and factories on the one hand, and to schoolrooms and drawing rooms on the other. Educational opportunities were also expanding. From the 1870s when it was first made compulsory for working-class children, both girls and boys went to elementary school. Simultaneously, rapid growth in the provision of secondary education offered new opportunities both to a small proportion of working-class girls and to numbers of middle-class and upper-class girls. The growth in the education system itself greatly expanded women's employment opportunities, as did health and welfare reform. This chapter focuses on the rise of clerical employment in that larger context of economic and cultural change, on the girls and young women drawn into such work, and on the meanings that it held for them.

New Prospects for Girls

As the commercial and distributive sectors of the British economy grew in the second half of the nineteenth century, and as bureaucracy in business and government became increasingly complex, more and more office workers were required. Men's clerical employment grew fast, but employers also drew a new and cheaper female workforce.[1] There were similar developments in retailing. While the new department stores had male supervisors, shopwalkers, and managers, neatly dressed young women worked as counter staff, cashiers, models, clerks, packers, and sewing hands,[2] and female attendants serviced the ladies visiting Harrod's "elegant and restful waiting and retiring rooms . . . , writing rooms . . . , club room, fitting rooms," as well as the "hairdressing, manicure and chiropody courts," the Ladies Club, and the Grand Restaurant with its orchestra.[3] Other neat young women served ladies of more modest means in the proliferating teashops.[4]

Simultaneously, the expansion of the education and healthcare systems provided new opportunities for young women professionals. Some of these worked as teachers in elementary, secondary, and evening schools or in the new "commercial" schools that provided instruction on typing, shorthand, and bookkeeping. Others held positions as doctors and nurses attached to hospitals, schools, and clinics; as midwives and health visitors; or as factory, sanitary, Poor Law, and health inspectors.[5] Even in the voluntary sectors there were women in paid posts. By the early twentieth century much work previously done by working-class men or lady volunteers had been taken over by middle-class female employees.[6]

Qualifications, wages, conditions, and expectations varied across the range of the new forms of employment, but the jobs had certain shared aspects. First, they were generally perceived as "superior" to other forms of female employment, especially domestic service and factory work. The employees in the new jobs were supposedly "young ladies," conforming to genteel conventions in their dress and manners and entitled to being addressed as Miss Whatever, not as Mary or Lizzie. Secondly, wage rates, if well below those of comparable male employees, were better than those of servants and factory workers. Thirdly, employment practices in these fields tended to be paternalist, aimed at securing the alleged welfare of the young ladies, reassuring their parents, and guaranteeing the satisfaction of the employers. Such work was respectable even for a lady.

The meanings of clerical work varied according to social background. For the bright working-class girl whose aspirant parents had kept her at school as long as they could afford, it was an assertion of superiority and opened possibilities of economic and social advancement. Girls from the uncertain boundary zone between the working class and the middle class could secure and perhaps improve their position through such employment. And for "young ladies" brought up in middle-class homes but nonetheless obliged, or determined, to earn their own living, it provided a respectable option. In general, then, office work met the need for respectable employment for young women. It was not dirty or heavy, it required education, and the work environment was feminine. It was an obvious recourse both for young ladies eager to escape inactivity and for girls eager to support themselves or help the family but averse to work as a servant or factory hand.

New Employments

Young women worked for the London post and telegraph companies already in the 1850s, both as counterwomen (serving the public with stamps, taking in telegram forms, etc.) and as telegraphists (sending the messages on a mechanical instrument). When the civil service took over post and telegraphs in 1870, their numbers tripled.[7] The official in charge, Frank Scudamore, reasoned that women's dexterity made them particularly skillful manipulators of the new machines, that they took more kindly to sedentary work than men or boys, and that they bore long confinement with more patience. He concluded that they were a better value since "the wages which will draw male operators from but an inferior class of the community, will draw female operators from a superior class." They would therefore write and spell better and raise the tone of the whole staff. Scudamore also believed them to be less disposed than men "to combine for the purpose of extorting higher wages." Finally, most would marry and so relieve the pension list.[8] That the low cost of female labor was the most important of these considerations is clear both from Scudamore's arguments and from later civil service discussions.[9] However, young women were eager for the posts. When, for example, eleven positions as counterwomen were advertised in 1873, some 2,000 neatly dressed and eager applicants appeared for interview, blocking the city street.[10] Similarly, when telegraphy schools were set up, "a superabundance of applications" followed although the initial two-month training period was unpaid and the female probationer's wage was only eight shillings per week. In the first year of their existence, these schools produced 269 female 154 male telegraphists.[11]

Despite opposition from male clerks, women's employment in the civil service quickly increased.[12] Office work in other departments of the post office, for example, soon opened their doors to women. As the volume of work grew, the treasury urged economy, and women were both cheaper than men and, with "the solidity of grown-up persons," better than boys.[13] By the end of the century 45 percent of telegraphists and telephonists were women, and 25 percent of civil service clerks.[14]

This dramatic expansion was accompanied by increasing stratification among young female employees. The civil service authorities expected telegraph applicants to be the "children of the lower middle class." In the words of one lady writer, the work was suited to "young girls who would otherwise go behind the counter." [15] Still, telegraphy was advocated as "respectable, light, pleasant and remunerative" and thus suitable also for young ladies. The advertisements of one private telegraph school asserted that telegraphy was "the most easily acquired and remunerative occupation for Ladies in existence." [16] This was perhaps true in the early years, but the job had drawbacks for the genteel: telegraphists sometimes worked alongside men, and counterwomen dealt with the public. As a result, most counterwomen and telegraphists were probably from the upper working class or the lower middle class. The age of acceptance, typically between fourteen and eighteen, was simply too young for girls of higher standing. Besides, public elementary school education might be enough to pass the mandatory examinations in dictation, writing, and arithmetic. [17]

Young ladies of well-to-do backgrounds who wanted to enter the civil service generally applied later (at the age of eighteen and over) and they typically sought more strictly "clerical" work. In contrast to counterwomen and telegraphists, they often had several years of secondary education at the new high schools, the improved charity schools, or at private girls' schools. A few had even been to the university. Clerkships in the savings bank department, which carried higher salaries and status and shorter hours, were initially reserved for "gentlewomen of limited means, daughters of officers in the Army and Navy, of civil officers of the Crown, of those engaged in the clerical, legal and medical professions, of literary men and artists." [18] After 1881 entry was by competition, and schools and colleges provided specialized preparation for the civil service exams. [19] Yet, despite such emphasis on qualifications the work was routine—copying and filing letters, sorting cuttings, writing addresses—and the main requirements were accuracy and clear handwriting. Competition for the jobs nevertheless remained intense and the required qualifications were periodically raised, perhaps in part to reduce applicants. [20] Interestingly, the requirements were not only academic. In 1903, ladies applying for post office clerkships had to be over five feet tall, and they had to pass a medical exam. Moreover, they had to agree to live at home. However, the benefits associated with such clerkships were considerable. There was a clear structure for incremental pay rises and possible promotion: a few lady clerks rose rapidly. [21] The civil service also provided pensions for women, unknown elsewhere. In addition, medical attention was free, and facilities were good. Still, upon marriage women had to resign and lost their pension rights, though in some parts of the civil service a marriage bonus was paid out in lieu.

Further distinguishing the position of lady clerks from that of the humble telegraphists was the fact that the former worked "entirely apart from clerks of the male sex," and the Civil Service Inquiry Commissioners insisted that employment of women be conditional on "separate rooms, under proper female supervision." [22] Such segregation was necessary to maintain gentility, and gentility, whether of birth or of aspiration, was useful to employers. A "lady" would supposedly avoid unseemly wrangling or confrontation and put up with difficulties as best she could. Besides, women clerks in the civil service, with its excellent long-term prospects, might well be especially reluctant to jeopardize their jobs.

Girls also entered the private sector of the economy. In the business world, the insurance industry was first to employ women clerks, in the early 1870s. City firms, banks, and railways soon followed their lead.[23] By 1891, there were 6,793 female commercial clerks in London; by 1911, 31,920.[24] Their tasks tended to be repetitive and undemanding. As in the civil service, the best jobs required references establishing superior class background, applicants were older, and work was characterized by shorter hours, better facilities, and better pay.

The Prudential Assurance Company, for example, used female labor from 1873, accepting only the daughters of professional men. Some sixty or seventy clerks in 1875 were "copying letters and other documents and writing out dockets connected with the life policies issued to the poorer classes."[25] By 1890 the company employed two hundred such young ladies, of whom more and more could type. Employment began at the age of eighteen for girls and only fifteen for boys; pay and prospects for girls were inferior to those for boys.[26] By 1880, "a considerable number of ladies" worked at Rothschild's sorting coupons, needing only "an ordinary English education and good references."[27] The women who counted and registered bank notes at the Bank of England had to be nominated by a director and to pass an exam.[28] In general, then, social and academic requirements excluded working- or lower-middle-class applicants from such positions.

Other companies accepted younger girls, but pay and working conditions were worse. Girls with basic reading skills and "perfectly legible handwriting" could start work at the age of fourteen at Kelly's Post Office Directories, where they earned eight shillings a week, increasing by two shillings every year.[29] Press-cutting agencies used girl school-leavers, "generally the daughters of tradesmen"; cutters in 1880 earned from seven to ten shillings, while thirty to forty shillings could be earned by those graduated to be readers.[30] Baring's coupon-sorting female clerks were engaged by the week at fifteen shillings for juniors, one pound to twenty-five shillings for seniors.[31] "Lady ledger-keepers" at the National Penny Bank had to be accustomed to books and to have legible writing and figures; their weekly salary working from 9:00 A.M. to 6:15 P.M. was fifteen shillings (rising to twenty-five), or ten shillings for working from 4:00 P.M. to 9:30 P.M.[32]

New Technology, New Skills

Technology played an important part in the expansion of female employment, with the telegraph transmitter from the 1850s, the typewriter from the 1880s, and the telephone, whose use spread in the 1890s. However, the typewriter was especially significant, both in the enlargement of the field of female employment and in its stratification. Upon the introduction of the typewriter both men and women became "operators"—or sometimes "typewriters," before a clear separation was made between machine and typist.[33] Nonetheless, the work was often perceived as particularly suited for young women, with their (allegedly universal) deft hands and experience of playing the piano.[34] The establishment of typing as women's work was also helped along by typewriting agencies, often run by women. Such agencies provided individual instruction in a safe feminine atmosphere. They supplied a copying service for businesses and the public, with work done by women sometimes on the premises and sometimes freelance at home. In addition, they sold typewriters or hired them out by the day, or week, or longer, often with an operator. In this way the control of entrance to clerical positions through advertisements, interviews, and references was completely bypassed. Although "the coming of girls into offices perturbed many people deeply," with the typewriter as Trojan horse the city sanctum was irrevocably invaded by females.[35]

Women were certainly eager for the new skill. They may also have been more available than men, and they were cheaper. Consequently, men soon abandoned the typewriter for shorthand, defined as a more "masculine" skill. As young women flocked into the field, typing became not only a female occupation but also an overstocked one, where basic wages could be kept low. In 1904, in an article entitled "Typewriting Fetish," one journalist thus claimed that there was a shortage of sewing hands because girls had a "mania for employment in the city," though wage levels were comparable.[36] Many such criticisms described young women's eagerness for the new jobs as a "craze," "mania," or "fetish," suggesting that the newcomers were undereducated and aiming absurdly above their capacities and their status. In the words of one such critic, "brainless duties would better have suited their capacities."[37]

It is not surprising that many young girls preferred clerical work even when wages elsewhere were comparable. The work had its clear advantages. Hours were generally shorter than in other female employment. There was no seasonal unemployment, and wages were paid during summer holidays and bank holidays.[38] Moreover, unlike department store employees, girls did not have to live in hostels. Summarizing the attractions of clerical work, the girls in a central London club in the early twentieth century explained that they found it

> more varied and interesting than the sewing trades, and they are often too well acquainted with the harsh conditions of the sewing trades in their own homes. They have seen the long period of slackness that causes such insecurity among working tailors and makes the objectionable credit system necessary.[39]

In addition to such socioeconomic considerations, the work held other, less tangible appeals. For some, the very modernity of the work was part of its attraction. In the 1890s, the decade of the "New Woman," to be a "business girl" was to reject tradition, perhaps to break with convention, and certainly to identify with new technology and the modern world. Glamour was another attraction. Neatly dressed lady operators promoted typewriting agencies or the rival firms that sold the machines. Seated demurely at the machine in the large win-

Fig. 13. Illustration of a woman at a typewriter, 1894. The description of the new technology of typing suggests that the typist is imagined as a proper young woman. Reproduced from Bates Torrey, *Practical Typewriting*, 3d ed. (New York: Fowler and Wells, 1894).

dows of Holborn Viaduct businesses, or at exhibitions and lectures, they were simultaneously example and bait. Mrs. Bartle, for example, remembered walking along Holborn Viaduct as a girl in the 1890s and seeing in a window an elegant young lady in a black dress typing diligently. Mrs. Bartle came from a respectable working-class family with an ambitious mother; when the issue of what she should do came up she rejected training as a teacher because she wanted to type. So she was sent to Pitman's school, learned shorthand and typing, and became a clerical worker.[40]

As typists became more numerous, advice literature placed increasing emphasis on the importance of other office skills. Learning to type was only a start.

After six weeks of instruction at a typewriting office, a writer in the *Phonographer and Typist* advised in 1895, "the pupil will be but ill prepared for active service." The writer recommended another six months of practice, preferably at the office. The competent typist should not only be qualified in "quick and efficient manipulation of the machine," she should also be able "to decipher manuscripts dealing with any subject under or beyond the sun," however badly written, "to prepare stencils for the copying machine," "to typewrite at high speed from dictation," and to possess "a thorough knowledge of the proper form in which the multifarious documents which fall to be dealt with in a copying office must be set out."[41]

As wages for basic typing dropped, further qualifications were recommended for young ladies wanting to earn a proper wage. Acquisition of shorthand, for example, became increasingly desirable. According to one specialist in the field, "Typewriting and shorthand are twin arts, and young ladies who aspire to succeed in one of them must make themselves proficient in the other. A typist who cannot write shorthand is very much like a pianist who cannot read music."[42] Without shorthand, a girl typist in a business house would earn fifteen to twenty shillings a week. With shorthand, she could earn thirty shillings and upward.[43]

Classes and schools sprang up to meet the demand for training, and the list of London schools published in *Pitman's Year Book*—no doubt incomplete— quickly grew. In 1892, twelve schools were listed, in 1894 eighteen, in 1898 twenty-six, in 1899 thirty-nine, and so on. Pitman's school was said to take 2,000 young ladies a year at the turn of the century.[44] The larger establishments had elaborate syllabuses, large staffs of specialized teachers, day and evening classes, and separate tuition for ladies, gentlemen, and youths. All schools referred to pupils as ladies and gentlemen. One was still more specific. The Kensington School of Shorthand offered "high class instruction by means of private lessons or small select classes . . . to the sons and daughters of gentlemen and gentlewomen careful as to surroundings and associations." Their minimum charge for a course in typewriting was two guineas, payable in advance. At the Southeastern School of Shorthand in Newington Causeway, on the other hand, thirteen weekly lessons cost seven shillings and sixpence, or a three-month proficiency course with unlimited practice twenty-five shillings.[45] At smaller schools negotiation might be possible: Miss Edith Bailey of the Strand Typewriting Company, in Fleet Street, agreed to reduce her five-guinea fee to two for a student who had already learned the theory of shorthand.[46] Some schools were highly profitable: the London College of Shorthand was reported in 1887 to have realized a net profit of over 30 percent on the capital employed.[47]

Besides shorthand, the acquisition of foreign languages was also recommended. Miss Maud Polak, for example, added languages to her shorthand; she could write eight words in French and seventy words in German a minute, and gave demonstrations at Evening Continuation Schools and the Battersea Polytechnic.[48] Lady clerks with such superior qualifications took dictation from businessmen, writers, and politicians and rose to be secretaries with considerable responsibility. According to a writer in *Business Life* in 1903, highly-qualified young women "would earn much more in business life than in Government Service," especially in the first six to eight years, but civil service clerkships would always be attractive to "those who seek a secure position, which they may be able to retain for very many years."[49] Women with such skills also did literary work as translators, journalists, researchers, authors, and secretaries.

Some women built careers based on their new skills, whether in teaching, lecturing, or publishing or as entrepreneurs. The most successful became involved in running schools and agencies, often combined. When the House of Commons brought in four "exceptionally accomplished" young ladies as stenographers and typists the contract was arranged with the "Westminster firm" of Miss Ashworth, who had trained them.[50] Some women moved from one success to another: Mrs. Marion Marshall, for instance, started the Ladies Typewriting Office in Chancery Lane in 1884. She later sold it, set up another in Cambridge, and worked as an academic phonographer at meetings of the British Medical Association and the British Association. In 1891, the Society of Arts appointed her Examiner. In 1900, she sold the Cambridge business and accepted a private secretaryship in London.[51]

The Office as Workplace

It is hard to establish an intimate understanding of office life, its practices, and relationships. Press descriptions of women's office work, often rather general, tended to focus on its newness while stressing its suitability, as did the advice literature on work for women.[52] Such writings reinforce the impression of stratification. Some dwelt on the select character of lady clerks, their segregation from men, and the admirable provision made by paternalist employers. At the Prudential, for example,

> the comfort of the lady clerks has been studied to a very great extent, an excellent library and piano are provided for their use, and a refreshment room where they can obtain luncheon at a moderate price. The flat roof has been converted into terraces, where they may take exercise during their luncheon hour, and they have a separate staircase to that used by the male clerks.[53]

Others focused on less privileged workers. The author of "Healthy Lives for Working Girls," for instance, in the *Girls' Own Paper* in 1886, deplored the impact of clerical work on girls who worked for eight to ten hours a day sitting in stuffy rooms—loss of appetite, lassitude, anxiety, fatigue, indigestion, and backache. She recommended exercises in the office, a good lunch, walking at least part of the way to and from work, no stays, comfortable clothes and shoes, and that girls avoid rushing.[54] In similar vein, *Truth* criticized long hours in the post office, describing cases where "unfortunate" girls had worked ninety-five and a hundred hours a week.[55]

Some press contributions purported to be written by women workers in real work situations. In 1895 the *Phonographer and Typist,* for example, printed an extract from a "long and pleasantly chatty article," originally published in the *Girls' Own Paper,* about typists in a busy copying office. The girls worked from 9:30 A.M. to 5:30 P.M., with breaks for lunch and tea. They usually stayed in for lunch and always for tea. They celebrated birthdays and anniversaries of arrival at the office and held lively "funeral teas" when anyone left, usually to get married. Their piecework rates varied; "about thirty shillings would be a good average for the week," excluding holidays.[56]

Dorothy Wallis, a purportedly autobiographical novel published in 1892, described work in a Fenchurch Street office, "a room filled with desks and large volumes on stands" from which women were copying out addresses. It had a washstand for inky hands, a fire for kettle and toast, and pegs for coats and hats.[57] Most girls brought in their lunch, reading or working as they ate. According to the novel, "the common complaint was the head," doubtless because of gaslight and poor ventilation.[58] The girls were paid piece rates, with deductions for errors such as repetition or omission, occasional overtime "to oblige the manager when he is busy," and days laid off if work was short.[59] Maximum earnings required writing 850 addresses on weekdays and 500 on Saturdays. When business was "in full swing" the staff numbered 120 girls. The author portrays relations with the manager as mixed. The workers were anxious about being laid off, but "his courteous consideration of his employees [was] such as to command grateful recognition." She notes, however, that "his success is due to female labour": an earlier enterprise staffed by men had failed.[60]

This semifictional account of an all-female, relatively unskilled workplace is positive overall: the long and tiring day was offset by amicable relations and the pleasure of getting home to "our own room" and of preparing "the one meal of the day we thoroughly enjoy, for it is the one meal we have really time to eat."[61] Despite occasional didacticism and stereotypes, the detail suggests actual experience. However, office relations were not always so easy. The educated and high-powered lady clerks who serviced the Royal Commission on Labour in the mid-1890s, for example, were subjected to petty workplace bullying about their dress, hair, and appearance, which made daily life a misery. Those who stood against it lost their jobs, and fear of publicity and of checking the progress of women hamstrung the others.[62]

Perhaps in part because of the "lady clerks" of the 1870s, clerical employment continued to suggest a genteel and ladylike status even when it became clear that recruits were coming from more diverse backgrounds. The visibility of neatly dressed young ladies on their way to and from work—on the underground, in the bus or train, and walking or even cycling in the city streets—functioned to reinforce that impression. Class distinction may have been to some extent obscured by the similar clothing they increasingly wore—white blouse, tight belt, and dark skirt—though differences in quality and fashionable detail were no doubt also to be observed by those who knew. At all levels of clerical, retail, and professional employment women had to meet expectations of appearance and dress, however tight their budgets.

Fig. 14. Illustration showing young woman cyclist, 1897. Reproduced from *Scribner's*, June 1895.

Both femininity and class status mattered to female clerks. They affected education, choice of job, pay, and opportunities for career and pension. As women they were always paid less than men, and they were always subordinate to men, even if socially superior. Class, gender, and femininity also inflected the meaning of work. Clerical workers might be bettering themselves, or they might be doing work for which they were overqualified and underpaid. But they were part of a new wave of women who had won themselves more education, pushed back boundaries of employment, and made themselves a place in the modern world. As "city girls" seized their new and shared identity they were developing a sense of achievement and of individuality, making new claims for themselves. Not surprisingly, they were well represented in the feminist ranks.

Notes

1. See especially Meta Zimmeck, "Jobs for the Girls: The Expansion of Clerical Work for Women, 1850–1914," in *Unequal Opportunities: Women's Employment in England 1800–1918*, ed. Angela V. John (Oxford: Blackwell, 1986), 152–177; and Zimmeck, "Strategies and Stratagems for the Employment of Women in the British Civil Service, 1919–39," *Historical Journal* 27 (1984): 901–924.

2. James B. Jefferys, *Retail Trading in Britain, 1850–1959* (Cambridge: Cambridge University Press, 1954); for shopworkers, see Lee Holcombe, *Victorian Ladies at Work: Middle-Class Working Women in England and Wales, 1850–1914* (Newton Abbot: David and Charles, 1973), chapter 5; and Wilfred B. Whitaker, *Victorian and Edwardian Shop Workers: The Struggle to Obtain Better Conditions and a Half-Holiday* (Newton Abbot: David and Charles, 1973).

3. Alison Adburgham, *Shops and Shopping: 1800–1914: Where, and in What Manner the Well-Dressed Englishwoman Bought Her Clothes* (London: Allen and Unwin, 1964), esp. 271–274.

4. Mrs. C. S. Peel, *A Hundred Wonderful Years: Social and Domestic Life of a Century, 1820–1920* (London: John Lane, 1926), 18–19; and see Barbara Drake, "The Tea-Shop Girl," *Women's Industrial News* 17, no. 61 (April 1913).

5. Dora M. Jones, "The Cheapness of Women," *Englishwoman's Review*, October 1909 (reprinted in Janet Horowitz Murray, *Strong-Minded Women and Other Lost Voices from 19th-Century England* [Harmondsworth: Penguin, 1982, 322–325). See also Mary Drake McFeely, *Lady Inspectors: The Campaign for a Better Workplace, 1893–1921* (Oxford: Blackwell, 1988).

6. See Eileen Janes Yeo, *The Context for Social Science: Relations and Representations of Gender and Class* (London: Rivers Oram, 1996), chapter 8 (esp. table 8:1, 220); and Patricia Hollis, *Women in Public: The Women's Movement, 1850–1900* (London: Allen and Unwin, 1979).

7. Report on the Reorganization of the Telegraph System of the United Kingdom, PP 1871 xxxvii (c.304), 58. Female employees rose from 479 to 1,535

(male 2,035 to 3,370). Night work ensured continuing employment of men. See also Anna Davin, "Women Telegraphists and Typists, 1870–90," in *Women in Industry and Technology (Prehistoric–Present): Current Research and the Museum Experience,* ed. Barbara Wood (London: Museum of London, 1986), 213–223.

8.   Report on Telegraph, 78.

9.   For example, Report of Select Committee on the Post Office (Telegraph Department), PP 1876 xiii, 357.

10.   *Victoria Times,* 10 May 1873 (letter from J. Kent, who taught telegraphy).

11.   Report on Telegraph, 154–156; Public Record Office (hereafter cited as PRO) T.19, vol. 8, p. 2, letter from Treasury, 26 September 1873.

12.   For opposition see Civil Service Inquiry Commission, PP 1875 28 (c.1113), App. B, Evidence Charles Hope Johnston (Post Office Foreign Branch), qq. 3,999–4,002; Patrick J. Comyns (Returned Letters), qq. 4,081–4,099; A. C. Wilson (Post Office Savings Bank Office), qq. 4,465–4,471 (q. 4,467; and App. C, Supplement to Statement of the Clerical Staff of the Savings Bank Dept, GPO, 314.

13.   Women joined the Returned Letters Branch from 1873, the Clearing House Branch from 1874, the Savings Bank from 1875. On salaries, see, for instance, Civil Service Inquiry Commission, PP 1875 28 (c.1113), 1st Report, App. B, evidence of George Chetwynd, qq. 4,599–4,601. Quotation from evidence of Mr. Grisdale (senior clerk in the Telegraph Account Branch of the Post Office Receiver and Accountant General's Office), q. 4,421.

14.   David Rubinstein, *Before the Suffragettes: Women's Emancipation in the 1890s* (Brighton: Harvester, 1986).

15.   Mrs. M. J. Loftie, "Work for Women," in her *Social Twitters* (London: Saturday Review, 1879), 140.

16.   Advertisements in *Victoria Times or Woman's Advocate and Advertiser,* 26 April 1873.

17.   Postmaster General's 21st annual report, PP 1877 xxvii (c.1867), App. 3. The examination was made harder in 1885 by the addition of a fourth subject, "Elementary Geography of the United Kingdom," and the substitution of "first four rules, simple and compound," for "easy sums in the first four rules" in arithmetic (PRO T.19, vol.17, p.118; 5 June 1885).

18.   "Employment of Women in the Public Service," *Quarterly Review* 151 (1881): 185.

19.   Hilda Martindale, in *Women Servants of the State* (London: Allen and Unwin, 1938), 28, attributes this change to Henry Fawcett, Postmaster General 1880–1884. Fawcett opposed patronage and supported women's employment: see *Dictionary of National Biography* entry and Georgiana Hill, *Women in English Life,* vol. 2 (London: Bentley, 1976), 179.

20.   This was asserted by *Business Life* both in May (p. 132) and September (p. 35) 1903. In 1902 it had reported four hundred applicants for forty places as lady clerks in the post office, despite the addition of shorthand as a requirement.

21.   Maude Arundel-Colliver started as a telegraph clerk at under a pound a week; her salary as head of the Post Office Clearing House rose from £250 to an amazing £400 by her retirement. *Phonographer and Typist* 3, no. 1 (October 1893): 12.

22.   *Fraser's Magazine* 12 (September 1875), 335; and Civil Service Inquiry Commission, PP 1875 28 (c.1113), 18.

23.   See Holcombe, chapter 7; Davin; Margaret Mulvihill, "The White-Bloused Revolution: Privately-Employed Female Clerks in London, 1890–1914" (master's research essay, Birkbeck College, 1981).

24.   Gregory Anderson, *Victorian Clerks* (Manchester: Manchester University Press, 1976), table 7, 57.

25.   *Fraser's Magazine* 12 (September 1875): 340.

26.   Mulvihill, 18, from figures supplied by the company. In 1906 boys started at £20 a year; by eighteen they could reach £50 a year; by twenty-six £150. Girls started at £32, and could never pass £62 (1909 scale).

27.   Mercy Grogan, *How Women May Earn a Living* (London: Cassell, Petter, 1880), 87.

28.   Leonora Philipps, *Dictionary of Employments Open to Women* (London: Women's Institute, 1898), 37.

29.   Grogan, 86.

30.   Veva Karsland, *Women and Their Work* (London: Sampson Low, 1891), 126–128.

31.   Grogan, 87.

32.   *Woman's Gazette* 5 (March 1880), 81.

33.   Clementina Black spells out the difference in "Typewriting and Journalism for Women," in *Our Boys and Girls and What to Do with Them*, ed. John Watson (London: Ward Lock, 1892), 35.

34.   The *Phonetic Journal* often made this connection: see 24 December 1887, 624 ("Typewriting requires no harder labour and no more skill than playing the piano"); 14 January 1888; and 2 February 1889, 49.

35.   Peel, 19.

36.   "Typewriting Fetish: Girls' Mania for Employment in the City," *Typist's Review*, July 1904 (reprinted from *Daily Express*).

37.   "Women's Lives: The Typist," *Phonographer and Typist* 4, no. 10 (July 1895), 1 (in "The Girls' Own Corner," interestingly on the front page). See also *Trades for London Girls and How to Enter Them* (London: Longman, 1909), 118; or *Young Woman* 4 (December 1895): 106.

38.   *Trades for Girls*, 118.

39.   Lily H. Montagu, *My Club and I: the Story of the West Central Jewish Club* (London: Joseph, 1944), 62, makes this point.

40.   Tape recording (June 1973) with Mrs. "Bartle," born Poplar 1882. In author's possession.

41.   "Women's Lives: the Typist," 1.

42.   *Phonetic Journal*, 4 April 1891, 209.

43.   *Counting House*, September 1892, 228.

44.   *Typist's Review*, March 1902. See also PP 1911 (Cd. 5693) xxii.

45.   *Pitman's Shorthand and Year Book* (London: Pitman, 1892).

46.   *Typist's Review*, March 1904, 160.

47.   *Phonetic Journal*, 1887.

48.   *Typist's Review* 1, no. 2 (November 1903): 39.

49.   *Business Life*, May 1903, 132.

50.   *Phonographer and Typist* 4, no. 7 (April 1895): 83.

51.   She was originally compelled by "home troubles" to earn her own living

so learned typing and shorthand. *Phonetic Journal* 11 (November 1893): 707–708; obituary, *Incorporated Phonographic Society Quarterly Journal,* May 1901, 40.

52. Besides endless magazine articles, see Grogan; Karsland; Watson; J. E. Davidson, *What Our Daughters Can Do for Themselves: A Handbook of Women's Employment* (London: Smith Elder, 1894); Philipps; and *Trades for Girls.*

53. Grogan, 86–87.

54. "Healthy Lives for Working Girls," *Girls' Own Paper,* 31 October 1886, 16–19.

55. *Truth,* 3 August 1893 (reprinted *Phonetic Journal,* 19 August 1893, 515, and also by post office magazine *St Martin's-le-Grand,* October 1893, 404.)

56. *Phonographer and Typist* 4 (1895).

57. Dorothy Wallis, *Dorothy Wallis, an Autobiography* (London: Longman, 1892), 35–38. The introduction by Walter Besant, the documentary style, and the sometimes didactic tone may mean that the account is a composite rather than an autobiography. Besant in the 1880s was much concerned with young women's work; see, for instance, his essay "The Endowment of Daughters," in *As We Are and As We May Be* (London: Chatto and Windus, 1888).

58. Ibid., 37, 50, 67, 42.

59. Ibid., 50.

60. Ibid., 43.

61. Ibid., 67.

62. See PRO, HO 45/9837/B10296/102. This file includes various correspondence and a pamphlet put together by the (stockbroker?) father of a dismissed lady clerk, whose main content is the daughter's account: "Statement of I.W." See also Janet Hogarth (later Courtney), *Recollected in Tranquillity* (London: Heinemann 1926); and Rubinstein, 73.

14 Girls in Court: *Mägde* versus Their Employers in Saxony, 1880–1914

Elizabeth Bright Jones

Elizabeth Jones's chapter returns to young women "in service" introduced in chapter 1. Drawing on evidence from court cases in Saxony, Jones offers new insights into the working life and changing expectations of girls who worked as Mägde *(that is, live-in farm servants under the authority of the farmer who employed them) in Germany in the decades before World War I. Were they "New Women," similar to young women who worked in modern sectors such as retail and clerical work, Jones asks? Perhaps not, yet many of these cases highlight young women's awareness of other employment opportunities, whether in a more desirable position as a* Magd *or a job in the city.* Mägde *displayed awareness and determination that contradict the stereotype of them as country girls cowed by their employers and anxious to please. While the evidence presented here is local, the numerous official reports on the shortage of young women's agricultural labor across Europe during these decades suggest new possibilities for research into the lives of this vast pool of young working women in the generation before 1914.*

Beginning in the late 1880s, girls employed as agricultural hired hands, or *Mägde*, began showing up in local police courts in the southeast German Kingdom of Saxony.[1] They were accused of such offenses as mistreating animals or running away from their employers; their testimony in court is evidence of their determination to redefine and improve their work relationships. In their statements in court, *Mägde* justified their transgressions with vivid accounts of physical punishment, verbal or sexual abuse, late wage payments, insufficient food, or being forced to perform tasks that did not fall under the job description. Their testimonies reveal a clear set of expectations about work and a familiarity with the particular laws regulating their employment (called *Gesindeordnungen*) that belie stereotypes about ignorant and docile country girls.[2] Farmers objected loudly to girls' new audacity and couched their demands for local and state officials' assistance in tracking down and punishing wayward *Mägde* in economic and moral terms. While the courts often ruled in favor of employers and punished runaway *Mägde* with cash fines or even prison sentences, some girls persuaded the authorities of the rightness of their actions and escaped punishment—and agricultural work—altogether.

The audacity of these servant girls was rooted in the growing demand for women's labor as a means of intensifying and diversifying agriculture in northwestern and central Europe, especially on family farms, in the late nineteenth century. The impetus for agricultural intensification on European family farms was twofold. First, sharply declining prices for grains during the depression that began in the 1870s made diversification key to their survival. Second, as the race to industrialize intensified, European state officials recognized that producing more and better foodstuffs for expanding urban populations was essential for building and maintaining economic strength. Significantly, girls and women—including *Mägde*—remained vital for the production of meat, milk, and butter on European family farms as well as for the cultivation of fodder crops that allowed the expansion of livestock holdings.

The emerging recognition that young rural women were key contributors to the nation's political economy in turn-of-the-century Europe frames the conflicting perceptions of agricultural work by adolescent girls, social welfare reformers, and state officials. While contemporary studies from Scotland to Austria occasionally speculated about young women's reasons for leaving agricultural work, others made young women's decision to flee the farm central to their arguments about the dangers of industrialization for the future generation of mothers. At the same time, these accounts offer detailed descriptions of the enormous labor burden borne by farmwomen of all ages by the early twentieth century.

In the decades before World War I, the battles over young women's labor in Saxony highlight the tensions between European states' twin agendas of promoting industrial growth and ensuring a vital agricultural sector based on prosperous farm families. Saxony was an early leader in the German textile industry and consequently a site of long-standing and fierce competition between farm and factory for girls' labor. While acknowledging that the textile industry was the economic lifeblood of the region, state officials could easily justify their anxieties about young women's decisions to leave the farm by pointing to the increased urban demand for meat, milk, and butter. Complicating this dilemma was the moral status attached to farm families and farm labor by conservative German politicians, who warned that young rural women were the future of the nation, both as mothers and workers. At the local level, the court cases from the Saxon district of Oschatz offer a unique window onto rural girls' responses to their increasing labor burden and employers' demands; court records also provide some rare insights into girls' perceptions of their future employment opportunities and family responsibilities. While the numbers of male and female hired hands were roughly equal, girls and young women appeared as plaintiffs in at least two-thirds of the Oschatz records. Moreover, the urgent debates over individual cases highlight the increasingly gendered vocabulary rural social welfare reformers and state officials used to negotiate many aspects of Germany's transition from agrarian to industrial state.

Historians have frequently used changes in women's employment in the modern period to explore the impacts of industrialization, war, and the rise of the welfare state on women's autonomy, and there is a large and growing scholarship on women's employment during and after the First World War. The studies show that the emancipatory glow of women's war work faded almost immediately after the armistice and military demobilization in 1918. Nevertheless, this work emphasizes women's agency as they navigated the social dislocations, economic hardships, and politicization of women's work that shaped both the war and its aftermath.[3] Within this tradition, others have identified the New Woman, whom contemporary observers condemned for her "self-centeredness" and "independence," as a distinctive postwar phenomenon in western Europe.[4] Whether symbolic or real—and she was both—the New Woman provoked widespread anxieties about women's work as a potential threat to postwar society's morality and prosperity.

Despite the significant shifts in gender relations during World War I, however, my evidence suggests that a rebellion against constraining notions of female subservience in rural labor had begun before the dislocations of the war. What are the legacies left by prewar generations in this regard? Studying farm women's work in late nineteenth- and early twentieth-century northwestern and central Europe offers historians a perspective on female labor that is important both in terms of the large numbers of women still employed in agriculture and also in terms of young women's contributions to the survival and indeed prosperity of family farms in the modern period. Moreover, far from suggesting that female youth in rural Saxony were alone in developing strategies for controlling their labor, part of this chapter's purpose is to highlight how a view from the countryside complements, and complicates, existing research on the debates over youth, gender, social welfare, work, political economy, and modernity that marked the beginning of the twentieth century in Europe.

Young Women's Agricultural Work in the Era of Industrialization, 1870–1914

Except for Britain and the Low Countries, just over half the European population was employed in agriculture in 1870, even as the Industrial Revolution was in full swing.[5] While this number fell to 46 percent by 1910, agriculture still employed more workers than any other economic sector in Europe until the

Fig. 15. "Neubert's Rose with a Sheaf of Wheat," Farm servant, Germany, ca. 1870. Reproduced from Ernst Hirsch, Matthias Griebel, Volkmar Herre, eds., *August Kotzsch, 1836–1910: Photograph in Loschwitz bei Dresden* (Dresden: Verlag der Kunst, 1986), 218.

First World War. Two major shifts associated with the nineteenth-century agricultural revolution in western and central Europe had a major impact on the demand for female labor and caused a tightening of the labor market for female hired hands and wage laborers.[6] First, the shift to more diverse crop rotations that included root crops like turnips, potatoes, and sugar beets demanded more work; women and children supplied the bulk of the labor for planting, weeding, hoeing, and digging these crops, even on large estates.[7] Contemporary agricul-

Fig. 16. "Near Felsner's Well," Farm servant, Germany, ca. 1870.
Reproduced from Ernst Hirsch, Matthias Griebel, Volkmar Herre, eds., *August Kotzsch, 1836–1910: Photograph in Loschwitz bei Dresden* (Dresden: Verlag der Kunst, 1986), 85.

tural experts and laymen alike emphasized the connection between female labor and root crops. As one German observer argued in 1913,

> There are tasks that women do as efficiently as men, sometimes even more so, especially those requiring dexterity as opposed to brute strength. So we see in spring-

time women hoeing root crops and grains, planting potatoes, and weeding . . . and in the fall harvesting potatoes and fodder beet.[8]

Others expressed this prejudice more baldly: "a Lothian ploughman would feel insulted if asked to pull turnips."[9] Besides providing more food per acre for human consumption, especially potatoes, the increased cultivation of root crops like fodder beet was a necessary prerequisite for the second major development in European agriculture in the late nineteenth century: the expansion of livestock raising and dairying. During the 1880s and 1890s, European farm families expanded their livestock holdings and invested in dairying as a means of weathering the agricultural depression caused by low grain prices.[10] In some countries, Denmark being the best example, farmers' shift from grain cultivation to dairying guaranteed not merely the survival but the prosperity of the primary sector.[11] Just as with "light," repetitive fieldwork, women were considered essential for livestock care.[12]

Thus between about 1870 and the outbreak of the First World War, complaints about the shortages of women's agricultural labor, especially long-term hired labor, resounded throughout much of western and central Europe.[13] The observers who commented on this trend framed it as both a moral and an economic crisis. For example, Edward Wilkinson lamented in his 1893 report on agricultural labor in Berwickshire and Roxburghshire counties (Scotland) that

> The distaste for fieldwork alluded to above, has, I fear, its origin in personal vanity. The workers, though said to be fast deteriorating are still, as a rule, a very fine set of young women, strong, straight of limb and upright in carriage. The possession of these attributes, which one would like to see in all the mothers of the generations to come, unfortunately seems to be considered by many to be incompatible with refinement.[14]

Here Wilkinson purposefully links young women's aversion to fieldwork not only to the morality of the British nation, expressed in girls' inappropriate preoccupation with vanity and refinement, but also to increased worries about the declining health, and with it the birthrate, of the nation. Certainly western European anxieties about the declining birthrate reached a highpoint after World War I, but British, French, German, and Austrian observers, among others, had already before 1914 begun to discuss female adolescents as a social category ripe for reform and guidance. By turning their attention to the countryside, state officials and social welfare reformers sought to preserve and protect the notion that agricultural work was the healthiest, most appropriate work for young women.

Adolescent Girls as a New Social Category in German-Speaking Europe, 1880–1914

In 1912, conservative social reformer Elisabeth Gnauck-Kühne observed regretfully that, for the girl finished with school,

> Everything is new. . . . New not merely in the subjective sense but in abso-
> lute terms, so that in no form of employment has tradition been able to carry
> the day . . . the relationship between hired hand and employer must now be
> negotiated individually, for the old spirit has faded away.[15]

Her remarks betray nostalgia for a world in which young women knew their place and respected their employers' guidance and demands. Gnauck-Kühne's apprehensions about young women's responses to what she termed the "discontinuities of our time" foreshadow the broad public perception of gender chaos that followed the outbreak of the First World War a few years later. Indeed, in 1905, the German Agricultural Chamber published a detailed study of the migration of female youth from the countryside to the cities of Leipzig and Halle based on the cohort of girls born from 1884 to 1888.[16] The study drew wide-ranging conclusions about the reasons for girls' resistance to agricultural work and the threat that posed to national stability if the trend continued. In particular, the author emphasized the political implications of young women's rural flight and its potential to erode the rural economy and weaken the state.[17] Between 1880 and 1914, the numbers of German girls employed in factories increased steadily, and the perceived social and moral decline of urban working-class girls attracted a great deal of notice from these same experts.[18] Gnauck-Kühne's conclusions about the value of agricultural work for girls' health and morals, especially as a means of instilling respect for authority of all kinds, capped several decades of increasing conflict between *Mägde* and their employers on family farms and large estates.

Recent studies have explored how social welfare reformers and state officials constructed the problem of female youth in Wilhelmine and Weimar Germany, especially focusing on the state's efforts to regulate urban, working-class girls' behavior.[19] In particular, this work traces emergent prewar debates over young women's work, sexuality, and future roles as mothers and how the war increased the contradiction, both ideological and actual, between young women's contributions to the war economy and their maternal sensibilities. For example, one historian concludes that youth welfare reformers focused their considerable energies and resources on herding girls into home economics courses rather than pressing for reforms of their working conditions.[20] Yet there is comparatively little historical work on children's agricultural labor in nineteenth- and twentieth-century Europe.[21] Existing studies in most instances treat youth as an ungendered category.[22] At the same time, rural girls had emerged as a "social problem" in turn-of-the-century Germany and Austria, provoking particular concern among contemporary social welfare reformers and agricultural experts.[23] This perception stemmed directly from girls' increasing refusal to work in agriculture, as marked by a rash of contract breaking among *Mägde*. In 1873 Robert Schorer, in a speech to fellow German agricultural experts, lamented:

> When today one speaks of political or social questions, it is always with the
> assumption that there is a way of straightening out, improving, or healing what-
> ever is crooked and unhealthy, unhealthy or lazy. In this regard the hired-hand

situation, especially the relationship between master and hired hand, has in many regions become a question . . . [it is as if] a certain spirit of unbridled selfishness has overtaken this entire class.[24]

Moreover, contemporary social welfare experts who studied prostitution and criminality among hired hands took care to emphasize that rural girls, too, often possessed the same rebellious and immoral propensities as their urban counterparts.[25]

Girls in Court: *Mägde* versus Their Employers in Saxony, 1880–1914

Between 1882 and 1910, the numbers of *Mägde* in Saxony declined by just over half, from 7,820 to 3,890, but at the turn of the century, young women still comprised the majority of all agricultural hired hands.[26] Most of the evidence here, about thirty cases, is from Oschatz district, which lies between Leipzig and Dresden in the northern part of Saxony. While each case reveals singular details about individual relationships between farm owners and *Mägde,* there are also patterns of language and behavior that reveal young women's efforts to shape the terms of their employment. Some of the cases are fragmentary, and some contain multiple accounts of what occurred according to different witnesses, including the girl's coworkers, the owner or his wife, or the young woman's parents or guardian. Young women's ages are often, though not always, given, and range from fourteen to twenty-five. In every case, a *Magd's* statement of complaint was written out by a local court official and signed by the young woman herself. Her employment book (*Dienstbuch*), which contained a record of the girl's previous positions, if any, and her references, was kept by her employer once she accepted a position. If she sought to leave her job legally and seek another, giving the required one month's notice, then her *Dienstbuch* was turned over to her without question.

Conflicts arose in almost every case, because most young women were accused of running away without any reason and "of their own accord," which provoked many employers to withhold the *Dienstbuch* until the case was settled. Often a *Magd* appeared in court to demand that her *Dienstbuch* be returned, using the opportunity to air longstanding complaints about her working conditions, her employer, or a coworker as her reason for running away. This was the case with Emilie A., eighteen years old, who, on 22 May 1894

> appeared in court to demand the return of her *Dienstbuch* from owner M. having given the requisite four-week notice. She complained that a male hired-hand came into her room every night, which she could not lock, and drove her from her bed by lighting matches.[27]

Emilie stated that she had complained several times about the harassment to her employer to no avail, so she simply left. The court subsequently ordered M. to return the *Dienstbuch* to her within two days. Another case where a young woman succeeded in persuading the court to order the return of her *Dienstbuch* because of abuse is the case of Louise K., who testified that she ran away after her employer had beaten her and thrown her against the wall.[28] He contradicted her vociferously in his statement, maintaining that "he had never gone after her" and that she had left without notice. In this case the plaintiff also succeeded in making her case and the court ordered the return of her *Dienstbuch*. A year later, *Magd* Anna Maria G. appeared in court and stated that she had run away because her employer beat her repeatedly and called her a "whore."[29] This was the second time she had run away; the first time she was "escorted back by the town watchman." In this case there is no contravening testimony from the employer and the state official in charge of the case reported that her *Dienstbuch* and personal items were returned. Similarly, Lina B. testified in December 1895 that she had been "driven from her job" by her employer without any reason but that "now he refuses to return any of my things."[30] She stated that she had no means and needed to care for her illegitimate child. In addition to her *Dienstbuch*, Lina demanded the return of her clothing, "so necessary at this time of year," and back wages. In this case the court ruled that the employer-worker relationship had been dissolved and ordered the return of her *Dienstbuch*, wages, and belongings.

The importance of securing the return of the *Dienstbuch*, whether or not a young woman intended to continue working in agriculture, emerges in the case of Anna Z. Like Lina B., she too had an illegitimate child and in July 1895 testified that the delivery of her baby had forced her to leave her job as *Magd*. She stated that her boyfriend, a carpenter, wanted to marry her and adopt the child but that she needed her *Dienstbuch* back "in order to seek other employment to help support the family."[31] One Karl K. testified on her behalf that Anna was an orphan and needed the *Dienstbuch* because "the *girl must raise the child* on her own" and that maintaining custody of her child depended on its return.[32] In response, the employer's wife stated that she had paid Anna the higher wages she had "demanded" for three weeks after the baby was born, but that when Anna had refused to return to the job she had decided to withhold the *Dienstbuch* until Anna paid the wages back.

In cases of employers' physical and verbal abuse of these young women, however ambiguous, the court usually ruled in favor of the *Magd*. Yet there are also incidents of young women accused by their employers of deviousness, bad behavior, and running away without cause. Although her statement is missing, in the case of *Magd* Maria R., her employer testified bitterly that

> all is not as she says. She and her mother are both inveterate liars . . . she is 21, not 18, and left her previous position not because the work was too hard but because she was egged on by her fellow hired hands, for example during meals, that she should strive for something better. . . . Moreover she has left jobs [without notice] before . . . and I have proof from a doctor that she faked illness the last time she ran away.[33]

A year later, in April 1896, two sisters, Minna and Auguste S., appeared in court to accuse the owner's wife of beating them, asserting, moreover, that "there is hair in the soup and that the meat tastes like petroleum."[34] Senior hired hands testified that there was "nothing wrong with the food" and that the girls were "trouble, liars who are just trying to leave their jobs." Another maintained that if the girls washed their hands properly before meals, the meat wouldn't taste like petroleum. Finally, the owner and his wife added that Auguste was "especially immoral" and was a bad influence on the other hired hands. While we do not know the fate of these sisters, the court ordered Linna M. to remain in her present job despite the ongoing conflicts between her and her employer's daughter.[35] In this case owner P.'s wife and daughter, Malita, appeared in court to testify that Linna

> treats the cows under her care very badly and abuses them. This has led to fights but M. is very ill-tempered and complains a lot. She beats the cows repeatedly with a pitchfork or a broom. [One time] The daughter Malita took her by the shoulder and scolded her, whereupon M. took up a pail, threw it at her feet and shouted "I can go anytime!" In response Malita is to have said, "If it's up to me you can go anytime; I'm not holding you back."

P.'s wife nevertheless maintained that neither she nor her husband had given permission for Linna to go and that her daughter had no authority to fire a *Magd*. Furthermore she would continue to withhold Linna's *Dienstbuch* as a means of compelling her to return.

In several cases, a young woman's grievance specifically addressed an increased or unfair workload that she felt unable or unwilling to bear. In May 1893, Maria N. ran away because "her employer made her do all the work."[36] In the same year, *Magd* Anna S., apparently under pressure from her fellow *Mägde*, came forward to complain that the food they were served tasted all right but that it was "insubstantial" and "not filling." She added that "given the long hours, from 3 A.M. to 8 P.M., this is a serious problem."[37] A few years later, Auguste Marie B. came before the court to complain that she had taken a job as *Magd* in January 1897 with the understanding that she not work in the fields or the barn, given her poor health.[38] She explained further that because of an illness contracted in her previous job as a *Magd*, the doctor had ordered her to perform "only light work." At the time of her interview with her present employer, owner K., she was told that there were four other *Mägde* and that this would be no problem but, according to the court's report, "she soon realized that she had been lied to. Except for her, there was no other *Magd* . . . and she was made to perform every kind of task, mainly threshing in the barn." Marie became very ill, was first taken home, then spent several weeks in the hospital suffering from "overwork." She was forced to return to her job, ordered once more to the threshing floor, again fell ill, and returned home. At that point her mother begged the doctor to issue her a release from agricultural work, which the doctor refused to do. In April, Marie appealed to K. for the return of her *Dienstbuch*, and he retorted, "she could have it at Christmas [when most hired-hand contracts were renewed or struck], but not before." Her mother's personal appeal to him for its return also went unheeded. As the court explained, without it she could not leave the village of Pelzen, where K.'s farm was located, and apply for health insurance in her parents' village. Finally, after another six weeks of wrangling, the court ordered K. to return the *Dienstbuch* and let her go.

Many cases reveal that girls had solid knowledge of the laws regulating the employment of *Mägde* as evident, for example, in their repeated requests to have mandatory prison sentences for running away "without cause" commuted into cash fines. In July 1900 the court turned down a request by *Magd* Theres K., from Bavaria, who requested that her sentence of three days' imprisonment for running away be commuted to a cash fine.[39] In this case the Leipzig court noted that the Saxon district court of Rochlitz had already turned her down, and "since they did not at present know the whereabouts of K.," they ordered the sentence enforced. In January 1902 the court considered the request of Frieda Rosa A. to have her sentence of three days' imprisonment reduced to a cash fine.[40] In their decision for leniency, the court authorities noted that this was the third time she had run away, but that given her young age the first time— having just turned fourteen, newly confirmed, only recently having left school, and having caused no previous trouble—that she should not be punished. Moreover, they added that she was clearly under the influence of her parents, for her father, "a mining invalid," had helped her run away the first time. Nevertheless, the court concluded by recommending that her parents be prosecuted under Paragraph 28 of the *Gesindeordnungen.*

By 1907, young women's requests to have their prison sentences converted to cash fines were less likely to be approved. This was the case with Franziska N., whose request to be freed from two days' imprisonment was turned down abruptly by the court. In the next few years, similar pleas by runaway *Mägde* Ida B., Frieda H., and Hedwig U. were all turned down.[41] Ida was turned down due to her "morally questionable behavior in the past," as was Hedwig, who "had refused heavy work" though she maintained she had been hired only to care for the pigs and that her wages had not been paid on time. In July 1913, *Magd* Monika S., from Bavaria, was fined twenty marks for running away without cause from her job.[42] In January 1914, the authorities reported that because efforts to collect the fine had been unsuccessful, even though it had been reduced to five marks, the sentence had automatically reverted to a ten-day prison sentence. Though her father wrote requesting leniency for his daughter, the court ruled that "since S. shows no inclination to pay the fine" and because "the labor shortage in the countryside was worse than ever" (!), the sentence would stand, presumably as an example.

The Saxon court cases offer tantalizing glimpses into the working life and social relationships of girls in the agricultural labor force in turn-of-the-century Germany. Were they "New Women"? Certainly not in the sense that the term is used by European gender historians of the interwar period. Yet many of these cases highlight young women's awareness of other employment opportunities, whether in a more desirable position as *Magd* or a job in the city. Girls often ran away to escape miserable, abusive working conditions but just as often their motives seem less driven by desperation and more by some measure of self-assurance. Moreover, their awareness of the terms and conditions of their employment and their determination to control their resources, ranging from their labor to their reputations in the form of the *Dienstbuch,* contradicts the stereotype of country girls cowed by their employers and anxious to please. While the evidence presented here is local, the numerous official reports on the shortage of young women's agricultural labor across Europe during these decades suggest new possibilities for research into the lives of the majority of young working women in the generation before 1914.

Notes

1. Ministerium des Innern (hereafter cited as MdI) 15875, 15876, "das Gesindewesen," Sächsisches Hauptstaatsarchiv (hereafter cited as SäHSTA) Amtshauptmannschaft (hereafter cited as AH) Oschatz 1114, "einzelne Gesindepolizeisachen betreffend," Sächsisches Staatsarchiv Leipzig (hereafter cited as StAL). The courts I am referring to here are those of the police charged with enforcing the laws regulating disputes between agricultural hired hands and their employers, the *Gesindepolizei.* See Wilhelm Kähler, *Gesindewesen und Gesinderecht in Deutschland* (Jena: Verlag Gustav Fischer, 1898), 186–189.

2. For a discussion of the *Gesindeordnungen* in Germany, see Kähler. For an excellent discussion of the recent literature on gender relations in early modern rural Germany, see Barbara Krug-Richter, "Agrargeschichte der fruehen Neuzeit in geschlechtergeschichtlicher Perspektive. Anmerkungen zu einem Forschungsdesiderat," in *Agrargeschichte: Positionen und Perspektiven,* ed. Werner Trossbach and Clemens Zimmerman (Stuttgart: Lucius & Lucius, 1998), 33–50; Dorothee Wierling uses both oral interviews and archival sources to argue that German rural girls taking their first jobs as housemaids in late nineteenth-century Berlin or Frankfurt were not "empty vessel[s] waiting to be filled up with bourgeois values." See Dorothee Wierling, "Vom Mädchen zum Dienstmädchen: Kindliche Sozialisation und Beruf im Kaiserreich," in *Geschichte im Alltag—Alltag in der Geschichte,* ed. Klaus Bergmann and Rolf Schörken (Düsseldorf: Pädagogischer Verlag Schwann, 1982), 57–87, here 57. Regina Schulte also explores how young rural women, mainly *Mägde,* used the courts to plead their causes in cases of infanticide in late nineteenth-century Bavaria. See Regina Schulte, *Das Dorf im Verhör. Brandstifter, Kindsmörderinnen und Wilderer vor den Schranken des bürgerlichen Gerichts* (Hamburg: Rowohlt, 1989). For Austria, see Maria Woitsche, "Gesindewesen in Tirol im 19. Jahrhundert. Dienstbotenlieder, Dienstbotenrecht-mit einem Versuch über das Verhältnis zwischen Dienstboten und Gemeinde" (Diplomarbeit, Institut für Volkskunde/Europäische Ethnologie, Innsbruck, 1989).

3. Belinda J. Davis, *Home Fires Burning: Food, Politics, and Everyday Life in World War I Berlin* (Chapel Hill: University of North Carolina Press,

2000); Ute Daniel, *Arbeiterfrauen in der Kriegsgesellschaft: Beruf, Familie, und Politik im Ersten Weltkrieg* (Göttingen: Vandenhoek & Ruprecht, 1989); Christiane Eifert and Susanne Rouette, *Unter allen Umständen: Frauengeschichte(n) in Berlin* (Berlin: Rotation, 1986); Margaret H. Darrow, *French Women and the First World War: War Stories of the Home Front* (Oxford: Berg Publishers, 2000); and Deborah Thom, *Nice Girls and Rude Girls: Women Workers in World War I* (London: I. B. Tauris, 1998).

4.   Atina Grossmann, "*Girlkultur* or Thoroughly Rationalized Female: A New Woman in Weimar Germany?" in *Women in Culture and Politics: A Century of Change,* ed. Judith Friedlander et al. (Bloomington: Indiana University Press, 1986), 62–80; Mary-Louise Roberts, *Civilization without Sexes: Reconstructing Gender in Post-war France, 1917–1927* (Chicago: University of Chicago Press, 1994); Katharina von Ankum, ed., *Women in the Metropolis: Gender and Modernity in Weimar Culture* (Berkeley: University of California Press, 1997); Elizabeth Wilson, *The Sphinx in the City: Urban Life, the Control of Disorder, and Women* (Berkeley: University of California Press, 1991); and Christina Benninghaus, "Mothers' Toil and Daughters' Leisure: Working-Class Girls and Time in 1920s Germany," *History Workshop Journal* 50 (2000): 45–72. On rural girls in particular, see Elizabeth Jones, "A New Stage of Life? Young Women's Changing Expectations and Aspirations about Work in Weimar Saxony," *German History* 19, no. 4 (2001): 549–570; and Jones, "The Gendering of the Post-war Agricultural Labor Shortage in Saxony, 1918–1925," *Central European History* 32, no. 3 (1999): 311–329.

5.   Included here are Austria, Denmark, France, Germany, Hungary, Italy, Ireland, Norway, Poland, Russia, Sweden, and Switzerland. See J. L. van Zanden, "The First Green Revolution: The Growth of Production and Productivity in European Agriculture, 1870–1914," *Economic History Review* 44, no. 2 (1991): 215–239; Michael Tracy, *Agriculture in Western Europe: Challenge and Response, 1880–1980,* 2d ed. (London: Granada Publishing, 1982), 53; and Edward Higgs, "Occupational Censuses and the Agricultural Workforce in Victorian England and Wales," *Economic History Review* 48 (November 1995): 700–716.

6.   See Deborah Simonton, *A History of European Women's Work 1700 to the Present* (London: Routledge & Kegan Paul, 1998), 112–132.

7.   See, for example, von Berlepsch to von Fidler, 14.1.1905, Geheimes Staatsarchiv Preussischer Kulturbesitz, Rep. 92 von Berlepsch, Nr. 12, 1–11; W. R. Lee, "Women's Work and the Family: Some Demographic Implications of Gender-Specific Rural Work Patterns in Nineteenth-Century Germany," in *Women's Work and the Family Economy in Historical Perspective,* ed. W. R. Lee and Pat Hudson (Manchester: Manchester University Press, 1990), 50–75; and T. M. Devine, "Temporary Migration and the Scottish Highlands in the Nineteenth Century," *Economic History Review* 32, no. 3 (1979): 344–359.

8.   Karl Müller, *Die Frauenarbeit in der Landwirtschaft* (Mönchen: Gladbach, 1913), 18.

9.   Cited in T. M. Devine, ed., *Farm Servants and Labour in Lowland Scotland 1770–1914* (Edinburgh: John Donald Publishers, 1984), 100.

10.   Tracy, 1–123; and T. M. Devine, "Scottish Farm Labour in the Era of Agricultural Depression, 1875–1900," in Devine ed., *Farm Servants and Labour*

in *Lowland Scotland 1770–1914* (Edinburgh: John Donald Publishers, 1984), 243–255.

11.   Tracy, 113–121. For England, see Joan Thirsk, *Alternative Agriculture: A History from the Black Death to the Present Day* (Oxford: Oxford University Press, 1997), esp. 165–169. See also Cormac Ó Gráda, "The Beginnings of the Irish Creamery System, 1880–1914," *Economic History Review* 30, no. 2 (May 1977): 284–305.

12.   Simonton, 113–114, 122–125; Deborah Valenze, "Women's Work and the Dairy Industry, c. 1740–1840," *Past and Present* 130 (1991): 142–169; and Richard Breen, "Farm Servanthood in Ireland, 1900–1940," *Economic History Review* 36, no. 2 (February 1983): 87–102, esp. 91.

13.   See, for example, "Die Lohn-und sonstigen Verhältnissen der land- und forstwirtschaftlichen Arbeiter Österreichs nach den Ergebnissen der Erherbungen der Landeskulturräte vom Jahre 1897," in *Statistische Monatsschrift*, ed. K. K. statistischen Zentral-Kommission, Neue Folge, 9. Jahrgang (Wien, 1904): 466–602; *Staatscommissie voor den Landbouw, ingesteld bij K.B. van 20 Juni 1906*, no. 72 "Verslagen betreffende den oeconomischen toestand der landarbeiders in Nederland," antwoorden ob vraag II.g.2. 2 dln.'s Gravenhage, 1908; and R. Hunter Pringle, Royal Commission on Labour, "The Agricultural Labourer, Vol. III, Part II. Scotland. Report on the Counties of Fife, Kinross, and Clackmannan," 50–52, 116–117, 142. Hereafter cited as *R.C. on Labour*.

14.   Edward Wilkinson, *R.C. on Labour*, report on the counties of Berwickshire and Roxburghshire, 197.

15.   Elisabeth Gnauck-Kühne, "Die allgemeine Bedeutung und Notwendigkeit des Ausbaus der weiblichen Jugendpflege," *Schriften der Zentralstelle für Volkswohlfahrt* 9 (Berlin, 1912), 186–198, here 186.

16.   Deutscher Landwirtschaftsrat, "Sesshaftigkeit und Abwanderung der weiblichen Jugend vom Lande," *Sonderabdruck aus dem Archiv des Deutschen Landwirtschaftsrats* 29 (Berlin, 1905): 103–185.

17.   Deutscher Landwirtschaftsrat, 166.

18.   See, for example, Helene Simon, "Der Anteil der Frau an der deutschen Industrie nach den Ergebnissen der Berufszahlen von 1907," vol. 2, *Schriften des ständigen Ausschüsses zur Förderung der Arbeiterinnen-Interessen* (Jena: Gustav Fischer, 1910), 55–56.

19.   Christina Benninghaus, *Die anderen Jugendlichen: Arbeitermädchen in der Weimarer Republik* (Frankfurt/New York: Campus Verlag, 1997); Derek Linton, *"Who Has the Youth, Has the Future": The Campaign to Save Young Workers in Imperial Germany* (Cambridge: Cambridge University Press, 1991); and Elizabeth Harvey, *Youth and the Welfare State in Weimar Germany* (Oxford: Clarendon Press, 1993).

20.   Derek Linton, "Between School and Marriage, Workshop and Household: Young Working Women as a Social Problem in Late Imperial Germany," *European History Quarterly* 18 (1988): 387–408, esp. 404.

21.   One exception is Mats Sjöberg, "Working Rural Children: Herding, Child Labour and Childhood in the Swedish Rural Environment 1850-1950," in *Industrious Children: Work and Childhood in the Nordic Countries 1850–1990*, ed. Ning de Coninck-Smith et al. (Odense: Odense University Press, 1997), 106–128.

22. Andreas Gestrich, *Traditionelle Jugendkultur und Industrialisierung. Sozial-geschichte der Jugend in einer ländlichen Arbeitergemeinde Württembergs, 1800–1920* (Göttingen: Vandenhoek & Ruprecht, 1986); Siegfried Becker, *Arbeit und Gerät als Zeichensetzung bäuerlicher Familienstrukturen: Zur Stel-lung der Kinder im Sozialgefüge landwirtschaftlicher Betriebe des hessischen Hinterlandes zu Beginn des 20. Jahrhunderts* (inaugural diss., Universität Marburg/Lahn, 1985).

23. Johannes Corvey, "Arbeitermangel in der sächsischen Landwirtschaft," *Der Arbeiterfreund* (Berlin, 1902), 395–404; "Die Leutenot in sächsischen Dörfern," *Leipziger Tageblatt und Anzeiger*, 24 Dezember 1902, MdI 15924, SäHStA, Bl. 85; "Vorschläge zur Bekämpfung des Mangels an landwirt-schaftlichen Arbeitern und Dienstboten in Österreich," *Soziale Rundschau* (Wien, 1902), 900–903; "Zur Dienstbotennot in Bauernwirtschaften," *Wiener Landwirtschaftliche Zeitung*, 29 April 1911.

24. Robert Schorer, "Die ländliche Dienstbotenfrage," *Vortrag gehalten in der Versammlung des ökonomischen-gemeinnützigen Gesellschaft des Amtsbezirks Burgdorf, zu Krauchtal*, 7 Dezember 1873, 97–113, here 98–99.

25. Dr. E. Hurwicz, "Kriminalität und Prostitution unter weiblichen Dienst-boten," *Archiv für Kriminalanthropologie* 65/66 (Berlin, 1916), 185–251. Hurwicz compares France, Germany, England, Italy, and Austria between 1895 and 1907.

26. "Dienstboten in Sachsen," *Dresdner Volkszeitung* 48, 1 March 1910, MdI 15876, SäHStA, Bl. 44. The total number of hired female labor in the King-dom of Saxony in 1910, whether employed in agriculture or urban house-holds, was 80,688. Seven hundred thirty-six were under age fourteen and 62,246 under age twenty-five. All but 4,036 were born in Germany, the majority in Saxony, and the vast bulk of foreign female hired labor came from Bohemia and Austria-Hungary, totaling 3,500. Kähler, 96.

27. AH Oschatz 1114, StAL, Bl. 24 folio.

28. AH Oschatz 1114, 30 April 1896, StAL, Bl. 102 folio.

29. AH Oschatz 1114, 12 March 1897, StAL, Bl. 142 folio.

30. AH Oschatz 1114, 11 December 1895, StAL, Bl. 94 folio.

31. AH Oschatz 1114, 8 July 1895, StAL, Bl. 55 folio.

32. Statement of Karl K., 7 July 1895, AH Oschatz, StAL, Bl. 56, emphasis mine.

33. Statement of R. Däbritz, AH Oschatz 1114, 22 April 1895, StAL, Bl. 44 folio.

34. AH Oschatz 1114, 21 April 1896, StAL, Bl. 100 folio.

35. AH Oschatz 1114, 27 June 1896, StAL, Bl. 117 folio.

36. AH Oschatz 1114, 21 July 1893 letter from Frau M. Maria N. StAL, Bl. 15.

37. AH Oschatz 1114, 30 June 1893, StAL, Bl. 9.

38. AH Oschatz 1114, 19 May 1897, StAL, Bl. 175 folio.

39. MdI 15875, SäHStA, 3 July 1900, Bl. 146 folio.

40. MdI 15875, SäHStA, 4 January 1902, Bl. 164 folio.

41. MdI 15876, SäHStA, Bl. 2 folio, 8 folio, 89 folio.

42. MdI 15876, SäHStA, 28 January 1914, Bl. 68 folio.

15 "Something for the Girls": Organized Leisure in Europe, 1890–1939

Tammy M. Proctor

Tammy Proctor's chapter focuses on the variety of organized leisure activities created by adults for girls in the early twentieth century. Most of these groups, such as the Girl Guides, struggled to shape girls to be eventual "good mothers" but also to satisfy girls' new demands for the kinds of "adventures" their brothers enjoyed. Despite the broad range of ideological frames that shaped organizations for girls and young women in the early twentieth century—from liberal or socialist to right wing and nationalist, from avowedly secular to militantly Christian—girls' experiences in these organizations were the results of adults' agendas and young women's increasing demand for "something for the girls."

The official mythology of Girl Guiding cites a September 1909 rally at London's Crystal Palace as the point when Boy Scout founder Robert Baden-Powell was first introduced to a contingent of girls who wanted to be Boy Scouts.[1] At this time the Scouts had achieved a membership in the London vicinity of more than eleven thousand boys, and among the ranks were also a considerable number of girls, some of whom showed up at the 1909 demonstration calling themselves the "Girl Scouts." Wearing borrowed hats and uniforms copied from the boys, the girls demanded inspection by the founder as well.[2] This story is indicative of the demand made by European girls of the late nineteenth and early twentieth century for a "boyhood" for themselves.[3] That is, girls were demanding a period of youthful freedom between school leaving and marriage. Gradually, this demand helped to foster female youth organizations, sporting, and social clubs, and eventually a teen culture of magazines, fiction, film, and memorabilia. Female educators and social reformers, for their own purposes, joined the cry for clubs that targeted girls, and they helped create and run such organizations in the period between the 1890s and the 1930s.

Youth movements originated in the late nineteenth century as ways of channeling boys' energies and controlling their behavior.[4] Gradually girls were included in club schemes as well, but almost always in separate sections. Unlike the British youth subcultures of the post–World War II period that have been the focus of many studies, the youth subcultures of the first thirty years of the twentieth century were perceived to be respectable, service oriented, and politicized phenomena.[5] These subcultures attempted to define themselves against the fragmentation of class communities and the growth of hedonistic pursuits by using regimented dress and secret rituals to create a sense of belonging.

Within female youth organizations, girls were fed a mixed message, especially in the 1920s. In order to appeal to both parents and girls, successful youth movements had to create a multifaceted program and image that would simultaneously satisfy adult concerns about girls' respectability and girls' desires for fun. In most cases, this mission of addressing both girls and their parents focused on activities for learning efficient home skills that would make adolescent girls into good wives and mothers of the future. In addition, however, girls were also encouraged to break free from constraining female roles and to play games, to learn self-sufficiency, and to value themselves as individuals and as women, not just companions for males. Girls sought to fulfill their own desire for adventure and to be boyish, with license for mischief and activity, even if only for a brief moment in their lives. While adult founders of such organizations generally sought to promote gender-appropriate leisure activities for boys and girls, young members often appropriated such social spaces for their own ends, transforming them to better meet youthful interests that frequently clashed with adult intentions.

The Origins of Youth Organizations: Religious Service Organizations

In Britain, as elsewhere, the model for the modern youth organization was designed by religious groups for boys. The Boys' Brigade, a Christian service club targeting working-class lads from Nonconformist backgrounds, was launched in 1883, followed in the early 1890s by the (Anglican) Church Lads Brigade, the Jewish Lads Brigade, and the Catholic Lads Brigade. These brigades emphasized religious instruction and drill, and they provided free uniforms to the working-class boys they recruited as members.[6] Other such organizations for boys, whether founded by schools, churches, or missions, used uniforms as well, echoing the general militarization that occurred as British authorities battled societal "degeneration." The uniform, a hallmark of modern youth organizations, also served to mask class differences among members and create a sense of common identity. As Britain built its empire abroad, it sought to stamp out social disorder at home and enhance national integration. These new organizations seemed to fit this purpose; boy "hooligans" were particular objects of reform for these new brigades.[7]

Girls were not initially targeted by youth organizations because they were seen as less disruptive. The idea of a female adolescent threat did not gain much press coverage until the post–World War I period, when flappers, "modern girls," and "khaki-mad" hoydens (so called because of their aggressive pursuit of boys in uniforms) became perceived as a serious problem in many European countries. Generally, though, girls had more constraints on their time and more parental supervision than boys. Consequently, "girls never constituted a youth problem to anything like the same degree as boys, partly because they were not seen in the same kind of problematic contexts, and partly because, in general, they were not deemed to be capable of male forms of behaviour and thought."[8] Girls only constituted a problem for youth workers and social reformers when they were perceived to be "aping" boys or claiming boys' activities for themselves.

Nonetheless, some organizations for girls had already emerged in Victorian England, if on a different model than the boys' organizations. In 1875, for example, Anglican laywomen created the Girls' Friendly Society, in which upper- and middle-class girls were paired with working-class counterparts in an attempt to foster cross-class friendships, while also teaching poor girls manners, respectability, morality, and piety. Unlike later youth groups, this organization functioned more as a mentoring program than a social club, but it did create a network of girls organized together.[9]

Despite this early experiment with organizing girls, the first real youth clubs for British girls did not appear until the turn of the twentieth century, more than a decade after the emergence of similar organizations for boys. Among the earliest girls' organizations was the Girls' Guildry, founded in 1900. The Guildry adopted the Boys' Brigade program of drill and religious instruction, and feminized forms of the uniform were created. The movement, which began in Scotland, spread in the early years of the century and throughout the First World War. The Girls' Guildry sought to inculcate "womanly helpfulness," which translated into home training and nursing, the major features of the program. Like the boys' movements, the Guildry and the imitators that followed (e.g., Girls' Life Brigade) targeted working-class girls between school-leaving age and adulthood and tried to make leisure provisions for them as they moved through youth.[10]

New Forms of Youth Organizations in the Early Twentieth Century: Nature, Sports, and Exercise

At about the same time as the Girls' Guildry was getting off the ground in Glasgow, a new model of organizing male youth was emerging in Germany. The *Wandervogel* started in Berlin in 1901.[11] The *Wandervogel* eventually splintered into a variety of different groups for boys and girls, but its core values remained intact. Unlike the British organizations of the nineteenth century, the *Wandervogel* was solidly middle class in its membership, and it harkened back to the romanticism of the early nineteenth century. The youth of the *Wandervogel* embraced hiking, camping, and nature worship, but they also resurrected and reinterpreted historical rituals and symbols from the European, and especially the medieval, past. Emphasis on folklore, anti-materialism, and the rejection of the corruption of the adult world led to the creation of informal havens for youth who held a wide range of political views.[12] Most historians agree that these German youth movements, despite their political differences, shared a strong anti-authoritarian streak and a clear nostalgia for an imagined and beautiful rural past.[13] In contrast with the military model, the *Wandervogel* emphasized youth self-organization; uniforms as such were generally shunned although belonging was marked by apparel such as leather shorts and Alpine hats.

Girls were not originally allowed into these *Männerbund,* or communities of males, but many longed for the same opportunities to ramble and find meaning in such organized movements.[14] Girls' and coed troops of *Wandervogel* emerged by 1905. The female *Wandervogel* did not necessarily transgress women's roles as nurturers and mothers.[15] Nonetheless, these organizations allowed girls freedom of movement and expression, and their emphasis on nudity, body culture, and sunbathing permitted female members to share in the emancipation of bodily expression so central to the boys' movements.[16]

Bodies, whether nude as in some of the Wandervogel troops or uniformed as among Scouts and Guides, had become a central focus of many organizations for youth throughout Europe by the 1920s. Bodily health was equated with national strength and virtue; youth were encouraged to mold and transform their bodies. Simultaneously, sunbathing, tanning, dieting, and slimming entered the vocabulary and pastimes of youth. Physical culture and gymnastics had been a part of British society since the late nineteenth century, but physical training became more commercial in the 1920s and 1930s with the advent of "Keep Fit."[17]

Combining Discipline and Adventure: Scouting and Guiding

The largest voluntary international youth movement ever created, namely the Boy Scouts and the Girl Guides, successfully combined elements from the early uniformed Christian service organizations and the adventurous, nature-loving *Wandervogel.* When the Boy Scout movement was first founded in Britain in 1908, it was intended as an organization that would create "men of character." Reflecting the efforts of other social reformers of the period, its founder Robert Baden-Powell sought to build a cross-class male community within the Scout movement. He wanted to encourage upper- and middle-class boys to use their leadership skills, and he wanted to inculcate loyalty and selflessness in working-class boys.

Scouting, like the *Wandervogel,* promised "adventure" to urban youth. Even as urban living and indoor work threatened traditional forms of masculinity, the thrills of military campaigns or imperial explorations offered new forms. (Indeed, since the eighteenth-century popularity of Robinson Crusoe, Europeans associated masculine "adventure" with exploration and savagery in opposition to the feminized world of "civilization.") Adventure was central to the Scout ethos, and the movement appeared to many boys a great game. Scouting made effective use of gadgets, clothing, weapons, and mysterious secrets as encouragement for boys. In an essay submitted to Scout headquarters for a 1909 competition, thirteen-year-old Robert Black expressed his excitement about Scouting:

> Just imagine for one moment what it means, to get the order from your chief, to carry dispatches [*sic*] through the enemys [*sic*] lines and country to their destination. You know for sure that it means life or death to you, if you are caught. While I am writing I may say that there are scores of scores of people who have only a very hazy idea of the hardships and hair breadth escapes a scout has to go through.[18]

The movement, its literature, and its heroes seemed to embody adventure and to embrace a life of imagination. Beyond the adventures, the service ethic also drew members to Scouting by selling the idea of patriotic participation in the nation to boys. In short, the movement offered both fun and competition along with a sense of purpose and usefulness.

It is hardly surprising that the activities that attracted boys to Scouting also appealed to many girls. Regardless of sex, large numbers of young people seemed to love the idea of Scouting, and after reading *Scouting for Boys* at least some girls "soon became possessed with a violent desire to be Scouts too."[19] Girls bought Scout manuals and paraphernalia from the time of the first installments of *Scouting for Boys* in 1908 into the early years of the Girl Guides. One early female enthusiast's memories encapsulate how Baden-Powell's manual had inspired girls:

> Six of us decided that we should like to be Scouts, and very soon formed ourselves into a patrol, the Night Hawks. We bought hats, jerseys, haversacks, poles, belts, knives and whistles from Boy Scout Headquarters. We started to build a hut for ourselves, following word for word the instructions given in *Scouting for Boys.* The result was most successful: the hut became our headquarters, and lasted, with repairs, for many years.[20]

This account, along with others, points to a twofold development of Guiding. Girls themselves negotiated and shaped the movement that became Guiding long before male and female leaders worked out the official outlines. In the early years, the loose structure of the organization also made it easy for boys and girls to start mixed-sex troops. The following letter to Baden-Powell from ten-year-old "scout" Robert Harrison illustrates this phenomenon:

My sister, Jenny aged 11½, and I are running a troop of young boys and girls, the members are Magdalen Ogle, age 11, Jack McDougall, age 8, Martin Ogle, age 6, Kathleen Southey, age 11, Nancie McDougall age 6½, Mary Holdgate, age 13, and Evelyn Holdgate, age 11. . . . The girls are not allowed to go out with out a grownup with them, so can you think of any outdoore games we do not have to scatter much. We would love to be reviewed. We usely meet on Saturday afternoons at our house. Also can you somehow design a uniform for boys and girls.[21]

From the founding of the Boy Scouts in 1908, such letters and other reports suggesting the popularity of Scouting among female youth flooded into Scout headquarters from schools, churches, and girls themselves, making it clear that girls from across the country were creating all-female Scouting troops. When denied access to the accoutrements of Scouting, some girls designed and sewed their own uniforms. Other girls simply applied for badges and other materials by mail, registering as Scouts and signing up using only their initials. Early Guide histories estimate that several thousand girls registered as Scouts using this method.[22] Still other girls used brothers or male friends as fronts for their activities, sending them to get materials or badges. For example, Gladys Commander's brother enrolled her as a Scout in 1909, and she soon started her own Scout patrol of girls. Elizabeth de Beaumont formed an unofficial group with her brother and her governess. In a few cases, schoolmistresses began Scouting programs for girls in order to build their character and teach them responsibility in a fun way.[23] Simply put, the early "girl Scouts" got the same thrill and sense of usefulness as the boys did from Scouting:

We got our first precious copy of *Scouting for Boys* by the Chief Scout and read all we could lay hands on, about Scoutcraft. We had Scout hats and poles and scarves and belts. We were the Seal Patrol and were desperately in earnest about it all. It was a wonderful game, so full of something that was utterly lacking in any other![24]

Such female enthusiasm for Scouting became the focus of public attention at the September 1909 London Boy Scout rally mentioned previously when a contingent of girls showed up and demanded inspection by Baden-Powell. When Baden-Powell told them "[t]hat's impossible, this is only for the boys" the girls pleaded their case, asking him to come up with "something for the girls, please?"[25] This demand posed a dilemma for the adult male Scout leadership. Not only was Scouting defined as a male activity, inappropriate for girls; the potential inclusion of girls in the organization might make it seem less appealing to boys. Worse yet, it might threaten the respectability of the Scout movement in parents' eyes. Coeducational meetings and hikes and especially mixed-sex camps would certainly undermine the all-male community of Scouting and potentially threaten the moral purpose of the organization. Nonetheless, many girls obviously wanted to be Scouts, forcing the leadership to deal with the "girl question."

The creation of a separate, female version of Scouting seemed the only option. Consequently, the notion of Girl Guides was introduced in late 1909. Although in later years Baden-Powell would maintain that he always had planned for a girls' movement, he wrote little about girls before World War I, and the Girl Guides were not created until almost two years after the publication of *Scouting for Boys*. Nevertheless, by establishing a separate, single-sex organization for girls, and giving girls and boys some similar activities but different identities, the leadership managed to circumvent public criticism of gender-mixed activities, while simultaneously incorporating both sexes into the Scouting movement.

In general, "Girl Scouts" reacted unfavorably to the idea of the Girl Guides. Fearing, and realistically so, that their programs were about to change, "Girl Scouts" insisted on continuing their exciting activities: "Armed with staves the Girl Scouts set off to look for adventure. It was found in leaping over dykes, and crawling about in fields on hands and knees, or even on one's tummy."[26] As members of the Girl Guides (as imagined by Scout adult leadership), they would no longer undertake such daring adventures. Instead, they would be taught feminine virtues. As part of this feminization of girls' activities, they would no longer have animal mascots but instead be expected to sport the flower emblems of the Guides. The stated aim of the new organization was "to get girls to learn how to be women—self-helpful, happy, prosperous, and capable of keeping good homes and of bringing up good children."[27] One "Girl Scout" later recounted her reaction to being told of the conversion to Guiding: "One can still remember the feeling of anti-climax, of being let-down, almost insulted. Who wanted to be womanly at our age?"[28] Girls wanted adventure, not "home training."

Apparently, most girls submitted to the changes, although in retrospect they often insisted that the Scout ethic remain alive in the Guides. They combined the new womanly activities with rifle shooting, cycling, and signaling, and they absolutely refused to give up their distinctive Scout hats from the early days. Moreover, because the Guide movement remained relatively unorganized in the years prior to World War I, girls were often able to shape the activities to suit their needs. In fact, Baden-Powell was still receiving letters about unofficial "Girl Scouts" as late as 1916.[29]

Guiding, along with other youth movements for girls, had to walk a careful line between respectability and adventure. To maintain the support of adults and girls, youth movements such as the Guides embraced the vision of complementarity, arguing that girls needed their own versions of boys' movements for learning appropriate feminine skills. In this script of complementary youth roles, boys and girls were "equal" in their access to adventure and service, but they also learned their sex-assigned roles and followed them. For leaders, it meant the empowerment of a single-sex organization and the appearance of respectability. Baden-Powell explained this relationship between boys' and girls' movements for parents:

> But, just as that rib [referring to Adam] grew in the end to become the important partner of the man (apart from the incident of nearly wrecking his career), and to be mother of the human race, so, too, the Girl Guide Movement has grown up

Fig. 17. Baden-Powell family, model Boy Scouts and Girl Guides, England, 1920s. From the top left, clockwise: Olave is the Guider (leader), Robert the Scouter (leader), and the children Peter (Scout), Betty (Brownie), and Heather (Guide).
Courtesy of the Scout Association.

automatically, in equal strength with the Boy Scouts, to develop individual character in the girlhood, not only of our own race, but of our neighbor nations about the world.[30]

As the Guides developed in the 1920s, they became the largest girls' organization in Britain. By the 1930s, the organization boasted a membership of more than half a million girls from working- and middle-class backgrounds. In the course of the 1920s, Guiding for girls also gained success internationally, gradually introducing branches in every European nation and dozens of other countries around the world. This process of international expansion formally began when Olave Baden-Powell, Robert's young wife, founded two new entities in February 1919: the Guide International Council and the Imperial Council, "for the purpose of carrying assistance and inspiration to those countries newer and consequently smaller and less experienced in the world of Boy Scouting and Girl Guiding."[31] In 1928, the World Association of Girl Guides and Girl Scouts (WAGGGS) was formed at the World Conference in Hungary, with twenty-eight founder member countries.[32]

Guiding and Girl Scouting (the name for some national versions of the move-

Fig. 18. Jewish Girl Guides, at Camp Dorking, England, 1927.
Reprinted by kind permission of the Guide Association.

ment) succeeded throughout Europe because of the flexibility of its program, its international ties, and its amalgamation of several earlier forms of youth movement. The Guides allowed flexibility to accommodate separate denominational organizations in countries where dissent developed. France was one such nation, where the *Guides de France* (Catholic) and the *Eclaireuses* (Protestant) co-existed in the 1920s, with both groups attending international gatherings as "official" representatives from France. Moreover, the international gatherings of the 1920s in places such as England, the United States, and Hungary tapped into the postwar rhetoric of cooperation and peace. Finally, the movement incorporated many of the attractions of earlier youth movements and in some cases totally swallowed up those movements. Guides and Girl Scouts hiked and camped as did the *Wandervogel*, they attended church parades and wore uniforms like the Girls' Guildry, they held sporting competitions, they built an international hostel in Switzerland, and they encouraged consumption of leisure items and movement literature.

Alternative Forms of Youth Organizations: Political Groups

Another form of youth organization to develop in the first quarter of the twentieth century was the political youth group. By the 1930s, significant uniformed and explicitly political youth movements existed in every European country, organized by left-wing, right-wing, and centrist political parties. These organizations shared with the international Scout and Guide movements an interest in mass rallies, parades, uniforms, and spectacles; like the *Wandervogel*, they celebrated youth as a viable and vital force in the future of Europe.

Socialist parties in Germany and France sponsored youth clubs and gymnastic societies alongside activities for adults as they built their strength before the First World War.[33] Contrary to most other youth groups in the early twentieth century, many left-wing organizations were committed to coeducational activities. Although some parents disapproved of such gender mixing, Socialists proclaimed female emancipation as one of their goals; many girls seemed to get a thrill out of organizing with the male youth. As one female member recalled, "We had a little band of girls in the local groups who were very emancipated, they went round with red scarves, a bit tomboyish in appearance, but that wasn't at all the usual thing for girls at the time."[34] Despite such enthusiastic reports from some girls, however, the mixed-sex nature of these groups meant that girls did not have the autonomy or the authority they gained in single-sex organizations. In most cases, girls were marginalized and excluded from leadership roles, and gender-mixed groups generally remained male dominated.

At the same time as Socialists and Communists were targeting youth, the Catholic Church began sponsoring clubs to attract young people away from the Left. Hoping to promote Christian political and social responsibility as well as appropriate morality, Catholic political youth groups focused their efforts in a number of European countries during and after World War I. In Italy, the political coalition Catholic Action developed organizations first for boys and then for girls in the late 1910s. The first girls' organization, *Gioventù femminile cattolica italiana*, was founded in 1918 specifically to help counter socialism in Milan. Only a decade later, Catholic Action's youth organizations for boys and girls boasted a membership of almost one hundred thousand.[35] In Belgium and France, the *Jeunesse Ouvrière Catholique* for boys was started in the early 1920s, followed by separate girls' sections later in the decade. As was the case with the Italian organizations, the French *Jeunesse Ouvrière Chrétienne Féminine* (the girls' section) sought to inculcate self-reliance, but within a gendered framework of Christian duty and morality and through separate-sex activities.[36]

By the 1920s, extreme right-wing organizations had joined the battle for youth loyalties. During the interwar era, the two movements that gained the most members were the Italian Fascist and German National Socialist (Nazi) youth movements. Fascist and Nazi party leaders recognized that the inculcation of values in youth might help strengthen the parties with a cadre of loyal young people. The youth organizations started slowly in both countries, but the rise of each party to power ultimately made it possible to compel young people to join. By 1929 in Italy, the Fascist youth organizing body, the *Opera nazionale balilla*, claimed "a virtual monopoly over children's after-school activities," with separate sections for boys and girls.[37]

As was the case with most other European youth organizations, *Balilla* attempted to reinforce sexual norms and conventional gender roles for boys and girls. Girls were taught rhythmic exercises, nurturing and homemaking skills, and charity, while boys engaged in war training and sporting competitions. Boys practiced military drill while girls engaged in "doll drill," which meant marching around holding dolls in the "correct manner of a mother."[38] Yet although the party hoped to inculcate traditionally feminine qualities, girls in the Fascist movement learned competitiveness, self-reliance, and physical activity. One female member described her time in the Fascist youth thus:

> At times, on my way, I imagined adventurous dreams of glory. Often, because of my quick response and diabolically clever intuition, I saved the beloved Duce from assassination attempts, accidents, drowning, and for every feat there was a solemn ceremony at which another shining metal cross was pinned on my white shirt, making me walk even more with my chest out and my stomach pulled in.[39]

Although the organization was designed to create a loyal cadre of Fascist youth, this recollection suggests that Fascist leaders were unable to control girls' thoughts and imaginations. On the contrary, many girls seem to have used *Balilla* as a means to escape the confines of the home and the constraints of domesticity, as an opportunity for fun, as a forum for building friendships, and as a pretext for fantasies about being meaningful citizens.

Like the Italian Fascists, German National Socialists strove to incorporate youth into the societal vision they molded in the interwar years. In 1933, there were approximately five to six million members of German youth organizations. By the end of 1934, these organizations had been outlawed in favor of the *Hitler-Jugend* (HJ) and its female counterpart, the *Bund Deutscher Mädel* (BDM).[40] Like *Balilla*, the HJ and BDM were uniformed movement modeled on the Scouts, emphasizing outdoor activities, character building, and a clear moral/ethical code. Originally founded in 1930, the BDM, in following with the National Socialist political program, sought to promote motherhood and devotion to family, but many girls found that membership in the organization and participation in some of its many activities provided opportunities to escape from domestic responsibilities. Moreover, many girls gained unprecedented freedom of movement and self-reliance through the BDM, and even discrimination against women within the Nazi party did not stop some of these girls from assuming leadership roles.[41] Indeed, involvement in youth organizations such as the BDM politicized girls to a previously unparalleled extent in Germany and linked them to the Nazi state in a gender- and generationally specific fashion.

The political youth organizations of the interwar period were a product of the highly charged post–World War I atmosphere and its concern with families, youth, and gender roles. Despite embracing modern notions of propaganda and flashy technology, these political organizations followed established patterns of targeting first boys and later girls for "appropriate" sex role socialization activities. With the establishment of separate sections for females, Catholic, Communist, and Fascist organizations each sought to shape girls according to their particular ideals of womanhood. Yet girls themselves ensured that they gained a measure of autonomy, leadership training, and adventure, largely unanticipated by the creators of these organizations. At least in part as a result of the demands of their female members, political youth groups for girls offered a mixed bag of motherhood training and female emancipation, and of both obedience to and resistance to authority.

Despite the obvious popularity of youth organizations, most groups continued to struggle with the central difficulty facing all youth movements involving girls: how to create "good mothers" who would literally reproduce the nation while simultaneously attracting girls who wanted adventure and autonomy. Clubs for girls constantly strove for a balance between maintaining respectability and providing activities that would attract and hold the attention of girls, who increasingly were demanding some measure of autonomy.

Clearly, European girls were attracted to youth organizations for the same reasons that boys wanted to join: fun, adventure, travel, companionship, international affiliation, and a sense of belonging. In youth movements, whether Christian service clubs, social groups, political entities, or Scouting, girls from a host of European countries seemed to find such opportunities in a space apart from their homes and workplaces. When interviewed in the 1990s, many British Girl Guides from the 1920s and 1930s described the sense of liberation and freedom they found in girls' youth organizations. Describing their experiences as life changing, they recalled the movement as "a sort of emancipation" and a means of "fighting petticoats." As one elderly Guide remarked in an interview, "I don't know what I would have done if I hadn't been in guiding." Another woman expressed this sentiment even more strongly, claiming that "without guiding my life would have been nothing."[42] Ironically, women who were members of the Nazi BDM often later recall a similar temporary liberation it offered from the usual constraints of femininity.[43] The Nazi movement and regime embodied a political backlash against female emancipation, but its female youth movement left a more contradictory and complex political legacy to its members. Despite the broad range of ideological frames that shaped organizations for girls and young women in the early twentieth century—from liberal or socialist to right wing and nationalist, from avowedly secular to militantly Christian—girls' experiences in these organizations were the results of adults' agendas and young women's increasing demand for "something for the girls."

Notes

1.   Parts of this paper are drawn from my book *On My Honour: Guides and Scouts in Interwar Britain* (Philadelphia: American Philosophical Society, 2002).

2.   "Girl Scouts: A Popular Contingent," *Illustrated London News,* 11 September 1909, 356. Other accounts also suggest early girl scouts attended Scout ral-

lies. For example, Mary Royden and Sybil Canadine, "Early Days of Guiding" box, Girl Guides Association (hereafter cited as GGA).

3. Sally Mitchell, *The New Girl: Girls' Culture in England, 1880–1915* (New York: Columbia University Press, 1995), 103–105.

4. Michael Mitterauer, *A History of Youth*, trans. Graeme Dunphy (Oxford and Cambridge, Mass.: Blackwell, 1992).

5. A rich literature on youth subcultures emerged from the work of the Centre for Contemporary Cultural Studies at Birmingham University, for example: Phil Cohen, *Subcultural Conflict and Working-Class Community* (Birmingham: Centre for Contemporary Cultural Studies, 1972); Stuart Hall and Tony Jefferson, eds., *Resistance through Rituals* (London: Hutchinson, 1977); Dick Hebdige, *Subculture: The Meaning of Style* (London: Methuen, 1979); and Angela McRobbie and Mica Nava, eds., *Gender and Generation* (London: Macmillan, 1984). For information on the movements for national efficiency and for worries about degenerated youth, see John Gillis, *Youth and History* (New York: Academic Press, 1974); Harry Hendrick, *Images of Youth: Age, Class and the Male Youth Problem, 1880–1920* (Oxford: Clarendon Press, 1990); Michael Rosenthal, *The Character Factory* (New York: Pantheon Press, 1986); John Springhall, *Youth, Empire and Society: British Youth Movements, 1883–1940* (London: Croom Helm, 1977); Allen Warren, "Mothers for the Empire," in *Making Imperial Mentalities,* ed. J. A. Mangan (Manchester: Manchester University Press, 1990); Warren, "Citizens of the Empire," in *Imperialism and Popular Culture,* ed. John Mackenzie (Manchester: Manchester University Press, 1986); and Paul Wilkinson, "English Youth Movements, 1908–1930," *Journal of Contemporary History* 4, no. 2 (April 1969): 3–23.

6. Springhall, 24–37.

7. Geoffrey Pearson, *Hooligan: A History of Respectable Fears* (London: Macmillan, 1983), 74.

8. Harry Hendrick, *Images of Youth: Age, Class and the Male Youth Problem, 1880–1920* (Oxford: Clarendon Press, 1990), 8.

9. Ray Fabes and Alison Skinner, "The Girls' Friendly Society and the Development of Rural Youth Work, 1850–1900," in *Essays in the History of Community and Youth Work,* ed. Ruth Gilchrist, Tony Jeffs, and Jean Spence (Leicester: Youth Work Press, 2001), 66–67.

10. Springhall, 130–131; and Anne Summers, *Angels and Citizens: British Women as Military Nurses* (London: Routledge & Kegan Paul, 1988), 278.

11. Walter Laqueur, *Young Germany: A History of the German Youth Movement* (New York: Basic Books, 1962), 3.

12. Reuven Kahane, *The Origins of Postmodern Youth: Informal Youth Movements in a Comparative Perspective* (Berlin and New York: Walter de Gruyter, 1997), 47–50.

13. Laqueur, 5–7, 12, 16; and John Neubauer, *The Fin-de-Siecle Culture of Adolescence* (New Haven, Conn., and London: Yale University Press, 1992), 189–190.

14. George Mosse, *Nationalism and Sexuality: Middle-Class Morality and Sexual Norms in Modern Europe* (Madison: University of Wisconsin Press, 1985), 45.

15. Marion E. P. De Ras, *Körper, Eros und Weibliche Kultur: Mädchen im Wandervogel und in der Bündischen Jugend 1900–1933* (Pfaffenweiler: Centaurus-

Verl.-Ges., 1988), 7, 22. See also Sabine Andresen, *Mädchen und Frauen in der bürgerlichen Jugendbewegung: Soziale Konstruktion von Mädchenjugend* (Neuwied: Luchterhand, 1997).

16. Mosse, 51–53.

17. Michael Budd's work on this subject suggests that a major transformation in the understanding and articulation of physical culture took place after World War I, especially in regard to youth. Michael Anton Budd, *The Sculpture Machine: Physical Culture and Body Politics in the Age of Empire* (New York: New York University Press, 1997). For other works on the body and consumption, see Jill Julius Matthews, "They Had Such a Lot of Fun: The Women's League of Health and Beauty between the Wars," *History Workshop* 30 (autumn 1990): 22–54; and Sally Alexander, "Becoming a Woman in London in the 1920s and 1930s," in *Metropolis London: Histories and Representations since 1800,* ed. Gareth Stedman Jones and David Feldman (London: Routledge & Kegan Paul, 1989), 262.

18. Robert Black, "An Essay on Scouting" [handwritten manuscript], 27 August 1909, TC/42, Scout Association (hereafter cited as SA).

19. Marguerite de Beaumont, "From the Beginning," *The Leader's Opinions* 4 (April/May 1921): 39. This was a typewritten magazine of the 5th Lone Guide Company, GGA.

20. Rose Kerr, *The Story of the Girl Guides* (London: GGA, 1940), 155.

21. Robert C. Harrison to Robert Baden-Powell, 12 July 1916, TC/42, SA.

22. Kerr, *Girl Guides,* 30.

23. Gladys Commander's 1954 Thinking Day speech and Elizabeth de Beaumont's reminiscences dated 20 October 1931, "Early Days of Guiding" box, GGA.

24. Marguerite de Beaumont, 39.

25. "Girl Scouts: A Popular Contingent," 356.

26. Kerr, *Girl Guides,* 39.

27. Agnes Baden-Powell, *The Handbook for Girl Guides, or How Girls Can Help Build the Empire* (London: Thomas Nelson & Sons, 1912), vii.

28. Evelyn Goshawk, "Early Days of Guiding" box, GGA.

29. Lady Betty Balfour to Robert Baden-Powell, 26 March 1916, TC/42, SA.

30. Robert Baden-Powell, "Introduction," (to 1932 edition and reprinted in subsequent editions) in Kerr, *Girl Guides,* 5.

31. Mrs. Herbert Hoover, "The Girl Guide International Council," TS, 14 May 1926, WAGGGS—International Council folder, Girl Scouts of the USA, New York.

32. Rose Kerr, *The Story of A Million Girls* (London: GGA, 1936), 388–390.

33. Derek S. Linton, *"Who Has the Youth, Has the Future": The Campaign to Save Young Workers in Imperial Germany* (Cambridge: Cambridge University Press, 1991), 120, 167–168.

34. Colette Jobard, as quoted in Siân Reynolds, *France between the Wars: Gender and Politics* (London/New York: Routledge, 1996), 58.

35. Victoria de Grazia, *How Fascism Ruled Women: Italy, 1922–1945* (Berkeley: University of California Press, 1992), 140–143.

36. Reynolds, 54–55.

37. de Grazia, 141.

38. Ibid., 158.

39. Ibid., 159.

40. Kahane, 52; and Dagmar Reese, "Emancipation or Social Incorporation: Girls in the Bund Deutscher Mädel," in *Education and Fascism: Political Identity and Social Education in Nazi Germany,* ed. Heinz Sünker and Hans-Uwe Otto (London: Falmer Press, 1997), 116.

41. Detlev Peukert, *Inside Nazi Germany: Conformity, Opposition, and Racism in Everyday Life* (New Haven, Conn., and London: Yale University Press, 1987), 150–151.

42. Interview with Jeanne Holloway in London, 27 January 1993; interview with B. Cobb in Bushey, Hertsfordshire, 24 March 1993; and interview with Muriel Brown in Cudham, 28 April 1993. Alice Behrens's lecture on "Rules of Health" presented at the Foxlease General Training Week, 22–29 November 1922—recorded in the GGA Training Book Log of Miss Doris Mason.

43. See Michelle Mouton, "From Nurturing the Nation to Purifying the *Volk:* Conflicts in the Implementation of German Family Policy, 1918–1945" (Ph.D. diss., University of Minnesota, 1997).

16 Employment and Enjoyment: Female Coming-of-Age Experiences in Denmark, 1880s–1930s

Birgitte Søland

Birgitte Søland uses memoirs to explore Danish working-class women's recollections of their youth. She finds an interesting combination of continuities and changes in these documents. Memoirs written by women who grew up in the late nineteenth century demonstrate little awareness of youth as a distinct phase in life that differed, or ought to differ, from adulthood. Authors who came of age between 1900 and 1920 were more likely to recall these years as a unique stage between childhood and full adult responsibilities that they tended to devote to various, often unsuccessful, projects of self-realization in the labor market. Women who reached adolescence in the 1920s and 1930s typically portrayed those years as primarily devoted to the pursuit of fun and entertainment. Despite the persistent reality over the whole period between 1880 and 1930 of full-time labor as the lot of working-class girls, in their later memoirs, youth gradually came to be associated with leisure and enjoyment.

The decades around the turn of the twentieth century mark a critical transitional moment in the history of European girlhood. These years witnessed a significant expansion in the educational opportunities for girls and young women, while a broad range of new jobs provided previously unknown options in the labor market. Yet, how did these changes affect the lives and experiences of young girls coming of age during these decades? Did these changes influence girls' perceptions of themselves and their possibilities for the future, or their expectations of their youth?

Women's Memoirs as Historical Sources

This chapter seeks to answer some of these questions through an analysis of approximately eleven hundred unpublished memoirs written by Danish women born in the decades between the 1880s and the 1930.[1] As historical sources, such personal narratives are of course problematic: the ways in which individuals recall their past should not be confused with the past itself. Nonetheless, memoirs provide access to experiential dimensions of the past otherwise difficult to discern, and the existence of recurrent patterns, common themes, and structural similarities in women's recollections may call attention to key features of female coming-of-age experiences.

Moreover, the specific memoirs from these three archival collections share a number of characteristics that make them particularly intriguing as historical sources. First, with very few exceptions, they were written by women who grew up in poverty.[2] Marriage rarely provided an opportunity for upward social mobility; in the overwhelming majority of cases narrators married men of their own class. Consequently, these women generally lived their entire lives as part of the least-privileged groups in Danish society, a fact that set their stories apart from most published memoirs and other sources about girlhood. Secondly, unlike most autobiographers whose recollections have been published, these women did not make the self-confident decision to write down their life stories unsolicited.[3] On the contrary, they only chose to put pen to paper in response to a request from archivists. Not surprisingly, many of their memoirs thus include self-deprecating apologies for "not having much to tell" or "not being somebody important." Others insisted on anonymity or expressed their delight in the promised twenty-five-year moratorium on public access to the documents.[4] These narrators may therefore best be described as "accidental autobiographers," as individuals who came to write their life stories without having given much thought to such a project prior to being asked to do so.[5] This does not mean that their memoirs are less "constructed" or more "authentic" than other personal narratives, but it does mean that their stories offer insights into the ways in which a particular group of historical subjects (whose voices might otherwise easily have been lost) recalled, explained, and made sense of their past. This extraordinary set of historical sources therefore permits a unique opportunity for tracing continuities and changes over time in the recollections of a broad group of "ordinary" Danish women who came of age in the decades around the turn of the twentieth century.

Limited Lives: Continuities in Women's Memoirs

At first glance these memoirs seem to attest to remarkable continuities in the lives of young women growing up between the 1880s and the 1930s. Some experiences certainly seemed to change only little over the half century in question. For example, whether born in the 1870s or in the 1920s, most autobiographers recall the continued realities of limited educational opportunities that characterized their youth. Throughout this period the overwhelming majority of all Danish children left school at the age of thirteen or fourteen. Less than 10 percent would ever receive any formal education beyond the compulsory, seven-year primary school curriculum.[6] Instead, the overwhelming majority of young adolescents would fairly quickly move into full-time work.

By school-leaving age a large number of the autobiographers had already had their first experiences in the labor market.[7] Nonetheless, when recalling their teen years, the end of school attendance generally played a significant role in the life stories. When school ended, so did childhood. Especially for the many narrators who recalled their schooling with fondness, coming of age was therefore an experience tinged with loss and melancholic recognition of the limitations poverty placed on their lives. Ellen Hansen, for example, recalled that her "schooling went well. I was, I suppose, what you would call rather intelligent." As a result she was awarded a tuition scholarship but, she added, "because there was no assistance for that sort of thing, the idea had to be abandoned. You were supposed to be fairly well-dressed and my parents' budget couldn't handle that." Instead she had to take a job in a shoe factory.[8] Ellen Mortensen, another successful student, had similar memories. In her family, she bitterly noted, "there wasn't much talk about [the value] of knowledge acquired in school, work was the only thing that mattered." Like so many other bright working-class girls, she was placed in domestic service immediately after leaving school.[9]

Surely, poverty was a key factor in determining a child's future, but female memoirists were keenly aware of the ways in which gender expectations contributed to shaping their lives. Throughout the decades under investigation here, girls were expected to grow up to marry. As a result few working-class parents thought it a wise investment to allow their daughters to pursue formal apprenticeship training, much less secondary education. Such privileges were reserved for sons. As Edith Jansen reported, "I did very well in school but study [beyond elementary education]—'no,' said my father, it was only the boys who were to go on [and receive apprenticeships]. It was of no use that my teacher, Miss Struve, spoke to father and mother about my [intellectual] abilities etc."[10]

In spite of the generational differences among them, most of these narrators also seemed to share a number of experiences related to work and wages. First, their earnings were of great importance. Even decades later, almost all writers listed the specific amount of money they were paid for every single job they held in their youth. Secondly, throughout the half century recalled in these memoirs, the earnings of girls and young women remained so low that an independent existence was practically impossible. Even as young adults in their early- to mid-twenties, only a handful of narrators were able to establish their own households. Instead, teenaged girls and young women typically lived with parents or relatives or in the homes of their employers until marriage. Finally, it remained the norm into the 1930s that unmarried daughters, irrespective of their site of residence, contributed at least part of their earnings to their parents. In the poorest of families and while girls were still in their teens, they were generally granted only little spending money, but as daughters reached adulthood and/or family incomes rose, they were typically allowed to keep greater portions of their own wages.

Parents, and especially mothers, played a central role in the work lives of daughters, particularly during the first few years after leaving school. However, as girls grew older, they were more likely to find employment themselves, whether through friends and acquaintances or by scrutinizing newspaper advertisements.[11] Gradually, then, parents seemed to lose or relinquish control over children's work lives, and by the time a daughter turned eighteen and legally came of age, parents no longer claimed any formal authority over children. Many narrators thus recall their eighteenth birthday as another important transitional moment during their youth, and many report having left behind jobs in which their parents had placed them or leaving the countryside for the city at exactly this time in their lives.

Obviously, then, many fundamental characteristics of young women's lives seem to change very little between the 1880s and the 1930s. Limited formal education, paid labor from an early age, and considerable parental control over adolescent daughters and their wages are experiences recalled by large numbers of women who grew up during these decades. Yet despite these shared features of their life stories, women who came of age in the 1880s and 1890s seem to recall their youth quite differently than women who reached adolescence in the 1920s and 1930s. The role of work in their lives, for example, seems strikingly different. So does the relative importance of family and friends. Prospects and possibilities, dreams and desires are also recalled in remarkably different ways, suggesting that in spite of significant continuities in girls' lives, female coming-of-age experiences may in fact have been changing in subtle but significant ways in the decades around the turn of the twentieth century.

In order to explore these seemingly generational differences in women's memoirs, I divided the memoirs into three groups based on narrators' year of birth. The first group includes a total of 221 life stories written by women who came of age in the 1880s and 1890s; the second, 626 life stories written by women who came of age in the first two decades of the twentieth century; and the third, 83 life stories written by women who came of age in the 1920s and 1930s.[12] This allows me to compare women's recollections of their coming of age in three different periods.

Coming of Age in the 1880s and 1890s

As may be expected, the most dramatic accounts of abject poverty derive from women who grew up in the late nineteenth century. Even under the best of circumstances, when fathers were skilled workers, had steady jobs, did not drink, and brought home their earnings, narrators describe childhoods characterized by scarcity. In less-fortunate homes, low wages, periodic unemployment, physical illness, and alcoholism made matters much worse, and in the numerous cases where fathers had died or simply abandoned their families, hunger was not an unfamiliar occurrence. Under such circumstances, many parents had to place their children in part-time jobs while still in school.

Though some poor families somehow managed to keep their children outside the labor market until they reached adolescence, full-time work was the unequivocal norm and expectation once a child's mandatory schooling was completed. Even narrators who recall having been successful in school generally expected to support themselves from their early adolescence, and as a result they quickly settled into the new realities of their lives. Kirstine Hansen, for example, briefly recalled her childhood dream of becoming a teacher before she matter-of-factly proceeded: "But then I left school and then I got a job in a cardboard box factory and then I took a liking to that [job]."[13]

Like Hansen, a large number of narrators from this generation repeatedly use the phrase "and then," recalling their lives as if they consisted of a series of consecutive, discrete events, about which they do not find personal reflections necessary or appropriate.[14] However, there is one notable exception to this general rule: when speaking of work many narrators were uncharacteristically forthcoming, carefully recalling the options they had, the choices they made, and the motivations that informed their decisions. Surely, those options were severely limited and wages were always minimal, but, as these narrators point out, each job had its own advantages and disadvantages, which were carefully considered.

Domestic service, for example, offered room and board, which was an important consideration for young women who either could not or did not want to live at home. For girls from the countryside, it was often the only way to move to urban areas, and for those who had grown up in the direst of poverty, the prospect of (relative) physical comfort and regular meals was appealing. As Mrs. A. Enevoldsen recalled, "I was fortunate to go into service and got wonderful food, and my, how I enjoyed it, being able to eat until I was full."[15] Yet such advantages had to be measured against the hard physical labor, long hours, miserly pay, constant surveillance by employers, and loneliness many young girls experienced as the only domestic servant in a household.

Factory work had other pros and cons. Though housing was not provided, wages were generally higher than in domestic service. Working conditions were more regulated, and even though many young female workers faced ten- to twelve-hour workdays, they typically agreed with Kirstine Krath, who found it "awfully good to have every evening free."[16] Others remembered appreciating the company of their coworkers and enjoying that "while you were working you could sing or discuss [matters] with each other."[17] Narrators who came of age in the 1880s therefore tended to consider themselves fairly fortunate if they managed to obtain a factory job.

Beyond such stories about work, narrators who grew up in the late nineteenth century are remarkably quiet about their youth. A small number of writers, including Augusta C. Christiansen, recalled that they liked to "get out among people" after a long day of work.[18] A handful noted that they occasionally went dancing, a couple that they attended evening classes in gymnastics, and a few that they spent evenings going for walks. Though the vast majority would marry while in their twenties, only one person spoke of the courtship that preceded her marriage, and none mentioned their husband by name. Surely, the quest for entertainment and pleasure and the pursuit of romance must have been part of the experiences of many women of this generation, but these aspects of their youth have left very few traces in their memoirs.

Interpreting such silences is of course problematic. It may well be that some narrators simply believed that such "private" matters would be of no interest to archivists. However, the fact that several writers include similarly "private" stories about fathers who spent their wages on drink, boyfriends who left them when they became pregnant, and abusive husbands who neglected their financial responsibilities suggests that this is not the entire explanation. It may also be that leisure and enjoyment were such marginal phenomena during their youth that narrators simply did not think to include it in their stories. Given their low wages, limited spending money, long workdays, and the domestic responsibilities many girls were assigned as long as they lived with their parents, that certainly seems possible. Yet most girls and young women must have had at least some time to themselves, and at some point they obviously met and decided to marry their future husbands. More likely, then, is the explanation that the narrators simply did not see entertainment, pleasure, and romance as in any way central to the story about their youth. In their experience, wage labor was the key feature of this phase of life, the daily reality with which they had had to contend, the sine qua non. Even in retrospect, they recalled no sense of disappointment and demonstrated little awareness that things could, or should, have been different. Never expecting their teens and early twenties to be without paid employment, financial responsibilities, and familial obligations, they did not seem to harbor any sense of having been deprived of a "proper" youth.

Coming of Age in the 1900s and 1910s

Such pragmatic accounts of growing up poor are much rarer in memoirs written by women who came of age the first two decades of the twentieth century. Even though this "second" generation of narrators came from the same socioeconomic background and the same cultural milieus as the previous group, their stories are strikingly different. In general, their tone is much gloomier; comments like that of Olga Schutz, who wearily declared that her life had not been "a bed of roses," are much more common.[19] Moreover, their stories are far more likely to contain expressions of resentment over the limited opportunities afforded young girls from poor homes. Whereas the previous group of narrators tended to focus their discussions on the pros and cons of the different jobs available to them, this later generation of writers frequently included references to opportunities they did not have, paths they were not permitted to take, and dreams they were forced to abandon. Apparently familiar with a broader array of options for women than their predecessors, or at least better able to envision alternative life courses for themselves, this generation of narrators was therefore more likely to experience frustrations and disappointments, and when writing their memoirs they were more likely to recall dashed hopes, unfulfilled desires, and thwarted aspirations.

Contrary to what might be expected for women who came of age during a time characterized by rising wages, a gradual shortening of the workday, and the emergence of new forms of commercial leisure and entertainment, these narrators recall no more personal freedom and enjoyment than the generation before them.[20] In fact, among the 626 memoirs written by women who reached puberty between 1900 and 1920, only 43(!) mention any form of leisure activities or other forms of enjoyment in their youth. Among this minority, Vera Carla Pedersen recalled Sunday bicycle trips with coworkers.[21] Ella Marie Christensen remembered going to dances sponsored by the local YWCA.[22] Thora A. J. Huss remembered evening walks and the thrills of window shopping with friends.[23] Yet these were the exceptions. Perhaps Anna Marie Petersen's experience was common. As a domestic servant with only one half day off a week, she recalled having "no time to learn anything about life (. . .) and about what was going on in the city."[24] Others, who had a little more free time, encountered other obstacles. Helga Jensen, for example, liked going dancing but, she explained, "it did not happen very often, it cost money, and we did not have any."[25] Still others may simply have chosen not to write about it. Yet no matter what the explanation may be, the most striking aspect of this absence is that the lack of personal freedom and enjoyment only very rarely surfaces as a source of regret or resentment. Anna Hansen was one of very few writers who noted with bitterness that "there was so such thing as entertainment [in her youth]. All that mattered was work."[26] As was the case for the previous generation, these narrators described leisure, pleasure, courtship, and romance as marginal to their youth, and much like their predecessors, they did not seem to harbor a sense of having missed out on fun and enjoyment during their adolescence and early adulthood.

However, in marked contrast to narrators who grew up in the nineteenth century, members of this younger generation often recall other personal wishes and ambitions. Whereas narrators who grew up in the nineteenth century occasionally mentioned their childhood fantasies of staying in school past their fourteenth birthday, hardly any of them articulated other dreams and desires. In comparison, almost two-thirds of writers who grew up during the first two decades of the twentieth century recalled having specific aspirations in their youth. Frequently, they voice such dreams only briefly, as a casual aside in the midst of another story, but memories of individual ambitions still permeate their accounts. Amalie Nielsen, for example, recalled spending much of her youth in the countryside, dreaming of the day she could leave farm labor behind and "travel to Copenhagen and [get a job as a domestic servant] in the home of a wealthy family."[27] Anna Margrethe Lindskoug remembered her desire to leave her job as a laundress for more skilled and satisfying work.[28] Vera Carla Pedersen dreamed of becoming a seamstress,[29] while Anine Hamre longed for a job as a milliner.[30] Other writers recalled dreams of becoming sales clerks, stenographers, typists, office workers, bookkeepers, accountants, nurses, and teachers.

In light of the fact that the overwhelming majority of these women grew up poor, it is hardly surprising that none of them recalled dreams of higher education. Even to the brightest and most ambitious of these writers, primary school teaching seemed the ultimate social and educational achievement imaginable. Yet, in spite of the obvious limitations poverty placed on their lives, and in spite of the fact that most girls were taught to place duty, obligations, and devotion to family above individual desires and self-fulfillment, these recollections suggest that many girls nourished private dreams and ambitions that defied social restrictions and negated cultural expectations of feminine self-sacrifice. Thus, among the 626 writers who grew up between 1900 and 1920, fully 402 narrators recalled what may best be described as dreams of "making something" of themselves, dreams of fulfilling individual potential, of developing personal talents and abilities. Even more strikingly, 391 of these 402 narrators tied such dreams of self-improvement and self-realization to activities in the labor market. Surely, their dreams and ambitions were generally modest, and they rarely broke gender conventions. Most "merely" hoped for less arduous, more skilled, and/or more pleasant jobs within the category of work deemed appropriate for women. Yet, these were clearly matters of importance to the narrators, and their memoirs are filled with moving stories about youthful struggles to obtain desirable jobs, expand their knowledge, acquire marketable skills, and get some form of vocational training.

It is significant that so many of these women recall specific youthful desires and aspirations as well as their efforts to translate these dreams into reality. This is particularly striking when compared to the recollections of women who came of age in the late nineteenth century. Among this older generation such individual desires were hardly ever voiced, and even though they attempted to maneuver as best they could within a very limited framework, they never expressed the same sense of personal goals as did women who came of age just a decade or two later. For the older generation, the overriding concern was sheer economic survival. By the early twentieth century, rising wages allowed greater numbers of poor and working-class families to keep the direst threats of outright starvation at the door, which may well explain why daughters were even able to contemplate their wishes. Besides, expansion in commerce, industry, and the service sector was producing new employment opportunities, giving young girls more options to ponder and explore and raising their expectations of youth as a period in their lives when they might pursue individual aspirations and establish an identity not entirely determined by their familial status.

Such raised expectations undoubtedly account for the gloominess and sense of regret that permeate so many of the memoirs written by this second generation of narrators. Conscious of the increasing scope of educational and employment opportunities open to women, yet unable to take advantage of these opportunities because of the continued realities of familial poverty and limiting gender conventions, these writers often speak of their youth with a bitterness virtually absent in the memoirs of the previous generation. Elise Jensen, for example, recalled longings to escape domestic service, preferably for a job in an office where she could be "neat and chicly dressed." But, she explained, "of course I had to stay. All girls from poor families did. We never got a chance [to do] anything else."[31]

Despite such rising expectations, very few of the narrators recalled their youthful attempts to expand their knowledge and enhance their practical skills as means to long-term financial independence or economic self-reliance. Even fewer seemed to have contemplated the possibility of a life that did not include marriage and motherhood. On the contrary, the vast majority of narrators seemed to have hoped to marry husbands who would be able to provide for them while they devoted their lives to housewifery and childrearing, and when they did marry such husbands, they abandoned the labor market without regret. In this light, the urgency with which so many narrators recall having pursued individual aspirations as young girls may seem paradoxical. If they never envisioned their adolescent efforts to "improve" themselves as shaping the rest of their lives, why did it matter so much to them? If they did not imagine the knowledge, skills, and training they recalled trying so hard to obtain as benefiting their adult futures, why did the acquisition of these qualities seem so important to young girls?

The answer to these questions may lie in their perception of the female life course in general and in their perception of female adolescence in particular. In contrast to the earlier generation of narrators who seemed to have no particular conception of youth as a specific life phase that was, or ought to be, qualitatively different than adulthood, writers who came of age in the early twentieth century seemed to perceive the years between leaving school and entering marriage quite differently. In their memoirs, they typically represented these years as a unique period of time, as a chapter of their lives with its own features and characteristics. In so doing their memoirs reflect changing cultural and intellectual perceptions of youth, but unlike many experts of their day, these women did not describe their adolescence as a conflicted transition from girlhood to womanhood. Rather, they seemed to understand these years as a window of opportunity, a brief moment in a woman's life cycle that allowed for self-realization and for establishing an independent identity. At this particular moment, wedged between childhood dependence and adult obligations, when social expectations were perhaps less clearly defined than at any other time in their lives, these women recall having harbored a sense of possibility for individual accomplishments. Nonetheless, because they perceived marriage to be a "natural" part of a woman's life, and because they accepted a construction of the female life course as fundamentally fragmented, the fact that their entry into marriage marked the temporal endpoint to this moment of opportunity did not seem to produce any serious reservations about relinquishing other ambitions. As a matter of course, they seemed to accept that marriage marked the abrupt end of one chapter in life and the beginning of another.

Coming of Age in the 1920s and 1930s

The differences in the recollections of women who came of age in the late nineteenth century and women who came of age in the first two decades of the twentieth century are quite striking, but in spite of their differences these two sets of memoirs share one central theme: they focus on labor market experiences. In fundamental ways, this sets the memoirs of women who grew up between 1880 and 1920 apart from those written by women who reached adolescence in the 1920s and 1930s. Though children of the same social strata, this latter group of women tells entirely different stories about being young. Theirs are stories featuring life outside the world of work—stories of leisure, entertainment, hobbies, and other pleasurable pastimes.

This remarkable difference in emphasis defies simple explanation. Like older generations of writers, these narrators worked for wages for several years in their youth, and they held the same kind of jobs. Like their predecessors, they toiled as farmhands and domestic servants, as seamstresses and garment workers, as factory employees, shop assistants, and office workers, and as women before them, they received measly compensation for their labor. Even though Danish workers in 1919 had won the right to an eight-hour workday, many of these women worked in sectors of the economy where this legislation was not applicable or enforced. Into the 1930s many of them would therefore continue to work up to ten hours a day, six days a week. Obviously, then, paid labor occupied a great deal of time, but when recalling their youth they generally devoted very little attention to this aspect of their lives.

In some cases narrators simply noted that they held one or more jobs in their youth, typically mentioning their salary but rarely indicating what kind of work they performed. If this "third generation" did in fact take pleasure and pride in enhancing their knowledge or acquiring new skills in the labor market, they rarely mention it. On the contrary, the few narrators who speak of their workplace experiences at any length do so only to tell tales of the hardships they encountered and the indignities and exploitation they suffered. The memoirs of Dagny Helene Jensine Nielsen, for example, included the following outburst:

> When I was fourteen years old I was sent into service on a farm for Dkr. 250 for a year I had to get up at six o'clock in the morning milk 5–6 cows wash the buckets and then inside and eat porridge one cup of coffee and then back out in the fields until 11 o'clock then back home and help with the cooking and the dishes while the others took a nap then out in the field and hoe sugar beets weed carrots dig potatoes and sugar beets that was all done by hand in the year 1920–21. . . . I came to work for a baker for six months and then on a big farm with 32 cows where I had to assist with milking but I still had to get up at six o'clock and cook . . . we were 16-year old two servant girls who took turns in the kitchen . . . then I returned to my first position it was my mother who decided that because I was only 17 years old, but as soon as I turned 18 years old I went to stay with my foster parents who were good to me.[32]

Thora Anine Skov also recalled her heavy workload as a domestic servant: "There was much to do, it was a big house [. . .] and everything had to be done, and it was me who had to do all the work and cook all the food and at the same time answer the phone."[33] According to Karen Andersen, office work was not much better. It might be less physically strenuous, but "you had to ask the boss for permission for everything. For example, you had to ask whether you were allowed to cut your hair short, you were not allowed to smoke during working hours etc."[34] Surely, such experiences, however exploitative and insulting, were no more egregious than those encountered by earlier generations of women, but looking back at their youth in the 1920s and 1930s these narrators obviously felt more aggrieved than did their older counterparts.

In the memoirs of this third generation of narrators, work is generally represented as at best marginal or insignificant to the stories of their youth, or at worst as exploitative or outright abusive. Yet paradoxically, the general tone of these recollections tends to be much more cheerful and upbeat than that characterizing memoirs written by older narrators. Whereas older generations recalled their youth as dominated by work, rarely mentioning other activities, practically every single woman who grew up in the 1920s and 1930s included stories about leisure activities. Even Dagny Helene Jensine Nielsen, whose recollections of her grueling physical labor were quoted previously, went on to tell stories of bicycle trips with friends and Saturday night dances that lasted until five in the morning.[35] Others recounted the good times they had at local markets and fairs and the enjoyable evenings they spent at the movies. Some told of card-playing clubs, coffee klatches, and gatherings where they joined friends in song. A few remembered spending their free time with like-minded friends in organizations such as the YWCA or the Social Democratic Youth movement, while others recalled the pleasures of going dancing. According to Edith Andersen, you might be a "worker bee" all week long, but come Saturday, "every trace of exhaustion was gone."[36]

On average, women who came of age in the 1920s and 1930s probably had shorter workdays and more leisure time than those who grew up between 1880 and 1920. They probably also had more money at their disposal. It is certainly telling that only two of the eighty-three narrators in this cohort recall having to hand over their entire pay packet to their parents. Before the turn of the century, this was the case for almost two-thirds of the narrators, while approximately 25 percent of writers who came of age between 1900 and 1920 recalled having to do so. To the extent that free time and disposable income were requirements for the pleasures recalled by women who grew up in the interwar years, this may offer part of the explanation why leisure activities were so central to their recollections of their youth. Yet it does not explain why hardly any of these women recall accomplishments in the labor market as a potential source of personal joy and satisfaction. It could of course be that only very few women of this generation were able to find any enjoyment in what continued to be relatively limited options for young female workers. It may also be that the delights of leisure

Fig. 19. Girls on the Copenhagen main train station on their way to London. By the 1920s many girls and young women were able to take part in sports and other organized leisure activities. The young women belonged to a gymnastics team.
Courtesy Royal Library Photo Archives, Copenhagen.

simply outweighed the pleasures derived from the world of work, thus "crowding out" the latter. Yet this would seem to suggest a more profound and abrupt social and economic change from the prewar to the postwar years than actually occurred. After all, wages had been rising since the turn of the century, and already before 1919 the length of the workweek had been shortened. Moreover, with the exception of movies, the forms of entertainment adolescent girls and young women enjoyed in the 1920s and 1930s had all been part of popular culture since the nineteenth century.

Consequently, it seems that this remarkable shift in emphasis from work to leisure in women's recollections of their youth reflects shifting cultural expectations at least as much as it does changing social and economic circumstances. By the 1920s, it was not only physicians, psychologists, sociologists, and other experts who had come to understand youth as a distinct phase in life, replete with its own features, emotions, and characteristics. Apparently, much broader segments of society, including many parents, had adopted this view, allowing girls a transitional period of time during their adolescence rather than expecting their lives to change seamlessly from childhood to adulthood. And if we are to believe the memoirs of women who came of age during the interwar years, adolescent girls and young women seemed to identify that transitional period primarily as one that permitted leisure and personal enjoyment before the onset of "serious" adulthood, which occurred at the time of marriage.

Danish women's memoirs suggest both fundamental continuities and profound changes in the experiences of women who came of age between the 1880s and the 1930s. Throughout this half century, early school leaving, limited educational opportunities, low-paid wage labor, long workdays, and considerable parental control over their lives seemed to remain the reality for most girls who grew up in poor and working-class households. Yet during these same decades girls' perceptions and expectations of what it meant to be young and female seemed to change considerably. Whereas the memoirs written by women who grew up in the nineteenth century demonstrated little awareness of youth as a distinct phase in life that differed, or ought to differ, from adulthood, narrators who came of age between 1900 and 1920 were more likely to recall these years as an interlude in their lives, a unique stage between childhood and full adult responsibilities that they tended to devote to various, often unsuccessful, projects of self-realization in the labor market. The last group of narrators represented in this sample, women who reached adolescence in the 1920s and 1930s, also tended to represent youth as a distinct phase in life, but unlike their immediate predecessors they typically portrayed those years as primarily devoted to the pursuit of fun and entertainment. In spite of the harsh realities of full-time labor they encountered as adolescent girls and young women, youth, it seemed, had in their memory become associated with leisure and enjoyment, not work and obligations.

Notes

1.   These memoirs were collected by three Danish archives at three different points in time over a period of twenty-five years. The first of these three sets was collected in 1955 by the Danish National Museum after they issued a widely publicized call for memoirs written by working people of all trades. From hundreds of submissions, I sampled 250 memoirs written by women, most of whom were born in the 1870s and 1880s. These are in the Labor Movement Archives (hereafter cited as LMA), Copenhagen. The second set was collected in 1969. That year the Copenhagen City Archives sent out a letter to all retirees in the greater metropolitan area, urging recipients to write and submit their life stories. Approximately 2,000 people submitted their memoirs, of which I sampled 750 contributions written by women, the majority of whom were born between 1890 and 1910. These are in the Copenhagen City Archives (hereafter cited as CCA), Copenhagen. The third collection came into existence in 1980 in response to an announcement by the Regional Archives of Northern Jutland calling for memoirs by local residents. From among the approximately 350 submissions, I sampled

100 female memoirs, whose authors generally were born in the 1910s and 1920s. These are held by the Regional Archives of Northern Jutland (hereafter cited as RANJ), Aalborg.

2. Not all memoirs contain enough information to determine narrators' class background. However, fully 88 percent of the eleven hundred authors recount childhoods in poor and/or working-class families.

3. Recently Mitchell B. Hart has argued that "autobiography is a presumptuous act. It presumes a life lived in such a way that it deserves to be told" (Mitchell B. Hart, "The Historian's Past in Three Recent Jewish Autobiographies," *Jewish Social Studies: History, Culture, Society* 5, no. 3 [1999]: 132). While this may be true for authors who anticipate their memoirs to be published, it is much less true for the women who contributed their life stories to archival collections.

4. Both the National Museum and the Copenhagen City Archives assured potential contributors that all manuscripts would be kept confidential for at least twenty-five years. The Regional Archives for Northern Jutland gave contributors the options of requesting a twenty-five-year ban on public access to the documents.

5. I have borrowed the term "accidental autobiographers" from Mary Jo Maynes, *Taking the Hard Road: Life Course in French and German Workers' Autobiographies in the Era of Industrialization* (Chapel Hill: University of North Carolina Press, 1995).

6. Compulsory school attendance for all children between the ages of seven and fourteen had been required by Danish law since 1814. If parents requested special permission, children were frequently allowed to leave school at the age of thirteen. See Søren Mørck, *Den nye Danmarkshistorie 1880–1960* (Copenhagen: Gyldendal, 1982), 136; see also Ning de Coninck-Smith, "The Struggle for the Child's Time—All the Time: School and Children's Work in Town and Country in Denmark from 1900 to the 1960s," in Ning de Coninck-Smith et al., eds., *Industrious Children: Work and Childhood in the Nordic Countries 1850–1990* (Odense: Odense University Press, 1997), 129–159.

7. Writers who grew up in urban areas recalled a broad range of casual labor for preteen girls, including running errands, delivering goods, doing laundry and other domestic work, baby-sitting, selling and delivering newspapers, and selling food products. Some also mention having taken part in domestic industry in the home. Women who grew up in the countryside recall doing domestic work, shepherding animals, and milking cows for wages before reaching puberty.

8. CCA, file 496/1969.

9. CCA, file 1000/1969.

10. CCA, file 2002/1969.

11. Key studies of Danish women's labor history include Tinne Vammen, *Rent og urent. Hovedstadens piger og fruer 1880–1920* (Copenhagen: Akademisk forlag, 1986); Kirsten Geertsen, *Arbejderkvinder i Danmark 1914–1924* (Grenaa, Denmark: GMT [*sic*], 1977); Geertsen, *Arbejderkvinder i Danmark. Vilkaar og kamp 1924–1939* (Copenhagen: Akademisk forlag, 1982); and Geertsen, *Dannet ung Pige søges. Kvinder paa kontor 1900–1940* (Copenhagen: Akademisk forlag, 1982).

12. In 170 cases it was not possible to determine the year of birth, or even the decade in which the narrators were born, which explains the discrepancy between the total of 1,100 memoirs on which this study is based and the 930 memoirs on which the following discussion is based.

13. LMA, file 1829/1955.

14. This pattern of telling life stories is not unique to these narrators. As literary scholars of female autobiography have pointed out, women's life stories are typically written in ways that diverge from the textual model established by their male counterparts. In contrast to men, women tend to describe their lives as fragmented, consisting of distinct segments or chapters. See, for instance, Carolyn Heilbrun, *Writing a Woman's Life* (New York: Norton, 1988); Shari Benstock, ed., *The Private Self: Theory and Practice of Women's Autobiographical Writings* (Chapel Hill: University of North Carolina Press, 1988); and Martine Watson Brownley and Allison B. Kimmick, eds., *Women and Autobiography* (Wilmington, Del.: SR Books, 1999).

15. CCA, file 550/1969.

16. LMA, file 2093/1955.

17. CCA, file 1026/1969.

18. LMA, file 1253/1955.

19. LMA, file 1699/1955.

20. For a brief account of social, cultural, and economic developments in Denmark in the early years of the twentieth century, see Birgitte Søland, *Becoming Modern: Young Women and the Reconstruction of Womanhood in the 1920s* (Princeton, N.J.: Princeton University Press, 2000), 3–17.

21. LMA, file 691/1953.

22. LMA, file 1315/1955.

23. LMA, file 1285/1955.

24. CCA, file 1002/1069.

25. RANJ, file 1981/3252.

26. CCA, file 421/1969.

27. CCA, file 200/1969.

28. CCA, file 145/1969.

29. LMA, file 691/1953.

30. RANJ, file 1983/3318.

31. CCA, file 777/1969.

32. RANJ, file 1980/3032.

33. RANJ, file 1980/3100.

34. CCA, file 1024/1969.

35. RANJ, file 1980/3023.

36. RANJ, file 1980/3042.

17 Leisure, Pleasure, and Courtship: Young Women in England, 1920–1960

Claire Langhamer

Claire Langhamer also explores female leisure, calling upon oral histories to supplement documentary evidence. She suggests that women who came of age in England between the 1920s and the 1960s experienced their youth as a "golden age," a period in the female life cycle when the pursuit of personal pleasure had come to be both legitimate and possible. Freedom and independence in youthful leisure was made possible by a range of factors that combined to create a cultural consensus around the notion of earned leisure as a counterpart to paid labor. With regards to leisure and personal pleasure English girlhood was indeed distinct from married womanhood. Certainly oral testimony suggests that women were, on the whole, far more likely to complain about constraints on their leisure in youth than they were to object to its virtual absence later in married life.

> You can't live the same way all the time. I mean there's different chapters in your life. Always look on it as different chapters. Like when you're a child and then you're in your teens and that's a different chapter and then you get in your twenties and you've different ideas then, and you're married, that's another chapter. And then you have your family, another sort of different life, another chapter.[1]

That girlhood represents a distinct, although historically and culturally specific, chapter in a woman's life is a central argument in this book. This chapter contributes to the history of European female youth through an exploration of the changing meanings of personal pleasure for working-class and lower middle-class young women in England between 1920 and 1960. I argue that leisure reveals much about the distinctiveness of youth as a stage in the female life cycle *and* that attention to social constructions of girlhood helps us to understand the relationship between women and work and leisure.

The time frame of this study starts just after the upheavals of the First World War and ends on the eve of the so-called "swinging sixties," defined by some as a period of sexual revolution. While the Second World War undeniably acted as a force of dislocation, this frame enables comparisons between the youth cultures of the interwar and postwar periods and offers an opportunity to assess both continuity and change. This periodization also allows for the use of oral history evidence. In addition to social surveys and print media sources, this chapter draws upon life history interviews conducted with twenty-three working-class and lower middle-class Manchester women, born between 1907 and 1936.

This chapter begins by exploring the common perception of girlhood as a "golden age" for leisure. It investigates when and how girls' leisure came to be seen as a legitimate expectation for girls and explores the emergence of "youth" and "teenage" culture.[2] I also add a note of caution, however, showing that control as well as autonomy characterized youthful leisure in England. I outline the parameters within which pleasure was pursued and assess the resources of time and money available to young women throughout the four decades in question. I then explore the nature and meaning of leisure in young women's lives. Particular attention is paid to the cinema and dance hall as the dominant leisure venues of the period, but other forms of pleasure are surveyed. Finally, I examine heterosexual courtship and the extent to which potential and actual relations between young men and women provided a subtext to particular leisure forms. The evidence suggests that, ultimately, such relations could blur the lines between leisure, pleasure, and work in young women's lives, and even though girls could resist and remake gender roles through leisure, it was also an arena within which they were schooled into, and rehearsed, prescribed versions of acceptable womanhood.

Youth and Female Leisure

Youth was frequently seen as the preeminent period of leisure in the lives of twentieth-century Englishwomen. Richard Hoggart described it as a "brief flowering period" for working-class girls.[3] Oral testimony often characterizes the years between leaving school and marrying as a time of unparalleled freedom and independence—a period with no major responsibilities and no developed sense of duty to others. In effect, youth constituted a period of legitimate leisure. As Dorothy put it: "I'm awfully sorry that really my leisure ended when I started my family which was 1948. But I thought you might just be interested in, you know, before that."[4]

The experience of earning a wage and being engaged in clearly defined hours of work seems to have engendered an assumption among young women of this era that they were entitled to time for themselves. As Pearl Jephcott observed of the 152 elementary school educated "working girls" who responded to her wartime questionnaire, "The girls say that when you begin to work you want to go out at night."[5] Apparently, the paid work of a woman's youth endowed her with a sense of earned leisure. In contrast the unpaid work of married life was only infrequently conceptualized as work deserving of a leisure reward.[6] These shifting discourses legitimizing leisure are central to understanding the relationship between women and leisure across the life cycle and over time.

Documentary sources provide evidence both of the association between leisure and youthfulness and of a national preoccupation with the leisure choices of young people throughout this period. Young women's leisure attracted the attentions of a number of researchers. Moreover, it was not unusual for the local and national press to reflect upon the state of youth through an assessment of leisure practice alone, with activity in this realm regarded as constituting grounds for general assessments of young women's behavior and status. In the interwar period, a characterization of the young female worker as a reckless consumer was regularly employed as a vehicle to express a more fundamental unease concerning perceived shifts in gender roles.[7] By the 1950s, young women as well as young men were actively courted by the press as a distinct leisure class, as evidenced in the emergence of "teenagers' pages" with items on dancing, clothes, music, fashion, and sport.[8]

By the end of the 1950s, identifiable patterns of "distinctive teenage spending for distinctive teenage ends in a distinctive teenage world" had developed.[9] However, youth culture was not an invention of the postwar period, nor did the consumption of leisure goods, by which it is often defined, emerge only after the Second World War.[10] The success of commercial entertainment in the interwar period was, in large part, predicated upon the existence of a youthful clientele eager, and able, to assert their own leisure choices. Indeed, one historian has suggested that girls, rather than boys, were the driving force behind an interwar "teenage" culture.[11] There is certainly clear evidence of the existence in Britain of a distinct youth culture, within which girls played an instrumental role, prior to the 1950s—the decade identified with the emergence of such a culture in other regions of Europe.[12] Trends already apparent in interwar England only deepened after the Second World War, as the visibility of youth as a social category was heightened. Consumer culture became increasingly attractive to young people, who spent their money on a wide range of leisure goods and commercial entertainments. Besides, in the postwar era, girls were less likely than previously to be asked to contribute to the running of the home, thus increasing the time potentially spent in pursuit of personal pleasures.[13] Newspaper evidence points to an intensified characterization of youth as a leisured age, and an acceptance that young people of both sexes possessed the money with which to finance their pursuits.[14] In the case of women, the intensity of "youth" was compounded by the reality that this period of relative independence was becoming shorter, a consequence of the fall in the mean age at first marriage.[15]

The Limits of Female Leisure

While the association between youth and leisure remained strong throughout the years between 1920 and 1960, youth was rarely a period of unencumbered leisure for women. As Pearl Jephcott acknowledged of the girls she surveyed in 1945,

> The status gained by working, or rather by earning, carries the right to spend your non-working hours more or less as you like, and not as your mother dictates. That is the theory. In practice the girls' own good nature, pressing family needs and in some cases very definite parental control, mean that many are not nearly so free to come and go in their non-working hours as might be supposed from the hair-raising time-tables of an occasional one or two.[16]

Indeed, for young women there were two main limitations upon the expression of leisure choices, namely the availability of money and time. In addition, dominant constructions of femininity provide a context within which leisure behavior and opportunities must be understood. The time available to young women for leisure activities depended in large part upon the nature and hours of their paid work. However, the family could make other demands and, even if these demands were less burdensome than previously, they still rested more heavily on girls than on boys. Evidence suggests that young women, across class lines, regularly had to perform housework and other duties, and that they often held particular responsibility for younger siblings, seriously curtailing girls' time for personal leisure outside the hours of paid work. As Margaret, a working-class interviewee born in 1917, noted, there was often a stark gender inequality in the allocation of chores within a family. This typically meant that brothers and sisters had access to different levels of "free" time: "Well a girl was supposed to be in the kitchen, put it that way. A boy didn't have to wash up, or do things like that, that was unmanly."[17] Friday night, in particular, was often a time when girls, but rarely boys, stayed at home to perform household chores.

Even those young women with time on their hands could find their leisure choices restricted by parental discipline. Parents might attempt to control a daughter's leisure-time destinations or personal appearance. Alice, for example, recalled her elder sister's stories of furtively applied makeup in the lobby of their home during the 1920s: "She darn't put it on if my mam saw her you see in those days, to go out to the dances."[18] Parental concern over leisure companions was also frequently expressed. Dorothy, for example, was warned by her father not to be seen with American servicemen, a demand she partly acquiesced to by dancing with, but not being taken home by, such men.[19] Parental control was perhaps most evident in the rules governing the time that girls came in at night. As the King George's Jubilee Trust survey concluded in 1954, "Parental rulings were still surprisingly strict in many homes, especially as to the hour a daughter had to be home at night."[20]

By examining the issue of time in relation to paid work, unpaid chores and parental control, we can identify some of the factors that acted as a brake upon unmitigated personal freedom in leisure among young working women. However, the issue of wages and, more pertinently, "spends" must be added to the contextual framework for young women's leisure. While the level of wages could be of crucial importance to the young woman and her family, of more direct importance to the girl herself was the level of pocket money, or "spends," designated as her share of that wage. As Pearl Jephcott observed, "Wages, to the girl of fifteen mean pocket money and a regular amount to spend on pictures, dancing, cigarettes and bus fares. Pocket money, in its turn, depends on home circumstances and may vary widely among girls who are earning identical wages."[21]

Most of the women I interviewed remembered "tipping up" their wages to their mothers and receiving an amount of "spends" in return. Often the pay packet was handed over unopened. As Joan explained,

> *And did you tip your money up to your mother?* Oh yes, of course, unopened. And I remember in the end, towards the end, she gave me, I don't know whether it was, when the war had already broken out, no. I think it was about 1938, she said you can keep yourself now. So she gave me five shillings a week. But I kept within the five shillings and I, I was so proud of it, you know, to know that I'd got five shillings to myself and I could manage on it in my own way, you know. It was wonderful.[22]

While boys more often paid board rather than tipping up the whole wage, girls might continue to hand over their wages, even up to their wedding day. Nonetheless, neither social investigators nor oral history interviewees suggest that young women's leisure choices were unduly constrained by their spending power. Indeed, as a recent study of girls in interwar Bermondsey has shown, working-class "teenagers" often exhibited considerable resourcefulness in order to access consumer goods and commercial leisure venues.[23] And yet, material circumstances clearly did structure leisure choices. Levels of spends determined, among other things, the types of cinemas and dance halls young women could visit, the frequency of these visits, the extent to which they could follow fashion, the geographical scope of rambling excursions, and their ability to learn to play a musical instrument.

Arenas of Female Leisure

The cinema constituted one of the major leisure resources available to young women throughout these decades. As Freda observed, "dancing and pictures were the two main ways of enjoying yourself."[24] Studies of Manchester conducted in the interwar period suggested that all but a fraction of the city's young women attended the cinema at least once a week, many more frequently.[25] A survey of the civilian cinema audience during World War II found young female wage earners most numerous among cinema enthusiasts, while B. Seebohn Rowntree and G. R. Lavers's 1951 national leisure study found cinema audiences composed of a disproportionate number of young people.[26]

The popularity of the cinema among young women was partially based on its affordability. In the 1940s, local cinema prices ranged from a few pence for the cheaper seats to just over a shilling for the more comfortable ones, and prices were reduced for matinee performances. Price of admission had a direct impact on the type of cinema to which girls would go and the seats they would occupy, thus maintaining class distinctions amongst the cinema-going public.[27] Irene, a particularly keen cinemagoer, recalled one Ardwick cinema of the 1930s, the Coliseum, which had prices as low as tuppence. Her description of its interior confirms the link between cost of admittance and quality of experience: "It was a huge barn of a place and the doors opened straight out into the street and if, of course we used to get fog years ago and if it was foggy the fog'd come seeping in and you couldn't see. You couldn't see anything." She also remembered usherettes spraying disinfectant in the air and insisted that "you could hardly see the screen for cigarette smoke sometimes."[28]

For those able to pay the slightly higher prices charged by city center picture houses, a world of glamour and luxury replaced the seeping fog and sprayed disinfectant. The "supercinemas" of this age were sumptuous evidence of the vitality of commercial entertainment, and in periods of momentary affluence a trip to the cinema allowed working-class girls access to a physical environment that differed markedly from their home experiences. As Irene explained,

> Well you see . . . , our homes weren't very comfortable. . . . [J]ust a two up and two down. We had no . . . hot water and the outside toilet. . . . [J]ust gas light and especially if you went to the Odeon, or the Paramount cinema, they were like palaces, so you could spend two or three hours just going inside, cos they were wonderful, especially the . . . Paramount. They were, they were, just like palaces inside. And . . . you'd be taken out of your, well it was a bit of a miserable environment for two or three hours, go to this lovely palace and sit in a comfortable seat and see . . . well it, going to the pictures as it was called.[29]

Visits to the cinema offered good value for the money, providing a whole afternoon's or evening's entertainment, which included forthcoming attractions, the news, cartoons, and a "B" film as well as the main picture. The cinema also provided other forms of leisure experiences appealing to the young women, although, once again, these attractions were subject to class differentiation, particularly in the interwar period. Mary, for example, remembered the social aspect of visits to the cinemas of Didsbury and Withington: "All the picture houses they had cafes and you met your friends there and you had a coffee before you went into the pictures."[30] Other cinemas offered variety acts as part of the program, music from the electric organ, orchestral interludes, or even mid-program talent shows.

Despite this plethora of attractions, the entertainment provided by a cinema was not always the chief motivation for attendance. Young women used this leisure space for a variety of ends. While films provided girls with a window on changing fashions and behavior, the cinema itself was a space to meet potential

Fig. 20. London Bobbies Restraining Female Crowd, 1937. A sign of new forms of youth leisure, London's young female cinemagoers try to push their way toward American actor Robert Taylor as he arrived at Waterloo Station, London.
Photo © Bettman Archive/Corbis.

boyfriends and an invaluable arena for courtship activity away from parental supervision.[31] Indeed, in 1960, the *Times* reported a "Cinema Ban on Girls":

> A Coventry cinema manager, Mr. John King, who claims that teenage girls use his cinema—the Standard—as a meeting place to look for boyfriends, has banned girls between 13 and 18 permanently from it. He said to-day that the ban did not apply to boys, who behaved themselves when the girls were not there to "spur them on."[32]

While this report shows that women were by no means passive actors within the rituals of courtship, it also illustrates the common belief that women of all ages were responsible for the leisure behavior of men.

Preeminent among the alternative commercial leisure venues vying for the time and money of young women was the dance hall. In 1925, the *Manchester Evening News* reported that "dancing is, undoubtedly, getting a firmer grip of the people every day. New dance halls are being opened everywhere, and old and young spend happy hours gliding around to the strains of syncopated melodies."[33] By 1951, there were 450 dance halls in the United Kingdom admitting three million, predominantly young, dancers per week and charging admission fees ranging from one shilling and six pence to two shillings and six pence.[34]

Like the cinema, dancing constituted an escape for young women, allowing them access to a world of comfort and glamour that many ordinarily had little opportunity to experience.[35] In her 1942 study of Manchester girls, Olive Morgan explained the attraction of the dance hall by reference to the bright lights and loud dance music that provided a contrast to conditions at home.[36] She also noted that dancing presented an opportunity for girls to show off new items of clothing.[37] Certainly the act of dressing up contributed significantly to the pleasure Freda derived from attending the Chorlton Palais de Dance in the 1920s: "Well if you didn't get any partners, at least you knew you were looking nice."[38] A twenty-three-old typist from Liverpool told Mass-Observation in 1939 that "preparing for a dance is half the fun to my mind."[39] Dancing was a complex leisure experience that transcended the dance venue itself. Appearance, consumption, sexuality, and friendship as well as music and physical movement were aspects of the overall experience.

While public dance halls remained popular throughout these years, other venues for dancing were available and catered to young women of different social backgrounds. Sunday school socials, works dances, and private parties also offered opportunities to dance.[40] The predominantly middle-class young women who replied to the Mass-Observation Directive of January 1939 mentioned private dances given by friends in addition to club, hotel, and restaurant dances; college dances; and private charity dances.[41] In fact, some parents did not allow their daughters to attend public dance halls, especially where these were licensed, because of concerns about respectability.[42] Evidence of such parental control comes from women of all backgrounds and supports Davies's understanding of respectability as "a complex and multi-layered category."[43] Joan, for example, recalled that her parents restricted her dancing to ticketed affairs:

> You couldn't go to a public dance, my mother and father wouldn't let you. Now that was a dance where you can just go in, . . . pay money and go in. They would only let you go to a dance that had tickets. Church dance or, a charity dance or something like that you know. Because of who you'd meet. Places like the Ritz, . . . but . . . there were local places like that, it didn't have to be in town. But those places, no way. *Why, what was th'?* They thought you'd meet the wrong type of person there. *What rough or?* Rough and perhaps dangerous, you know.[44]

Middle-class attitudes toward public dance halls could be particularly harsh. In 1939, one twenty-four-year-old unmarried BBC employee insisted that "I've never been in a dance hall—if by that you mean the shady looking places usually in the neighborhood of Charring Cross Road and thereabouts where you can go and dance. Or more local Palais de Danse halls, like the one in Hammersmith. I think of them as haunts of the less desirable sections of the lower classes."[45]

Social researchers of the period uniformly emphasized the attraction of the dance, regardless of venue, as an arena for meeting boys. This aspect of dance hall culture appears to have become particularly pronounced in the postwar era, as traditional methods of "picking up," such as the Sunday evening "monkey walk," began to die out.[46] Ordinarily, a woman was not expected to ask a man to dance; they simply waited to be asked. However, "excuse me" or "buzz-off" dances did provide an opportunity for girls to choose their partners. Margaret recalled that "they used to have a ladies' excuse me, we weren't as forward as you lot . . . no, we were very hopeful, we'd think oh I like him over there, you know, you would . . . never dream of going. They used to stand, the fellas ogling and then they'd amble over, and some of them were very nice."[47] Nonetheless, any suggestion that young women danced *only* to gain contact with the opposite sex would be inaccurate. As Jephcott observed, "Girls generally go dancing in twos and are often quite content to dance with each other, as well as a boy partner."[48] The dance hall thus represented "one of the few mixed leisure environments where men were not necessary to women's enjoyment, though women were vital to men's."[49]

Despite the overwhelming popularity of dancing and cinema going as leisure activities for young women, personal pleasure was pursued in a variety of other contexts both outside and inside the home.[50] The nature and meaning of these pleasures were subject to change over time. The years between 1920 and 1960 witnessed, for example, significant shifts in young women's public house attendance, which reached a high point during the Second World War when significant numbers of young women, drawing upon wartime discourses of sexual equality, challenged the masculine identity of the English pub.[51] Organizations and clubs offered another space for socializing for young girls, though their appeal to working-class girls seemed limited. In an attempt to respond more directly to the interests of these girls, many introduced significant changes in their emphasis. Other young women devoted their leisure time to sports. In general, the life cycle stage was a crucial determinant of both participation in physical activity and spectatorship of organized sport.[52] Throughout these years and across class lines, rambling, cycling, swimming, and tennis were particularly popular, but female spectators attended a variety of other sporting events, including football matches.[53] Some young women also found pleasure in reading at home, in listening to the radio, and in doing home crafts, an activity that might under other circumstances or at a different stage in the life cycle be more accurately described as work.

Many of the activities in which young women participated were valued for the opportunities they provided for socializing and friendship. A postwar survey of Birmingham youth concluded that visiting relatives and prospective in-laws accounted for a considerable amount of young women's leisure time,[54] while Jephcott's national survey emphasized the importance of "my mate" as a companion for leisure activity.[55] Oral testimony demonstrates that the company of friends could translate particular activities such as shopping, particular spaces such as coffee bars, and particular moments of unoccupied time into personal leisure and/or pleasure.

Leisure and Courtship

Relationships with boys constituted another crucial context for young women's experiences of leisure. Within a society where adolescent girlhood was constructed in terms of active heterosexuality, the realm of leisure was closely related to boy-girl relationships. Moreover, while finding a "good" husband remained a young woman's primary task, pleasurable leisure could merge into hard, time-consuming work. Many of the activities young women engaged in were chosen at least in part because of the opportunities they provided for meeting boyfriends. In fact, the way in which leisure arenas were designed to accommodate heterosexual couples frequently functioned to marginalize those who were not part of such a unit. Dancing and even cinema going were recognized arenas for partner finding; societies and clubs also acted as unofficial dating agencies. Particularly in the interwar years, less formal activities such as an evening walk were used to gain introductions. Margaret remembered what she termed the "walkabout": "In those days Langford Park, which is in Stretford used to be (laughs), the walkabout. There used to be a band there on a Sunday, and people used to go there and stroll and, pick up, like you do today at a jive. But we used to go in the park walking and eyeing up the boys and the boys eyeing up us."[56] Girls also adapted other forms of leisure to the purpose of courting. The King George's Jubilee Trust survey called attention to cycling, for example, as a way of picking up men, noting that "a cycle was regarded as essential for making encounters, since it is quite in order to pick up boys if one is on a bike—an altogether different matter from going after them on foot."[57]

For young girls in receipt of moderate spends, courtship could help to finance leisure activities, at least in the short term. As Jephcott observed,

> Weekly spending drops most gratifyingly when the girl has a boy. The fair return, when the matter is serious, is for her to put by, for their future home, the money that she personally has saved. . . . On the other side of the picture are those girls who really do prefer to pay for themselves when they go out with a boy, "then they don't expect anything of you"; but this seems to apply more in the case of a fairly casual relationship than of a serious courting.[58]

Certainly, oral testimony calls attention both to the common practice of boys paying for courting activity and to the way in which this arrangement enabled limited spends to go further. Celia was clear in her acknowledgement that going out with a boy carried such benefits: "If anybody asked you out well that was alright then. You know it didn't cost any money then."[59] While there was not uniform support for this practice (for example, in 1930 the issue of paying generated significant debate on the letters pages of one local newspaper[60]), this arrangement did not simply reflect cultural expectation. The custom had a material basis in the higher wages that young men could expect from their work and the higher amount they retained for personal expenditure. As Jephcott noted of the girls she surveyed, "They grow up in the knowledge that the boy does not have to do any of the housework, and that he has a better wage and more pocket money than they have."[61]

Throughout these decades certain forms of leisure activity were directly dependent on heterosexual couples. As a result, a boyfriend was a useful partner with whom to engage in such activity, regardless of any expectation of marriage or whether he paid. In the *Manchester Evening News* of 1935, a "modern girl" defended her right to go out with a boy she had no intention of marrying, arguing that "I want to go out. There are heaps of places—dances for instance—which are scarcely any fun at all without an escort."[62] One of the women I interviewed took advantage of her relationship with a young man in a similar manner: "I'm afraid I was a bit naughty really, I just used him to take me out, to dances and things and you know, I wasn't really that interested, but it was somebody to go out with."[63] Clearly, leisure preferences that necessitated a male partner could be sustained through recourse to courting, providing evidence that the experience itself, rather than the opportunities it presented for meeting the opposite sex, sometimes provided the real appeal to young women.

The onset of courting often functioned to disrupt already established leisure patterns, and it often absorbed a great deal of a young woman's spare time. Edith, for example, recalled her movement away from close girlfriends toward a reliance upon a boyfriend: "And then . . . we all got boyfriends. . . . So we, we seemed to drift apart then."[64] Courtship could ultimately transform a young woman's leisure. Both written and oral sources document the phenomenon of young women rejecting favored ways of spending their time because of a boyfriend. Jean recalled trips to see Oldham Athletic play football: "I'm not saying that I was an enthusiast you know, I suppose it was just one of those give and take things, well, you know."[65] Moreover, the fact that many arenas were identified as places to meet boyfriends ensured that once courting, a girl felt obliged to forgo them since she had already found her mate. The association of dancing with the act of finding a partner, for example, controlled access to the dance hall itself. In a study of working-class districts in 1950s Liverpool, Madeline Kerr noted that "dancing is extremely popular with the girls until marriage, when it is dropped at once."[66]

Still, some women refused to tailor their leisure activities to fit the demands of courting, providing examples of the ways in which women resisted prescribed gender roles. Margaret, for example, temporarily parted with the man she would eventually marry because he would not accept her right to separate leisure choices. As she explained, "He didn't like the idea of me (pause) not, having a date with him, rather than swimming for the RAF."[67] In 1949, Mass-Observation interviewed one eighteen-year-old clerical worker who similarly refused to sacrifice her own varied interests for the sake of a boyfriend. "I go to the jazz club, dancing, tennis, swimming, and listening to gramophone records. On Saturday, I went to the Bebop club in the evening and shopped in the afternoon, then a party at night . . . I packed my boyfriend last week because he didn't like my going to bop clubs."[68]

The evidence suggests that women who came of age between the 1920s and the 1960s experienced their youth as a golden age, a period in the female life cycle when the pursuit of personal pleasure was felt to be both legitimate and possible. Freedom and independence in youthful leisure was made possible by a range of factors that combined to create a cultural consensus around the notion of earned leisure as a counterpart to paid labor. Nonetheless, leisure experiences remained for young women subject to limitations throughout these years. Time and money were not always available. Moreover, courting activities frequently precipitated a move away from much-loved activities, thus functioning as a transition to adulthood, where the leisure preferences of others often took precedence in women's lives. Yet despite a range of obstacles, which operated in different ways depending on class and historical decade, the nature of the work/leisure relationship was such that women themselves perceived their youth to be a period of legitimate personal leisure.

Young women pursued personal pleasures in a variety of spheres. The relative popularity of particular pastimes clearly changed over time, as did cultural perceptions of legitimate leisure activities for young women, but a considerable degree of continuity in the representation and practice of youthful leisure is apparent across this forty-year period. For example, a distinct youth culture—created by and catering to young women as well as young men—predated the advent of the 1950s "teenager." Moreover, the assumption that youth constituted a period of legitimate leisure for women, an assumption emergent not just in post–World War I England but also in 1920s Denmark and in Weimar Germany, remained central to the understanding of this stage in the female life cycle for the remainder of the period in question.[69] In regard to leisure and personal pleasure, English girlhood was indeed distinct from married womanhood, and it remained so at least until the 1960s. Certainly, oral testimony suggests that women were, on the whole, far more likely to complain about constraints on their leisure in youth than they were to object to its virtual absence in married life. Once married, and particularly after the birth of children, the relationship between women and leisure changed markedly; personal leisure preferences were subsumed into those of the family, with leisure becoming a vehicle for service to husband and children.

Notes

This chapter draws on my book *Women's Leisure in England, 1920–1960* (Manchester: Manchester University Press, 2000), which explores understandings, representations, and experiences of leisure across the life cycle, in Manchester and the national context. The book also provides a full bibliography on this topic.

1.   Interview with Mary, who was born in 1911 to lower middle-class parents and worked as an insurance clerk until her marriage in 1939.

2.   Although "teenager" is a term generally used in the years after the Second World War, both David Fowler and Katherine Milcoy use it in their studies of youth in interwar Britain. In fact, as Fowler points out, "young people 'in their teens' have been recognised as a distinct group in Britain since the seventeenth century." David Fowler, *The First Teenagers: The Lifestyle of Young Wage-Earners in Interwar Britain* (London: Woburn, 1995), 2–3. See also Katherine Milcoy, "Image and Reality: Working-Class Teenage Girls' Leisure in Bermondsey during the Interwar Years" (Ph.D. diss., University of Sussex, 2000).

3.   Richard Hoggart, *The Uses of Literacy* (London: Penguin, 1992), 51.

4.   Interview with Dorothy, who was born in 1925 to working-class parents and employed in clerical work and munitions until her marriage in 1946.

5.   Agnes Pearl Jephcott, *Girls Growing Up* (London: Faber & Faber, 1942), 56. Jephcott distributed her questionnaire throughout England and Wales between September 1941 and March 1942.

6.   Claire Langhamer, *Women's Leisure in England, 1920–1960* (Manchester: Manchester University Press, 2000), chapter 5.

7.   See, for example, an article in the *Manchester Evening News* that, under the headline "Dressy Mill Girls. Saturday Afternoon House Parties. Money to Burn. Chocolates, Cinema and the Hesitation Waltz," expressed a fear of the economically independent working-class woman by "exposing" her leisure behavior. *Manchester Evening News* (hereafter cited as *MEN*), 3 May 1920, 4.

8.   See, for example, *MEN*, 7 January 1955, 2.

9.   Mark Abrams, *Teenage Consumer Spending in 1959 (Part II): Middle Class and Working Class Boys and Girls* (London: London Press Exchange, 1961), 5.

10.   Fowler, 93–115.

11.   Milcoy, 225.

12.   See, for example, Karin Schmidlechner's chapter in this book.

13.   Elizabeth Roberts, *Women and Families: An Oral History, 1940–1970* (Oxford: Blackwell, 1995), 33–34.

14.   See, for example, *MEN*, 28 October 1955, 8.

15.   In 1921 the mean age at first marriage stood at 25.5, in 1941 at 24.6, and by 1961 stood at 23.1.

16.   Agnes Pearl Jephcott, *Rising Twenty* (London: Faber & Faber, 1948), 142. In this study, Jephcott explored the leisure experiences of girls in London, a northern town, and a pit village.

17.   Interview with Margaret, who was born in 1917 to working-class parents and worked in a tea factory and then the WAAF before marrying in 1946.

18.   Interview with Alice, who was born in 1926 to working-class parents and worked in service and then nursing until her marriage in 1957.

19.   Interview with Dorothy.

20.   Agnes Pearl Jephcott, *Some Young People* (London: George Allen and Unwin, 1954), 55–56. This study, sponsored by the King's Jubilee Trust, surveyed young boys and girls in parts of central London, Nottingham, and four villages in Oxfordshire in 1950–1952.

21.   Jephcott, *Girls Growing Up*, 93.

22.   Interview with Joan, who was born in 1920 to working-class parents and worked in a biscuit factory until her marriage in 1940.

23.   Milcoy, 175–180.

24. Interview with Freda, who was born in 1909 to lower middle-class parents and worked in clerical occupations throughout her life. She did not marry.

25. Joan Harley claimed that 90 percent of the girls surveyed attended the cinema at least once a week. "Report of an Enquiry into the Occupations, Further Education and Leisure Interests of a Number of Girl Wage-Earners from Elementary and Central Schools in the Manchester District, with Special Reference to the Influence of School Training on Their Use of Leisure" (M.Ed. diss., University of Manchester, 1937), 202. Olive Morgan claimed that 84 percent of the fourteen to eighteen year olds she surveyed attended the cinema twice or more every week in "A Study of the Training for Leisure Occupations in a Senior Girls School in an Industrial Area, Together with an Enquiry into the Use Made of This Training by the Girls, after Their Entry into Employment" (M.Ed. diss., University of Manchester, 1942), 60.

26. Louis Moss and Kathleen Box, "The Cinema Audience: An Enquiry Made by the Wartime Social Survey for the Ministry of Information" (July 1943), 13, Mass-Observation Archive (hereafter cited as M-O A): File Report 1871; and B. Seebohn Rowntree and G. R. Lavers, *English Life and Leisure: A Social Study* (London: Longmans, 1951), 230.

27. Richards notes that cinema audiences were not classless and that classes rarely mixed at cinemas. Jeffrey Richards, *The Age of the Dream Palace: Cinema And Society in Britain, 1930–1939* (London: Routledge & Kegan Paul, 1984), 17.

28. Interview with Irene, who was born in 1922 to working-class parents and employed in clerical work and munitions before marrying in 1952.

29. Interview with Irene.

30. Interview with Mary.

31. Jephcott, *Rising Twenty*, 155.

32. *Times,* 1 February 1960, 7.

33. *MEN,* 17 April 1925, 7.

34. Rowntree and Lavers, 279–280.

35. "Escape" is used here in a literal sense, meaning a release from a particularly harsh material environment or set of domestic circumstances.

36. Morgan, 114.

37. Ibid.

38. Interview with Freda.

39. M-O A: Directive Respondent 1040, reply to January 1939 Directive. For more on Mass-Observation see Dorothy Sheridan, Brian Street, and David Bloome, *Writing Ourselves: Mass-Observation and Literary Practices* (Cresskill: Hampton Press, 2000).

40. Morgan, 118.

41. M-O A: replies to January 1939 Directive.

42. Morgan, 115.

43. Andrew Davies, *Leisure, Gender and Poverty: Working-Class Culture in Salford and Manchester, 1900–1939* (Buckingham: Open University Press, 1992), 172.

44. Interview with Joan.

45. M-O A: Directive Respondent 1086, reply to July 1939 Directive.

46. *MEN,* 7 January 1955, 2.

47. Interview with Margaret.

48. Jephcott, *Girls Growing Up*, 121.
49. Michele Abendstern, "Expression and Control: A Study of Working Class Leisure and Gender, 1918–1939—A Case Study of Rochdale Using Oral History Methods" (Ph.D. diss., University of Essex, 1986), 215.
50. See Langhamer, chapter 3, for an extended discussion.
51. See Claire Langhamer, " 'A public house is for all classes, men and women alike': Women, Leisure and Drink in Second World War England," *Women's History Review* 12, no. 3 (2003): 423–444.
52. Jennifer Hargreaves, *Sporting Females: Critical Issues in the History and Sociology of Women's Sports* (London: Routledge & Kegan Paul, 1994), 113.
53. See, for example, a series of football and rugby crowd counts conducted by Mass-Observation in April/May 1947, which found that between 2 and 24 percent of the crowds sampled were female. M-O A: Topic Collection Leisure, 80/1/C, Football/rugby counts, April/May 1947.
54. Bryan H. Reed, ed., *Eighty Thousand Adolescents* (London: George Allen and Unwin, 1950), 130.
55. Jephcott, *Rising Twenty*, 159.
56. Interview with Margaret.
57. Jephcott, *Some Young People*, 58.
58. Jephcott, *Rising Twenty*, 74–75.
59. Interview with Celia, who was born in 1929 to working-class parents and held clerical occupations until her marriage in 1951.
60. *MEN*, 8 May 1930, 6; *MEN*, 10 May 1930, 4; *MEN*, 12 May 1930, 6; and *MEN*, 15 May 1930, 6.
61. Jephcott, *Girls Growing Up*, 39.
62. *MEN*, 3 January 1935, 3.
63. Interview with Amy, who was born in 1936 to lower middle-class parents and studied domestic science at college before marrying in 1959.
64. Interview with Edith, who was born in 1911 to working-class parents and worked in a foundry throughout her life. She married in 1931.
65. Interview with Jean, who was born to lower middle-class parents in 1930 and held clerical positions until her marriage in 1955.
66. Madeline Kerr, *The People of Ship Street* (London: Routledge & Kegan Paul, 1958), 32.
67. Interview with Margaret.
68. M-O A: File Report 3150, "Teen-age Girls," August 1949, 2–3.
69. In a study of 1920s Germany, Christina Benninghaus has argued that within this context too, "free time was regarded as a privilege of youth" and was incompatible with available models of adult womanhood. Christina Benninghaus, "Mothers' Toil and Daughters' Leisure: Working-Class Girls and Time in 1920s Germany," *History Workshop Journal* 50 (2000): 64. In her study of womanhood in 1920s Denmark, Birgitte Søland demonstrates that self-expression through leisure constituted a significant aspect of newly emergent "modern" female identities. Birgitte Søland, *Becoming Modern: Young Women and the Reconstruction of Womanhood in the 1920s* (Princeton, N.J.: Princeton University Press, 2000).

18 The Emergence of the Modern Teenage Girl in Postwar Austria

Karin Schmidlechner

According to Karin Schmidlechner, gender relations in postwar Austria reflected a need to reestablish "normality," including a heavy dose of domesticity aimed at rechanneling girls' aspirations toward marriage and motherhood. With the arrival of American mass culture in Austria, a new type of girl was introduced—the "teenage." Teenage girls of the fifties distinguished themselves in clothing, hairstyle, behavior, and pastimes from the conventional Austrian girls whose appearance and behavior were still heavily influenced by Nazi ideals, featuring peasant dress, country shoes, braided hair, and no makeup. The emergence of the teenage girl on the cultural scene immediately triggered adult efforts to minimize the oppositional elements of the new style, resulting, Schmidlechner argues, in a "domestication" of teenage girl culture, even if these girls of the fifties, when grown up, would imagine alternative futures for their own daughters.

The world of postwar Austria was an unlikely setting, at first glance, for the emergence of a modern teenage girl culture. It was paternalistic, authoritarian, and pious.[1] In the immediate postwar period Austria witnessed a strengthening of traditional religious institutions in the context of post-Nazism and the emergent cold war. In rural areas in particular, the church defined the rhythms of people's everyday life and holidays.[2] The influence of the church on the population only began to wane in the middle of the 1950s, a development related to the triumph of consumer and leisure culture.[3] In this conservative context, women were viewed primarily as mothers and housewives whose place was in the nuclear family. After the temporary disruption of gender roles in the immediate postwar era when women had had to perform all sorts of tasks, a reinstatement of gender polarization moved to the center of the political agenda in the 1950s.[4] The family was regarded as a shelter from the pressures of the outside world and as a protective retreat from questions about Austria's recent Nazi past and its political taint. This way of life—idealized and propagandized—addressed the needs of a large portion of the population after the strain of the war and the immediate postwar period. Women's economic independence and self-realization was not part of this model.[5]

Once postwar economic recovery was underway, women's employment was increasingly accepted only as a supplement and only when economic circumstances required it. The presence of mothers in the labor force was regarded as a societal failing, a "waste of the best population power."[6] Professional work ruined the character of young women; it corrupted women's values and special characteristics, their "essential disposition towards marriage and the desire for a man."[7] Unmarried and childless women were denied their gender identity, and professional and career-oriented women were stigmatized as sick. Women who wanted to be seen as "real" women had to fit the prescribed norm. Statistics indicate that many did. A boom in marriage, nuclear families, and births soon occurred.[8] The socialization of female youth played a major role in this development, as this chapter will demonstrate.

Girlhood and Gender Order

As part of the Austrian reconstruction of gender order, briefly threatened in the immediate postwar era, prewar notions of girlhood were revived. Parents' attitudes toward raising their daughters reflected their own socialization experiences. Order and cleanliness were the most important virtues, equally valued across classes.[9] The dominant social ideal encouraged socialization of young women around a single worthwhile goal—namely, marriage. In preparation for future marriage, girls were trained to do housework starting at a very young age. The emphasis on marriage as the proper destiny for girls was reflected in Austrian films produced during these years.[10] Most of these films presented a narrow repertoire of female roles. There was the young girl from a good family who married well and evinced the traits of fine lady and loving mother. In contrast with her, there was the young girl from a simpler home; she was naive and silly and very much interested in "marriageable" men. Then there was the emancipated and elegant young woman who was career oriented and stubborn but who ultimately was "tamed" by love. Finally, the "femme fatale" was most often depicted in a negative or comical light as a mature woman with lots of experience who exploited men. There were no models available with which young women could identify that offered goals other than marriage or reliance on men.[11]

Socialization in schools also reinforced this emphasis on marriage as a primary goal. Anni O., who came of age in the 1950s, recalled in an interview that "it was drummed into you, that you had to get married and that you wanted to have a family—that much was made clear. It naturally became your goal."[12] Schools also helped girls prepare for their all-important household duties through sex-segregated classes and gender-appropriate curricular plans.[13] To this end, the participants in a 1955 conference on family policy organized by the Ministry of Education unanimously passed a proposal to promote subjects such as cooking, housework, sewing, handicrafts, child care, and childrearing in higher grade-level school instruction of girls (and girls only). This proposal was justified on the grounds that assuring Austria's economic and social existence depended on healthy, child-centered families and that the neglect of the domestic sphere by wives and mothers represented a grave danger.[14]

For working-class girls, marriage was important not only for social but also for economic reasons; a life without a partner was nearly impossible because of low wages. Marriage was often seen as offering the opportunity to escape the unattractive jobs open to these girls. The fact that a large number of young women had to continue working outside of the home after marriage was rarely acknowledged in postwar public discourse.

Since girls were dependent on the marriage market, they had to make sure to position themselves for it in the best way possible. This still meant, in addition to moral prerequisites and the ability to run a household, accumulating a dowry. The dowry that a girl customarily brought to a marriage, which consisted mainly of household items like dishes, kitchen utensils, bedding, and furniture, was of considerable importance. In some families, starting to collect items for the dowry began at the time of a daughter's birth.[15] As soon as a girl began to earn her own money, a portion was used for the purchase of the dowry goods that would be so important for her future life as a wife. In contrast, young men typically spent their money on radios, motorcycles, and sporting goods.[16]

Respectability and the Suppression of Sexuality

"Respectability" (*Anstand*) was the catchword of Austrian society in the 1950s. "Respectable" behavior was the decisive precondition for upward social mobility and was therefore more important than ever before. Hardly surprisingly, "respectable behavior" for young women was incompatible with sexual activity. This was the message provided by the advice books for young people that appeared in large numbers on the Austrian market. Questions regarding the body and sexuality were either not addressed in these books and brochures, or else they were treated in a purely negative way. The prescribed rules of sexual behavior for girls were unambiguous: "Nothing adorns a girl like restraint. . . . Especially in matters of love, one expects measured restraint from a girl. The girl who gives in too quickly rarely gets engaged."[17] Premarital sex was treated as dangerous and sinful: "Girls don't realize that intercourse reduces her value to others; an upstanding young man—often even one who is not—wants to embrace an untouched girl after the wedding."[18] Sexuality was also a taboo topic in the school's official curriculum.[19]

Public hostility to sex found its counterpart in the family, where parents were responsible for this aspect of socialization. According to popular understandings, this responsibility was largely confined to protecting daughters against the dangers of sexuality. For this reason, young women were often kept at home after they reached puberty, in contrast with their childhood during the war and the immediate postwar period when girls enjoyed a relatively high degree of freedom outside of the home.[20] Because families avoided the subject of sexuality, girls, like most boys, were largely ignorant. According to one recollection,

As far as sex education is concerned, I must honestly say, I was denied it. It was just not discussed at all. Oh, maybe a little bit in school in the 4th or 5th grade, but actually, I must say that there was complete silence.[21]

Instead of a sound sexual education, girls were indoctrinated with fear of men and of sexuality: "You were not educated as a girl, you were afraid; you somehow were scared of every touch."[22]

Because a respectable girl was not supposed to engage in premarital sexuality, getting pregnant was a constant source of anxiety. Pregnant girls were outcasts even from their own families. Girls were constantly reminded that they would never be allowed to come home again in the event of a pregnancy. Maria M. thus recalled:

My parents had always been very strict. My father had said when I first went out, he said, young lady, I'm telling you, as long as you stay respectable and good you can come home, but if not, then don't even bother to come to the door. That's what he told me before I went out. It really hurt me.[23]

That these were not empty threats is demonstrated by the fact that numerous homes for unmarried mothers were established to alleviate the plight of girls cast off by their families.[24]

But it wasn't just pregnancy that girls risked through encounters with boys; they also had to fear for their reputation and their future chances for marriage. The only possibility for saving their good reputation in the event of pregnancy was a quick marriage. Sex with a "fiancé" was the only even implicitly tolerated form of premarital sex because a potential husband was already lined up. Very often, sex was even traded for the promise of a steady relationship with the ultimate goal of marriage. But as demonstrated by the fact that in the mid-1950s approximately 20 percent of all Austrian children were born to unmarried women, pregnancy did not always lead to marriage, at least not immediately. It is striking that the shame associated with unmarried motherhood persisted despite these relatively high levels.[25]

Working Before Marriage, Waiting for Marriage

In Austrian society, very clear ideas prevailed about proper jobs for girls in the time before marriage—namely, work either in agriculture or in the service sector. Higher education was viewed with suspicion because it seemed to direct girls toward the wrong goals. J. Ponsold, a member of the State Parliament, insisted,

There are three universities in Vienna, Graz and Innsbruck, 4,000 female students studying philosophy. Just imagine what difficulties lie ahead for them once they graduate. I would like to know where the tiny country of Austria will accommodate them all? Maybe 2,000 of them will find a husband. (Amusement) See, this is how the story works in reality. If I had 2,000 stable hands I could place them in a week. (Much laughter and amusement in the chamber) People are always complaining at assemblies that farmers don't have enough milkmaids, usually only an old lady in her sixties or seventies . . . among farmers' kids . . . one schoolgirl says to the other: "What do you want to be? I want something better because I go to high school!" She no longer wants to work on the land.[26]

Professional education was seen as unnecessary since women would withdraw from the labor market after marriage anyway; instead, the expansion of home economics courses accelerated. In 1950, Maria Matzner, the Styrian state secretary for social affairs argued, "This is not only a means to combat the waywardness among young women, but these courses also hold significance for state economic interests. Young women growing up will become mothers, and much depends on the manner in which they manage their households."[27]

Films produced in Austria in the early 1950s also reinforced the general belief that women were not destined for occupations outside of the home. Married working women were hardly ever depicted; working mothers were almost invisible.[28] Independent professional women were condemned as unfeminine and stereotyped as temporarily insane and egotistical. Viewers never saw female employment as normal, not to mention satisfying. Only chambermaids, housemaids, farmwomen, farmhands, waitresses, and seamstresses were presented in a positive light.[29]

In fact, girls in the early 1950s had few occupational choices. High rates of unemployment prevailed among youth in general, affecting a significant proportion of the roughly 80,000 annual secondary school graduates, and especially girls.[30] As Hermine B., who worked in a grocery store, recalled, "I was very interested in fashion, but there wasn't even a chance that I could get an apprenticeship. Apprenticeships were available only in grocery stores. But I would have liked to have learned the textile field, or to have gone on in school."[31]

Nevertheless, many girls did resist societal prejudices and worked outside of agriculture. One of these, Theresia S., who eventually became a servant, later recalled,

> It was difficult to get away from farming. Quite simply, they needed people for the field work. But in my view, there was no future there; at that time, they used to say that a girl didn't need to study because she'd marry without that. But from beginning I fought tooth and nail to avoid marrying a farmer. I wanted out; I wanted to get away from farming, from all of that. It was too difficult for me, too primitive.[32]

Many girls either worked in unskilled, poorly paid training positions or in low-status, typical women's professions such as the caring professions. Besides the unfavorable working conditions, these paid extremely poorly and offered no chance for promotion.[33] According to Hermine B., who worked in a grocery store, "I had to save an entire month to buy a pair of shoes because (my job) paid so little."[34]

A position as a secretary, the dream job of many girls, was next to impossible to obtain. In contrast with the period around 1900, when educated girls from the upper and middle classes monopolized clerical occupations, girls from the working class could also make their way into these jobs in the 1950s. But they were getting overcrowded.[35] It was also extremely difficult to get an apprenticeship as a seamstress or hairdresser. Limited financial means often ruled out the chance of further education. For many girls, factory work was the only option. In the words of Hermine B., "Apprenticeships were tough back then, but in the factory, you could always find work."[36] However, the decision to work in a factory was not just the result of the lack of other opportunities; girls could earn more there than in jobs requiring apprenticeship.[37] As unskilled workers, they were in a better position to afford the increasing number of goods offered to girls by the consumer economy that took off beginning in the mid-1950s.[38]

Economic Growth and "American" Consumer Culture

Never before in the economic history of Austria was there as rapid growth as in the early 1950s. The primary goal of economic policy was to make the Austrian economy competitive, to improve the international balance of trade, and to secure "a socially acceptable standard of living" for the population.[39] "The standard of living" became the new mantra, according to which the individual was to be pushed toward greater achievement and personal effort for the good of the national economy.[40]

This campaign was apparently successful.[41] As happened in the course of Germany's postwar "economic miracle," in Austria too economic opportunities increased as never before.[42] In 1956, the living standards were double what they had been in 1950.[43] Private consumption increased by 71 percent in the decade between 1950 and 1960.[44] Spending for basic necessities and semi-luxury goods rose by 50 percent, for clothing by 68 percent, for education and entertainment by 81 percent, and for transportation by 169 percent during the same decade.[45] The development of the welfare state also made progress during this era. In 1955, the general social insurance law was passed; five years later, the forty-five-hour week was established.[46]

With the increased leisure time and the economic upswing came the breakthrough to an Americanized consumer culture, which contributed in a significant way to the changes in everyday life.[47] American food and consumer goods became essential components of the quality of life in Austria. For young people in particular, American popular culture symbolized freedom and independence, and consumer goods became an essential part of their lifestyle and everyday cultural practices, signaling a new attitude toward life.[48]

The "Teenager" Arrives in Austria

With the arrival of American mass culture in Austria, a new type of girl was introduced under the label "teenager."[49] In the newly established teenage leisure market, girls emerged as a new and attractive target group—especially young working girls who, for the first time, had money of their own to spend. Teenage girls distinguished themselves in clothing, hairstyle, behavior, and pastimes from the conventional Austrian girls whose appearance and behavior were still heavily influenced by Nazi ideals, featuring peasant dress, country shoes, braided hair, and a face without makeup. The new teenagers were interested in fashion and enjoyed spending money on clothing, cosmetics, accessories, movie tickets, and records. Information about these new products and styles was transmitted primarily by the mass media.[50]

The media also transmitted images about the "ideal female body" for which American actresses like Jayne Mansfield and Marilyn Monroe served as models. Through the mass media, young girls learned not only how to attain and keep the perfect body but also how important it was to have a perfect appearance and, to that end, the right clothing and appropriate makeup. This required money and new forms of discipline and self-control. However, the measure of their success was, as before, the attention and recognition they received from men.[51]

Music also belonged to the American way of life, especially rock 'n' roll, which, given its expressiveness, offered girls a possible outlet for their sexuality and a means of protesting existing norms about masculinity and femininity.[52] Many girls also cherished American teen rebel films that could be viewed in Austria by the mid-1950s. They offered stiff competition to German and Austrian films. Going to the movie theater played an especially important role in girls' free time. A newspaper poll found that the top ways boys spent their time was doing sports, going to the movies, or hiking, while for girls it was dancing, going to the movies, and reading.[53] American movie stars like James Dean and Marlon Brando were not just trendsetters in music and fashion; they also sparked a new willingness among boys and girls to protest against social norms, despite the absence of specifically female role models. American teen film culture promoted a heightened tendency toward protest among girls and contributed to the preference for "rebels" as boyfriends.

The fact that the attractions of American mass culture offered girls new opportunities to articulate their protest against authoritarian structures and conventional expectations made them all the more appealing. Through the American style of life, girls had at their disposal an alternative to the morality of self-denial and the traditional image of girlhood. Thus American mass culture undoubtedly offered girls one of their first possibilities for self-determination, even if this was an unintended effect and in spite of the fact that it operated for a limited time only.

Girls and Gang Rebellion

Female hooligans (*Halbstarke*) offered girls a model of resistance at a time when all forms of oppositional behavior were discouraged and society gave girls very clear signals to behave and conform. In Austria the term "hooligans" was applied primarily to young working-class men affiliated with gangs. In the 1950s they made up a kind of vanguard working-class youth who articulated their protest against society and their rejection of dominant societal values primarily through the adoption of American mass culture.[54] The actions of hooligan gangs were defined by masculine norms of interaction, even though a few of these gangs included girls, most of whom participated only for a short period of time and not as members in their own right but as the girlfriends of boy members.[55] Nevertheless, solely by reason of the fact that they undertook activities in common with the boys, these girls called into question dominant gender norms. Yet ironically, even though boy gang members rejected many social values, they accepted some of the conventional moral standards established for girls. A girl who wanted to marry a hooligan was still supposed to be obedient and respectable. Female "buddies"—girls with minds and wills of their own, girls with whom one could have fun—might make attractive companions, but they were never considered future wives. Neither were the attractive, curvy, and sexually permissive girls. They were most desired as sex objects but remained morally suspect.[56]

Adults almost unanimously condemned hooligans for their behavior. Not surprisingly the parents of girls associated with the gangs objected to their daughters' blatant rebellion.[57] Therefore, they often resorted to drastic measures in order to keep their daughters from joining gangs. According to one informant, "many girls were beaten violently by their fathers back then because they rebelled against paternal commands . . . and there was one girl, who used to look after me when I was a kid, she was horribly beaten, she was around 16 then, because she was running around in those circles."[58] Nonetheless, not all girls were intimidated by such repressive tactics. The same informant recalled, "I even know of one case where they had shaven a girl's hair, I mean, had completely shaved her bald, so that she would certainly no longer go out, but she put on a scarf and went out anyway."[59]

At the time, popular consensus blamed the new trends adopted from America for the problems with young people.[60] Anxieties generally centered on the displacement of national culture by types from Hollywood. According to Tito Pölzl, a member of the Styrian State Parliament, "we know that our youth are unusually strongly influenced by trashy American movies." Still, movies were only one part of the problem. According to Pölzl, Austria's youth was "being flooded with trashy literature . . . designed to turn the thoughts, feelings and fantasies of our young people in the worst direction."[61] Other observers feared the potential contamination of youth "through striptease as a means of American propaganda" and indicted "half-naked pin-ups as a cunning form of sexual provocation" and as a "moral danger."[62] Crime stories and Wild West novels were also suspected of leading young people into trouble, possibly even criminal activity.

For the guardians of order and morality, attempts to combat these new currents were crucial. The war against "trash and filth" (*Schmutz und Schund*), primarily conducted by the church, schools, and youth organizations, constituted one such attempt. Other means to curb the "moral decadence" of the young in general and hooligans in particular fell into two different categories. The first of these was a series of legal measures enacted in this era, including youth protection laws designed to protect minors from "the dangers of the street, patronizing bars and establishments, from the use of alcohol and nicotine, and from all harmful influences from the outside including movies."[63]

Attempts to organize young people's leisure time constituted the second means of combating the dangers of waywardness. Efforts were undertaken by a variety of institutions, interest groups, and organizations such as the church, political parties, and schools to keep young people from becoming too influenced by commercial culture and the leisure industry. In 1957, a deputy to a provincial assembly thus declared that "We have the duty not just to hold young people accountable for small infractions, but also to provide them with possibilities for free time activities in centers, clubs, and so on, so that the youth does not need to go to banned films, so that he does not have to hang out on the street, but instead can spend his free time usefully at specific organizations or facilities."[64] Unfortunately for the reformers, young people's enthusiasm for spending their free time in such organizations was limited.

The Domestication of the Teenage Girl

The emergence of the teenage girl on the cultural scene immediately triggered efforts to minimize the oppositional elements of the new style. In 1956, the German youth magazine *Bravo*, for example, started a campaign "against the reprehensible erotic star image, advocating instead the modest home-loving and girlish teenage-type who would rather wear skirts than blue jeans."[65] Brochures aimed at girls featured the image of the ladylike teenager who kept her body under control and behaved according to "civilized standards."[66] Efforts were also made to tame rock 'n' roll by robbing it of its expressiveness. Thus altered, it was elevated to the status of an acceptable form of social dancing, taught in dance schools along with the foxtrot and the waltz. The American rebel films and songs were replaced with less-threatening German variants with the revival of the German entertainment industry.[67]

The result of these developments was that by the end of the 1950s an indigenous cross-class female teenage subculture had begun to establish itself, a culture existing largely "within the walls." That is, it played itself out largely at home, where girls would listen to music, read magazines, and chat with friends. The activities were those that could "be readily fit into the traditionally defined cultural space of the home, organized through . . . same-age groups."[68] In this way, the female teenager in Austria was "domesticated" in the course of the late 1950s and her rebellious potential curtailed. Consequently, the emergence of the female teenager can be seen as a reconstruction of girlhood, albeit in somewhat more modern form, and thus more appropriate to the altered social and political conditions.

There was one difference between this new model of the teenager and the model of girlhood in the prewar and immediate postwar period in Austria—namely the attitude toward girls' employment. By the late 1950s, acceptable work for girls was no longer limited to agriculture, domestic service, and occupations related to child care, and it was no longer seen as merely filling the waiting period before the actual goal of marriage and motherhood. Rather, work came to be seen as part of a long-term strategy, acceptable even after marriage. Alternatives to the "housewife only" image appeared in advertising and film that began to present women as successful employees, particularly in clerical positions. This new attitude was not necessarily the result of changing values alone but also a response to the changing needs of the labor market.[69]

Despite the short-lived rebellion of a minority of Austrian teenage girls in the 1950s, the values and conventions of the interwar years and the Nazi era still predominated in Austria. There were many efforts to combat this deviation from the earlier model of girlhood. Still, girls took up fashions, leisure activities, and ways of thinking about the body made available to them through American consumer culture. In doing so, they interrupted the cultural continuity and seeming "naturalness" that surrounded girlhood. In addition, cultural rebellion was reinforced by discontinuities in the realm of gender roles in the labor market. While Austrian society in the immediate postwar years held on to gender expectations established in the prewar period, girls in the 1950s succeeded in exploding at least some of these repressive constraints. It was not easy for girls to bring about dramatic changes or to follow unconventional directions in their lives. Nonetheless, many of these girls of the 1950s passed on to their daughters a new perspective. Their daughters in turn would belong to the first generation of women who, because of a widening range of educational and training opportunities, could develop a life plan that did not necessarily focus on marriage.[70]

Notes

1. See Karin M. Schmidlechner, *Frauenleben in Männerwelten. Ein Beitrag zur Geschichte der steirischen Frauen in der Nachkriegszeit* (Vienna: Döcker Verlag, 1997).

2. Ernst Grissemann and Hans Veigl, eds., *Testbild, Twen und Nierentisch. Unser Lebensgefühl in den 50er Jahren* (Vienna, Cologne, and Weimar: Böhlau Verlag. 2002); and Hans Veigl, *Die 50er und 60er Jahre: Geplantes Glück zwischen Motorroller und Minirock* (Vienna: Ueberreuter, 1996), 36.

3. Ernst Hanisch, *Der Lange Schatten des Staates* (Vienna: Böhlau, 1994), 247.

4.   Schmidlechner, 209.

5.   Erika Thurner, "Die stabile Innenseite der Politik. Geschlechterbeziehungen und Rollenverhalten," in *Österreich in den Fünfzigern,* ed. Thomas Albrich et al. (Vienna-Innsbruck: Österreichischer Studien-Verlag, 1995), 53–66.

6.   Franz M. Kapfhammer, ed., *Die Frau und Ihre Welt* (Vienna: 1952), cited in Edith Saurer, "Schweißblätter. Gedankenfetzen zu Frauengeschichte in den fünfziger Jahren," in *Die 'wilden' fünfziger Jahre. Gesellschaft, Formen und Gefühle eines Jahrzehnts in Österreich,* ed. Gerhard Jagschitz and Klaus-Dieter Mulley (St. Pölten/Vienna: Verlag Niederösterreichisches Pressehaus, 1985), 42.

7.   Gertrude Weitgruber, *Das Bild der Frau in der Öffentlichkeit in Österreich, Deutschland und Amerika in den Nachkriegsjahren (1945–1953)* (Ph.D. diss., Universität Salzburg, 1982). Cited in Saurer, 43.

8.   In the years between 1950 and 1960, the annual number of marriages was between 54,000 and 64,000. Between 1953 and 1963, the birthrate increased by 20 percent. Central Statistical Office of Austria, *Republic of Austria, 1945–1995* (Vienna: Bundesverlag, 1995), 23–26.

9.   Schmidlechner, 246.

10.   Christine Leinfellner, "Silberwald, Sissi und Sexbomben," in *Die 'wilden' fünfziger Jahre. Gesellschaft, Formen und Gefühle eines Jahrzehnts in Österreich,* ed. Gerhard Jagschitz and Klaus-Dieter Mulley (St. Pölten/Vienna: Verlag Niederösterreichisches Pressehaus, 1985), 54. Forty to 50 percent of films shown in Austria originated in the United States. Reinhold Wagnleitner, "Die Kinder von Schmal(t)z und Coca Cola," in Jagschitz and Mulley, 148.

11.   Leinfellner, 56–58.

12.   Anni O., born 1931, held several jobs in the service industry. Interview in Graz, 15 March 1993. This and subsequently cited interviews were conducted by the author.

13.   Saurer, 44.

14.   Kapfhammer, 205. Needlework instruction was mandatory only for girls in elementary and secondary school, and cooking lessons in secondary school until the 1980s.

15.   Karla B., born 1934, worked in a factory, married in 1960. Interview in Kalsdorf, Styria, 6 April 1993.

16.   *Die Frau,* no. 20 (1954): 20; and Erica Carter, "Alice in the Consumer Wonderland: West German Case Studies in Gender and Consumer Culture," in *Gender and Generations,* ed. Angela McRobbie and Mica Nava (Basingstoke: Macmillan, 1984).

17.   Gertraud Von Hilgendorff, *Gutes Benehmen Dein Erfolg* (Stuttgart and Vienna: Humboldt Verlag, 1953), 180. Peter Huemer, "Die Anst vor der Freiheit" in *Die 'wilden' fünfziger Jahre. Gesellschaft, Formen und Gefühle eines Jahrzehnts in Österreich,* ed. Gerhard Jagschitz and Klaus-Dieter Mulley (St. Pölten/Vienna: Verlag Niederösterreichisches Pressehaus, 1985), 212.

18.   Pius Frank, *Führung durch die Reifejahre* (Linz: Veritas, 1956), 68, cited in Huemer, 212.

19.   Huemer, 208.

20.   Schmidlechner, 255. Yvonne Schütze and Dieter Geulen, "Die 'Nachkriegskinder' und die 'Konsumkiner': Kindheitsverläufe zweier Generationen,"

in *Kriegskinder, Konsumkinder, Krisenkinder: Zur Sozialisationsgeschichte seit dem Zweiten Weltkrieg,* ed. Ulf Preuss-Lausitz et al. (Basel: Beltz, 1999), 29–58.

21.   Anni O., interview in Graz, Styria, 3 March 1993.

22.   Ibid.

23.   Maria M., born in 1930, worked as a waitress, got married in 1952. Interview in Kalsdorf, Styria, 23 May 1993.

24.   *Neue Zeit,* 5 June 1955.

25.   In fact, levels of illegitimacy had been extremely high in Austria and southern Germany throughout the nineteenth century. For a comparative European historical discussion of illegitimacy and its decline, see Edward Shorter, John Knodel, and Etienne van de Walle, "The Decline of Non-marital Fertility in Europe, 1880–1940," *Population Studies* 25 (1971): 375–393; and Michael Mitterauer, *Ledige Mütter. Zur Geschichte illegitimer Geburten in Europa* (Munich: Beck, 1983).

26.   Johann Ponsold, Stenographic Protocol of the Styrian State Parliament (hereafter cited as SPSSP), 24.S., I.P., 25 November 1947, 396.

27.   Maria Matzner, SPSSP, 7.S. II.P., 25 April 1950, 129.

28.   This despite the fact that the rate of women's employment was 40 percent and more than 25 percent of working women were mothers. Leinfellner, 60.

29.   Ibid.

30.   Veigl, 36.

31.   Hermine B., born in 1938, worked in different stores and factories. Interview in Graz, Styria, 16 June 1993.

32.   Theresia Sch., born in 1934, left her parents' farm and went to Graz where she became a maid until she got married in 1954. Interview in Graz, Styria, 8 January 1993.

33.   *Neue Zeit,* 4 July 1957.

34.   Interview with Hermine B.

35.   Erna Appelt, *Von Ladenmädchen, Schreibfräulein, und Gouvernanten: Die Weiblichen Angestellten Wiens zwischen 1900 und 1934* (Vienna: Verlag für Gesellschaftskritik, 1985). At the end of 1949, there were 659 open positions in office jobs and 1,470 people looking for this kind of work (of whom 1,071 were female). *Frau* 1949, 2 and 28. In 1951, the percentage of female trainees in professional occupations in Styria stood at 1.5. Thirty-five percent of girls wanted to be seamstresses, 30percent salespeople, and somewhat fewer hairdressers. Schmidlechner, 198.

36.   Interview with Hermine B.

37.   Dorothea-Luise Scharmann, *Konsumentenverhalten von Jugendlichen* (Munich: Juventa Verlag, 1965), 25.

38.   Saurer, 48; and Thurner, 60.

39.   Klaus-Dieter Mulley, "Wo ist das Proletariat? Überlegungen zu, Lebensstandard und Bewußtsein' in den fünfziger Jahren," in *Die 'wilden' fünfziger Jahre. Gesellschaft, Formen und Gefühle eines Jahrzehnts in Österreich,* ed. Gerhard Jagschitz and Klaus-Dieter Mulley (St. Pölten/Vienna: Verlag Niederösterreichisches Pressehaus, 1985), 22.

40.   Mulley, 22.

41.   Between 1950 and 1960, the gross national product of Austria grew by nearly 75 percent, resulting in a higher standard of living for practically all

Austrians. AK-Wien, "Der Lebensstandard von Wiener Arbeitnehmerfamilien im Lichte langfristiger Familienbudgetuntersuchungen," *Arbeit und Wirtschaft* 13, no. 10 (1959): 10. Cited in Mulley, 25.

42. Between 1958 and 1961, the per capita income increased 21 percent in real terms. In the years 1954 to 1960 alone, the net per capita wages of workers increased over 30 percent. At the same time, the workforce increased so quickly that private consumer spending increased by 45 percent. Bernd Riessland, "Das 'Wirtschaftswunder,'" in *Die 'wilden' fünfziger Jahre. Gesellschaft, Formen und Gefühle eines Jahrzehnts in Österreich*, ed. Gerhard Jagschitz and Klaus-Dieter Mulley (St. Pölten/Vienna: Verlag Niederösterreichisches Pressehaus, 1985), 94.

43. Hanisch, 440.

44. Roman Sandgruber, "Vom Hunger zum Massenkonsum," in *Die 'wilden' fünfziger Jahre. Gesellschaft, Formen und Gefühle eines Jahrzehnts in Österreich*, ed. Gerhard Jagschitz and Klaus-Dieter Mulley (St. Pölten/Vienna: Verlag Niederösterreichisches Pressehaus, 1985), 118. Arnold Sywottek, "From Starvation to Excess? Trends in the Consumer Society from the 1940s to the 1970s," in *The Miracle Years: A Cultural History of West Germany, 1949–1968*, ed. Hanna Schissler (Princeton, N.J., and Oxford: Princeton University Press, 2001), 341–358.

45. In the immediate postwar years, the main demand had been for food items, but the demand shifted to textiles in 1950 and to shoes in 1951. Beginning in 1954, the demand focused on consumer durables, especially motor vehicles, electronics, and other household furnishings. Between 1950 and 1960, the scooter and the motorcycle symbolized success and the spirit of the times. The number of motorcycles increased by 204,000 (from 123,000 to 327,000). Riessland, 96.

46. Hanisch, 440.

47. Without a doubt, this growth of American business interests came very opportunely and was fiercely and heavily driven by the relevant American institutions. Reinhold Wagnleitner, *Coca-Colonisation und Kalter Krieg: Die Kulturmission der USA in Österreich nach dem zweiten Weltkrieg* (Vienna: Böhlau Verlag, 1991).

48. Kasper Maase, "Establishing Cultural Democracy: Youth 'Americanization' and the Irresistible Rise of Popular Culture," in *The Miracle Years: A Cultural History of West Germany, 1949–1968*, ed. Hanna Schissler (Princeton, N.J., and Oxford: Princeton University Press, 2001), 428–450.

49. In Germany initially only the female Elvis Presley fans were labeled as teenagers, but beginning in 1957, female youth in general were being classified in this way. Only slightly later, beginning in 1959, did male youth begin to be labeled teenagers. Uta G. Poiger, *Jazz, Rock, and Rebels: Cold War Politics and American Culture in a Divided Germany* (Berkeley and Los Angeles: University of California Press, 2000), 191. In Austria, this terminology is part of oral tradition but is not yet documented.

50. Mulley, 24.

51. Leinfellner, 60; and Mulley, 25. Erica Carter, *How German Is She? Postwar German Reconstruction and the Consuming Woman* (Ann Arbor: University of Michigan Press, 1997). Victoria De Grazia and Ellen Furlough, *The Sex of Things: Gender and Consumption in Historical Perspective* (Berkeley: Univer-

sity of California Press, 1996); and Carter, "Alice in the Consumer Wonderland," 205.

52. Peter Zimmermann, "Aufwachsen mit Rockmusik—Rockgeschichte und Sozialisation," in *Kriegskinder, Konsumkinder, Krisenkinder: Zur Sozialisationsgeschichte seit dem Zweiten Weltkrieg*, ed. Ulf Preuss-Lausitz et al. (Basel: Beltz, 1999), 109; Heinz-Hermann Krüger and C. Bartram, eds. *Vom Backfisch zum Teenager, Mädchensozialisation in den 50er Jahren* (Opladen: Leske und Budrich, 1985), 100; and Poiger, 180.

53. Leopold Rosenmayr, Eva Köckeis, and Heinrich Kreutz, *Kulturelle Interessen von Jugendlichen: Eine soziologische Untersuching an jungen Arbeitern und höheren Schülern* (Vienna and Munich: Hollinek, 1996), 171. Oral reports suggest that urban girls preferred American protest films, while girls from rural areas mostly attended Austrian and West German films. The groups enjoyed musicals equally.

54. There were hooligans throughout Europe. Jürgen Zinnecker, *Jugendkultur 1940–1985* (Opladen: Leske und Budrich, 1986), 19. In Austria, the predecessors can be found in the "Schlurfs" of the 1930s—male working-class youth who gravitated toward American styles. Christian Gerbel et al., "Die 'Schlurfs': Verweigerung und Opposition von Wiener Arbeiterjugendlichen im Dritten Reich," in *NS-Herrschaften in Östereich 1938–1945*, ed. Emmerich Talos et al. (Vienna: Verlag für Gesellschaftskritik, 1988), 243–268.

55. Marina Fischer-Kowalski and Elisabeth Wiesbauer, " 'Früchterln' und was sie fruchten," in *Die 'wilden' fünfziger Jahre. Gesellschaft, Formen und Gefühle eines Jahrzehnts in Österreich*, ed. Gerhard Jagschitz and Klaus-Dieter Mulley (St. Pölten/Vienna: Verlag Niederösterreichisches Pressehaus, 1985), 76.

56. Ibid.

57. Ibid.; and Poiger, 179.

58. Ferdinand St., born in 1942. Interview in Graz, Styria, 15 May 1992.

59. Ibid.

60. Thurner, 60.

61. Tito Pölzl, SPSSP, III Period, 37th session, 19–29 December 1955, 846–847. This position of a Styrian elected official against Americanization may be considered atypical as the official positions on these issues were generally reserved.

62. Kasper Maase, " 'Antiamerikanismus ist lächerlich, vor allem aber dumm;' Über Gramsci, Amerikanisierung von unten und kulturelle Hegemonie," in *Kulturen der Widerstands: Texte zu Antonio Gramsci*, ed. Johanna Borek, Birge Krondorfer, and Julius Mende (Vienna: Verlag für Gesellschaftskritik, 1993), 27.

63. SPSSP, IV Period, 12th session, 4 December 1957, 100.

64. SPSSP, 103.

65. Krüger and Bartram, 94.

66. Ibid.

67. Maase, "Antiamerikanismus," 168.

68. Angela Robbie and Jennie Garber, "Mädchen in den Subkulturen," in *Jugendkultur als Widerstand*, 2d ed., ed. John Clark (Frankfurt am Main: Syndikat, 1981), 224.

69. Thurner traces the change in view back to the fact that sales possibilities for consumer products needed to be created in the mid-1950s. Thurner, 59.

70. Life history interviews with the daughters (and sons) of women born between 1923 and 1940 indicate that the mothers not only placed a great value on a foundational education for their daughters but also passed on critical ideas about marriage.

Contributors

Kathleen Alaimo is Professor of History at Saint Xavier University in Chicago, where she teaches world history and European history. She is the coeditor of *Children as Equals: Exploring the Rights of the Child.* Her research focuses on adolescence in modern Europe, especially France, and on the history of children's rights. (alaimo@sxu.edu)

Christina Benninghaus teaches history at the University of Bielefeld, Germany. She is the author of *Die anderen Jugendlichen. Arbeitermädchen in der Weimarer Republik.* Her current research focuses on the history of infertility in Germany (1750–1950). (cbenning@geschichte.uni-bielefeld.de)

Pamela Cox is a lecturer in the Department of Sociology at the University of Essex, England. She teaches and researches in the areas of cultural and social history, gender relations, criminal justice, and public policy. Her recent publications include *Gender, Justice and Welfare: Bad Girls in Britain 1900–1950; Crime in Modern Britain;* and *Becoming Delinquent: British and European Youth 1650–1950.* (pamcox@essex.ac.uk)

Clare Crowston is Associate Professor of History at the University of Illinois at Urbana-Champaign. Her area of specialization is early modern France, with interests in the history of work, women and gender, fashion, and material culture. She is the author of *Fabricating Women: The Seamstresses of Old Regime France, 1675–1791,* which was awarded the Berkshire Prize and the Hagley Prize. Her current project focuses on credit, fashion, and sex in eighteenth-century France. (crowston@uiuc.edu)

Anna Davin is a founding member of the editorial collective of *History Workshop Journal.* From her research into the history of women and children and of London, her published work includes "Imperialism and Motherhood" (*History Workshop Journal* 5 [spring 1978]) and *Growing Up Poor: Home, School and Street in London 1870–1914* (London: Rivers Oram Press, 1996). Her current research interests include Irish life in New Zealand in the first half of the twentieth century and mid-century new migration to Britain.

Andreas Gestrich is Professor of History at the University of Trier, Germany, where he teaches modern European history. Together with Jens-Uwe Krause and Michael Mitterauer he is the coauthor of *Geschichte der Familie.* His current research focuses on pauper families and family networks in nineteenth- and twentieth-century Germany and Britain as well as the social history of youth. (gestrich@uni-trier.de)

Céline Grasser is a translator, currently living in Paris and writing her Ph.D. thesis on gardens and bourgeois cultures in France and England (1780s–1870s). Her research focuses on national and gendered identities expressed through gardens. (cgrasser@wanadoo.fr)

Irene Hardach-Pinke is a sociologist and lives in Marburg, Germany. Her publications include books and articles on the history of childhood, intercultural relations, and the history of women. She is the author of *Bleichsucht und Blütenträume. Junge Mädchen 1750–1850* and is currently finishing a biography of Ottilie von Goethe. (IHardach@aol.com)

Elizabeth Bright Jones is Assistant Professor of Modern European Social History and Comparative World History at Colorado State University. She is the author of several articles on gender and agricultural work in Weimar Saxony. Her current project is a book-length study of gender, politics, and agricultural crisis in Germany before, during, and after the First World War. (elizabeth. jones@colostate.edu)

Claire Langhamer is Senior Lecturer in the Department of History at Sussex University, England, where she teaches twentieth-century British history. She is the author of *Women's Leisure in England, 1920–1960.* Her current research focuses on love and courtship in twentieth-century England. (C.L.Langhamer@sussex. ac.uk)

Mary Jo Maynes is Professor of History at the University of Minnesota. She is currently involved in two research projects: a history of young women spinners in early modern and modern Europe, and an interdisciplinary project on the use of personal narratives in the social sciences. Her books include *Taking the Hard Road: Life Course in French and German Workers' Autobiographies in the Era of Industrialization* and *Gender, Kinship and Power: A Comparative and Interdisciplinary History* (co-edited with Ann Waltner, Birgitte Søland, and Ulrike Strasser). (mayne001@umn.edu)

Carol E. Morgan is the author of *Women Workers and Gender Identities, 1853–1913.* She has been a Visiting Scholar at the Center for Advanced Feminist Studies, University of Minnesota, and has published articles on women in the cotton and chain-making industries in *Social History; International Labor and Working Class History;* and *Women's History Review.* (cemorgan@forbin.net)

Tammy M. Proctor is Associate Professor and Chair of History at Wittenberg University, Ohio, where she teaches European history. She is the author of *Female Intelligence: Women and Espionage in the First World War* and *On My Hon-*

our: Guides and Scouts in Interwar Britain. Her current research focuses on civilians and the First World War. (tproctor@wittenberg.edu)

Rebecca Rogers is maître de conférences at the University of Marc Bloch in Strasbourg, France, where she teaches modern French history and comparative European history. She is the author of *Les demoiselles de la Légion d'honneur. Les maisons d'éducation de la Légion d'honneur au XIX siècle* as well as numerous articles on the history of girls' education. (rrogers@umb.u-strasbg.fr)

Karin Schmidlechner is Professor of Contemporary History and Gender Studies at the University of Graz, Austria, and editor of the *Grazer Gender Studies.* She teaches contemporary history and women's and gender history. Her current research interests include intercultural marriages and youth cultures. Most recently she has published, with Jim Miller, *Die Liebe war starker als das Heimweh: Heiratsmigration in die USA nach 1945.*

Deborah Simonton lectures in History and Women's Studies at the University of Aberdeen, Scotland. She has published *A History of European Women's Work, 1700 to the Present* and numerous articles on the history of gender, labor, and education in the eighteenth century. Her research focuses on gender, childhood, education, and work, and she is currently completing *Women in European Culture and Society.* (d.l.simonton@abdn.ac.uk)

Birgitte Søland is Associate Professor of History at The Ohio State University, where she teaches European women's history. She is the author of *Becoming Modern: Young Women and the Reconstruction of Womanhood in the 1920s* and *Gender, Kinship and Power: A Comparative and Interdisciplinary History* (co-edited with Mary Jo Maynes, Ann Waltner, and Ulrike Strasser). Her current research focuses on the history of children's rights in nineteenth- and twentieth-century western Europe. (Soland.1@osu.edu)

Mary Lynn Stewart is Professor of History and Women's Studies at Simon Fraser University in Burnaby, B.C., Canada. Her most recent monograph is *For Health and Beauty: Physical Culture for Frenchwomen, 1880s–1930s.* Her current research project is entitled "Dressing Modern Frenchwomen, 1919–1939," and she has published portions of what will be a book on fashion theory and textile history. (mstewart@popserver.sfu.ca)

Index

Page numbers in italics refer to illustrations.

abandonment, and early service, 25

abortion, 107, 172

accountants, 261

adolescence, 105, 112n18, 150–153; concept of, 128n3; as a developmental stage of life, 16–17n12, 150; extensive literature on, 151–152, 153, 179–180; and family relationships, 180–181, 188; and lack of sex education, 164; and strict constraints, 194. *See also* youth

Adolescence: Its Psychology and Its Relations to Physiology, Anthropology, Sociology, Sex, Crime, Religion and Education (Hall), 151

advice literature, 101–102, 104, 107, 108–109, 113n35, 164; and emphasis on office skills, 215–216; and emphasis on religion, 117–118; and message of respectability, 286; and suggestions for entertainment, 104

agricultural work. *See* farm work

alcoholism, 257

American mass culture, 289–290, 296n47

apprenticeships, 7, 23, 29, 32–35, 288; age when beginning, 76; areas available, 78; charity support of, 73; concept and practice of, 34; contracts of, 12, 24, 72, 73; distribution of trades by sex, *33;* as an enhancement of options, 32–33, 183; and family involvement, 72, 73; and "female" work for girls, 33; hairdressers, 289, 295n35; and immediate earning power, 34; and learning a trade, 26–27, 34; length of, 33, 34, 72; limited opportunities of, 33–34; male, 32, 33, 77, 78; of paupers, 34; replaced by simple hiring agreements, 34–35; seamstresses, 71, 72, 77, 78, 81n9, 289, 295n35; sources of records of, 33

Arachne and Pallas, 38–39, 51

architecture, and instruction of boys, 74

Ariès, Philippe, *Centuries of Childhood,* 1

Association for Christian Marriage, 168, 173

"*Aufsatz-Methode,*" 180

Backfisch, 104, 105, 107, 112n12

Backfischkultur, 105

Baden-Powell, Betty, *246*

Baden-Powell, Heather, *246*

Baden-Powell, Olave, 246, *246*

Baden-Powell, Peter, *246*

Baden-Powell, Robert, 239, 242, 243, 244, 245, 246, *246*

Baden-Powell family, *246*

Balzac, Honoré de, 117

Bank of England, 213

Beale, Dorothy, 121

Beauvoir, Simone de, 169

Benninghaus, Christina, 283n69

Berg, Maxine, 43

"Between Purchasing Power and the World of Goods . . . " (de Vries), 51–52n10

bicycling, 10, 157, *219,* 260, 264, 277; and courtship, 278

birth control, 8, 107, 171, 172, 175n31

birthrate: decline in, 4, 10, 229; increase in, 294n8

births, illegitimate, 63, 68n43, 109–111

"Blooming maiden," of Catholic France, 132–137, 142, 143n4

Blum, Léon, 171

boarding schools: activities criticized, 117; advertisements for, 120; and Christian education, 120; comic images of, *118, 119;* and control of entire day, 121, 124; and dangers of excessive religiosity, 122; emphasis on memorization, 121; in England, 116, 126; and forming of friendships, 124–125; in France, 115–127, 128n5; and a group identity, 123, 126; guidelines for, 120; and incompatible subjects, 120; and influence of adult women, 122–123; and lack of privacy, 121–123, 124, 126; and lesbian behavior, 117, 122, 124; and male teachers, 117; and outside contacts, 122, 123, 126; and prize-giving ceremonies, 120, 122; regarded as "prisons," 123–124; and restrictions on reading, 121; as secure and moral environments, 120, 122; and sex education, 172; and sexuality, 124–126; and sleeping arrangements, 121; stereotypes about, 117; and theatrical productions, 120

"A Boarding-school girl's dreams," *119*

book trade, 26–27
bookkeepers, 261
Bourdieu, Pierre, 9
Boy Scouts, 239, 242, 243, 244, *246;* and attempt by girls to join, 239; London rally (1909), 239, 244
Boys' Brigade, 240, 241
Bravo, 292
British Association, 217
British Mail, 88
British Medical Association, 217
Brontë, Charlotte, 115
Bund Deutscher Mädel (BDM), 249, 250
Burney, Fanny, *Evelina,* 2
Burt, Cyril, 195, 201
Business Life, 217
button making, 84, 85, 87
Byron, Lord, 105

Cadbury, Edward, 95
Campbell, Janet, 159
Campe, Joachim Heinrich, *Fatherly Advice for My Daughter,* 107
card playing, 104, 264
caring professions, 288
Catholic Action, 248
Catholic Lads Brigade, 240
Centuries of Childhood (Ariès), 1
chain manufacture. *See* nail and chain manufacture
chandlery, 32
charity schools: curriculum, 74; and vocational training, 73–76. *See also* boarding schools
chastity, 105–108; exaggeration of, and boarding schools, 124; premarital, 171; youth as a period of, 101
Chateaubriand, 121
Child Guidance Council, 200
child labor, 6, 16n11, 50, 150
child protection movement, 151
Childhood and Society (Erikson), 1
Children's Branch of the Home Office, 200, 201
Children's Employment Commission. *See* Royal Commission on Children's Employment
chlorosis, 156
Church Lads Brigade (Anglican), 240
cinema. *See* movies
civil service employment, 211, 212, 221n13; and resignation after marriage, 212
Civil Service Inquiry Commission, 212
clerical work. *See* office work

clothing and dress, 9–10, 157, 160, 179, 271; "above rank," 47, 48; adoption of adult, 3; chaste in design, 167, 168; and conventional Nazi ideals, 290; and fashion, 47, 48, 271
coffee bars, 277
coffee klatches, 264
Colbert, Jean-Baptiste, 71, 77
Commercial and Agricultural Magazine, 31
communications and administration, workers in, 6
Communists, and youth groups, 248
companions, and parental concern, 272
Compayré, Gabriel, 154, 156, 158
"*condition prédisposante,*" 154
confirmation, 3, 182; Protestant, 102–103
consumer products, and growth in demand, 71
contraception. *See* birth control
"convent-factory," 46
Copenhagen City Archives, unpublished memoirs, 266–267n1, 267n4
correspondence, monitoring of, 121
cottage industries, 27; nail and chain manufacture, 90; sewing, knitting and crochet work, 62
"cotton craze," 40
cotton manufacture. *See* textile production, cotton
Courbet, Gustave, *The Hammock,* 135, *136*
courtship, 62, 63, 64; and boy paying, 278, 279; and leisure activities, 278–279; and *Lichtstuben,* 62–65; not mentioned in Danish memoirs, 259
Cowie, John, 193, 195, 196, 201
crochet work, 62
Crowston, Clare, 32
Curo, Marie, *Etudes morales et religieuses,* 118
cycling. *See* bicycling

dairying and dairy products: grain cultivation shift to, 229; increase in demand for, 225, 229
dance halls, 275–277
dancing, 10, 104, 105, 111, 167, 258, 260, 264, 270, 271, 273, 275–277, 290, 292; with American servicemen, 272; and courtship, 278, 279; forbidden on holidays, 68n45; to show off new clothes, 276
Danish National Musuem, and unpublished memoirs, 266–267n1, 267n4
Dayus, Kathleen, 94, 95
De Vries, Jan, 71; "Between Purchasing Power and the World of Goods . . . ," 51–52n10
death of a parent, and early service, 25
death rate, premature, 102, 112n5

delinquency, 150, 153; and approved schools for delinquents, 193, 203n7; and expert diagnoses, 200–202; and female sexuality, 197–199; and genetic factors, 194–195; and inferior family relationships, 195; medical explanations for, 194–195; pathological explanations for, 194–196; and physical appearance, 195–196; predominance of male, 193, 203n4; and property crimes, 194; social explanations of, 196–197; and social relationships, 195; sociological explanations of, 199–200

department stores, and gender-specific positions, 210

dexterity: and clerical employment, 211; and nail and chain manufacture, 91

Dienstbuch: importance of, 231, 232, 235; withholding of, by employers, 231–234

diet, 157, 160

doctors, 210

domestic service, 4, 5, 6–7, 23, 260, 263, 264; advantages and disadvantages of, 258; age at entering, 24, 256; chambermaids, 30; cleaning, 27, 30; cooking, 27, 30, 70; duties and gender, 6, 272, example of agreement for, 28; as a first step, 28; as the ideal female job, 29, 210; increased demand for, 29; ironing, 30; lady's maid, 30; laundering, 27, 30, 260; and length of stay, 28, 29; locations of, 29; and loneliness, 30; nanny, 30; and number employed by the household, 29–30; and preference for country girls, 28; rarity of written records of, 12; reasons for entering, 28; and sexual vulnerability, 29

dowries, 24, 27, 28, 48; Austria, 286; unaffordable, in France, 168

dress. *See* clothing and dress

dressmakers: and femininity, 186; and social status, 183

Eclaireuses (Protestant), 247

Edgeworth, Maria, 137

education, 3, 24; aesthetic, 9; and charity schools, 73–76; Christian, and boarding schools, 120; and employment opportunities, 210; expansion of, 150, 151, 152, 209, 254, 256, 267n6; and gender, 3, 33, 152, 159–160, 184; and gender-appropriate curriculum, 27, 284–285, 294n14; higher, 178, 183, 261, 287–288; home, 13, 26; limited by financal means, 289; professional, seen as unnecessary, 288; records of, 12, 13; secondary, expansion of, 209–210; and segregated classes, 284; and socialization, 284; training

by mothers of daughters, 26, 93, 298n70; of upper-class female youths, 104; value of, 158–160; vocational training, 4, 70–71, 77, 78, 79, 82n26, 184

electronics, demand for, 296n45

electroplate manufacture, 85

embroidery, 78, 82n24; instruction in, 74, 75, 77; of muslins, 27

employment, 5, 6, 25; age at time of, 86; alongside men, 86, 90; in banking, 212, 213; before marriage, 44, 185–186, 287–288; changing attitude toward, 293; and clothing, 92; contractual, 24; desires and aspirations, 260–261; and employee's workshops, 79; as end of childhood, 182; in insurance industry, 213; and labor legislation records, 13; mobility of labor force, 43–44; of mothers, 93, 284; opportunities, 4, 261; and paternalistic control, 88; and protoindustrial activity, 42–43; sex-segregated, 86, 90, 93, 212–213; and skilled workers, 7, 24, 32, 35, 92; and social hierarchy of workers, 95; supervised, 51–52n10; training of workers, 26, 94; and unequal workload between women and men, 64; and unskilled workers, 183, 190n21; and working conditions, 88, 94, 183, 184; and workplace clubs, 94–95. *See also* civil service employment; domestic service; factory work; farm work; office work; post office employment; textile production

enamelers, 78, 82n24

Encyclopédie, 78

engraving, 26

entertainment. *See* leisure activities

entrée, as a gender-specific rite of passage, 103, 104

epilepsy, 156, 195

Erikson, Erik, *Childhood and Society,* 1

"Essay to Encourage and Extend the Linen-Manufacture in Ireland" (Prior), 41–42

estate management, 138

Etudes morales et religieuses (Curo), 118

eugenics movement, 153

"European Marriage Patterns in Perspective" (Hajnal), 15n2

evangelical revival movement, and supervision of youth, 63

Evelina (Burney), 2

Evening Continuation Schools, 216

experimental psychology, emergence of, 152

"factory girls," 10, 45–46

factory work, 4, 29, 46, 51–52n10, 210, 263; advantages and disadvantages, 258; and competition with farm work for girls' labor, 225, 227; increase in employment, 230; as only option, 289; and owner's paternalism, 46

families: challenges to authority of, 197; and controls, 8; devotion to, 261; major influences of, 25; neglect by, 93; quality of, as highly important, 196; and protection against the dangers of sexuality, 286; social status of, 9; stability of, as importance, 196–197; and treatment of girls in gangs, 291

family workshops, contributions to, 70

fan makers, 78, 82n24

farm work, 4, 23, 29, 30–31, 263, 287; age at entering, 24; and children, 230; and competition with factory work for girls' labor, 225, 227; and dairymaids, 30; and day laborers, 30, 31; decline of, in eighteenth century, 31; description of, 31; difficulty of avoiding, 288; duties of, 5; example of staff needed, 30–31; growing demand for, 225; hierarchy among, 31; hired annually, 31; numbers involved in, 225–226, 236n5, 238n26; reasons for leaving, 225, 234–235; and resident servants, 30, 31; resistance to, 230; workers, *227, 228*

farming: and crop rotation, 227; and diversification, 225; and root crops, 227–229

Fascist movement, and youth groups, 248–249

Fatherly Advice for My Daughter (Campe), 107

Fathers, death of or abandonment by, 257–258

Faute de l'abbé Mouret (Zola), 137

Feminine Education Committee, 173

femininity: and clerical employment, 218, 220; conflicting notions of, 185; and dressmakers, 186; and manual labor, 185; and metal manufacture, 84, 86; and nail and chain manufacture, 91; and working married women, 93–94

feminist movements, in England and France, 137–138

Filles de Sainte-Agnès, 74–76, 77–78

First Communion. 102–103; preparation for, 116

First World War. *See* World War I

Fischer, Anna, 170; *Woman, Family Doctor,* 169, 175n31

flappers, 241

flirting, 168

flowers, artificial, makers of, 78, 82n24

food crisis of 1846–1847, and Germany, 55

football, 277, 283n53

Francillon, Marthe, 154, 155, 156, 158, 166

Frank, Johann Peter, 107, 108

"free love," 172

French Association of Women Doctors, 173

French League against the Venereal Peril, 173

French Revolution, 34, 40, 64

French Union for Women's Suffrage, 173

friendships, forming of, and boarding schools, 124–125

"furiosi," 105

gangs, 153, 291

gardens, 2, 132, 142

  English: and building of personality, 137; and contemplation, 138, 140; involvement in all activities of gardening, 138; and self-education, 137; as study of God's creation, 140; and tactile and visual senses, 141; visiting and social activities, 140; walking, reading, and exercising in, 137

  French: attention to details, 138; and bringing friends together, 135–136; and emotional religion, 134; as meeting place for engaged couples, 136–137; as outlet for a repressed sensuality, 134, 135; as place of contemplation and meditation, 133–134, 140; and self-centered activities, 140; and senses of smell and touch by imagination, 141

garment workers, 263

Gaskell, Elizabeth, *Wives and Daughters,* 140

generational conflict, 181–182

genitals, 166, 169

Gesindeordnungen, 225, 234

Gibbens, Trevor, 198, 201

Gillis, John, *Youth and History,* 1

Gillott, Joseph, 87

Gioventú femminile cattolica italiana, 248

Girl Guides, 239, 242, 243, 244–245, 246–247, *246,* 250; Jewish, *247*

Girls Scouts and Girl Scouting, 13, 239, 245, 246–247

"girl," use of term, 15n1

girls, definition of, 1

Girls' Friendly Society, 241

Girls' Guildry, 241

Girls' Life Brigade, 241

Girls' Own Paper, 217, 218

Glover, Edward, 200

Glueck, Eleanor, 195

Glueck, Sheldon, 195

Gnauck-Kühne, Elisabeth, 229, 230

Goethe, Ottilie von, 109

"good girl" of Protestant England, 132, 137–142, 143n4

Goupil, E. A., 166, 170
Grimshaw, Atkinson, *The Rector's Garden: Queen of the Lilies,* 141–142, *141*
gross national product, Austria, 295–296n41
Guide International Council, 246
Guides de France (Catholic), 247
guilds, 34; control of, 79; embroiderers, 69, 79; entry into difficult, 76; female, in Paris and Rouen, 70, 71; flower sellers, 70; and formal apprenticeship contracts, 72; formation of, 71, 77; linen drapers, 70; male domination of, 70; midwives, 70; records of, as sources, 69–70; regulations by, 69; seamstresses, 70, 71–72; status in, 32; tailors, 69, 71

hairdressers, and social status, 183
hairstyles, and conventional Nazi ideals, 290
Hajnal, John, "European Marriage Patterns in Perspective," 15n2
Hall, G. Stanley, 158; *Adolescence: Its Psychology and Its Relations to Physiology, Anthropology, Sociology, Sex, Crime, Religion and Education,* 151
Hall, Gladys, 198
The Hammock (Courbet), 135, *136*
Hanawalt, Barbara, 16–17n12
Hart, Mitchell B., 267n3
health manuals, 164, 173n2
healthcare systems, and employment opportunities, 210
"Healthy Lives for Working Girls," 217
historical records, 11–14
Hitler-Jugend (HJ), 249
Hoggart, Richard, 270
Homer, Thomas, 93
homosexuality, 108, 113n351; lesbians, 117, 122, 124
hooligans (*Halbstarke*): female, 290–292, 293, 297n54; male, 291
Horne, R. H., 90, 91
hours of work, 184, 263, 264, 265; forty-five-hour workweek, 239; and legislation to regulate, 93; metal manufacture, 84; nail and chain manufacture, 90; reduction in, 183, 260; and time available for leisure, 272
household furnishings, demand for, 296n45
"housewifery," 27, 31
Hugo, Victor, *Les misérables,* 135
hunger, 50, 257, 261

illegitimate children, 107; in *Mägde* court cases, 232
Imperial Council, 246
independence, 47, 89, 95, 167, 240

India, textile industry of, 39, 40
Industrial Revolution, 14, 71, 82n26, 226
industrialization, as competition with farm work, 225
"industrious revolution," 71, 79, 82n26
industry, expansion in, 261
"industry schools," founding of, 41
Institute for the Scientific Treatment of Delinquency (ISTD), 200
interest groups, and protection of young people, 292
International Congress on Penitentiary and Penal Science, 152
International Congress on Protection of Children, 152
International Congress on School Hygiene, 152, 161n8; Third, 172
Irish Linen Board, 41

Jephcott, Pearl, 271, 273, 277, 278, 281n5
Jeunesse Ouvrière Chrétienne Féminine, 248
jewelry, 167
jewelry trade, 85, 87
Jewish Lads Brigade, 240
Juggins, Richard, 92, 93

Kensington School of Shorthand, 216
"khaki-mad" hoydens, 241
King George's Jubilee Trust survey, 272, 278
kissing, 168
knitting, 27; instruction in, 74; schools for teaching of, 41

Labour Tribune, 90–91
lace making, instruction in, 74, 75, 77
Laclos, Choderlos de, *Les Liaisons Dangereuses,* 108
lacquerers and lacquering, 84, 85, 95
"ladder of life," metaphor of, 24
Ladies Typewriting Office, 217
Lajolais, Nathalie de, 116, 118, 121
languages, 104, 105, 111
lathe work, and metal manufacture, 94
lay communities, Catholic, and education of the poor, 71
League for the Rights of Women, 173
left-wing organizations, and youth groups, 248
legal age of eighteen, as transitional point, 257
Legrand, Louis, 127
Leighton, Lord, *Sisters,* 138, *139*
Leipzig High School for Women's Occupations, 187
leisure activities, 10–11, 54, 104, 242, 260, 264; and courtship, 278–279; gender-

specific, 104; not mentioned in Danish memoirs, 259; and rural youth culture, 54; as a sense of earned time, 271; sports, *265;* time for, 4, 63–64, 272. *See also specific activities*

lesbian behavior, and boarding schools, 117, 122, 124

Les Liaisons Dangereuses (Laclos), 108

Lichtstuben, 56–64; and boys' school-leaving years, 64; and courtship, 62–65; documentation of, 58; and end of official control, 60; and girls as family and neighborhood oriented, 64; history and custom of, 56–57, 61; household heads' organization of meetings, 58; and illegal male attendance, 57–58, 59–60, 62; makeup of attendee groups, 56–57, 58, 66n23, 67nn24,31; and non-attendance by some girls, 58, 60, 61; and pious evangelical prayer group, 59; regulations and fines, 57, 59; and separation of the sexes, 62; three types of, 58–59; traditional opening dates, 66n11; and widows, 67n24; and work done for own profit, 61

"The Life & Age of Woman: Stages of Woman's Life from the Cradle to the Grave," 25

life cycles, *26*

lighting costs, saved by many working in one room, 56, 57

linen. *See* textile production, linen

Linnaeus, Carolus, 166

literacy, increase in, 153

literature: American, influence of, 291; campaigns against cheap, 10; erotic, 117; juvenile, proliferation of, 150; pedagogical, 117; prescriptive, 102, 105, 116, 164; romantic, 116, 167. *See also* advice literature

livestock raising, increase in, 229

lock making, 85

London College of Shorthand, 216

London School of Economics, 201

Louis XIV, 77

luxury fabrics, worn by poorer classes, 48

Mägde: and conflicts with employers, 230–235; and contract breaking, 230; court cases of, 224–235, 235n2; decline in number of, 231; definition of, 224; essential for farm production, 225; and knowledge of employment laws, 234, 235; and livestock care, 229; in more court cases than men, 225; and root crops, 227–229; shortage of, in agricultural labor, 229; as a "social problem," 230

"maids of all work": duties of, 30

Maistre, Xavier de, 121

makeup, 167, 168, 272, 290

Malraux, Clara, 167

Manchester Evening News, 275, 279

Männerbund, 242

mantua making, 31

Marion, Henri, 156, 158, 159

marriage: age of first, 1, 103, 271, 281n15; choices dictated by fathers, 70; early, 66n9; emphasis on, 284–285; as end of childhood, 35; as end of employment, 212; as end of opportunity, 262; as end of youth, 3; expected of girls, 256, 262; and gaining of adult status, 103; late, 1, 15n2, 16n3, 56, 259; legal age of, 107; numbers of, 284, 294n8; postponement of, as long as possible, 56; and working women, 288, 295n28

mass media: and the "ideal female body," 290, 293

Mass-Observation Directive, 276, 283n53

masturbation, 108, 157, 201

Maynes, Mary Jo, 267n5

McKendrick, Neil, 82n26

memoirs, unpublished Danish, 255, 266–267n1, 268n12

memorization, emphasis on, and boarding schools, 121

men, unmarried, recognition of, as citizens, 65n6

Mendousse, Pierre, 154, 156

menstruation, 8, 102, 134–135, 153, 165–166; age of first, 3, 106, 154, 155, 165; as confidential between mother and daughter, 165, 166; education about, 106; impact of, on behavior, 155–156; lack of knowledge about, 164, 165; management of, 155–156; and physical activities, 165; and sexual maturation, 105–106; side effects of, 116; theories about, 105–106, 111; unpreparedness for onset of, 165

metal manufacture, 83–95; age at time of employment, 86; and female laborers, 6, 83, 85; and femininity, 84, 86; hours of labor, 84; and lathe work, 94; and machine attendants, 84; and morality, 84, 91–92, 93; products produced, 83; polishing and buffing, 85; and working conditions, 85, 94

Michelet, Jules, *The Women,* 134

midwives, 210

migration to the cities, 230

military service, records of, 12

milliners and millinery, 31, 261

Les misérables (Hugo), 135

Mitchell, Sally, *The New Girl,* 15n1
"modern girl," 192, 241
monastery, Protestant, of unmarrieds, 63
Monet, Claude, *A Woman Reading or Spring-time,* 133, *133*
money, 271; availability of, and leisure, 164, 272–273, 257, 290; spending of, by young men, 286
moral code, imposition of, 86
moralists, Catholic, 168
morality, 6, 10, 11; and metal manufacture, 84, 91–92, 93–95; strict preservation of, 46
mothers: absence of, and delinquency, 197; central role of, 257; information concerning, 181–182, 190n12; responsibility of, for daughters' sex education, 168, 169, 171, 172; unmarried, 3, 7, 62–63, 87, 107, 109–111, 287, 295n25
motor vehicles, demand for, 296n45
motorcycles, demand for, 296n45
moviegoers, *275*
movies, 264, 265, 270, 273–275, 282nn25,27; American, 291, 294n10; American teen rebel films, 290, 292, 297n53; Austrian, and female roles, 284, 294n10; campaigns against, 10; and courtship, 274–275, 278; frequency of attendance, 273, 282n25; as good value for the money, 274
music, 104, 111, 271; and American culture, 290, 292

nail and chain manufacture, 85; and age restrictions, 92; and expertness and dexterity, 90–91; and femininity, 91; hours of labor, 90; and importance of female labor, 92–93; manufacture described, *87,* 91, 90–93, 97n39; wages, 90, 97n39; and work clothing, 92
National Socialist (Nazi) movement: and youth groups, 248, 249
needlework and needleworkers, 27, 70, 71
Nelfrand, Nelly, *What Every Young Girl Should Know at Puberty,* 171
neurasthenia, 156
The New Girl (Mitchell), 15n1
"New Woman," 179, 192, 214, 226, 234
nudity, 242
nurses and nursing, 210, 261

occupations: choices of, 183, 288; dreams of, 260–261
office work, 4, 10, 213, 261, 263, 264; advantages of, 214; and foreign languages, 216–217; and gender appropriateness, 186–187; and higher wage rates, 210; intense competition for, 212, 289, 295n35; and males, 210, 211; paternalistic and respectable, 210, 211; and social status, 183, 211, 212, 218, 220; via trade schools, 187, 216; and the workplace environment, 211, 217–218, 220
orphanages, records of, 13
orphanhood, and early service, 25
Ovid, 38–39, 51

painters and sculptors, 70
Pankhurst, Sylvia, 90, 92
paper makers, 78, 82n24
peer group organizations, 54; male, 55–56, 66n9
pen making, 85, 87–88, *89*
penal system, records of, 12
personal appearance, 9–10, 11. *See also* clothing and dress; makeup
personal freedom, lack of, 260
Phonographer and Typist, 216, 217
physical activities, 153, 157–158, 160, 172, 242, 252n17
physiological maturation, 154
Pietism: influence of, 60; and *Lichtstuben,* 55, 59, 60–61, 63
pin making, 84
"Place your girls in boarding schools!" *118*
Pölzl, Tito, 291, 297n61
Portlaw mill, 44–45
post office employment, 211–212, 221nn13,17,20,21; clerkships, 212, 221nn17,20
postwar "economic miracle," 289, 295–296n41
pottery manufacture, 34–35
poverty, 256, 257–258
pregnancy outside marriage, 107, 108, 109–111, 287
press-cutting agencies, 213
press work, 87; description of, 88
Prior, Thomas, "Essay to Encourage and Extend the Linen-Manufacture in Ireland," 41–42
prison sentences, and conversion to cash fines, 234
privacy, lack of, and boarding schools, 121, 123, 124
private consumption, increase in, 289, 296n42
prize-giving ceremonies, and boarding schools, 120
Proczek, Casimire, 159
professions, access to, 178, 183
pronatalism, 153
prostitution, 7, 195–196, 197, 198–199

protests, within context of religious movements, 64
Prudential Assurance Company, 213, 217, 222n26
puberty, 8, 102, 116; and concerns about morality, 157; and hygienic recommendations, 157; and intensified supervision, 165; management of, 157–160; nervous disorders brought on by, 156–157; onset of, 150; as opening stage of adolescence, 154; and physical activities, 157; physical changes involved in, 154–155, 156, 166–167; psychological changes, 166; social-sexual importance of, 154; and stress, 106, 156; understandings of, 153–157
public house attendance, 277
Puliga, Countess, 121, 125, 129n25

Raciborski, A, 158, 166; *Treatise on Menstruation*, 155
radio listening, 277
railway employment, 213
rank, and transmitting of orders, 138
reading, 153, 277, 290; restrictions on, 121, 158. *See also* literature
rebelliousness, 105, 192–193
The Rector's Garden: Queen of the Lilies (Grimshaw), 141–142, *141*
Red Cross, 173
reform schools, 12, 13; for boys, 12
Regional Archives of Northern Jutland, unpublished memoirs in, 266–267n1
religiosity, excessive, dangers of, 122
religious communities, female, and education, 74–76, 81n18
religious institutions, strengthening of, 284
religious instruction, in charity schools, 74
religious service organizations, 240, 242
reproductive organs, growth of, 154
residence, until marriage, 256
respectability, 6, 12; *Anstand*, 286–287; defense of, 185–186
rest, 157, 160
Richardson, Helen, 195, 196, 201
right to vote, 178
right-wing organizations, and youth groups, 248
Robinson Crusoe, 243
Roche, Daniel, 79
role models, 185
Rousseau, Jean-Jacques, 108
Rowntree, B. Seebohn, 273
Royal Commission on Children's Employment: 1843, 86; 1864, 84, 85, 86, 87

Royal Commission on Labour, 218
Russell, Dora, 200
Rylett, Rev. Harold, 91

saddlers, 78, 82n24
saleswomen, 4, 183, 261
Sand, George, 124, 132
Schilfarth, Else, 181, 183
school hygiene movement, international, 151
school leaving, 3; as end of childhood, 182, 256; and full-time work, 256, 257, 258, 267n7
Scouting for Boys, 243, 244, 245
screw making, 84, 85, 86
sculpture, instruction in, for boys, 74
seamstresses, 263; apprenticeships, 71, 72, 77, 78, 81n9, 289, 295n35; and request for guild status, 70, 71–72
Second World War. *See* World War II
seduction, prevention of: Catholic or French method, 108–109; Protestant method, 108–109
servants: as a reflection on their household, 30; in non-parental households, 56
service trades, 70, 261, 287
sewing, 41, 56, 62, 74
sex and sexuality, 7–9, 134–135; appeal, seen as an asset, 198–199; and delinquency, 194; fantasy, 157; ignorance of, 4, 164, 168–171, 287; manuals on, 170–171; period of revolution, 270; and promiscuity, 117; and prudery about the pubic area, 169–170; social-scientific study of, 152; suppression of, 286–287; used for material and emotional gains, 198, 199; vulnerability, in domestic service, 29
sex education, 8, 107, 108, 109; absence of, 286, 287; for males, 172; promoted by socialists, 171–172; and public education, 172
sex, premarital, 7, 107; as dangerous and sinful, 286; with a "fiancé," 63, 287
sexual activity: and boys' involvement, 62–63; control of, 7–8; and parental knowledge of, 63
shoe factory work, 256
shoes, demand for, 296n45
shop assistants, 263
shopping, 260, 277
shorthand, 214, 215, 216, 217
silk manufacture. *See* textile production, silk
silkworkers, C. J. Bonnet Company, *47*
silkworm disease, 50
Siredey, Armand, 154, 155, 159
Sisters (Leighton), 138, *139*

skeletal growth, 166

Søland, Birgitte, 283n69

social background, and expectations regarding work, 187–188

Social Democratic Youth, 264

social inequality, 184

social insurance law, passage of, 289

Socialists, and youth groups, 248

socialization, 25–26, 33, 104; clubs for, 277; and passing along of traditions and skills, 27

societies and clubs, and courtship, 278

Society for Sanitary and Moral Protection, 171

Society of Arts, 217

Soeurs de la Communauté Sainte-Geneviève, 76, 81–82n18

spectator sports, 277

Spencer, Herbert, 159

spending money/"spends." *See* money

spinners and spinning, 5, 27, 39, 52n17; domestic, 40; earnings of, 42; as a female occupation, 43; and flax spinners, 40, 61; mechanization of spinneries, 6, 44; movement from rural cottages to large spinneries, 43; recruitment and training of, 40; schools for teaching of, 41; and social gatherings, 56; unmarried older girls most reliable, 42

Spinnstuben, 56–64

sports activities, 157, 271, 277

Spring's Awakening (Wedekind), 3–4

status "cross-dressing," 10, 47

stenographers, 261

stocking makers, 78, 82n24

Strand Typewriting Company, 216

suicide, and men, 4

sumptuary laws, 47–48

surveillance, and boarding schools, 121–123, 126

Swift, Jonathan, 38

swimming, 157, 277

"swinging sixties," 270

tapestry making, instruction in, 74, 75, 77

Taylor, Robert, *275*

teachers and teaching, 210, 261

technology, and creation of new jobs, 209

"teenage" culture, 271, 280, 284, 292–293

"teenagers," 5, 270, 281n2; and American mass culture, 289–290, 296n49

"teenagers' pages," 271

telegraphists, 211, 212, 220–221n7; and sex segregation, 212–213

telegraphy schools, 211, 212

telephonists, 211–212

tennis, 277

textile production, 6, 70

age and gender division of labor, 43

cotton, 40, 61; and calico printing, 43

demand for, 296n45

discipline, severe and enforced by fines, 46

and the *Lichtstuben,* 61

linen: flax spinning, 40, 61, 74, 75; and gender division of labor, 42–43; and Germany, 40, 41, 42–43, 45, 50; and Ireland, 39–42

and participation of young women, 39, 46, 50

protoindustrial, 39–40

silk, 40–41, 43, *44,* 45, 46, 50–51; and the *fileuse,* 43, *44,* 45; Japanese domination of world trade in silk cocoons, 50; and the *tourneuse,* 43, *44;* unwinding of silk, *44*

and state intervention, 40, 41

weaving, 26, 43, 44

wool, 38, 39

theatrical productions, and boarding schools, 120

Third French Republic, 171

Thomas, William I., 198, 199; *The Unadjusted Girl,* 197–198

Times, 275

trade policy, English, 38, 39

trade unionists, 185

"trash and filth" (*Schmutz und Schund*), war against, 292

Treatise on Menstruation (Raciborski), 155

Truth, 217

typists and typing, 213–216, *215,* 261

The Unadjusted Girl (Thomas), 197–198

uniforms: and political youth groups, 248; and youth organizations, 240, 241, 242

unmarried, as virtuous, 63, 67n24

unruliness, 60, 67n29

valets, 30

venereal diseases, 171, 172, 173, 176n54

visiting relatives and prospective in-laws, 277

wage labor pools, 46–47

wages, 4, 7, 263, 273; and contribution of earnings to parents, 85, 184, 256–257, 264, 273; importance of, 256; and increased earning power, 50; increased, 289, 296n42; and independence, 89; lower for girls, 183, 184, 190n24, 211, 213, 222n26, 256; lowering of male wages, 91; nail and chain manufacture, 90, 97n39; portion of, retained by worker, 85; Prudential Assurance Company, 222n26; rising of, 260, 261, 265

"walkabout," 278

walks, 259, 260, 277

Wandervogel, 241–242, 243, 247, 248

Wedekind, Franz, *Spring's Awakening,* 3–4

Wedgwood, Josiah, 34–35; hiring agreement of, 35

Weiler, Amélie, 125

welfare state, development of, 289

Western European marriage pattern, 1

What Every Young Girl Should Know at Puberty (Nelfrand), 171

White, J. E., 85–86

wigmaker-barbers, 78, 82n24

Wives and Daughters (Gaskell), 140

Woman, Family Doctor (Fischer), 169, 175n31

A Woman Reading or Springtime (Monet), 133, *133*

Women: and instruction by other women in the household, 27; marriageable, and lack of eligible men, 168; married, criticism of, 6, 50; role of, 134; rural, and agricultural work, 225; scholarship on women's work, 18n20; and terms specific to age and gender, 3; unmarried, 1, 3, 4, 55; upper-class and working-class compared, 183; viewed primarily as mothers and housewives, 284; and women's movement, 152–153; and work outside the home, 288

The Women (Michelet), 134

Wood-Allen, Mary, 156

World Association of Girl Guides and Girl Scouts (WAGGGS), 246

World Conference, Hungary, 246

World War I, 22, 167, 168, 226, 270

World War II, 270, 271, 277, 281n2

Wright, J. S., 85, 89–90

Wurster, Maria Agnes, 59, 67n24

"young lady," use of term, 15n1

Young Women's Christian Association (YWCA), 13, 264

youth: attributes of, 105; and the choice of a husband, 104–105; as implying "unmarried," 55; considered happiest time of life, 103; as a period of chastity, 101; as a period of leisure and personal enjoyment, 104, 266, 269–280, 283n69; as a period to establish an independent identity, 262; as a phase of life, 3, 4, 95, 179, 182, 183, 270; portrayal of, in plays and novels, 3; as preparation for being wife and mother, 104; psychological concepts of, 182; as a social category, 271; sources for history of, 11–14; as a time of male preparation for a career, 104; work seen as marginal, 264. *See also* adolescence

Youth and History (Gillis), 1

youth movements and organizations: 11, 179, 188; as market for goods, 19n34; first appearance of, 241; participation in, ended at marriage, 56; political groups, 247–250; and religious instruction, 240; and a sense of belonging, 240; and uniforms, 240, 241, 242

youth protection laws, 292

youths: disciplining and punishing of, 150, 151; increased visibility of, 150–151

Zedler, Johann Heinrich, 112n18

Zola, Emile, *Faute de l'abbé Mouret,* 137